BEYOND HOLY RUSSIA

BEYOND HOLY RUSSIA

The Life and Times of Stephen Graham

Michael Hughes

www.openbookpublishers.com

© 2014 Michael Hughes

This work is licensed under a Creative Commons Attribution 4.0 International license (CC BY 4.0). This license allows you to share, copy, distribute and transmit the work; to adapt it and to make commercial use of it providing that attribution is made to the author (but not in any way that suggests that they endorse you or your use of the work). Attribution should include the following information:

Hughes, Michael, *Beyond Holy Russia: The Life and Times of Stephen Graham*. Cambridge, UK: Open Book Publishers, 2014. http://dx.doi.org/10.11647/OBP.0040

Further details about CC BY licenses are available at

http://creativecommons.org/licenses/by/4.0

Every effort has been made to identify and contact copyright holders; any omissions or errors will be corrected if notification is made to the publisher.

Digital material and resources associated with this volume are available from our website at:

http://www.openbookpublishers.com/isbn/9781783740123

ISBN Paperback: 978-1-78374-012-3
ISBN Hardback: 978-1-78374-013-0
ISBN Digital (PDF): 978-1-78374-014-7
ISBN Digital ebook (epub): 978-1-78374-015-4
ISBN Digital ebook (mobi): 978-1-78374-016-1
DOI: 10.11647/OBP.0040

Cover image: Mikhail Nesterov (1863-1942), *Holy Russia*, Russian Museum, St Petersburg. Wikimedia http://commons.wikimedia.org/wiki/File:Nesterov_SaintRussia.JPG

All paper used by Open Book Publishers is SFI (Sustainable Forestry Initiative), and PEFC (Programme for the Endorsement of Forest Certification Schemes) Certified.

Printed in the United Kingdom and United States by Lightning Source for Open Book Publishers

For my parents Anne and John Hughes

Contents

List of Illustrations		ix
Epigraph		xi
Acknowledgements		1
Introduction		3
1.	Chasing the Shadow	13
2.	Searching for the Soul of Russia	53
3.	The Slow Death of Holy Russia	85
4.	The Pilgrim in Uniform	133
5.	Searching for America	169
6.	A Rising or Setting Sun?	205
7.	New Horizons	237
8.	A Time of Strife	269
9.	The Pilgrim Reborn?	303
Final Thoughts		323
Bibliography		329
Index		345

List of Illustrations

Figure 1   Pen portrait of Stephen Graham by Vernon Hill, published in Stephen Graham, *Changing Russia* (London. John Lane, 1913), frontispiece.   p. 36

Figure 2   Photograph taken by Stephen Graham in the Terek Gorge of two Ingush women collecting water, published in Stephen Graham, *A Vagabond in the Caucasus* (London, John Lane, 1911), p. 140.   p. 39

Figure 3   Photograph taken by Stephen Graham at midnight of the inhabitants of a village near Archangel, published in Stephen Graham, *Undiscovered Russia* (London. John Lane, 1912), p. 24.   p. 48

Figure 4   Photograph taken by Stephen Graham of elderly Russian peasant woman on the banks of the Jordan, published by Stephen Graham, *With the Russian Pilgrims to Jerusalem* (London. Macmillan, 1913), p. 194.   p. 74

Figure 5   Two of the pictorial emblems appearing in Stephen Graham, *Priest of the Ideal* (London. Macmillan, 1917), pp. 151 and 165.   p. 115

Figure 6   Two of the illustrations by Vernon Hill in Stephen Graham, *Tramping with a Poet in the Rockies* (London. Macmillan, 1922), pp. 1 and 201.   p. 181

Figure 7   Press photograph of Vachel Lindsay and Stephen Graham (on the right) in 1921 (http://commons.wikimedia.org/wiki/File:Vachel_Lindsay_with_Stephen_Gwynne.jpg) [NB in the original Stephen Graham is mistakenly identified as Stephen Gwynne].   p. 186

Figure 8 Stephen Graham in 1926 (photographer unknown). p. 219
Courtesy National Portrait Gallery, © CC BY-NC-ND.

Figure 9 Photograph of Stephen and Vera Graham on the 13 p. 306
August 1957 (photographer unknown). Courtesy
Private Collection.

An Englishman ('To Stephen Graham')

I went an Englishman among the Russians,
Set out from Archangel and walked among them,
A hundred miles,
Another hundred miles,
A moujik among moujiks,
Dirty as earth is dirty.
And found them simple and devout and kind,
Met God among them in their houses –
And I returned to Englishmen, a Russian.

Witter Bynner, *A Canticle of Pan*

Умом Россию не понять,
Аршином общим не измерить.
У ней особенная стать,
В Россию можно только верить!

Fyodor Tiutchev

Acknowledgements

I have received a huge amount of help from around the world in writing this book. Financial support was provided at various points by the Harry Ransom Center (University of Texas), the British Academy, the University of Liverpool and the Scouloudi Foundation. I have benefitted from the generous help of archivists and librarians in more than a dozen institutions, and would like to acknowledge in particular the help of Bill Modrow and Burt Altman at the Strozier Library, Florida State University, along with Molly Schwartzburg and Bridget Gayle at the Harry Ransom Center in Austin. My work has also greatly benefitted from the feedback to papers I have presented in Athens GA, Cambridge, Canterbury, Liverpool, London, Moscow and Stockholm. I have received advice and help of various kinds from numerous other individuals including: Mike Bishop, Dr Phillip Ross Bullock, Professor Dennis Camp, Professor Anthony Cross (whose knowledge of Anglo-Russian cultural relations remains unrivalled), Professor Simon Dixon, Alan Freke, Lance Sergeant Kevin Gorman, Anil Gupta, Professor Marguerite Helmers, Dr Sam Johnson, Nicholas Lindsay, Javier Marias, Branco Omčikus, Marko Omčikus, Professor Predrag Palavestra, Dr Aleksandr Polunov, Professor Andrew Rigby, Paul Tomlinson and Mike Tyldesley (the latter representing the Mitrinović Foundation whose rich archive is housed at Bradford University). Sally Mills made generous use of her time and legal drafting skills to subject the manuscript to eagle-eyed scrutiny. Dr Alessandra Tosi at Open Book Publishers provided invaluable support and advice (and I am delighted to be associated with such an innovative enterprise). Many other people too numerous to mention have provided me with particular leads, and I hope they know how grateful I am to them. I am particularly grateful to those who have shared their memories of Graham with me. I would like to thank those who have given me permission to quote from material to which they own the copyright. Every effort has been made to trace holders of copyright material used in this book, and I would of course be happy to acknowledge any further copyright permissions in future editions. The publication of this book has been made possible by a generous grant from the Scouloudi Foundation in association with the Institute of Historical Research.

I owe as ever a huge debt to Katie who has yet again put up with a distracted husband whose mind must often have seen thousands of miles and many decades away. This book is dedicated with love and affection to my parents Anne and John Hughes.

Introduction

On 17 April 1975 a small congregation assembled on a drizzly grey day at St Margaret's Church, in Central London, to attend a memorial service in honour of the writer Stephen Graham. Graham had died a few weeks earlier, just four days before his ninety-first birthday, and his passing had been marked by substantial obituaries in *The Times* and the *Daily Telegraph*. It is perhaps odd that they appeared at all. Both obituaries suggested that Graham would be best remembered for the books he had written before 1917, describing his time in pre-revolutionary Russia, which in the words of *The Times* made him "probably more responsible than anyone else in this country for the cult of Holy Russia and the idealization of the Russian peasantry that were beginning to make headway here before 1914".[1] Although the two obituary writers acknowledged that Graham had in later life written numerous novels and travel books, as well as a series of biographies and historical works, he seemed in death to be frozen as a thirty-year old figure tramping across the vast spaces of the Tsarist Empire, in search of a half-mythical world of icons and golden cupolas. Recollections of him were bound up with hazy memories of the *Ballets Russes* and the cult of Tolstoy, which transfixed a swathe of the British intelligentsia on the eve of the First World War, convincing numerous artists and writers that Russia could become an unlikely source of a cultural and spiritual renaissance destined to sweep the world. Graham had certainly spent much of his time as a young man trying to persuade readers that Russia possessed a richness of spirit that had long since vanished in the industrial west. The photographs that appeared of him in the British press, dressed in a peasant blouse with soulful face turned away from the camera, hinted at an elusive *persona* bearing words of truth from another world. But Graham had, even

---

1   *The Times*, 20 March 1975.

http://dx.doi.org/10.11647/OBP.0040.11

when writing about Russia, always been a more complex and multi-faceted figure than his obituaries acknowledged. Nor did he disappear from public view for the last sixty years of his life, instead retaining his popularity as a writer long after the Bolshevik seizure of power, which separated him forever from the country that dominated his imagination as a young man. Graham's half-forgotten life consisted of much more than acting as a cheerleader for the religious rituals of a sprawling autocratic empire falling apart in the face of its own contradictions.

Graham first visited Russia in 1906 and spent much of his time there over the next ten years, writing a total of eight books about the country, along with countless articles in publications ranging from *Country Life* to the *Daily Mail*. He did not invent the term 'Holy Russia', which had been in use in the British press since at least the 1880s, and was for centuries a staple of debate in Russia itself about the country's imagined status as heir to the authentic tradition of Eastern Christianity. Nor was Graham alone in falling in love with a romanticised conception of the Russian Orthodox Church, one that revelled in the beauty of its architecture and liturgy, which seemed to hint at mysteries more profound than anything that could be sensed in the faintly suburban world of the Church of England. The Russian Church was for him, as for many other Britons, just one element in the picturesque tapestry of a land whose tantalising strangeness appeared as an intriguing enigma rather than a sinister threat. Russia was for Graham never just another country like France or Germany. It was instead a place that held out the hope of personal epiphany. He first travelled there in the years before the Great War as thousands of young hippies later went to Tibet and Nepal, seeking to overcome their sense of estrangement from the world into which they had been born. Perhaps all those who fall in love with a foreign country are to some extent prompted by dissatisfaction with their ordinary lives. Graham was no exception. Whilst it took him some time to realise it, he went to Russia as a pilgrim, searching for something that he could not name until he found it.

The Russia that Graham created for his readers in the years before 1917 was above all a kind of vast sacred space, a world whose people lived their lives attuned to metaphysical echoes that resonated through the landscape they inhabited. He certainly acknowledged that such awareness did not turn all Russians into saints – he was throughout his life powerfully attracted by Dostoevsky's belief that it was through experience of sin that true humility was found. Nor did Graham deny that the vast social and economic changes taking place in Russia by the start of the twentieth century were threatening to erode its unique spiritual heritage. He was nevertheless convinced that there could be found in the mundane lives of the ordinary Russian peasantry a precious kernel, an intuitive understanding of wholeness that transcended the material conditions of everyday life, and brought together the here and now with a sense of the eternal. The simple practices of popular piety – the light in front of the ikon, the urge to go on pilgrimage – were evidence for Graham not of superstition but of a rich interior religious life. During his massive tramps across the Tsarist Empire, which took him from Archangel to the Caucasus and Warsaw to the Altai Mountains, he was himself a wanderer in search of meaning. When he travelled with hundreds of Russian pilgrims to Jerusalem in 1912, he was convinced there was a powerful symbolism in the fact that his companions were drawn from the ranks of the peasantry, noting in the book he wrote about his experiences that "it is with these simple people that I have been journeying".[2] A tall blonde man, often to be found with a pipe in his mouth, Graham must have cut a strange figure when dressed in the costume of those he travelled with. He was nevertheless always an acute observer of the people he met and the places he visited. Much of his popularity can be explained by his skill at providing readers with colourful portraits of life in far-away and exotic countries. His books about Russia were not, however, simply works of descriptive travel literature. They were instead suffused by meditations on the sense of unease that defined the atmosphere of life in Britain during the years leading up the cataclysm of the Great War. Graham unwittingly carried within himself many of the contradictions of the age into which he was born. An intensely individual man, who in his early years felt most at ease when walking alone through an empty landscape, he idealised the kind of community whose members would have frowned at his thoroughly modern desire to cross the world in search of new horizons and experiences.

There still remains the danger of reducing Graham's long life to the ten years that he spent travelling to and from Russia. Within months of the February 1917 Revolution, he was conscripted into the Scots Guards, seeing action as a private soldier on the Western Front, before publishing a book about his experiences that was sufficiently critical to earn censure from Winston Churchill in the House of Commons. Over the next few years,

---

2   Stephen Graham, *With the Russian Pilgrims to Jerusalem* (London: Macmillan, 1913), p. 12, available at http://archive.org/details/withrussianpilgr00grahuoft.

Graham made several trips to America, walking through the South in 1919 in order to see at first hand the legacies of slavery, following up his trip two years later with a massive hike through the Rockies accompanied by the self-proclaimed "Prairie Troubador" Vachel Lindsay. A year later he spent six months exploring Mexico and the American south-west, mourning the death of his travelling companion Wilfrid Ewart in a freak accident, when the young novelist was shot through the eye on his hotel balcony by revellers firing into the air to celebrate New Year. In between these visits Graham established himself as something of a celebrity in New York, giving numerous lectures about his travels, and making friends amongst the city's literary elite. His trips to the United States were interspersed with a visit to the bleak battlefields of France and a long journey to the capitals of the new states of central Europe created by the Treaty of Versailles.

Before the 1920s were out, Graham had made four more visits to New York, and travelled down the eastern frontier of the USSR, as well as spending time with the various Russian émigré communities that sprang up across Europe after 1917. He also found the energy to write a number of novels and sketches about life on the streets of London, as well as publishing an elaborate *Credo,* setting down a new spiritual vision for life in the post-war world. Graham subsequently spent much of the 1930s in Yugoslavia, walking and fishing in some of its remotest regions, as well as retreating to the mountains of northern Slovenia to write several more novels. He spent the Second World War back in London working for the BBC, possibly on the fringe of operations carried out by the Political Warfare Executive to spread black propaganda in occupied Europe, as well as editing a newsletter designed to act as a clearing house for information about the Orthodox Churches in war-time. Although his pace slowed down following the end of hostilities in 1945, he still found time to publish another three books, as well as producing manuscripts of several more that never appeared. By the time he died, Graham had published more than fifty books, including nine novels and five biographies, as well as numerous travel books and a three-hundred page autobiography. He also found time to write a number of short fantasies on subjects ranging from the ghost of Lord Kitchener through to an imaginary war in which French and Italian airplanes bombed the heart out of London.

Graham once observed that no biography could capture the truth of a life. There was certainly something unrevealing about his own autobiography, *Part of the Wonderful Scene*, even though it is full of anecdotes about the countless people he met throughout his long life. Whilst much of Graham's writing was characterised by a confessional tone that made no effort to hide its author's emotions and sensibilities, he was always adept at concealing his private life from his readers. Graham's own background was decidedly un-Victorian, since his father abandoned his young family to set up a new home with a younger woman, whom he never married despite having two more children with her. Graham's own first marriage disintegrated in the late 1920s, with considerable anguish on both sides, although the marriage itself only formally ended in 1956 with the death of his wife. He was himself from the 1930s closely involved with a young Serbian woman, whose family looked askance at their relationship, and the two of them effectively lived together as man and wife until they were free to marry after Graham was widowed. No mention of these events appears in any version of Graham's autobiography (published or unpublished). This may in part simply have been the reticence of a decent man who had no desire to cause pain to anyone still alive. It may also have been that such irregularities sat uneasily with his conscience. They are in any case essentially private affairs, which appear in the following pages only to the extent that they cast light on the way that Graham's work reflected the concerns and preoccupations of the man himself. No person is ever fortunate enough to be taken solely at their own evaluation. But nor should a study of the achievements of any writer or artist automatically feel the need to delve too deeply into the private life of friends and family, except where the material can help to illuminate the public world of books and paintings.

It is in any case no easy matter to recreate Graham's life in full, even though this biography draws extensively on his private papers, which are scattered in numerous archives and libraries around the world. Most of his letters have been lost (particularly those written in Russian and Serbian). His surviving diaries and journals generally relate only to the years from 1918 to 1929. The manuscripts of his books give little away beyond showing that he was a remarkably fluent writer, who seldom felt the need to write detailed plans of his work before launching into a sea of prose. Graham's private papers do nevertheless provide insights into his life and work that could never be culled from his written works alone. In some cases this concerns little more than matters of basic chronology. There are numerous errors in the dates of Graham's own accounts of his travels, whilst he was in any case inclined to conflate different incidents and events in his books, redrawing their sequence in order to create a better story. His diaries and letters help to restore the jangled complexity that was sometimes missing from his published work. Graham's papers also help to gently undermine some of his own self-mythologising, perhaps most notably by showing how he was before the mid 1920s far more interested in the New Age world of Theosophy than he was later ready to acknowledge. They also show how the dramatic change in the tone of his writing during the second half of the 1920s was shaped by a deep sense of crisis in his personal life. There is by contrast little material available for the 1930s, although some of the documents hidden in the archives do show the extent of Graham's connections with the Yugoslavian political elite, which he used extensively when writing his study of the assassination of King Alexander in 1934. Graham never made any secret of his sympathy for the Serbian national cause, which meant that he was during the Second World War a strong supporter of General Mihailović's *Chetniks*, whose rumoured collaboration with the Nazi occupying forces caused huge controversy in London during the years before 1945. Although Graham never abandoned his Serbian loyalties, they may have been controversial enough to encourage him to say little about Yugoslavia in his memoirs, even though he readily acknowledged in *Part of the Wonderful Scene* that he spent almost as much time there as he did in Russia. He said still less about the final years of his life, which were mostly spent at his long-time home in Soho, a period when he was dogged by ill health and found it increasingly hard to come to terms with the changing landscape of modern Britain.

Graham has, like so many writers, suffered the indignity of becoming a forgotten person. It was indeed a fate that he suffered when still alive, for in the final decades of his life the market largely disappeared for the kinds of books he wanted to write. The middle-brow fiction he specialised in during the 1930s seemed almost unbearably quaint when he tried to reproduce the formula twenty years later. Word pictures of London appeared positively archaic when the British public could watch the coronation live on television. The ultimate indignity for Graham's legacy came at the end of the twentieth century, when the Spanish novelist Javier Marias wrote a book *Negra espalda del tiempo (Dark Back of Time)* which was largely woven around the relationship between Graham and his friends Wilfrid Ewart and John Gawsworth. It was precisely the fact that these characters had all but disappeared from memory, lurking only in the recesses of unread books, that intrigued Marias enough to weave a complex narrative around a trio who had lost their flesh and blood substance and been reduced to names on a page. Graham has on occasion attracted the attention of some other contemporary writers, including the environmentalist Annie Dillard in *Pilgrim at Tinker's Creek*, whilst Robert Macfarlane devoted several pages of his wonderful book *The Wild Places* to an affectionate review of Graham's descriptions of the joys of walking. In the 1990s, *The Times* journalist Giles Whittell followed the route of Graham's 1914 trek through central Asia to the Altai Mountains when writing his book *Extreme Continental*. Such references are, however, the exception rather than the rule. Graham has not even figured much in the dry pages of academic tomes, cropping up as the subject of a few articles by western and Russian scholars, and appearing in a few anthologies of travel-writing.[3] Numerous copies of his books still reside on the dusty shelves of libraries across Europe and North America, but their author has largely faded into obscurity, a name in a card index or an entry in a computerised catalogue linked to the keywords 'Russia' and 'tramping'. All of which raises the question of why Graham should still be of interest today?

The previous few pages have started to provide an answer. Graham had a high profile as a writer for much of his life. His articles in the press were almost invariably published with a note that he was a "famous" or "celebrated" travel writer; he was a familiar enough figure to appear as a caricature in some of the cartoons which appeared in the literary magazines of the inter-war years; and, of course, he was a hugely significant figure in shaping British attitudes towards Russia during the years before the 1917 Revolution. Graham's complex and at times convoluted philosophy of life is also of interest, since it illustrates neatly how the discontents of modernity can stimulate a search for ideas and ideals that offer a compensating sense of harmony. His descriptions of landscape, and his ruminations on the role of rural life in compensating for the artificiality of the city, speak directly

---

3 For recent Russian discussions of Graham see S. Nikolaevna Tret'iakova, 'Angliskii pisatel'-puteshestvennik Stefan Grekhem o Rossii nachala XX veka', *Voprosy istorii*, 11 (2002), pp. 156–60; S.N. Tret'iakova, 'Rossiia v tvorchestve i sud'be Stefana Grekhema', in A. B. Davidson (ed.), *Rossiia i Britaniia: Sviazi i vzaimnye predstavleniia XIX–XX veka* (Moscow, 2006), pp. 220-27; Olga Kaznina, *Russkie v Anglii* (Moscow: Nasledie, 1997), 104-06. In English see, for example, Michael Hughes, 'The Visionary Goes West: Stephen Graham's American Odyssey', *Studies in Travel Literature*, 14, 2 (2010), pp. 179-96; Michael Hughes, 'The Traveller's Search for Home: Stephen Graham and the Quest for London', *The London Journal*, 36, 3 (2011), pp. 211-24. Some of Graham's writings on New York have appeared in Philip Lopate (ed.), *Writing New York* (New York: Library of America, 1998), pp. 487-96. A valuable overview of Graham's publications can be found in Marguerite Helmers, 'Stephen Graham', *Dictionary of Literary Biography*, vol. 195, pp. 137-54.

to a contemporary world familiar with the imperatives of a green agenda that seeks to build a new relationship between humanity and the natural world. His ruminations on matters spiritual have a remarkable symmetry with many contemporary New Age preoccupations. Perhaps above all, though, Graham simply had a fascinating and incident-filled life. He was born at a time when William Gladstone was Prime Minister and Queen Victoria had yet to celebrate her golden jubilee. He died when Harold Wilson was in Downing Street and Queen Elizabeth II had been on the throne for more than twenty years. During that time Graham travelled on four continents. He met monarchs and politicians, bishops and authors, prostitutes and vagabonds. He survived a hit on his house in the London Blitz. He enjoyed, in short, both the slings and arrows of outrageous fortune. Graham's prodigious output as a writer is staggering even in an age of word processors and the internet. The life he both chronicled and concealed deserves a new audience.

The writing of a 'Life' is, it goes without saying, an intensely personal process. Any biographer who seeks to tell the story of someone they never met will know how their quarry manages to be both deeply familiar and strangely elusive at one and the same time. The challenge they face in recreating their subject is not simply the lack of sources capable of yielding definite insights and perspectives. It is instead the difficulty of entering into a private mental realm of assumptions and values that are by their very nature inchoate and uncertain. Nor is it ever a straightforward business to recreate a world – social, cultural, intellectual – whose contours have changed so greatly over time. In the words of Richard Holmes, that most distinguished practitioner of the biographer's art, you can pursue your quarry but never hope to catch them, but must instead be content to sketch out the "fleeting figure" who never stands still long enough to be caught.[4] This project started out, at least in its early stages, as a kind of modern travelogue designed to return to the places Graham knew in order to reflect on the changes that have taken place since the days he toured the world. It soon became apparent that such a bold plan was doomed to frustration. Graham travelled astonishing distances in an age before the dawn of widespread air travel (his first long-distance flight did not take place until he was in his eighties). To follow in his footsteps – from western

---

4 Richard Holmes, *Footsteps: Adventures of a Romantic Biographer* (London: Harper Perennial, 2005), p. 2

Russia to Siberia, from Europe to Africa, from Canada to Mexico – would be the work of years even in an age of motorways and jet aircraft. But, and perhaps more importantly, the world that Graham knew has in many respects changed so greatly that to follow his footsteps in such detail would constitute an exercise in mere cartography. It would give precedence to the idea of 'place' as a set of coordinates over 'place' as a complex amalgam of history and story refracted through the vision of the people who experience it. Graham was in his travel writing adept at painting vivid portraits of the people he met and the landscapes he passed through. But he was also always searching for a 'spirit of place' that lay beneath the surface, a spirit shaped both by the past *and* by a strong sense that the richness of human experience rested on something more profound and elusive than its material substratum. Much of his early travel writing in particular was less about place as a location in time and rather about place as a meeting of the eternal and the temporal. It was only after he left Russia behind – or rather that Russia left him behind – that his work began to focus more immediately on the things he heard and saw on his long journeys through Europe and North America.

I have been fortunate enough down the years to travel to many of the places Graham visited. Russia is, so to speak, at the heart of my professional *oekumene*, the place I have written about over many decades, living in and visiting the country many times in both its Soviet and post-Soviet guises. The cities of Europe and North America about which Graham wrote so copiously – Prague, Vienna, Warsaw, Berlin, Chicago, New York – have also countless times been on my itinerary. The south-western states of America similarly feature in the mouldering collection of airline tickets hidden away somewhere in a storage cupboard. Only the Rocky Mountains and the mountains of central Asia have remained for me entirely *terra incognita*. It would nevertheless by untruthful to claim with much passion that I have been able to find Graham in the places he visited. The worst slums of Chicago's West Side and the New York Bowery have long since disappeared. Soviet planners swept away much of old Moscow, leaving Red Square and the Kremlin as glorified museums, echoes in brick and stone of a world that has long vanished. The vagaries of time and war have changed places like Berlin, Prague and Constantinople beyond all recognition. Even Graham's long-time home at 60 Frith Street, in London's Soho, has been through so many incarnations since his death that its brick facade and black front door seem now to have no memory of his presence. If ghosts are – as some believe – electronic emanations of people long departed, then Graham seems to have had no desire to haunt the world. He lives instead in the numerous books and journals he left behind.

There is one exception to this rule. Not long before the completion of this manuscript, I was lucky enough to visit the Old Believer settlements that stretch along the shore of Lake Peipsi in modern Estonia. The Orthodox Old Believers, religious dissidents who rejected the church reforms introduced by Patriarch Nikon in the seventeenth century, fled central Russia in search of more remote areas where they could live their lives free from persecution. Their descendants who live today on the banks of Lake Peipsi maintain many of the Old Believer traditions, both secular and religious, and to wander through the wooden houses of their villages is to get a sense of the old Russia. Even the presence of cars and electric light – *de rigueur* in such a determinedly modern country as Estonia – cannot conceal altogether the shards of the past. At one point during the visit I stood on a rock on the shore of the lake, looking out across the water towards Russia, which remained stubbornly invisible in the haze of a fine September day. When Graham was a young man in London, Russia became for him a half-mythical place, a "Somewhere-Out-Beyond", where he believed that he could find a life more fulfilling than one that involved a daily commute from Essex into London where he worked as a junior civil servant. By the time he visited the Old Believer settlements in 1924, seven years after the Revolution, Russia was closed to him and he could do no more than search for echoes of the country he had loved so dearly. As I peered towards the horizon across Lake Peipsi, trying to catch a glimpse of the Russian shore, it occurred to me that Graham had like all true pilgrims spent his life in search of something that he was doomed never to find. Much of his work was driven by a desire to make actual in the world the ideals he saw in his imagination. The visions that he sought to portray sometimes seemed to him tantalisingly close. At other times they seemed far away. The following chapters will show that Graham was despite his much-vaunted 'idealism' – his sense that the world was shaped by forces more profound than could be discerned in the rhythms of ordinary life – surprisingly adept at using his pen to capture the foibles and idiosyncrasies of the people he lived amongst. Aware of two worlds, but at home in neither, Graham's story was in the deepest sense of the term a religious one.

1. Chasing the Shadow

Stephen Graham was born in Edinburgh in March 1884, in a house near Calton Hill, distinctive then as now for the Parthenon-like monument that caps its summit, designed by the architect William Playfair as a memorial for those who died in the Napoleonic wars. It was snowing heavily, not a particularly unusual event for the final weeks of winter in Scotland's capital city, but still rare enough for the young Stephen to be regaled throughout his childhood with stories of how the "big wet snow-flakes" had driven against the windows on the day he entered the world. He was still speculating eight decades later whether his fascination with snow had been one of the factors that first led him to Russia.

Graham's early life remains surprisingly impervious to even the most sleuth-like biographical inquiry, for despite the confessional style that became the hallmark of so much that he wrote, his apparent candour often concealed a good deal more than it exposed. His description of childhood fills fewer than three pages of the autobiography he published in 1964, and the few episodes he chose to recall have a slightly fantastic character about them, coloured both by the passing of the years and his life-long vivid imagination.[1] Stephen remembered himself as a toddler with "golden curly hair", dressed like a girl, who was stolen away by the gypsies to "begin a begging career". All came right, though, when he was found by the police and returned home, after which his father cut off his flowing locks and dressed him in an altogether more masculine sailor suit. Graham's other recollections of childhood were equally episodic if less exotic. He remembered being a chronic sleepwalker, his nocturnal ramblings often concluded by a swift clip round the ear from his father,

---

1 All quotations in this paragraph unless stated otherwise are from Stephen Graham, *Part of the Wonderful Scene* (London: Collins, 1964).

http://dx.doi.org/10.11647/OBP.0040.01

who was seemingly untroubled by the prospect of startling his son into wakefulness. He also recalled how his best friend Kenny Self helped to foster in him an interest in moths and other insects, that led him to become an avid youthful collector of lepidoptera, earning him the nickname "legs and wings" from his childhood friends.[2] "Our friendship lasted six or seven years. During that time I was in love with him, make of that what you will. At night I used to haunt the street where he lived, watching for a glimpse of his face at a window. I hoped that his house would burn down so that I might rush through the flames to save him". The two boys also acted together in a school production of *A Merchant of Venice*, Kenny taking the part of the maid Nerissa, and Stephen the role of Portia, who dons men's clothing in order to masquerade as a lawyer to defend Antonio from Shylock's bloodthirsty demand for his pound of flesh. It would be unwise to read too much into such memories. It was, after all, inevitable that boys would have to play female parts in an education system that was strictly segregated by sex. Graham's recollections cannot in any case always be trusted. An unwavering commitment to the accurate delineation of past events was never the hallmark of his literary work. The brief hotch-potch of childhood anecdotes recounted in the opening pages of the published version of *Part of the Wonderful Scene* was designed to provide colour rather than insight. It may also have been designed to conceal some of the oddities of his upbringing. The eighty-year old Graham had little real interest in regaling his readers with accurate remembrances of his eight-year old self.

The father who cut off young Stephen's golden hair was the journalist and future *Country Life* editor Peter Anderson Graham (invariably known professionally by the moniker P. Anderson Graham). Graham senior had been born in 1856, in the border town of Crookham in Northumbria, the second eldest of a family of four boys and one girl. The Graham clan subsequently moved to Edinburgh, where they settled in Arthur Street, just a few minutes from the city centre. The family circumstances were not particularly prosperous. The 1881 census, which noted Anderson Graham's profession as "journalist and leader writer", also recorded that

---

2 Graham Papers (Harry Ransom Center henceforth HRC), Works file, *Part of the Wonderful Scene* (autograph version). The pagination of the autograph version is unreliable and is therefore not included in the references. Note, too, the existence of a typescript version of *Part of the Wonderful Scene* in the same Works file which differs significantly both from the first handwritten draft and the final published version. For Graham's youthful notes on lepidoptery, see Graham Papers (Florida State University, Strozier Library, henceforth FSU), Box 578, 31.

two of his brothers were respectively a "press-maker" and a "journeyman ironmonger". The third was an apprentice draper. Their father worked as a "weigher" at one of Edinburgh's numerous train stations (although his profession was recorded in a later census as railway clerk). Despite this less than propitious background for a literary career, Anderson Graham was able to attend Edinburgh University, before subsequently establishing himself on the *Edinburgh Courant*, a Conservative paper whose contributors were committed to countering the Liberal influence of *The Scotsman* in "this Whig-ridden country".[3] Stephen Graham subsequently recalled that his father was always a "hot Tory".

Anderson Graham later belonged to the circle of young men who surrounded the celebrated writer and critic W.E. Henley, famous amongst other things for his assault on the aestheticism of Aubrey Beardsley and Oscar Wilde, as well as his memorable dismissal of socialism as the "dominion of the common fool".[4] Henley had first travelled to Edinburgh in 1873 to seek medical treatment from Joseph Lister, the pioneer of antiseptic surgery, during which time he became a close friend of the novelist and travel-writer Robert Louis Stevenson. He returned to Scotland at the end of the 1880s, as editor of the newly-established *Scots Observer*, before going back to London in 1892 to edit the paper under its new and more imposing title of the *National Observer*. It was during this period that he became celebrated for furthering the careers of a whole host of young writers including J.M. Barrie and Kenneth Grahame. It was also during this time that Anderson Graham came firmly into Henley's orbit, although the two men may have met earlier during the latter's previous sojourns in Edinburgh. Anderson had moved his family from Edinburgh to Gloucestershire soon after Stephen was born, to take up the editorship of the *Gloucestershire Echo*, a provincial paper of some importance, but within a short time he decided to give up his post in order to move to London and concentrate on his literary ambitions. Stephen later recalled that during this time, when the family lived in Hornsey, they were "very poor", with the result that he was expected to act as "shopper for the family, saving a penny there and a ha'penny here".[5] His memory of events may once again

---

3   On the Scottish press at this time, see Stephen Koss, *The Rise and Fall of the Political Press in Britain* (London: Hamilton, 1981), p. 207.
4   W.E. Henley, *Views and Reviews* (London: David Nutt, 1890), 32. On Henley see Kennedy Williamson, *W.E. Henley: A Memoir* (London: Harold Shaylor, 1930). See, too, Damian Atkinson (ed.), *The Selected Letters of W.E. Henley* (Aldershot: Ashgate, 2000).
5   Graham, *Wonderful Scene*, p. 11.

have been over-coloured; although the family's pecuniary circumstances imposed on them a frugal life-style, not least because there were by the mid 1890s six children to feed and clothe, there was still enough money to keep a maid. The area of London they lived in was in any case characterised more by genteel poverty than real material deprivation. The family's lifestyle would have been familiar to the fictional Mr Pooter, the pompously respectable clerk whose ruminations on life feature in George and Weedon Grossmith's comic classic *Diary of a Nobody*, first published in *Punch* at the end of the 1880s, when the Grahams were already resident in Hornsey.

Stephen's family was, then, a literary if impecunious one. His mother Jane (*née* Macleod) had been a librarian before her marriage to Anderson Graham in Edinburgh in 1881. Her son later spoke of how she "handled first editions of Ruskin and Browning" – two of his favourite childhood authors – although a moment's reflection suggests that, since both men were still alive when Jane was working, this was more a statement of fact than any indication that she once enjoyed privileged access to rare material.[6] Graham also recalled how his mother seemed to him as he grew up like a character in a Walter Scott novel – "unhappy, pure, romantic and heroic".[7] Jane certainly had a deep aversion to the mundane business of household management, preferring to bury her head in a book, which perhaps explains why Stephen was promoted at a young age to the status of the family's shopper-in-chief. It is also clear that she represented a potent presence in her son's life, even though he barely mentioned her in his autobiography. During a deep personal crisis in his mid-forties, soon after she died, he wrote private notes of anguish to her in the diary he kept detailing the depths of his despair.

The best portrait of Jane appears in Graham's 1934 novel *Lost Battle* which detailed, in a thinly-fictionalised form, the disintegration of his parents' marriage, as it collapsed around 1900 when Anderson Graham left home to establish a new life elsewhere. A shy and retiring woman, who had few relationships outside the home, Jane had a strong taste for "literary romanticism" and spent much of her time reading the novels of Scott. She also read a great deal of French and Italian literature. "Jeannie Macrimmon" – as she appears in *Lost Battle* – developed a close and even intense relationship with her eldest child Mark (the *alter ego* of Stephen Graham himself). The two often stayed up late whilst the mother read

---
6 Ibid, p. 9.
7 Graham Papers (FSU), Box 580, 13c ('From the Days of My Youth').

to her son, dreaming that he might one day become a celebrated writer, succeeding in the literary world that tantalized her so greatly but which always appeared so remote. Although "Jeannie" was devoted to her other five children – four girls and a boy – it was in Mark that she seemed to find a sympathetic spark for her "romantic and imaginative" nature. The relationship provided her with some kind of emotional compensation for what was, at least to the jaundiced eyes of Stephen Graham as he looked back from the vantage point of later years, his parents' joyless and empty marriage.

The portrait of Anderson Graham painted by his son in *Lost Battle* was far more acerbic. The character of John Rae Belfort – as Anderson appears in the book – could hardly have been more different from that of his wife. Whilst "Jeanie Macrimmon" was mild-mannered and other-worldly, "John Belfort" was a hard-drinking and irascible individual, who desperately aspired to a literary career, but was constantly frustrated at having to turn his hand to hack-work to support his large family. He also possessed a fierce temper that inspired considerable trepidation in his wife and children. When at home in Essex – where the real Graham family moved in the early 1890s – John Belfort spent most of his time alone in his study playing chess. He could also be heard from time to time pacing up and down his bedroom reciting old Scottish ballads for hours on end.

The fictional Belfort achieved some success by writing about agricultural issues – as did Anderson Graham – and his absence from home on periodic tours around Britain was welcomed by his wife and children who relished the peace that reigned when he was away. The brittle marriage that Stephen Graham portrayed in *Lost Battle* finally came to an end when Belfort left home for a much younger woman. The book traces how the grown-up Mark, by now a successful writer in his own right, gradually re-established a relationship with his father and his two children by his second "marriage" (Belfort, like Anderson, never formally divorced his first wife). It is difficult to know to what extent *Lost Battle* represented anything more than a thinly-fictionalised account of the Graham household. The census records show that by 1911 Anderson Graham was living apart from his family with two new children in St Albans, although he had left his first family many years earlier, probably when Stephen was about sixteen. In the years that followed he built a substantial house in large grounds near Hemel Hempstead in Hertfordshire, paid for by his earnings from *Country Life*, and a series of articles on rural affairs in publications including the *Morning Post* and the *St*

James' Gazette. The portrait of John Rae Belfort in *Lost Battle* certainly tallies with the little that is known of the biography and character of Anderson Graham himself. Stephen remarked in his diary after his father's death that there were many mysteries about his family that he could never fathom. The same uncertainties confront his biographer.

Anderson Graham was, like many of those who made up the world of late Victorian *belles lettres*, very much a *professional* writer, dependent on his pen to earn his living, rather than a gentleman of leisure blessed with the means to contribute to the press according to his particular whim and interest. His articles appeared in publications ranging from the *Evening Standard* and the *Morning Post* to *Longman's Magazine* and *The New Review*. Stephen later remembered that it was his father who "taught me to write", making him re-tell the story of *Kidnapped* in sentences of no more than sixteen words, an exercise designed to emphasise the importance of brevity in effective communication. Despite the acerbic portrait of Anderson Graham in *Lost Battle* he still seems to have had a significant influence on his son's early life, not least in helping him realise that a literary career would always involve as much grind as inspiration. Stephen's later work-ethic and pride in earning his living from his pen were doubtless inherited from his father – just as the more intuitive and instinctive side of his character seems to have been shaped by his mother.

Graham *père* also in later years provided his eldest son with valuable advice about publishing his work, and opened the columns of *Country Life* to him at a time when Stephen was still struggling to find a market for his writing (the two men seem to have re-established their relationship after the hiatus caused by Anderson's departure from the family home in Essex). Stephen later returned the favour by helping his father to publicise his now long-forgotten science fiction novel, *The Collapse of Homo Sapiens* (1923), which Anderson published when he was in his mid-sixties, long after any fame he once enjoyed had been eclipsed by his son's. Nor was Stephen the only child in the Graham household to inherit the literary gene. His younger sister Eleanor was in later life to achieve fame as a children's author, most notably with *The Children who Lived in a Barn*, as well as playing a key role in establishing the celebrated Puffin series of books, which published such classics as Barbara Euphan Todd's *Wurzel Gummidge* and Roger Lancelyn Green's version of *King Arthur and his Knights of the Round Table*.

Anderson Graham's influence on his son was not confined to advising him about the skills he would need to succeed as a professional writer.

He also propagated in him a suspicion of the modern world that was to become a defining motif in the books that Stephen later wrote about his time in pre-Revolutionary Russia. Anderson Graham was from a young age concerned about the declining health of rural Britain, fearing that the rhythms of traditional society were being undermined by the twin processes of industrialisation and urbanisation, a theme that ran through his 1892 book *The Rural Exodus*. Although he told his readers that addressing the problem should not become a matter of party politics, there was something profoundly Tory about his prescriptions, which were rooted in a sense that any changes should take place "slowly and gradually" and be rooted "in the hearts and minds of the people".[8] Nor was Anderson Graham's concern about the countryside simply a matter of economics and sociology. He also had a strong interest in the natural world (although this may in part have been prompted by his recognition that there was a ready market for books and articles on the subject). His first lengthy published work on *Nature in Books*, which appeared in 1891, contained essays on the naturalist Richard Jefferies and the American transcendentalist Henry David Thoreau. His third book, *All the Year with Nature* (1893), which was dedicated to W.E. Henley, contained a series of articles on topics ranging from 'Birds-Nesting' through to 'The Harvest Labour'. Although most of the pieces were quite light-hearted, if sometimes marred by a rather laboured whimsy, their author did occasionally intersperse his meditations with more serious reflections on the state of rural society. He also succumbed to a lyrical celebration of the English countryside, despite half-jestingly warning against such extravagance, writing movingly of his love of winter evenings when "the distant woods are visible in the last streaks of daylight, and the blackening train of crows are hurrying to cold perches on the oaks".[9]

The essays in *Nature in Books* were more serious in tone, suggesting that whilst all human beings would in time become weary of seeking fame or material possessions, the appeal of "the music and pageantry of earth" would never fail.[10] Although Anderson Graham did not share the nature-mysticism of Richard Jefferies, he provided a sensitive account of his work, showing how Jefferies' love of the countryside provided him with a sense of meaning missing elsewhere in his life. And, in his chapter on Wordsworth, Anderson firmly dismissed critics who failed to engage with

---

8   P. Anderson Graham, *The Rural Exodus* (London: Methuen, 1892), p. 208.
9   P. Anderson Graham, *All the Year with Nature* (London: Smith and Elden, 1893), p. 181.
10 P. Anderson Graham, *Nature in Books* (London: Methuen, 1891), p. x.

the poet's religious views or rejected them as incoherent and immature. He criticised those who refused to see in nature anything more than an impersonally bleak world, arguing that "Right as it is for us to know and feel something of the sadness and melancholy that cast their sober mantle over so much of the universe, it is no less desirable to avoid a too morbid gloating over them, and to feel and appreciate the joy that, in spite of artificial restraints, is awakened by the happy carol of a bird, the glow of sunshine, the gambol of younglings, the beauty of landscape".[11] Whilst Graham senior was reluctant to ascribe any definite metaphysical meaning to the natural world, he consciously rejected the post-Darwinian sense that the beauty of the countryside represented nothing more than the accidental by-product of natural selection. It was a view echoed many years later by his son, who found in his massive hikes through the Russian countryside a sense of mystery that hinted at realms of meaning lying far beyond the limited horizons of the material world.

The extent to which Anderson Graham was a real countryman is open to debate. Although he was born in rural Northumberland, his parents' move to Edinburgh took place when he was a young boy, and much of his life was spent in towns and cities. Whilst he discussed the rural economy quite knowledgeably in *The Rural Exodus*, there is little evidence that he had much real sense of the intricate practices of agriculture. Even though his observations of the natural world were often acute, they showed no real evidence of a deep knowledge of birds and animals. Anderson Graham was certainly a lover of dogs, and his family at various times owned a fox-terrier and a deer-hound called Fingal, presumably named for the character in *Ossian*, but though he wrote of shooting and hunting it is not clear that he was a passionate devotee of country sports.[12] Nor is it clear to what extent Stephen Graham's own early years were actively shaped by his father's uncertain interest in rural affairs. Anderson published a book called *Country Pastimes for Boys*,[13] when Stephen was thirteen, which contained various Boy's Own information on such topics as collecting birds' eggs and catching fish. The book was, however, written for an essentially suburban middle class readership, anxious to find ways of ensuring that their children had something to do in the holidays, rather

---

11 Ibid, p. 191.
12 Anderson Graham was, however, a sharp critic of those who opposed country sports. See P. Anderson Graham, 'The Abuse of Kindness', *National Observer*, 30 March 1895.
13 P. Anderson Graham, *Country Pastimes for Boys* (London: Longmans, 1897).

than an audience who already possessed an intimate knowledge of the countryside. Stephen's own interest in lepidoptery comes across as that of a child raised in the suburbs, rather than characteristic of a boy intimately familiar with the life of the fields, although a fictionalised account of his early childhood published in the early 1920s revealed the depth of his passion for the subject.[14] Anderson Graham may well have made a real attempt to inculcate a love of the English countryside in his children, but if he did it would necessarily have been the love of an outsider, given that the family's daily life was spent in north London and suburban Essex.

P. Anderson Graham's combination of skills and interests meant that he was a natural choice in 1900 for the post of editor of *Country Life*, established three years earlier, to capitalise on a wistful nostalgia for an imaginary rural past amongst a middle class readership that overwhelmingly derived its income from commerce and industry.[15] The Arts and Crafts movement had been in full swing in Britain from the 1880s, characterised by a search for a new aesthetic style in art and architecture, intended to counter the soulless products of a mechanised age which denigrated the craft principle in favour of industrial efficiency.[16] In a supreme irony, the search for the authentic and traditional quickly became big business, as magazines like *Country Life* promoted such products as wood panelling from Liberty's of London, designed to adorn the dining rooms of the expensive new country homes advertised in its property pages. The magazine also carried numerous articles about aspects of rural life, ranging from stock-breeding through to fox-hunting, as well as publishing more literary pieces about travel and politics.

Anderson Graham was well-suited to manage such an enterprise (he also contributed many of the magazine's articles and columns). He had for many years been a devotee of John Ruskin, who served as a kind of guru for the Arts and Crafts movement, whilst his own idealised view of the English countryside dovetailed neatly with the ethos that *Country Life* tried so hard to promote. Anderson also possessed the hard journalistic skills needed to ensure that the magazine was run professionally, and responded to the demands of its readership, who bought it precisely because they aspired

---

14 Stephen Graham, *Under-London* (London: Macmillan, 1923).
15 On *Country Life* (including some comments on Anderson Graham) see Sir Roy Strong, *Country Life, 1897-1997: An English Arcadia* (London: Country Life Books, 1997).
16 For a valuable international perspective on the Arts and Crafts Movement, see Rosalind Blakesley, *The Arts and Crafts Movement* (London: Phaidon, 2006).

to the life-style it promoted. The portrayal of the English countryside that appeared in *Country Life* under Anderson Graham's editorship was a commercial product, reflecting the financial imperatives of a journalism that pandered to the longings of a particular section of urban society. The Russia that Stephen Graham was later to place before his readers was also in large part a fictional product, reflecting the hopes and dreams of its author, whilst at the same time being carefully calculated to appeal to the instincts and yearnings of his audience. He was, like his father, adept at recognising that romantic nostalgia and distrust of the modern industrial world were marketable commodities, capable of appealing to an urban readership anxious to hear about worlds they could imagine but never inhabit.

The young Stephen Graham was educated at Sir George Monoux Grammar School in Chingford, where he proved an able if sometimes lazy student, who had to be bribed by his father to apply himself properly to his studies. He made his greatest mark on the Latin teacher, one Mr Adams, who took a shine to his young pupil and awarded him the highest grades of any boy in class, before abandoning his teaching career to take up farming. Graham was in his own words, "always fighting, playing practical jokes, committing juvenile crimes, and getting chased by the police", memories that he drew on many years later in his 1922 novel *Under-London*, which described the lives of a small group of boys growing up in an East London suburb at the end of the nineteenth century. Despite his various misdemeanours, Graham became School captain, a result he believed of his popularity with the other boys as well as many of the masters.[17] He left at fifteen because his father was too poor to send him to university – the lucrative *Country Life* appointment still lay a year ahead – and within a few months Stephen was commuting to work as a clerk in the Bankruptcy Court at Carey Street in central London.

Anderson Graham was instrumental in encouraging his son to join the Civil Service, pointing out the benefits of a regular income and pension denied to the freelance journalist. Graham's office duties were very dull, consisting of routine clerical work and the daily distribution of the mail, but he at least had time to pursue his interest in literature. Within a few years he progressed to a post as staff clerk at Somerset House, where the grind of office life was interspersed with games of table-tennis in the basement,

---

17 Graham Papers (HRC), *Wonderful Scene* (autograph).

along with debates amongst "a distinguished company of young men" about such topics as "the Basis of Love".

Graham fell in love with a series of young women during these years, although his idea of courtship seems to have been excruciatingly earnest, consisting largely of forays into the countryside to engage in discussion about the virtues of various poets. There was a good deal of interest in literary matters amongst the clerks at Somerset House, several of whom later progressed to careers in journalism, and they eagerly followed such contemporary controversies as the dispute between Hilaire Belloc and George Bernard Shaw that followed the publication of the former's *The Servile State*.[18] Graham himself read widely – Ruskin and Carlyle being particular favourites – but the course of his life changed one day when he found a battered copy of Dostoevsky's *Crime and Punishment* on sale in a barrow in central London. He was immediately captivated by the brooding story of the student Raskolnikov, whose life was haunted by remorse following his murder of an elderly female pawnbroker, undertaken in a desperate act of defiance to assert his autonomy from the moral claims of the world around him. The "grand discovery" of an author who had, in Graham's words, "passed into oblivion", prompted the start of his life-long love affair with all things Russian. He insisted on sharing his discovery with a girlfriend who was ten years his senior, another harbinger of his future life, for Graham was over the next few years repeatedly attracted to women considerably older than himself.

Graham was right in suggesting that Dostoevsky commanded little interest in Britain in the early 1900s. Although a number of his novels had been translated into French and English some years earlier – and subsequently became very popular during the First World War – the author of *Crime and Punishment* was not particularly widely read in Britain during the early years of the twentieth century.[19] Russia itself had for centuries been seen by many Britons as little more than a remote and sinister void on the periphery of Europe. The era of the Great Game – that curious nineteenth-century duel of British and Russian soldier-explorers played out in the remote deserts and mountains of central Asia – helped to fuel the idea that Tsarist Russia was a natural enemy of the British Empire.[20] Nor was Anglo-

---

18 Graham, *Wonderful Scene*, p. 13.
19 For further details on the reception of Dostoevsky in Britain, see Helen Muchnic, *Dostoevsky's English Reputation, 1881-1936* (New York: Octagon Books, 1969); William Leatherbarrow (ed.), *Dostoevskii and Britain* (Oxford: Berg, 1995).
20 On the Great Game see Peter Hopkirk, *The Great Game: The Struggle for Empire in*

Russian antagonism simply a matter of geopolitics. The final decades of the nineteenth century also witnessed a growing campaign by British radicals to warn their fellow-countrymen that the despotic Russian Government posed a major challenge to the liberties and security of the entire continent.[21] H.G. Wells, who in the years before the First World War shared this *bienpensant* distaste for the empire of the tsars, later summarised the situation accurately when he recalled that for many Britons, Russia had always seemed "a fabulous country […] a wilderness of wolves, knouts, serfdom, and cruelty [as well as] Bogey Russia, which had 'designs' – on India, on all the world".[22] This long tradition of Russophobia had nevertheless become subject to challenge by the time Graham picked up his translation of *Crime and Punishment* a few years into the twentieth century. The publication in 1877 of Donald Mackenzie Wallace's magisterial *Russia* had provided a British audience with a more substantial account of the country than the usual *pot-pourri* of travellers' tales that so often shaped popular views of Russia. The British Museum librarian William Ralston published an important volume of Russian folk tales in 1869,[23] as well as translating the work of Ivan Turgenev, who was himself offered an Honorary D.Litt by Oxford University in 1879.[24] New translations of the most important novels of the Russian golden age began to appear in considerable numbers during the 1880s and 1890s, which although not always of the best quality, gave their British audience an insight into a literary tradition so different from the ones with which they were familiar.[25] There was also a growing audience for Russian music, not least thanks to the work of the formidable writer and critic Rosa Newmarch, who had studied under Vladimir

---

Central Asia (London: John Murray, 2006). For a dated but useful analysis of the origins of Russophobia see John Howes Gleason, *The Genesis of Russophobia in Great Britain* (Cambridge, Mass: Harvard University Press, 1950).

21 See, for example, Barry Hollingsworth, 'The Society of Friends of Russian Freedom: English Liberals and Russian Socialists, 1890-1917', *Oxford Slavonic* Papers, 3 (1970), pp. 45-64.

22 Introduction by H.G. Wells to Denis Garston, *Friendly Russia* (London: Fisher Unwin, 1915), pp. 9-10.

23 W.R.S. Ralston, *Krilof and his Fables* (London: Strahan, 1869).

24 On Turgenev's links with Oxford see J.S.G. Simmons, 'Turgenev and Oxford', in *Ivan Turgenev and Britain*, ed. by Patrick Waddington (Oxford: Berg, 1995), pp. 208-12. See, too the relevant pages of M. Kizilov, 'Russkie v Oksforde: kratkii obzor istorii', in *Russkoe prisutstvie v Britanii*, ed. by N.V. Makarova and O.A. Morgunova (Moscow: Sovremennaia ekonomika i pravo, 2009), pp. 101-16.

25 For a biography of Constance Garnett, who played a vital role in bringing translations of the Russian classics to an English-language audience, see Richard Garnett, *Constance Garnett: An Heroic Life* (London: Faber and Faber, 2009).

Stasov in St Petersburg, and later wrote numerous programme notes for the annual Proms season in London.[26] The idea that Russian culture was somehow more youthful and vigorous than the culture of Western Europe was becoming deeply entrenched in at least some British literary and artistic circles by the end of the first decade of the twentieth century.[27] When the young Stephen Graham first became engrossed in the novels of Dostoevsky, he was travelling a road already well-trodden by many of his fellow-countrymen.

The appeal of Russia to a new generation of British Russophiles was bound up with its exotic and even oriental character, a place concealing behind its strange veneer a world distinguished by a brooding intensity. Graham was so taken by *Crime and Punishment* precisely because it was much "more profound" than a "murder story", adding that "There is a hidden x in it. Let x be the soul of man, or let x be the meaning of life, something not familiar to the Western mind but, once sensed, for ever haunting. I was on the trail of a religious philosophy more inspiring than Carlyle or Ibsen or Nietzsche".[28] The references to Carlyle and Nietzsche were not accidental. Graham's taste in reading as a young man focused on authors who sought to articulate a complete vision of life, and there was more than a hint of hero-worship in his attitude towards the writers he most admired, which he ruefully noted a few years later resembled that of "a young girl in love with a new history mistress".[29] The youthful Graham was, like so many men of his age, searching for a pattern of significance that he could not find in the daily bureaucratic round. He had from the age of fourteen become "secretly religious", although religion already appeared to him less a matter of doctrine and more a form of spiritual quest, which assumed that the meaning of life could never be reduced to its purely material aspect.[30] In an unpublished version of his autobiography, he wrote that he had from his school years developed a "philosophy of prayer" in which prayer was "addressed [to] a secret power inside yourself", which

---

26 On Newmarch, see Philip Ross Bullock, *Rosa Newmarch and Russian Music in Late Nineteenth and Early Twentieth-Century England* (Aldershot: Ashgate, 2009).
27 See, for example, Havelock Ellis, 'The Genius of Russia', *Contemporary Review*, 80 (1901), pp. 419-33.
28 Graham, *Wonderful Scene*, p. 14.
29 Stephen Graham, *A Vagabond in the Caucasus with Some Notes of his Experiences Among the Russians* (London: John Lane, 1911), p. 4, version available at http://archive.org/details/cu31924028754822.
30 Graham, *Wonderful Scene*, p. 11. On Graham's youthful religiosity see Graham Papers (FSU), Box 580, 13c ('In the Days of my Youth').

later manifested itself in a belief that the divine permeated all aspects of creation and was often best-found "within".[31] By the time he reached his early twenties, the idea of Russia had become for Graham a kind of intellectual and emotional lodestar – a mythical place glimpsed through the prism of literature, where life seemed to possess a richness that was missing in the tediously ordered world of Edwardian Britain, where he was confined to expressing his individuality by wearing his hair long under "strange-looking hats".[32] The Romantic streak he inherited from his mother – a yearning for places half-imagined but little known – was helping to shape his growing disenchantment with humdrum existence at Somerset House and in the suburbs of Essex.

Most Britons who developed a taste for Russian literature were content to rely on translations, but Graham was determined to learn the language himself, so he could read Tolstoy and Dostoevsky in the original. He tried to study alone, making notes from a Russian grammar book, but when the results proved disappointing he wrote to the Russian consul in London asking for details of possible tutors. It was in this way that he came into contact with Nikolai Lebedev, the twenty-year old son of a deacon in the Russian Orthodox Church, who had come to London from a village near Kharkov in order to improve his English. The two young men quickly became good friends, and the relaxed regime at Somerset House meant that lessons could take place during office hours, at least until the appointment of a less accommodating supervisor meant that they had to be deferred until lunch-time or evening (his predecessor fell down the steep office steps and broke his neck). The arrangement came to an end, at least temporarily, when Lebedev was offered lucrative work as a translator at the Vickers shipyards at Barrow-in-Furness, in north-west England, where a number of ships were being built for the Russian navy. The youthful friendship between the two men was nevertheless destined to have an important impact on Graham's future. When he finally decided to abandon his life in London in order to move to Russia, with the intention of earning his living as a writer, it was to the Lebedev house that he first travelled.

Graham's first trip to Russia took place in 1906, at the age of twenty two, when he booked four weeks leave from his Civil Service post in order to see the country with his own eyes. It was not a propitious time to visit. The defeats suffered by Russia during the recent war with Japan had prompted

---

31 Graham Papers (HRC), *Wonderful Scene* (typescript), p. 2.
32 *Daily Express*, 3 March 1930 (Graham article headed 'First You Must Live').

the start of major disturbances, and by the middle of 1905 it looked as though the country might be headed for a full-blown revolution. The concessions offered by Tsar Nicholas II in October helped to calm the public mood, but periodic unrest continued to erupt for many months to come, both in the cities and especially in the depths of the Russian countryside. Graham travelled to Russia by train through Holland and Germany, armed with a Kodak camera to record his impressions – the editor of *Black and White* said the magazine would publish any photographs of particular interest – but without the revolver offered by a well-meaning friend who believed that he might need it at a time when "the bombs were flying thick and fast".[33] He arrived in Warsaw, a city that was then within the Tsarist Empire, on the day a senior official was assassinated. Graham was himself arrested by a group of soldiers, who doubted his *bona fides*, and was taken under armed guard to the local jail. Although his incarceration was brief, the *Rus'* newspaper reported that he had been beaten severely, news that "somehow [...] came to England as the arrest and flogging of Mr Foster Fraser" (a well-known foreign correspondent of the time).[34]

After this excitement, Graham went to Moscow, where he once again attracted the attention of the local authorities, before heading on to the city of Nizhni Novgorod in order to see the annual fair there. He witnessed with some shock the activities of the local prostitutes, who sat with their legs apart on the steps of the brothels, canvassing for business from the numerous visitors to the town.[35] Graham himself was more taken with the "respectable" women who passed him on the streets of Moscow and Nizhni Novgorod, seeing in them "replicas of Turgenev's heroines". Despite his good looks and physical stature – Graham was well over six feet tall – none of them were attracted by an impoverished Englishman who could only speak their language with stuttering hesitation. He therefore consoled himself with the purchase of a scimitar and a filigree belt, along with a pair of scarlet and gold slippers, which he carried back to London at the end of his holiday. He arrived in Britain to be hailed by his friends and colleagues as "a local lion" who had ventured into the dangerous world of Russia and lived to tell of his experience.

It is hard to establish the chronology of Graham's first visit to Russia in much detail, not least because of several contradictions in his own accounts

---

33 Graham, *Vagabond*, p. 7.
34 Ibid, p. 8.
35 Graham, *Wonderful Scene* (autograph).

of the trip, but it is clear that he did not grasp (and perhaps did not want to grasp) the significance of the things he witnessed. The upheavals of 1905-6, which Lenin later described as a dress-rehearsal for 1917, provided stark evidence that Tsarist Russia was already going through rapid social and economic change. The country had become the fifth largest industrial power in the world, and large-scale urban growth was creating considerable social tension in cities like Moscow and St Petersburg, as millions of peasants migrated from the countryside to work in the newly-built factories. The Russia that Graham had fallen in love with back in London – the land of golden cupolas and country estates that provided the setting for the novels of Tolstoy and Dostoevsky – had always been a largely mythical place. Books such as *Crime and Punishment* and *Anna Karenina* no more offered a realistic portrayal of Russia in the 1860s and 1870s than *The Pickwick Papers* did of Britain in the 1830s. And, in any case, the social and political world portrayed in the novels of Russia's golden age had changed almost beyond recognition by the early years of the twentieth century. The turbulent events of the 1905-6 Revolution did not lead Graham to question the accuracy of the images of Russia that had formed in his mind long before he first set eyes on the country. He had already begun to create the mythological Holy Russia that was to feature so large in his writing in the years before 1917.

Graham found it difficult to settle back into the routines of his old life when he returned home to Britain from Moscow. Although he punctuated his work at Somerset House by giving occasional lectures on literary topics, he continued to yearn for "new life, broader horizons, deeper depths, higher heights".[36] He later recalled that his decision to "give up everything and go to Russia" had come to him one Sunday at St Ethelburga's Church, in the City of London, when he was inspired by the preacher's words that "No one has achieved much in life who has not at some time or other staked everything upon an act of faith". His superior at Somerset House warned against taking any rash step that might throw away "the substance for the shadow", pointing out that he could look forward to receiving a generous pension after another thirty five years of work. Graham was confident enough to resist such unappealing blandishments, insisting that "I am going after the shadow".[37] He nevertheless told few people about his

---

36 Graham, *Vagabond*, p. 10.
37 Ibid, p. 17. Graham used this incident as the basis of a short story, 'The Shadow', which appeared in Stephen Graham, *Quest of the Face* (London: Macmillan, 1918), pp. 231-52, version available at http://archive.org/details/questofface00grah.

intention, fearing that they might dissuade him, for he was more nervous than he admitted about making such a drastic move. Even so, whilst his decision to move to Russia in the hope of earning his living from his pen was undoubtedly brave, it was one he made knowing that his father was now in a position to offer a modest degree of financial support (*Country Life* paid its editor generously, and by the outbreak of the First World War Anderson Graham was rich enough to build a fine Lutyens-designed house in Hertfordshire). Graham was convinced that the growing public interest in Russia meant that there would be a ready market for his work, and he grandly hoped to popularise the country's literature and thought in the same way that Carlyle had interpreted the ideas of the German Idealists for a British audience two generations earlier. The self-confessed Romantic who determined to pursue the "shadow" was always realistic enough to think seriously about the practical business of earning a living.

Graham made the decision to quit his job in June, but he left for Russia only six months later, on the last day of 1907. He was headed for Lisitchansk, a town south-east of Kharkov in modern-day Ukraine, where he had been invited to stay by the family of his old friend Nikolai Lebedev. The journey was an eventful one, and provided him with an uncomfortable introduction to the harsh realities of life in the Tsarist Empire. Once Graham left the ordered world of Germany, where the trains were spotless and punctual, he was forced to confront the reality of third-class travel in Russia in a carriage that was "unspeakable filthy". He was nevertheless impressed by the smoothness of the Russian trains, which ran on broader gauges than the rolling stock of western Europe, giving a "pleasantly soothing" ride that allowed passengers to "slip easily into slumber".[38] A less soothing introduction to provincial Russia was provided by one of his travelling companions, who stole Graham's overcoat whilst he was asleep, no minor matter in the depths of a Russian winter. By the time he got to Kharkov, Graham only had a light coat to protect him against thirty degrees of frost, and his woes continued when it became clear that his luggage had also gone missing. The final leg of the train journey to Lisitchansk proved equally vexed, when the inebriated engine-driver insisted on breaking the journey, so that he could eat and drink with friends at a farmhouse located close to the railway line. Graham was thankful when he finally got to his

---

38 Graham, *Vagabond*, pp. 15-16.

destination where he was met by the familiar figure of Nikolai complete with horse and sleigh.

Graham arrived in Lisitchansk on Christmas Eve – the Orthodox Christmas took place thirteen days after the festival was celebrated in Western Europe in line with the Julian calendar – and the events of the following week gave him his first real insight into life in the provinces of the Tsarist Empire. The Lebedev family provided him with an old overcoat made of wolf-skin, to replace the one that had been stolen, so that he could join them in their sled trips around the countryside in festive visits to their neighbours. Christmas week passed in "an orgy of eating and drinking",[39] and Graham was suitably awe-struck by the capacity of the locals for alcohol, ruefully noting that he himself drank as much in ten days as he had in the rest of his life. On Boxing Day he joined the Lebedevs in a trip to a local manor house, where some of the visitors performed Leonid Andreev's *Life of Man*, which had enjoyed enormous success a few years earlier when it was first produced at Stanislavsky's Moscow Art Theatre. Numerous other trips took place to the homes of family friends and relatives who lived in far more humble surroundings. Graham was profoundly grateful for the kindness he received from the Lebedev family, which helped him orient himself in an unfamiliar land at a time when his mastery of the language was still quite rudimentary, but his original plan had always been to go to live in Moscow with Nikolai. The two men left Lisitchansk in late January and headed northwards by train to Russia's ancient capital. They were met by an old friend of Nikolai's, who led them to some squalid accommodation in a down-at-heel area near the *Sretinka vorota*. Graham now found himself a resident of the city which had for years served in his imagination as the living embodiment of Russia.

The city in which Graham arrived early in 1908 had changed a good deal over the previous few decades. The golden-domed cathedrals of the Kremlin still looked much as they had for hundreds of years, as did the ornate St Basil's cathedral situated just outside the Kremlin walls. Some others parts of the city had also not greatly altered since being rebuilt in stone following the great fire of 1812.[40] The city centre nevertheless boasted the usual appurtenances of modernity, ranging from electric light and trams to elaborate shop-window displays designed to entice the wealthier residents of the city. Dozens of new factories had also been built around the city over

---

39 Ibid, p. 29.
40 For a contemporary guide to the city see the relevant pages of Karl Baedeker, *Russia: A Handbook for Travellers* (London, 1914).

the previous twenty years. Moscow had in the eighteenth and nineteenth centuries been idealised by many Russians as the real capital of Russia, embodying the Orthodox national spirit far more completely than soulless St Petersburg, the new capital built on the banks of the Neva River in the early eighteenth century as part of Peter the Great's campaign to open a window to the west. Although this image of Moscow lasted into the early years of the twentieth century, by the time Graham arrived the city was firmly in the throes of massive change, its society and economy shaped as much by the demands of the new industrial and commercial economy as by older visions of the city as the spiritual heartland of Russia. There was certainly no shortage of those like Count Sergei Sheremetev, scion of one of the country's wealthiest noble families, who bitterly lamented how the old churches and houses were being swept away to create a new Moscow.[41] The city was becoming a curiously placeless place, suspended between the ancient and the modern, its traditional character wilting in the face of huge social and economic change. Graham was characteristically only ever inclined to see the contours of the world that was vanishing.

Neither Lebedev nor Graham had much money when they arrived in Moscow, and the next few weeks were spent in a succession of grimy lodgings, where they lived on an unappetising diet of black bread and fried pork. Nikolai rather bizarrely planned to earn his living as a professional card player, whilst Graham hoped to give English lessons, at least until he had established himself sufficiently as a journalist to rely on his pen for a living. Graham relished the liberation from his routine life in Britain, particularly as he began to have some minor successes in placing his articles with the London press (his first triumph was a review of a recent scholarly volume by Howard Kennard on *The Russian Peasant*). In the months that followed he contributed further pieces to the British press, including one to the *Evening Standard* on the Azev affair, which erupted when members of the Socialist Revolutionary Party discovered that one of their leading members was an *agent provocateur* planted by the tsarist secret police. He was, however, less successful in finding a publisher willing to take up his offer to provide translations of Dostoevsky.

The periodic arrival of money from Anderson Graham also helped to ease his son's financial plight, although he moved lodgings a good deal in an effort to reduce his rent, earning his keep by teaching English to the

---

41 Rachel Polonsky, *Molotov's Magic Lantern: A Journey in Russian History* (London: Faber and Faber, 2010), pp. 30-31.

children of wealthy merchants. He also took a number of live-in jobs as a tutor, but the experience was seldom satisfactory, since it placed too many limits on his freedom. Graham spent a good deal of time with Nikolai's student friends, even though he had little sympathy for the atheism and radicalism espoused by most of them, spending evening after evening in endless discussions on topics ranging from politics to philosophy (Nikolai himself seems to have become a somewhat paranoid figure, convinced that his every movement was being monitored by the secret police). Still more time was spent skating and tobogganing in Sokolniki Park, one of the oldest in Moscow, which had been landscaped in 1900 to include a labyrinth of small alleyways and paths winding through the birch trees. Graham also attended performances at the Moscow Art Theatre, founded ten years earlier by Stanislavsky, which was already famous across Russia for its innovative staging of the work of playwrights such as Chekhov and Gorky.[42] Together with Lebedev he visited many of the poorest areas of the city, including one trip to a doss-house with a single lavatory, in which men and women slept together on the floor in unbearably stuffy rooms where the windows were sealed by putty to keep out the cold.

Graham was repeatedly appalled by the poverty he encountered in Moscow, and although he later came to believe that the material deprivation of the Russian people was often combined with spiritual wealth, he found it difficult at first to reconcile himself to the presence of thousands of beggars who owned the streets like the "rats own the drains".[43] He also published a piece about Moscow beggars in *The New Age*, the literary journal edited by Alfred Orage, which played such a large role in promoting English modernism in the first two decades of the twentieth century.[44] His new life in Moscow certainly broke down the "prison walls" of convention that he felt had confined him back in London.

Graham realised soon after his arrival in Moscow that "Russia was different from the Russia in books written by Russians", acknowledging that Dostoevsky for all his brilliance "will never take you into a Russian Church, nor will he reveal the mystery of the ikons or the spell of Russian music". The moment of epiphany seems to have come during a trip to the

---

42 On the Moscow Art Theatre, see Nick Worral, *The Moscow Art Theatre* (London: Routledge, 1996).
43 Graham, *Vagabond*, p. 74.
44 *The New* Age, 2, 18 (1908), pp. 358-59. On Orage and *The New Age* see Wallace Martin, *The New Age under Orage* (Manchester: Manchester University Press, 1967); Philip Mairet, *A.R. Orage: A Memoir* (London: J.M. Dent, 1936).

city of Sergiev Posad, forty miles outside Moscow, where Graham stood hour after hour mesmerized by the sound of chanting in the cathedral church. He recalled more than half a century later that it had been "a moment in personal history", adding that "it is not an explanation of what led me to Russia for I knew nothing of the Church and its music when I was in London".[45]

The Russian soul that Graham had fallen in love with now began to acquire a more distinctively spiritual form. The process was not unexpected, given that his longing for Russia had always been fuelled by a search for the numinous that escaped him in the workaday world of London, although it was not so much the Orthodox Church itself that Graham was falling in love with as a more elusive idea of Holy Russia. The country increasingly appeared to him as a vast sacred space where the fabric of daily life was shaped by the pervasive presence of the infinite. A few years later he wrote about the impact on him of the Easter celebrations he witnessed in 1909, shortly before leaving Moscow for a long trip to southern Russia, describing how the city again became the "city of the old time" and a "strange mystery and sacredness which must have enwrapped it in ancient days is felt again in the streets. The shops are all shut and dark, the churches are all open and bright [...] Even the air is infected with church odours and the multitudinous domes of purple and gold rest above the houses in enigmatical solemnity – they might be tents and pavilions of spirits from another world".[46] Graham's fascination with Russia was increasingly bound up with his belief that daily life there retained a spiritual depth that had long vanished in the more advanced countries of Western Europe. The sense that he had developed when first reading Dostoevsky – that the Russian people retained an intuitive understanding of the meaning of life that had disappeared elsewhere – was taking a more definite religious colouring.

Although Graham was inclined in later life to emphasise that it was his attendance at Orthodox Church services that led him to the mystery of Holy Russia, he was from his youth also deeply interested in various forms of non-Christian mythological thought, a fascination with the exotic and esoteric that remained with him for the rest of his life. By the time he moved to Russia, he had developed a rather cumbersome personal philosophy that rested on an almost Platonic distinction between the "Little World" (his

---

45 Graham Papers (HRC), *Wonderful Scene* (autograph).
46 Graham, *Vagabond*, pp. 111-12.

phrase) of everyday life and a more authentic world of values and beliefs. Graham articulated these ideas in a short book manuscript *Ygdrasil*, a name taken from the immense ash tree of Norse mythology, which he used as a core image for a series of meditations on spirituality and philosophy.[47] He made no mention of the book in the published version of his memoirs, whilst in the draft of *Part of the Wonderful Scene* he dismissed it as "not very original", one of many examples of Graham's attempts in later life to dismiss his youthful interest in the occult. Although many of his ideas were disjointed, Graham sought in *Ygdrasil* to emphasise the organic nature of reality, in which there was a fundamental unity between sea and river, rock and earth, human and animal. He rejected a philosophy that relied on reason alone in favour of a kind of existentialist vision in which the spiritual state of the individual governed their ability to find meaning in the world around them. Graham criticised all formal doctrines and creeds as a source of "tyranny", and instead presented Christ as a metaphorical figure who was "the archetype of man", as well as the representative of "the vision of [God's] purpose" encountered internally by each individual, which allowed them to develop their "own spiritual language". The language and argument of *Ygdrasil* certainly leave a good deal to be desired from a scholarly point of view (much of what Graham had to say can be traced back to his reading of Carlyle on German Romantic philosophy). It does nevertheless illustrate the extent to which his idea of the sacred was rooted as much in a diffuse metaphysical instinct as in a more formal interest in Christianity in general or Orthodoxy in particular. Holy Russia was for Graham a place where the transcendent could be discerned within the confines of the finite world.

The manuscript of *Ygdrasil* is important for the light it casts on Graham's intellectual and emotional preoccupations during the years he spent in Russia before the 1917 Revolution. He was even in old age forthright in his commitment to "idealism", a term he never defined properly, instead using it to express his instinct that art and religion had the capacity to provide access to realms of meaning that could not be found in the material world. It will be seen later that the success of Graham's early books rested in large part on his skill at providing his readers with illuminating sketches of the Russian landscape, both natural and social, which he encountered during his long tramps through the country. Some reviewers were indeed inclined

---

47 The following quotations are all taken from Graham Papers (HRC), Works file, *Ygdrasil*.

to see his forays into philosophical and religious reverie as little more than an unnecessary distraction that detracted from his qualities as a travel writer. It was partly for this reason that Graham later toned down the esoteric style that characterised much of his earliest work. He nevertheless remained intellectually and emotionally rooted for many years in the world-view he sketched out in *Ygdrasil*. Graham the aspiring philosopher continued to view the "Little World" as a place that mattered since it provided evidence of the beyond. Graham the journalist and sketch-writer was by contrast enthralled by the scenes of everyday life. It was a dualism of matter and spirit that can be found even in the diaries and notebooks he kept as an old man of eighty.

One other important development took place in Graham's life during his first year in Moscow, before he left the city to spend a year tramping through the Caucasus Mountains. In March 1909 he married Rosa Savory at St Andrew's Anglican Church in Moscow.[48] Rosa was fifteen years older than her husband, and worked as "a trainer of teachers" when they met, although little else is known about her early life. She was born in 1869 in West London, the daughter of a carpenter who ran a small business employing a number of apprentices, and moved with her parents when they emigrated to Russia in the 1880s (there was always a steady demand for English craftsmen in Russia). She became fluent in Russian and later cooperated with her husband in translating a number of short stories by Alexander Kuprin into English.[49] The marriage between Stephen and Rosa lasted until Rosa's death in 1956, when she was eighty six, although it had in effect ended more than quarter of a century earlier. Graham wrote in his autobiography that they had been "deeply in love, spell-bound by inspiration", praising Rosa for being "content to play the part of Solveig to Peer Gynt", adding that "when I was off on new adventures [she] remained in the background and kept a candle burning".[50] The artist Vernon Hill described many years later how struck he had been by the pair when he first met them in London in 1911, recalling how Graham "still had that patina of snow-light [...] in [his] eyes", whilst behind him stood "a very

---

48 Regimental Museum of Guards (Service Record of Stephen Graham).
49 A.I. Kuprin, *A Slav Soul and Other Stories*, trans. Stephen and Rosa Graham (London: Constable, 1916).
50 Graham, *Wonderful Scene*, p. 66.

quiet, nun-like lady with a tray of coffee, shy as silence" (for a sketch of Graham by Hill see Figure 1).[51]

Figure 1: Pen portrait of Stephen Graham by Vernon Hill, published in Stephen Graham, *Changing Russia* (London: John Lane, 1913), frontispiece.

The sense that there was something other-worldly about Rosa was commented on by other people as well. The Serbian Orthodox Bishop Nikolai Velimirović called her "the most Christian of all souls".[52] Eve Farson, wife of the American travel-writer Negley Farson, recalled on hearing of Rosa's death that her old friend had "great sweetness and goodness about her always [...] I [was] very fond of her in the old days".[53]

There are hints in some of Graham's earlier relationships that he was often attracted to women who were a good deal older than himself. He certainly placed an enormous emphasis on marriage as a profound union that brought two people together in "body, spirit and intellect". In one of the more abstruse passages of *Ygdrasil*, he articulated his belief that there was "no such thing as a man exclusively man or a woman exclusively woman", adding that "male and female exist not only in animals but in trees and rocks", a statement that reflected his conviction that "everything is organic and spiritually connected".[54]

---

51 Graham Papers (HRC), Letters file, Hill to Graham, 25 October 1964.
52 Ibid, Velimirović to Graham, 10 August 1921.
53 Ibid, Eve Farson to Graham, 19 July 1956.
54 All quotations from *Ygdrasil* except "everything is organic and spiritually connected" which can be found in Graham Papers (HRC), *Wonderful* Scene (autograph).

Rosa's surviving diaries and letters suggest that she was well-placed to play the part allotted to her in the youthful Graham's emotional pageant. She was a highly-intelligent woman, with a keen interest in eastern religion and West European art, who was willing and able to provide the refuge which Graham returned to time and again from his travels abroad.[55] Graham's description of his marriage to Rosa in *Part of the Wonderful Scene* was nevertheless a highly idealised one. The Spanish novelist Javier Marias noted in *Dark Back of Time* that Graham made very few references to his wife in his writings, even in the years after the First World War, when she abandoned the role of hearth-keeper to travel the world with him,[56] making her a curiously anonymous presence in his books. Graham was perhaps too inclined to take the fidelity and loyalty of "Solveig" for granted, and their marriage faced growing difficulties in the mid 1920s, at a time when he was going through a personal crisis, and had begun to re-evaluate many of his earlier views about life.

It may say something about the relationship between Graham and Rosa that he was determined in the weeks before his marriage to leave Moscow as soon as the snows cleared "and the country lay open tempting me".[57] It is not obvious why he chose to live for a year in the Caucasus, a remote region that had only finally been absorbed into the Tsarist Empire during the middle of the nineteenth century, following the defeat of the resistance movement mounted by Moslem tribes under the leadership of Imam Shamil. Several epic journeys that he made on foot over the next few years took place in precisely such borderland areas, where Orthodox and Slavic Russia gave way to places inhabited by peoples of other religions and nationalities. Some of those living in the Caucasus were, like the Georgians, Christian by faith. Others were Muslim. The whole region was still widely perceived in Moscow and St Petersburg, even at the start of the twentieth century, as a wild frontier region where the writ of the imperial authorities barely reached beyond the main towns and cities.

Graham was warned on countless occasions before travelling to the Caucasus that he was taking his life in his hands. It is true that the rickety tsarist bureaucracy sometimes failed to operate effectively in areas far from the major metropolitan centres, but the dangers of travel in the region were probably

---

55 Fragments from Rosa's diaries and journals, giving an insight into her views, can be found in Bradford University Library Special Collections, Archives of the New Atlantis Foundation, 1/6/2/12 Book 4.
56 Javier Marias, *Dark Back of Time* (London: Vintage, 2004), p. 202.
57 Graham, *Vagabond*, p. 101.

exaggerated, particularly given that the institutions of civil and military rule were well-established in south Russia by the end of the nineteenth century. The image of the Caucasus as a remote and exotic region, a place of barbarism and intrigue, was nevertheless so deep-seated in the orientalist imagination of European Russians that it continued to shape perceptions of the area right down to 1917 and beyond. Graham himself was not averse to emphasising the dangerous character of the place. His first book, *A Vagabond in the Caucasus* (1911), detailed with relish the kidnappings and murders that took place in the area. He told how Nikolai and his friends tried to dissuade him from travelling to a region where robbery and violence were commonplace. He also regaled his readers with colourful stories he heard, including one which described how a party of well-to-do travellers were held by robbers and "despoiled of their clothing. The robbers covered them with guns and called on them to undress and throw all their possessions in a heap on the road or be shot. And they accordingly returned to town in Adam's raiment".[58] Nor should all Graham's stories be dismissed as bravado. The decision by a recently married young foreigner to tramp alone through such a remote area took a good deal of courage.

The genesis of Graham's trip to the Caucasus was rooted in his hope that there might be a market for a book about the region. Hilaire Belloc's recent *Path to Rome*, which detailed its author's epic journey on foot from Britain to Italy, had attracted a good deal of public acclaim. The success of other books like W.H. Davies's *Autobiography of a Supertramp* and William Locke's *Beloved Vagabond* also suggested there was considerable popular interest in the figure of the walker and vagabond. Graham was a great admirer of *Path to Rome*, and determined early on that the book he planned to write about his sojourn in the Caucasus would, like Belloc's book, be something more than a simple travelogue, instead containing reflections on a whole range of questions both religious and mundane. In a letter to his publisher John Lane, written whilst working on the final draft of *Vagabond*, Graham suggested that the book should have a sub-title of 'The Story of an Individual who Escaped from England to Russia'.[59] In another letter he emphasised that the story he wanted to tell was "the story of *my* new life", as well as "a story of new aspects and new possibilities in Russian life", with the result that his approach would "be new in English ears".[60] Graham was determined not simply to regale his

---
58 Ibid, p. 131.
59 John Lane papers (HRC), Box 17, Folder 4, Graham to Lane, 31 May 1910.
60 Ibid, Graham to Lane, 14 June 1910.

readers with descriptions of town and countryside, but rather to provide them with a rich mixture of anecdotes and observations, as well as offering a kind of confessional narrative about how he had been shaped by his experiences on the road. This style was to become a hallmark of the many travel books he wrote over the next few years. The accounts Graham wrote of his various journeys, including his first trip to the Caucasus in 1909-10, were typically highly impressionistic narratives – a jumble of reportage and introspection – which together formed a kind of picaresque autobiography containing his reflections on all he had thought and witnessed.

Figure 2: Photograph taken by Stephen Graham in the Terek Gorge of two Ingush women collecting water, published in Stephen Graham, *A Vagabond in the Caucasus* (London, John Lane, 1911), p. 140.

After travelling south in the spring of 1909, Graham arrived at the town of Vladikavkaz, founded during the reign of Catherine the Great as a fort to strengthen Russia's military presence in the region. He came well-prepared for his travels, complete with a sleeping bag and waterproof blanket, and a revolver to defend himself against the bandits whom anxious friends assured him he would meet by the score in his travels. Vladikavkaz was in many ways a thoroughly modern town, complete with hotels and trams, but Graham quickly realised that he was a long way from the heartland of European Russia. Most of the local population was made up of ethnic Russians and Georgians, but there were also significant minorities of people Graham referred to as Ossetines, Tatars, Persians and Ingooshi, reflecting the extent to which the whole Caucasus region represented a meeting place of different religions and ethnicities.

It was still too cold to sleep rough when Graham arrived in Vladikavkaz, so he booked into a local hotel, making occasional forays on foot to survey the neighbouring countryside. When he finally set out on his first long tramp, at the end of April, he deliberately avoided the well-engineered military roads in favour of rough tracks that would take him deep into the wilderness. He also wore Russian peasant dress in an effort to blend into the background and make it easier to talk to those he met along the way. Although Graham was not by his own estimation "rich prey for a robber", he slept at night in caves, or hidden behind rocks where he was unlikely to attract the attention of any passing bandits. The brooding threat of violence always seemed to be present, even in places like the remote Daria Gorge, where the mountain-sides were covered in a mantle of green fir trees and the summits capped by snow. It was here, in these idyllic surroundings, that Graham first saw the grim ruins of the castle of the Georgian Queen Tamara, whose twelfth-century reign was widely remembered in local folklore as a time of great bloodshed, even though she was later canonised as a saint by the Orthodox Church. The juxtaposition of stories of violence with scenes of great natural beauty was indeed a feature of *Vagabond in the Caucasus*. In between telling readers how "unfortunate victims" of Tamara's reign were thrown down the rocks "into the foaming river", he jotted down impressions of the animals and plants that crossed his path, describing how he walked through meadows filled with flowers and along ditches lined by "thistles, barberry, teasle, hollyhock and mallow".[61]

---

61 Graham, *Vagabond*, p. 129.

After a few weeks of sleeping rough, Graham rented two rooms from a Baptist pastor who combined his duties as minister with those of miller (it seems that Rosa later joined her husband there at least for a time). He bought a mattress and various household utensils, carefully writing down the cost in his notebook, and paid a local Russian woman to do his cooking. Graham feared that the growth of non-Orthodox sects in Russia signalled a decline in the hold of the Orthodox Church on the emotions of the Russian people, but he was full of admiration for the minister himself. He attended one of the pastor's services at the local chapel, a "little defiant, heterodox place so brave in its denial and protest", where the sermon was "direct" and the congregation sang "with a will and kept in tune".[62] Graham also took the opportunity to talk with neighbours who were practising Moslems, including one Ali Pasha, whom he first saw on a Saturday evening sitting in his porch drinking "crimson tea, coloured by an infusion of cranberry syrup". Ali was a Persian – yet more evidence of the rich ethnic mosaic that characterised the population between the Black and Caspian seas – and he wore a gorgeous costume of "slate-blue cloak, golden stockings and loose slippers". Graham later described his neighbour as "a noble man, by far the most refined and courteous of the dwellers at the mill". He went on to add that "I might almost add, though it would sound paradoxical, he was the most Christian. Nowadays surely all men are Christian, even Mahommedans, Buddhists and Confucians. It is only the name that they lack, the same religion is in all of them".[63] His words were telling. For all his burgeoning love of the Orthodox Church, Graham was as ever convinced that true religion was a matter of spirituality rather than doctrine, a belief he was to retain to a greater or lesser extent for the rest of his life.

Graham's wanderings attracted a good deal of interest from those he met on the road. There were few Britons in the southern provinces of the tsarist empire, at least outside major towns like Baku, where British engineers were playing a significant role in developing the Caspian oil wells. One Ingush speaker he met on the road refused to believe that Graham was from Britain on the grounds that all "the English travelled in flying machines".[64] In another Ingush village he was invited to a dinner of lamb-cutlet and millet bread by one of the elders, who was convinced that the English were a tribe who lived somewhere away to the north-west of

---
62 Ibid, pp. 237-38.
63 Ibid, pp. 252-53.
64 Ibid, p. 141.

the valley. Graham predictably fell foul of the local authorities on a number of occasions. The area through which he tramped had been one of the main settings of the Great Game, and British intelligence agents operated there well into the twentieth century, and perhaps even in the years following the 1907 Anglo-Russian agreement that was meant to put an end to such activities.[65] Graham's passport may have made him an object of suspicion, particularly to the local military authorities, for tension was running high in 1909 between London and St Petersburg over their respective spheres of influence in nearby Persia. When he was arrested, though, it was not by a soldier or policeman, but rather by a "hillman" near the town of Lisri in what is now North Ossetia, who handed him over to the local *ataman* when his prisoner refused to pay a bribe for his release. A bizarre few days followed. Graham was released into the care of a local Georgian priest, with whom he had interesting discussions about religion, before being taken to another village ten miles away, where he was left for a time to his own devices. A few days later, after a period of desultory captivity in a series of local towns, he was taken to Vladikavkaz where he was released by the Chief of Police. Graham's account of his arrest may have been rather highly-coloured, and he certainly came to no great harm during his brief detention in a verminous prison cell, complete with "rotten floors and no glass in the windows", but it captured the chaos that was a common feature of tsarist rule in the more remote reaches of the Russian Empire.

The discursive character of Graham's writing makes it difficult to reconstruct his itinerary with much precision (the diary he kept on the trip has not survived). He certainly ranged widely around the western part of the Caucasus region, including at least two crossings of the high mountain ranges, when he "climbed into winter" from the valleys below, spending nights in a *koutan* with shepherds tending their flocks in the high passes. The mill that he used as a basis for his tramps was located on the Terek river, probably close to Vladikavkaz, although its exact location is unclear. He spent a good deal of time in the area north of Georgia, usually travelling within a hundred miles or so of Vladikavkaz itself. He does not seem to have spent much time in the areas closer to the Caspian Sea.

The draft of *Vagabond in the Caucasus* that Graham sent to John Lane in 1910 set down a number of themes that were to define his writing about Russia right down to the 1917 Revolution. The first was the whole idea

---

[65] On this theme see Michael Hughes, 'Diplomacy or Drudgery? British Consuls in Russia during the Early Twentieth Century', *Diplomacy and Statecraft*, 6, 1 (1995), pp. 76-95.

of Holy Russia, although this was not a phrase that occurred in *Vagabond* itself, perhaps because so much of the book recounted Graham's travels in a region that was neither uniformly Russian nor Orthodox. *Vagabond* also reflected its author's sense that the natural world could serve as a pointer to something more fundamental and important. There was something distinctly pantheistic about Graham's description of nights spent in the mountains, when he felt as if he "had entered into a new world and come into communion with Nature in a way as yet unknown",[66] an idea he was to develop more fully two years later in his third book *A Tramp's Sketches*. A third theme that ran through *Vagabond* was Graham's conviction that tramping provided a way of gaining insights into realities that eluded those who lived more confined lives within the city. Graham recalled in *Vagabond* how in one remote area:

> I met a noble tramp, an Eden tramp. He came upon me at dawn with a wood smile on his old face. He was one of the society of tramps; he knew all Russia, its places and peoples, and he called himself Mr Adam. Why did he adopt that name, why had he thrown away the other name? These were questions he was not in a hurry to answer. They involved a story. Such a story! It sounded in my ears like a secret melody of the world.[67]

There was in fact something of a paradox at the heart of Graham's treatment both of the natural world and the whole idea of tramping. Although over the next few years he was to become increasingly in thrall to the ideal of Holy Russia, precisely because he believed that the country had maintained a sense of the need for a shared spiritual community, he was also deeply intrigued by the figures of the tramp and the pilgrim, wanderers across the landscape who found themselves strangers in the places through which they passed. Nor could Graham's belief that nature throbbed with a set of meanings, capable of providing the individual with a sense of consolation and identity, be easily reconciled with his lingering desire to emphasise the importance of religion in providing a collective context to personal experience. The young Stephen Graham – and perhaps the older one too – was always conscious of a tension between the desire to belong and the desire to escape. It is of course a familiar dilemma for the natural Romantic, whose yearning for the settled securities of the past has been shaped by a modern consciousness, itself characterised by a powerful sense of autonomy and individuality.

---

66 Graham, *Vagabond*, p. 134.
67 Ibid, p. 224.

The epilogue of *Vagabond* concluded with a description of its author's quest, in which his wanderings through the Caucasus became an expression of his pursuit of something more profound, a spiritual journey in search of truths that had eluded him in his earlier life:

> A youth steps forward on the road and a horizon goes forward. Sometimes slowly the horizon moves, sometimes in leaps and bounds. Slowly while mountains are approached, or when cities and markets crowd the skies to heaven, but suddenly and instantaneously when summits are achieved or when the outskirts dust of town or fair is passed. One day, at a highest point on that road of his, a view will be disclosed and lie before him – the furthest and most magical glance into the Future. Away, away in the far-distant grey will lie his newest and last horizon, in a place more fantastic and mystical than the dissolving city, which the eye builds out of sunset clouds.

Graham's experiences on the road – and his reflections on the landscapes he saw and the people he met – changed "the youth" as he began to develop a clearer insight into the elusive object he sought. "He awakened, or rather he and himself awakened, a self below himself had awakened, as if the soul had drawn curtains from two windows after a long custom of drawing from only one. A new being waking, blinked uneasily to find itself in the swing and motion of life".[68] The tone of Graham's epilogue contrasted sharply with much of what had gone before, perhaps because it was written later than the earlier chapters, which were often taken almost *verbatim* from articles he had sent to *Country Life* and the *Pall Mall Gazette* whilst still on the road. It was instead inspired by the same sentiments that had run through *Ygdrasil*. Graham's tramp through the Caucasus was fuelled, at least in part, by a search for transcendence. He was a pilgrim inspired by a search for new insights into his own soul. Graham's Russia was already well under way to becoming less a place of geography and history, and more a place where a mythologized religion and culture provided opportunities for developing a new understanding of life, richer than the one that prevailed in the countries of the commercialised west he had left behind.

In the late spring of 1910 "a wave of intense longing to see England" led Graham back home to Britain, and in June he once again found himself walking through the streets of central London, cutting a curious figure in his exotic "shabby soft black hat" and "furry overcoat" (it was presumably

---

68 Ibid, pp. 288-89, p. 291.

not a warm spring in London that year). He was also brought back to Britain by the need to develop new contacts with journalists and publishers. The visit was only brief. Graham quickly realised that his heart still remained in Russia – apparently Rosa did too at this stage – and he returned to the country once more at the start of August.

> I went to Russia to see the world, to see new life, to breathe in new life. In truth it was like escaping from a prison, and now when I take a walk in London streets it seems as if I am taking the regulation exercise in a prison yard. And the dirty rags of London sky look like a tramp's washing spread on the roofs to dry. Still, it is given that we live even in prisons and under such skies for certain purposes.[69]

Graham was already planning a late summer tramp from Archangel in the far north of Russia down to Moscow. The possibility of such a trip was first suggested to him in Vladikavkaz by a friend, Vera Merkurieva, an aspiring poet who was shortly to begin publishing verse in the journal *Vestnik Teosofy* (Herald of Theosophy). She subsequently moved to Moscow, where she became a figure of some note, publishing work in the broad tradition of the Russian Symbolist movement.[70] Merkurieva introduced Graham to the work of some major contemporary Russian writers, including Andrei Bely and Alexander Blok, as well as pointing out that the Caucasus were, for all its stark beauty, a strange place for a foreigner to seek the real Russia. She therefore suggested that he travel north to live among Russians who "had not interbred with the Tatars".[71]

Graham's tramp from Archangel to Moscow cannot have taken more than six weeks or so, but its brevity would not have been apparent to readers of *Undiscovered Russia*, the book he published about his experiences (extracts from which first appeared in *Country Life* and *St James' Gazette*). Graham was already *en route* to becoming such a productive writer that his sheer output often had the effect of exaggerating the timescale of the events he described, an impression heightened by his penchant for re-packaging material so that books and articles which appeared to be about one particular journey contained material collected at different times and in different places. *Undiscovered Russia* detailed its author's impressions of his journey southwards from Archangel, which followed a circuitous route, going in an easterly arc, which at one point took him as far as Vetluga, before an

---

69 Ibid, p. 287.
70 Vera Merkurieva, *Tshcheta: sobranie stikhotvoretii* (Moscow: Vodolei Publishers, 2007).
71 Graham, *Wonderful* Scene, p. 29.

outbreak of cholera in the district forced him back west again. Graham was not altogether successful at hiding the thinness of his experiences, which perhaps accounts for the fact that *Undiscovered Russia* was less of a detailed travel book than *Vagabond in the Caucasus*, instead containing more general reflections on some of the themes that had emerged in his first book. The most important of these was the contrast between Holy Russia and the spiritually barren societies of the West.

The frontispiece of *Undiscovered Russia* reproduced the artist Michael Nesterov's picture "Holy Russia", which depicted a group of pilgrims seeking spiritual healing from Christ, in a landscape that fused together a typically Russian background of snow and fir trees with more celestial elements designed to suggest the immanence of the divine presence. Nesterov had for many years toured the churches and monasteries of north Russia in search of artistic inspiration, painting numerous pictures characterised by a distinctive aura of mysticism and spirituality, and in the early twentieth century he became an important figure in the *Mir iskustva* (World of Art) movement. Graham first met him in Moscow, at a meeting of the Religious-Philosophical Society, and was immediately struck by the artist's "supremely calm face" which made him look "like a statue".[72] Graham was fascinated by Nesterov's work, which he believed captured a complex and profound truth about Russia's spiritual identity, and he planned at one time to write a biography of the artist.[73] He was determined to use *Undiscovered Russia* to persuade his British readers that Russia was not, as many of them thought, the home of "bomb-throwers" and "intolerable tyranny", but rather a place where the people were "obediently religious, seriously respectful to their elders, true to the soil they plough, content with the old implements of culture, not using machinery or machine-made things, but able themselves to fashion out of the pine all that they need". The Russia that Graham wanted to convey was a place where social life was still rooted in the traditional rituals of an agricultural economy, inhabited by people "true to the soil [and] mystically superstitious by reason of their unexplained mystery".[74]

---

72 Graham Papers (HRC), *Wonderful Scene* (typescript), p. 24.
73 On Nesterov, see Abbott Gleason, '*Russkii inok:* The Spiritual Landscape of Mikhail Nesterov', *Cultural Geographies*, 7, 3 (2000), pp. 299-312. For notes relating to the proposed biography, see Graham Papers (FSU), Box 576, 19 (Biographical Notes of M.V. Nesterov). Nesterov for his part seems to have been willing to cooperate in the proposed biography. See M.V. Nesterov, *Pis'ma* (Leningrad: Iskusstvo, 1988), Letter 432.
74 Stephen Graham, *Undiscovered Russia* (London, 1912), p. ix, version available at http://archive.org/details/undiscoveredruss00grahrich.

Whilst Graham was still in the Caucasus, Vera Merkurieva had provided him with an introduction to the artist Vasily Perepletchikov, best-known at the time for his landscapes of the Russian north, painted in a style that owed a good deal to the French impressionist movement that was immensely popular in Russia at this time. The two men first met in Archangel when it was still illuminated by the eerie half-light of the white nights. The city had been a major port hundreds of years before Peter the Great conceived of St Petersburg, and Graham had long wanted to visit the "remote town", even though its commercial importance had for two centuries been eclipsed by its new neighbour far to the south. He was at first disappointed by what he found, ruefully noting that "it is always a little saddening to exchange a dream for a reality",[75] but one evening, sitting in the twilight on a hill above the city, he sensed "a strange mystery [...] One felt one's self in a light of peace and calm, as in the depths of some holy mystery, perhaps the vision of Holy Russia; it was the light of a vision before the eyes, flooding and transfiguring the darkness, the light of many haloes, dream daylight".[76]

Graham was fascinated by the hordes of pilgrims heading towards the harbour to take a boat for the island monastery of Solovetsky, many of whom had walked a thousand miles to get to Archangel, begging as they went, in order to make the trip to one of Russia's "most holy shrines".[77] It is surprising that he did not join them, evidence perhaps of the limited time available to him, since he was determined to reach Moscow by the middle of September. Graham nevertheless spent a few days in the town, travelling on a steamer down the river to the run-down suburb of Salombola. He also had a meeting with the Vice-Governor, who gave him a letter of recommendation and numerous pamphlets about the areas he planned to tramp through. The following day, Graham and Perepletchikov left Archangel together, since the artist planned to spend some time painting the countryside to the south of the city, and they departed by rowing boat down the northern Dvina river. The two men set off in the evening, but the light of the northern summer night allowed them to navigate easily amongst the barges that littered the river, and it was only in the early hours

---

75 Ibid, p. 12.
76 Ibid, p. 14.
77 For a history of the monastery and the island on which it is situated see Roy R. Robson, *Solovki: The Story of Russia Told Through its Most Remarkable* Islands (New Haven: Yale University Press, 2004).

of the morning that they tied up at a landing stage at one of the villages scattered along the riverside.

Graham was fascinated by the forests and lakes of the north, along with the people who lived there, many of whom still lived in native communities where the Russian language was almost unknown. He told readers of *Undiscovered Russia* how "the Baltic Slavs still live by the streams and the lakes, and although Christianity has found them, they have cherished paganism along with it".[78] Graham as usual had his camera with him, and amongst the photographs that appeared in the book were two of 'Aborigines of North Russia', taken by natural light at midnight, which showed groups of peasants posed in front of their wooden huts in the traditional dress of the region.

Figure 3: Photograph taken by Stephen Graham at midnight of the inhabitants of a village near Archangel, published in Stephen Graham, *Undiscovered Russia* (London: John Lane, 1912), p. 24.

Another photograph showed 'A Man of the Woods Reputed to be a Magician', whilst a third provided a portrait of two forest-dwellers, the hunter Shangin and his companion Darya, standing above the body of a bear they had shot in the woods. As Graham moved southwards, the Samoyede faces and shamanic echoes of the people he met gradually gave way to the more familiar features and rituals of European Russia. He was

---

78 Graham, *Undiscovered Russia*, p. 25.

as ever convinced that the spirituality of the Russian peasantry permeated every aspect of their life.[79] Because the weather was unseasonably wet and cold, Graham often sought shelter in peasant villages, and was repeatedly struck by the reverence given towards the household icons that showed how for "the Russian [...] God is not locked up in the church". In *Undiscovered Russia* he took issue with foreign travellers who dismissed peasant religion as a form of superstition,[80] arguing that it instead represented a genuine reverence and a desire to "give the Infinite a name". Although Graham freely acknowledged that many priests were drunks, who neglected the needs of their congregation, he was still captivated by the "wonderful" services of the Orthodox Church. He also spoke warmly of the hospitality he received in the monasteries where he sought shelter. At the Cathedral of the Assumption in Ustiug, he attended a service of blessing for one of the wonder-working icons, marvelling at the strength of the faith of the congregation as they surged forward for a blessing. Graham himself joined the procession, and went up to receive the blessing of the priest who stood motionless in front of the altar, looking "like a figure that had just stepped out of an Ikon".[81]

Even so dedicated a devotee of Holy Russia as Graham could not altogether ignore the signs of social and political change that were taking place in the Tsarist Empire during the early years of the twentieth century. In the course of his journey southwards, he came across numerous young Russians who had been sentenced to internal exile for their involvement in radical political activity, even though the reforms set in motion by the 1905 Revolution had introduced a more liberal political atmosphere. In one small town in the far north he met a group of political exiles who, although cleared of any crimes in the courts, had been banished on the grounds that they were "not innocent" of dabbling in "terrorism and propagandism".[82] Whilst they were given a small grant by the Government, and permitted to wander a few miles from town, the young radicals were under almost constant supervision by the local police. In another town he met a second group of administrative exiles – "much the bitterest men and women I had ever met in Russia" – and as Graham sat with them he could not help

---

79 Ibid, p. 232.
80 For a vigorous critique of Russian Orthodoxy from a contemporary Protestant standpoint see R.S. Latimer, *Under Three Tsars* (London: Morgan and Scott, 1907).
81 Graham, *Undiscovered Russia*, p. 220.
82 Ibid, p. 57.

reflecting that their anger would one day drive them to become involved "in acts of assassination and violence".[83]

The young radicals Graham met spoke bitterly of the British Government's refusal to take up the cause of the victims of tsarist repression. They also refused to accept his suggestion that the dreary lives faced by industrial workers and office clerks in cities like London and Manchester were, in their own way, as bad as anything faced by Russian workers and peasants. Graham was ready enough to acknowledge the injustice imposed by administrative exile, but he steadfastly refused to accept that political violence could ever be acceptable, on the grounds that "when once murder has come to the reinforcement of a cause, the question of the inherent goodness of that cause is forced into the background".[84] By the time he completed the final draft of *Undiscovered Russia*, in the spring of 1911, Graham made no secret of his belief that Russia's well-being depended on strengthening "the hands of the Tsar and of all reactionaries".[85] Although he acknowledged that "It is sad to think of [...] young men and women executed or exiled", he feared that the triumph of the radical movement would simply impoverish the Russian nation spiritually, and lead the country down a path of development that was alien to all that was best in its traditions and culture. Graham's increasingly conservative outlook on life was already starting to become clear.

One of the most memorable meetings Graham had during his journey from Archangel to Moscow took place at a large estate near the village of Gagarina, where he sought refuge when the appalling summer weather forced him to abandon his original plan to head eastwards towards Nizhni Novgorod. The house where he spent the night was well-furnished, and his hostess's study boasted a carpet and English fireplace, complete with an array of comfortable armchairs and divans. Madame Odintsev spoke excellent English and proved to be formidably well-read. She was an ardent follower of the ideas put forward by Madame Blavatsky, the *doyenne* of the Theosophical movement, which caused such a stir across Europe in the late nineteenth and early twentieth centuries, with its claim that all religions were merely one aspect of a single true faith whose secrets had been preserved in the remote monasteries of the Himalayas.[86] The two spoke

---

83 Ibid, p. 177.
84 Ibid, p. 58.
85 Ibid, p. 207.
86 Amongst Blavatsky's writings see Helena Blavatsky, *The Secret Doctrine: the Synthesis of*

at length about modern Russian culture, including the symbolist poetry of Alexander Blok and the philosophical writings of Viacheslav Ivanov, which led them to a speculative discussion about the nature of "the mystic life". Mme Odinstsev suggested that her Theosophy consisted above all in learning to distinguish between the transient and the permanent, insisting that true love consisted of love for what was eternal rather than mere outward form, a position that echoed the one sketched out a few years earlier in *Ygdrasil* by Graham himself. The two then became engaged in a good-tempered but "barren argument" about the extent to which God was knowable. Although they never came to an agreement, Graham left the house in his own words as "a mystic perhaps just too self-conscious", yet assenting "eagerly" to his hostess's view that "all life is symbolism, our actions are all rites, our worlds are all mysteries".[87] There was, as ever, something about the young Graham's views that smacked of the esoteric. The notion that the physical world represented a mere expression or emanation of some deeper reality remained firmly entrenched as a central feature of his personal philosophy.

Graham told his publisher in September 1910, following his arrival in Moscow, that he had "spent the whole of the summer in the North, tramping south from Archangel in the guise of a pilgrim or a tramp, receiving each night the hospitality and the blessing of the peasants [...] I have had a life that might be thought very beautiful". Businesslike as ever, he also assured John Lane that after collecting some further material, he would soon be in a position to write "the newest book on Russia".[88] The book he referred to was, of course, *Undiscovered Russia*, which Graham eventually concluded with a passionate declaration that the country he had fallen in love with remained a place where the foreigner could "smooth out a ruffled mind and look upon the beauty of life".[89] He was also convinced that Russia had a vital role to play in the world at a time when so much of Europe and North America was plunged in a headlong rush for industrialisation:

Science, Religion and Philosophy (London: Theosophical Publishing Society, 1891). For a useful analysis of theosophy within the western esoteric tradition see Antoine Faivre, *Accès de l'ésotérisme occidental* (Paris: Gallimard, 1986). On theosophy in Russia during Graham's time see the memoir by E.F. Pisareva, *The Light of the Russian Soul* (Wheaton, IL: Quest, 2008). For a more general discussion of the occult in Russia, see Bernice Glatzer Rosenthal (ed.), *The Occult in Russian and Soviet* Culture (Ithaca: Cornell University Press, 1997), esp. the chapter by Maria Carlson, 'Fashionable Occultism', pp. 135-52.

87 Graham, *Undiscovered Russia*, pp. 289-91.
88 John Lane Papers (HRC), Box 17, Folder 4, Graham to Lane, 18 September 1910.
89 Graham, *Undiscovered Russia*, p. 327.

> Sometimes it seems to me that in any man lives all mankind, and that every man going to and fro upon the earth represents a self within myself, and that because each other man is living his peculiar life I can live mine freely. I live my little life and give my little contribution to the grand harmony, in the faith that all other people are fulfilling their parts and making their due contributions. And England also lives its peculiar life in the faith that other nations are living their peculiar lives. England needs Russia living on the soil in holiness and simplicity, needs it living so, as a man needs a woman, for the food she gives him and the prayers she offers.[90]

By the time Graham arrived in Moscow, at the end of his trek from the north, Russia had become for him something more than a source of potential personal epiphany. It was also a place that could provide a living model for a world that had become too captivated by an overly materialistic conception of progress. Graham had, as a young man in London, dreamed of escaping to a place where he could find a sense of solace and harmony that eluded him at home. After two or three years in Russia, he had become convinced that the "Somewhere-Out-Beyond" he had discovered possessed a wisdom which, although rooted in the particularities of time and place, was capable of offering some kind of universal truth to the world. He spent much of the next few years struggling to build on his insights in a series of books and articles that were designed to expand his audience and shape British views of Russia on the eve of the First World War.

---

90 Ibid, p. 328.

2. Searching for the Soul of Russia

Although Graham was disappointed by the sales of his first two books, he must have been cheered by the reviews, even if there was something faintly patronising about the descriptions of *Vagabond* and *Undiscovered Russia* as "charming" and "attractive".[1] Not only was there a growing public fascination with Russia in Britain during the years before the Great War. There was also a great interest in walking and tramping in all their guises. The success of books ranging from Belloc's *Path to Rome* to Locke's *Beloved Vagabond* reflected the fascination of an Edwardian readership for pastoral descriptions of unfamiliar landscapes and carefree lifestyles. Kenneth Grahame's *Wind in the Willows* was an immediate hit when it first appeared in 1908 precisely because its characters were able to lead lives of leisure in bucolic surroundings, untouched by the world of the city centre office and the suburban commute.

In 1910 a monthly journal called *The Tramp* was established in London, which published articles ranging from no-nonsense accounts of camping expeditions in the Lake District, through to mystical reveries about the hidden meanings encoded in particular landscapes.[2] The journal carried one of the warmest reviews of *Vagabond in the Caucasus*, written by the mystery-writer Algernon Blackwood, who had himself travelled through the Caucasus and was so entranced by the region that he used it as a setting

---

1   See, for example, *The Bookman*, December 1910, which described *Vagabond* as "a most charming and attractive book"; *Saturday Review of Literature, Politics, Science and Art* [hereafter *Saturday Review*], 13 January 1912, where *Undiscovered Russia* was again described as "charming".

2   See, for example, Dr E.A. Baker, 'Easter at the Lakes', *The Tramp*, March 1910, pp. 3-7; Harry Roberts, 'The Art of Vagabondage', *The Tramp*, March 1910, pp. 22-26.

http://dx.doi.org/10.11647/OBP.0040.02

for his supernatural novel *The Centaur*.³ Blackwood praised *Vagabond* in *The Tramp* for conveying:

> The spirit of the open air, the passion of the tramp, the poet's delight in the simple yet significant little things of forest, mountain, plain, that combine to charm [...] The beauty of this marvellous land of mountains between the Caspian and the Black Sea is utterly arresting. I myself spent some weeks there last summer, and it calls to me like strong music. To read this vital account of it all is to live over again my own adventures.

Nor was such praise limited to the columns of *The Tramp*. The *Manchester Courier* praised Graham as "one of the true literary tramps", whilst the *Academy* compared *Vagabond* to Stevenson's *Travels with a Donkey in the Cevennes* and (predictably) Belloc's *Path to Rome*.⁴

The publication of *Vagabond* and *Undiscovered Russia* established Graham as a leading writer on Russia at a time when the country was attracting greater attention in Britain than ever before. The Anglo-Russian entente of 1907 had increased interest in Russia as a diplomatic and commercial partner,⁵ leading to a slew of publications suggesting that it was gradually becoming a more normal place, which would in time come to resemble the countries of Western Europe.⁶ Such a prospect was not universally welcomed. Countless books and articles also appeared arguing that the real appeal of Russia was still to be found precisely in its alien quality. The huge appeal of Sergei Diaghilev's *Ballets Russes*, which first came to Britain in 1911, rested in large part on the way in which its elaborate oriental scenery and fantastic costumes confirmed many existing stereotypes about Russia.⁷ The growing demand for Russian art and peasant handicrafts in the galleries of Bond Street similarly testified to the demand for something that was different and exotic. The writer and former diplomat Maurice Baring wrote

---

3   Mike Ashley, *Starlight Man* (London: Constable, 2000), p. 157 ff.
4   *The Academy*, 21 January 1911.
5   On Anglo-Russian relations during this period see Keith Neilson, *Britain and the Last Tsar: British Policy and Russia, 1894-1917* (Cambridge: Cambridge University Press, 1995); Michael Hughes, *Diplomacy before the Russian Revolution: Britain, Russia and the Old Diplomacy, 1894-1917* (Basingstoke: Macmillan, 2000); Jennifer Siegel, *Endgame: Britain, Russia and the Final Struggle for Central Asia* (London: I.B. Tauris, 2002).
6   See, for example, Bernard Pares, *Russia and Reform* (London: Constable, 1907). See, too, *The Times Russian Supplement* that was published periodically between 1912 and 1917.
7   On Diaghilev see Sjeng Scheijen, *Diaghilev: A Life* (New York: Profile Books, 2009). For a typical review of a pre-war Diaghilev production at Covent Garden (in this case 'The Golden Cock') see *The Times*, 16 June 1914. Also see Sally Baner, 'Firebird and the Idea of Russianness', in *The Ballets Russes and its World*, ed. by Lynn Garafola and Nancy Van Norman Baer (New Haven: Yale University Press, 1999), pp. 117-34.

in his book *The Mainsprings of Russia* about an elusive Russian soul that, once encountered, inspired a lifelong passion from which "you will never be free [...] The aching melancholy song, which Gogol says wanders from sea to sea throughout the length and breadth of the land, will forever echo in your heart, and haunt the recesses of your memory".[8] Graham's early books expressed ideas and motifs that were already embedded in British views of Russia. Both *Vagabond* and *Undiscovered Russia*, in turn, shaped images of the country as a place of exotic landscapes inhabited by people who lived their lives with a spiritual intensity missing in the countries of the west.

Given how soon Graham's name was to become indelibly associated with Russia, it is perhaps ironic that he was back in London working for the *Evening Times* when *Vagabond* was first published at the start of 1911. The setting up of the *Evening Times* in 1910 represented an ambitious attempt to take on the established London press, and the paper attracted a number of Fleet Street heavyweights besides its editor, Charles Watney, including Bernard Falk and Edgar Wallace (best known today as the creator of King Kong). The paper never had strong financial backing – its main sponsor was a rather reclusive Conservative M.P. from Nottingham – and the lack of money meant it could never live up to the grand hopes of its founders. Its week-end edition only managed to survive thanks to Wallace's skill as a racing-tipster. The reputation of the paper was severely damaged just a few weeks after its launch by the events surrounding the sensational trial of Dr Crippen for the murder of his wife at their home in North London. Watney purchased a supposed admission of guilt, which he published on the day of Crippen's execution, even though the confession in reality consisted of little more than a selection of notes of doubtful provenance cobbled together at the office of his lawyer.[9] The incident damaged the *Evening Times's* reputation for serious journalism. Although one of its leading lights later described it as "a good paper which ought not to have perished",[10] there was always something uncertain about the quality of its journalism.

---

8 Maurice Baring, *The Mainsprings of Russia* (London: Nelson, 1914), p. 301. On Baring's time in Russia see, too, Maurice Baring, *The Puppet Show of Memory* (London: Cassel, 1987). For a useful biography of Baring, see Emma Letley, *Maurice Baring: A Citizen of Europe* (London: Constable, 1991).
9 Margaret Lane, *Edgar Wallace: Biography of a Phenomenon* (London: Book Club, 1938), p. 188 ff.
10 Bernard Falk, *He Laughed in Fleet Street* (London: Hutchinson, 1937), p. 122.

Watney invited Graham to join the *Evening Times* as a journalist rather than a Russian specialist, promising to make him a household name, a prospect that Graham was later honest enough to admit "was very flattering and I fell for it".[11] He quickly won the respect of his new colleagues, despite the fact that he was little known, for final publication of *Vagabond* still lay some months ahead when he joined the paper.[12] Graham did not abandon his Russian interests altogether, though, since he was working on the manuscript of *Undiscovered Russia* throughout his time at the paper. He also wrote a novel for serialisation in the *Evening Times*, "written in Russian style about a man who hated the human race and decided to destroy it", but decided against publishing it in book form since Watney insisted that it contained a love story that "ruined the original".[13] It was a good decision, since *The Second Coming* is, even when judged by the most sympathetic reader, little more than a loosely connected story peopled by characters lacking in any discernible personality. So bad was it, indeed, that Graham had almost forgotten about it when he came across the manuscript in an American archive more than fifty years later. Nor was a short story he contributed to Orage's *New Age*, a sentimental account of an elderly female beggar in Moscow, much better in quality.[14]

Graham's colleagues at the *Evening Times* believed that his real literary gift was for "lurid realism",[15] a striking paradox given the lyrical prose that characterised his writing about Russia, and a stark reminder that he was always a professional writer capable of adapting to the demands of a particular market. Although the articles in the paper were unsigned, making it difficult to identify exactly which pieces he wrote, Graham seems to have been responsible for many of the court reports, including one that appeared at the end of March 1911 on the travails of a "hen-pecked husband" who had been attacked by his wife with a broom-handle.[16] He provided accounts of numerous football matches, taking delight in describing the behaviour of the crowds, delirious in victory and devastated by defeat. He

---

11 Graham Papers (HRC), Works File, *Wonderful Scene* (typescript), p. 24.
12 Falk, *He Laughed in Fleet Street*, p. 126.
13 Stephen Graham, *Part of the Wonderful Scene* (London: Collins, 1964), p. 36. The original manuscript of *The Second Coming* can be found in the T.I.F. Armstrong (Gawsworth) Papers (HRC), Misc. files. Graham later published a short story based on the novel, 'Going the Rounds', in *Path and Pavement: Twenty New Tales of Britain*, ed. by John Rowland (London: E. Grant, 1937), pp. 185-200.
14 Stephen Graham, 'Russian Beggar', *New Age*, 8, 3 (1910), pp. 62-63.
15 Graham, *Wonderful Scene*, p. 34.
16 *Evening Times*, 30 March 1911 ('The Courts Day-by-Day').

also reported on the seamier side of life, touring the docks of the East End looking for stories, on one occasion even interviewing a burlesque artist in her dressing room.

Graham was also one of the *Evening Times* journalists responsible for covering the Siege of Sidney Street, which took place in January 1911, when two Latvian revolutionaries responsible for murdering a number of London policemen were cornered and forced into a dramatic fire-fight which ended in their deaths. Graham's nine months on the *Evening Times* helped to develop his skill at painting characters and situations in a few colourful words. He was in any case fascinated throughout his long life by the human drama of major cities, subsequently writing numerous sketches about life on the streets of London and New York, even whilst there was another part of him that deplored the noise and chaos of urban life. The dichotomy between the rural traveller, immersed in the beauty and mystery of the countryside, and the urban resident enthralled with the buzz of city life, was deeply-rooted in Graham's psyche from a young age.

Graham's surprising penchant for urban life was symbolised by his choice of living arrangements in London. The census returns show that he was living with Rosa in Kentish Town in 1911, during the time he was working on the *Evening Times*, whilst the following year he moved to a flat in a four-storey house in Soho. 60 Frith Street was to remain his home for more than six decades, until his death in 1975, although it was frequently sub-let when he was away from London on one of his overseas visits. The house itself was originally built in the seventeenth century.[17] In the 1840s a number of artists had exhibited from this address, including Thomas Musgrove Joy, who, amongst other commissions, painted a series of portraits of the Royal Family. 60 Frith Street had also been home at various times to members of the minor nobility, and was suitably grand inside, complete with a dog-leg staircase and ornate wooden panelling. By the time the Grahams moved in, though, the house's glory days were long gone. Each floor was divided into a number of flats, the top two storeys populated by families of German and Russian Jewish immigrants, who conducted various tailoring and laundry businesses. They, in turn, sublet rooms with the result that people were coming and going at all hours of the day and night ("Who lived in the house and who did not it was difficult to

---

17 The description of 60 Frith Street is taken from F.H.W. Sheppard (ed.), *Survey of London*, Vols 33-34: *St Anne Soho*, pp. 151-66, accessible at http://www.british-history.ac.uk/report.aspx?compid=41075.

say"). On the floor below the Grahams lived a bookmaker, who, within a few weeks of their arrival, disappeared without paying his overdue rent to the irate landlord. The streets around the house were "very disreputable" and full of "unsophisticated poverty", and the pavement in front of 60 Frith Street itself was often strewn with rubbish, dumped from the windows by residents of the upper floors.[18]

Stephen and Rosa were not daunted by their surroundings. The living room of their first-floor flat boasted an Adam ceiling and painted wooden doors. Rosa was largely responsible for the internal decoration, covering the walls with copies of paintings by Russian artists including Repin and Perepletchikov, along with reproductions of works by English pre-Raphaelites including Watts and Burne-Jones. Graham added a wooden bookcase and an antique editorial chair that he still used half a century later. Their choice of Soho as a place to live was striking. The area bounded by Oxford Street and Charing Cross Road had already acquired its reputation as a slightly raffish and bohemian place, attractive to writers and painters, and the Grahams wanted to live in an area where they could mix easily with others who shared their interest in literature and art (Graham read the main literary journals of the period, contributing to the *English Review* and *The New Age,* and was well-aware of controversies that raged around the phenomenon of English modernism in all its forms).[19] The Grahams' flat at 60 Frith Street even became celebrated enough as a meeting place to figure in the columns of some of the literary magazines of the 1920s. Graham believed throughout his life that "if a man who travels a good deal desires to have a permanent home in London, he may as well have it as the centre of things", but Frith Street itself quickly became much more to him than just a place to rest his head when returning from his trips around the world. In a sketch written in the early 1930s, he wrote how "I have remembered Frith Street under Central Asian and Rocky Mountain stars, in the trenches and on the sea. I have looked to it as toward Mecca".[20] He loved the house enough to acquire in time the lease for the whole building.

---

18 Stephen Graham, *Twice Round the London Clock and More London Nights* (London: Ernest Benn, 1933), pp. 200-4.
19 For a useful discussion of Bohemian society in London during this period see Peter Brooker, *Bohemia in London* (Basingstoke: Palgrave, 2007). Also see Hugh David, *The Fitzrovians: A Portait of a Bohemian Society, 1900-1950* (London: Michael Joseph, 1988). For a useful contemporary account by an author whose destiny was, like Graham's intimately bound up with Russia, see Arthur Ransome, *Bohemia in London* (London: Chapman and Hall, 1907).
20 Graham, *Twice Round the London Clock*, pp. 202-3.

Graham, like so many travellers, seemed to have a need for a place that he could return to and call home. The pastoral Romantic in him was, however, never entirely silent even during the times he lived in Britain. Whilst he was working at the *Evening Times*, he and Rosa regularly went out at weekends to the Essex countryside, where they spent time "lying and lazing in the fields".[21] A few years after moving into Frith Street, when his financial situation had become more secure, Graham also acquired a small cottage in rural Sussex, near Horsham, where he could write in the intervals between tending his garden and going for long walks through the local woods.[22] Even here, though, he never abandoned himself entirely to solitude and peace, becoming involved in a controversy between the local vicar and some of his critics who disliked their rector's particular brand of muscular Christianity.[23]

Graham's work at the *Evening Times* came to an end in the summer of 1911. The paper's finances were at a particularly low ebb by this stage, and Graham later recalled that although he was Charles Watney's "pet writer […] he had to discard me".[24] It seems equally likely that he had come to realise how much he still longed "for the silence of [the] vast empty spaces" of Russia.[25] Graham's correspondence shows that he was close to completing a third book, which he provisionally called *The Tramp's Philosophy*,[26] but was unable to find a publisher for it (John Lane rejected it on the grounds that it would not be a commercial success). He therefore decided to return to Russia to continue his tramping career in the south of the country, which he preferred to the bleaker regions of the north, through which he had passed the previous summer on his tramp from Archangel to Moscow.

It was not, though, only the "vast empty spaces" that appealed to Graham. He was also becoming more interested in the ferment of what has often been called Russia's 'Silver Age' of culture. Graham had been interested in

---

21 Graham Papers (FSU), Box 579, 43 (1911 notebook).
22 Graham Papers (in private hands), Graham to Lulu Smith, 22 March 1965 (looking back on his time in Rusper).
23 Gawsworth Papers (HRC), Misc. file ('The Rector of Rusper'). For the memories of the Rector himself see Edward Fitzgerald Synnott, *Five Years' Hell in a Country Parish* (London: Stanley Paul and Co, 1920).
24 Graham, *Wonderful Scene*, p. 37.
25 Stephen Graham, *A Tramp's Sketches* (London: Thomas Nelson, 1913), p. 18, version available at http://archive.org/details/trampssketches00grahiala.
26 John Lane Letters (HRC), Box 17, Folder 4, Graham to Lane, 18 June 1911.

developments in Russian theatre and literature from the time he first arrived in Moscow – he had after all first fallen in love with the country through reading Dostoevsky – but it was the artist Vasily Perepletchikov who persuaded him that "to understand Russia fully one must appreciate the art of the day and listen to the philosophers. Russia had a base of peasantry but also an apex of thought and culture".[27] Perepletchikov was responsible for introducing Graham to the Moscow Religious-Philosophical Society, which was first established in the early years of the twentieth century, and quickly became an important meeting place for artists and writers committed to developing Russia's religious and cultural traditions in new creative forms.[28] The members of the Society were particularly influenced by the ideas of the writer Vladimir Solov'ev who, before his death in 1900, had been a pivotal figure in the country's cultural life, not least in trying to articulate a new philosophical system capable of reconciling the best of the western and Russian intellectual traditions (Graham himself wrote a paper on Solov'ev some years later for the British Theosophist journal *Quest*).[29] Many of the luminaries of Russia's Silver Age were involved in the Society, including Nikolai Berdiaev and Evgeny Trubetskoi, and Graham met a number of its most prominent figures during his periodic visits to its meetings.

Graham was never particularly adept at understanding the subtleties of the creative explosion that took place in Russia during the Silver Age (he freely admitted that he struggled to understand many of the abstruse talks he heard at the Religious-Philosophical Society).[30] Nor did he have much grasp of the immense complexities and contradictions that characterised the work of individuals like the writer Dmitri Merezhkovsky and the philosopher-poet Viacheslav Ivanov,[31] instead interpreting them rather simplistically as representatives of an authentic Russian cultural

---

27 Graham, *Wonderful Scene*, p. 32.
28 For a detailed account of the Society see Kristiane Burchardi, *Die Moskauer Religiös-Philosophische Vladimir Solov'ev Gesellschaft, 1905-1918* (Wiesbaden: Harrassowitz, 1999).
29 On Solov'ev see Jonathan Sutton, *The Religious Philosophy of Vladimir Solovyov: Towards a Reassessment* (Basingstoke: Macmillan, 1988).
30 Graham Papers (HRC), Works File, *Wonderful Scene* (autograph).
31 Graham himself translated Ivanov's 'Theatre of the Future' in *English Review*, March 1912, pp. 634-50. On Ivanov see Robert Bird, *The Russian Prospero: The Creative Universe of Viacheslav Ivanov* (Madison: University of Wisconsin Press, 2006). For valuable interpretations of Russian Silver Age culture and thought see Stephen C. Hutchings, *Russian Modernism: The Transfiguration of the Everyday* (Cambridge: Cambridge University Press, 1997); Avril Pyman, *A History of Russian Symbolism* (Cambridge: Cambridge University Press, 1994).

tradition, shaped by the influence of Orthodoxy on all aspects of national life.[32] Graham did however possess a powerful intuitive sense of the forces that were helping to shape their intellectual and artistic development, even if there was something too simplistic in his claim that the "higher intelligentsia" in Russia was seeking "religion [...] on the other side of doubt and scepticism and eclecticism".[33]

The cultural ferment of Russia's Silver Age was part of a European-wide reaction against the sense of anomie created by industrialisation and the fading appeal of institutionalised Christianity. Graham himself was, at this stage of his life, still an avid fan of the works of Friedrich Nietzsche, whose insistence on acknowledging the Dionysian aspect of human nature captivated a generation of European intellectuals, disenchanted with the narrow cultural confines of bourgeois society. Across Europe – including Britain and Russia – there was a widespread fascination with the occult. The huge interest in Theosophy reflected a pervasive sense that there were certain truths and levels of experience that could not be grasped by reason and science alone.[34] Although many of the leading lights in the Moscow Religious-Philosophical Society were, in some sense, committed to Christianity – or at least to the search for God – most of them expressed ideas and attitudes that set them far apart from the mainstream Church. The whole Russian Symbolist movement, in poetry and art, was dedicated to finding ways of expressing insights into the nature of reality that could not be obtained from a naturalism that contented itself with depicting a world of surface appearances. Some leading journals of the period, like *Mir iskusstva*, regularly appeared with ornate front covers decorated with symbols inspired by astrology or freemasonry. The Moscow Religious-Philosophical Society itself devoted a whole session in 1909 to a discussion of Theosophy, and the idea that there was a single truth expressed in all

---

32 Ivanov was in fairness by 1910 going through a Slavophile phase articulating views that were perhaps not far removed from Graham's ideas. For details see Bird, *Russian Prospero*, p. 27.

33 Stephen Graham, 'One of the Higher Intelligentsia', *Russian Review*, 1, 4 (1912), pp. 120-30.

34 On this topic see, for example, Demetres P. Tryphonopolous, 'The History of the Occult Movement', in *Literary Modernism and the Occult Tradition*, ed. by Demetres P. Tryphonopolous and Leon Surette, (Orono, ME: National Poetry Foundation, 1996), pp. 19-49. For a more detailed account of the situation in Britain see Janet Oppenheim, *The Other World: Spiritualism and Psychical Research in England, 1850-1914* (Cambridge: Cambridge University Press, 1985). On the situation in Russia see Maria Carlson, 'Fashionable Occultism' in *The Occult in Russian and Soviet Culture*, ed. by Bernice Glatzer Rosenthal (Ithaca: Cornell University Press, 1997), pp. 135-52.

the world's main religions, which could only be known by those with access to hidden forms of knowledge. Such ideas had long had an appeal for Graham. He was also instinctively sympathetic to the notion that the artist and writer had a responsibility to provide insights into a reality that might otherwise remain hidden ("pictorial pointers" he later called them).[35] Graham's distinctive understanding of the nature of 'religion' helps to explain why he was able to combine a panegyric for Russian Orthodoxy with an assertion that different religions each had their own way of leading their adherents to God.

For all his interest in the cultural life of Moscow, Graham still yearned to revive his tramping career, and in the late summer of 1911 he left the city by rail heading southwards for a new hike along the northern coast of the Black Sea. Although his movements over the next few months are hard to follow, he seems to have travelled from east to west along the shoreline, spending most of his time walking on the sands, before arriving at Constantinople in February 1912, where he boarded a boat carrying hundreds of Russian pilgrims bound for Jerusalem. Graham revelled in the solitude he encountered in the countryside through which he passed. He lived for much of the time on fruit "and realized how wild I was when I stood in thickets and bit mouthfuls of grapes from the hanging vines".[36]

Graham's tramps along the Black Sea in the winter of 1911-12 produced two very different books – *A Tramp's Sketches* (1913) and *Changing Russia* (1913) – which together neatly reflected the two main aspects of his burgeoning philosophy of life. *A Tramp's Sketches* was concerned less with the state of Russia and more with the search for meaning in the world ("it is with life that this volume is concerned"). The whole process of tramping was portrayed as a kind of pilgrimage, which allowed the individual to develop new insights into their soul, as well as giving them an opportunity to unravel the meaning of the landscapes through which they passed. Its esoteric tone makes the book at times very hard to understand (Graham himself noted that the book was "written spontaneously and without study, and as such goes forth all that a seeker could put down of his visions, or could tell of what he sought").[37] *Changing Russia* was by contrast a lament for the decline of the old peasant world, which Graham had eulogised at length in *Undiscovered Russia*, and which he feared was facing destruction by

---
35 Stephen Graham, *The Gentle Art of Tramping* (New York: Appleton, 1926), p. 231.
36 Graham Papers (HRC), *Wonderful Scene* (typescript), p. 36.
37 Graham, *Tramp's Sketches*, p. 8.

the huge social and economic changes taking place in the country. Graham noted sadly in his Introduction to *Changing Russia* that his book was "like a timely painting made of someone we love, not long before death. When next the painter offers to paint her, the time will be past, and the loved one be departed".[38] The missionary element in his writing was now stronger than ever, as he sought to persuade readers of the wisdom both of his particular life-philosophy, and of his conviction that Russia possessed a unique spiritual identity from which the rest of the world could learn.

A Tramp's Sketches is one of the hardest of Graham's books to read. It does contain a number of vivid descriptive passages, including a detailed description of 'A Turkish Coffee House' in the Transcaucasus, full of impoverished clients dressed in "drab turbans" and "dingy red fez hats". The book was above all, though, "not so much a book about Russia as [...] the life of the wanderer and seeker, the walking hermit, the rebel against modern conditions and commercialism who has gone out into the wilderness".[39] It begins with a diatribe against life in the "evil city" – in practice London but intended as shorthand for every major urban centre – which in time "drove me into the wilderness to my mountains and valleys, by the side of the great sea and by the haunted forests [...] There I refound my God, and my being reexpressed itself to itself in terms of eternal Mysteries. I vowed I should never again belong to the town".[40]

Graham tried as far as possible to avoid the major Black Sea towns during his tramp, although he did visit places like Sochi, in order to write sketches for dispatch back to the London papers. Whilst his previous books had been full of stories about the people he had met, he was now engaged in a kind of solitary pilgrimage, choosing to sleep rough rather than seek lodgings in the cottages he passed. He worked hard to convey a sense of wonder in the places he passed through, describing them not simply in terms of their beauty, but emphasising how the individual who slept in the wild "has entered into new relationship with the world in which he lives, and has allowed the gentle creative hands of Nature to re-shape his soul".[41] Graham had been asked by a friend whether a solitary existence in the countryside could really provide a fully satisfying and human life – an

---

38 Stephen Graham, *Changing Russia* (London: John Lane, 1913), p. 11, version available at http://archive.org/details/changingrussia00grah.
39 Graham, *Tramp's Sketches*, p. 7.
40 Ibid, p. 20.
41 Ibid, p. 23

interesting point given that he himself chose to live in the heart of the city when resident in London – and he replied rather elusively that:

> The tramp does not want a world of tramps – that would never do. The tramps – better call them the rebels against modern life – are perhaps only the first searchers for new life. They know themselves as necessarily only a few, the pioneers. Let the townsman give the simple life its place. Everyone will benefit by a little more simplicity, and a little more living in communion with Nature, a little more of the country. I say, 'Come to Nature altogether,' but I am necessarily misunderstood by those who feel quickly bored. Good advice for all people is this – live the simple life as much as you can till you're bored. Some people are soon bored: others never are. Whoever has known Nature once and loved her will return again to her. Love to her becomes more and more.

He also insisted that the tramp, or perhaps better the pilgrim-tramp, was best-placed to understand how the joys of rural life were linked to more fundamental questions about the nature of existence. "Whoever has resolved the common illusions of the meaning of life, and has seen even in glimpses the naked mystery of our being, finds that he absolutely must live in the world which is outside city walls".[42]

The theme of Holy Russia, in the sense of Orthodox Russia, did not loom large in *A Tramp's Sketches*, although the book does contain a lengthy description of daily life at the New Athos Monastery, along with a number of other monasteries where Graham was given shelter. The informing philosophy was instead that of *Ygdrasil*: that the everyday world was a series of signs that showed the way out of the "Little World" and into a place of deeper meaning. Graham was once again sharply critical of all forms of established Christianity, suggesting that the medieval Church showed "much more hospitality than to-day. The crusader and the palmer needed no introduction to obtain entertainment at a strange man's house".[43] He also spent a good deal of time discussing the aesthetics of beauty, whether in the form of lovely scenery or great art, which he believed could provide an intimation of the divine almost as surely as participation in formal worship ("The knowledge of the beautiful is an affirmation").[44]

The final chapters of *A Tramp's Sketches* are at times almost incomprehensible, as Graham struggled to convey his sense of a universe that was profoundly mysterious and irreducible to neat formulae or

---
42 Ibid, p. 57.
43 Ibid, p. 201.
44 Ibid, p. 63.

description. He told the story – or perhaps the fable – of a young woman called Zenobia, with whom he once collected flowers on a "breathless" and "mysterious" summer night. Her beauty and her naturalness were eventually corrupted, though, when she moved to the city and began to enter into local society. Her looks faded to grey as a result of an indoor life lived with a "lack of sun" and a "lack of life", leaving Graham to lament how "in one place flowers rot and die; in another, bloom and live. The truth is that in this city they rot and die". The figure of Zenobia, whether real, mythical, or somewhere in between, served for Graham as a symbol of the way in which true beauty and liveliness were crushed in the man-made world of cities. In a passage replete with the kind of existential language that echoed Dostoevsky and Nietzsche, he passionately declared that "Life is not thoughts, is not calm, is not sights, is not reading or music, is not the refinement of the senses, Life is life. This is the great secret. This is the original truth, and if we had never begun to think, we should never have lost our instinctive knowledge".[45]

It is worth quoting at some length the passage that ended the main part of *A Tramp's Sketches*, since it conveys more clearly than anywhere else in Graham's early writings his understanding of the universe, couched in terms that owe more to a diffuse early twentieth-century esotericism than to any formal Christian doctrine:

> But beyond the universe, no scientist, not any of us, knows anything. On all shores of the universe washes the ocean of ignorance, the ocean of the inexplicable. We stand upon the confines of an explored world and gaze at many blank horizons. We yearn towards our natural home, the kingdom in which our spirits were begotten. We have rifled the world, and tumbled it upside down, and run our fingers through all its treasures, yet have not come upon the charter of our birth. We explored Beauty till we came to the shore of a great sea; we explored music, and came upon the outward shore of harmony and earthly truth, and found its limits.

He went on to note that:

> Some day for us shall come into that blank sky-horizon which is called the zenith, a stranger, a man or a god, perhaps not like ourselves, yet having affinities with ourselves, and correlating ourselves to some family of minor gods of which we are all lost children. We shall then know our universal function and find our universal orbit. As yet the True Sun stands in the antipodes, the great light is not vouchsafed. In the night of ignorance our

---

[45] Ibid, pp. 239-53.

little sun is shining and stars gleam upon our sky-horizons. But when the True Sun shines their brightness will be obscured, and we shall know a new day and a new night, a new heaven and a new earth.[46]

Such words represented a distinct, if melodramatic, response to the intellectual and emotional dilemmas that shaped the response of a whole generation of intellectuals, in Russia and elsewhere, to the challenge of modernity. Graham's response took the form of a search for an affirmation of meaning and life beyond the confines of the everyday. He believed that language could help to capture and convey a sense of the numinous that could not be defined or valued by the scientist or the businessman. The only hint in this passage of a specifically Christian understanding of these perplexities and dilemmas comes at the very end with the words: "It is written, 'When He appears we shall be like Him'".

Changing Russia was so different in tone from *A Tramp's Sketches* that it is hard to believe it was inspired by the same journey along the Black Sea shore. The contrasting character of the two books captured something of a division in Graham himself. During the five years before the 1917 Revolution, Graham continued to write *both* about the mystery of Holy Russia *and*, more prosaically, about a range of Russian social and economic questions. *Changing Russia* contained more in the way of anecdotes and pen portraits than *A Tramp's Sketches*, including a lively chapter headed 'At the Seaside in Russia', that first appeared in the *Evening Standard*, and described the "rather tedious" rituals of daily bathing and nightly gossiping among visitors to towns like Sochi and Gelendzhik. Most of the book, however, represented a sustained lament about the way the country was changing. Graham stayed at Rostov-on-Don early in his trip, a place he believed "shows what Russia is going to be if it follows along the commercial lines of the rest of Europe", adding that "in such towns lies the foundation of what is called 'democracy', but which is really [...] quarrelling over the hours and the wage".[47] He wrote with disdain about streets full of shops and warehouses selling foreign goods – there was extensive investment by British and Belgian firms in the area – and bemoaned the impact of commerce on the morality and taste of the city's residents. Although many of them went to Church, still more flocked to the new "electric theatre", where they watched shows that "are bloodthirsty, gruesome murder stories, stories of crime, of unfaithful husbands and wives, and

---

46 Ibid, pp. 326-27.
47 Graham, *Changing Russia*, p. 24.

of course the usual insane harlequinades".[48] The situation was not much better at other towns like Novorossisk, with its "cement factories and soap-works", although Graham was consoled by the fact that the surrounding countryside was still largely unspoiled. The Black Sea was an important commercial hub in Russia, and by the early twentieth century the main ports were closely integrated into the wider European economy. Graham himself was particularly concerned that the construction of a new railway line along the Black Sea shore would soon spread modern commerce into less populated and underdeveloped regions and damage still more the character of the whole area.

Some of the most vitriolic passages in *Changing Russia* were reserved for the Russian bourgeoisie, which Graham believed was the defining class of the new social and economic order, and he vigorously condemned its members' materialist outlook on life which meant that they "want to know the price of everything". He also criticised their lack of interest in spiritual matters, noting that any talk of "the mystery of Christ" created unease, as did any hint that "though you are poor you have no regard for money".[49] Graham was particularly concerned at the bourgeoisie's growing social and political influence, which he feared was "beginning to clamour in the press, to write, to define, to censure. It calls itself the democracy, and points out that it will pay for its likes, and that its sort of art and life will 'pay'. That a thing 'pays' is to the bourgeois the test of democratic approval".[50]

The vision of Russia's future supposedly held by members of this new class could hardly have been more different from that of Graham, who continued to believe that "Russia has an extraordinary greatness to be attained through her Church, through her national institutions, and by virtue of her national landscape [...] The cultivated and educated Russians must not lose their peasant souls [...] the peasant is the root, and the root draws up mysteriously from those depths that which is its own, that which God has provided".[51] The best hope for preserving this traditional Russia against the depredations of change rested, in Graham's view, on "the Tsar and his advisers, who are all Conservatives, that they truly conserve and keep the peasantry living simply and sweetly on the land".[52] Graham never

---

48 Ibid, p. 28.
49 Ibid, p. 117.
50 Ibid, p. 121.
51 Ibid, p. 210.
52 Ibid, p. 11.

really hid his doubts about the Constitutional Experiment that was set in motion after the 1905 Revolution, believing that any institution like the *Duma* (Assembly) would be manipulated by the new commercial class that was becoming ever more powerful in Russian life. He also expressed doubt about whether greater education and the bestowal of civic rights would make Russia a happier place:

> In ten or twenty years illiterate Russia will be half-educated Russia, and the difficulty will be to find conservative people at all. As soon as a peasant learns to read he begins to want new things from life; he sees that he is poor, as Adam saw that he was naked; he begins to compare himself with his kind in other countries; he finds the ready-made creed of the Socialist, and swallows it whole.

The high hopes placed by British and Russian liberals alike on the prospects for the further constitutional development of the Tsarist Empire were not, to put it mildly, shared by Graham.

There was one further theme in *Changing Russia* that was to become even more pronounced in Graham's books and articles during the years that followed: the question of Anglo-Russian relations. Graham was well-aware that British finance was playing a pivotal role in the rapid industrial development taking place across Russia. He was concerned that the materialism he so disliked at home was being exported to the very country to which he had "escaped", the place that served for him as the "Somewhere-Out-Beyond" as he expressed it in *A Tramp's Sketches*.[53] Graham was a strong advocate of the Anglo-Russian entente established in 1907, but his support had little to do with diplomatic or commercial matters. It instead flowed from his conviction that the British public was turning to Russia for "art, thought and action" of a kind missing in their own culture.[54] Although he recognised that recent tensions in Persia had created some suspicion in Britain about the imperial ambitions of Russia, Graham was confident that the warm reception accorded to a recent visit by a delegation of British dignitaries to Russia showed that there was the potential to build and maintain good official relations. He concluded *Changing Russia* with a call to the Liberal Party to make clear that its members supported the policy of the entente set in motion by the Foreign Secretary Sir Edward Grey. Whilst Graham remained convinced that Russia's real importance to Britain flowed from its role as a living reminder of an alternative vision of

---

53 Graham, *Tramp's Sketches*, p. 206.
54 Graham, *Changing Russia*, p. 3.

life, he had begun to consider the kinds of practical questions that were to command his attention more closely following the outbreak of war in 1914, when his opinions were increasingly sought by some of the most senior figures in the British Government.

Graham's tramp along the shores of the Black Sea during the autumn and winter of 1911-12 eventually led him to Constantinople, where he set sail for Jerusalem with hundreds of Russian pilgrims, in order to spend Easter in the Holy Land. The book that he subsequently wrote about his experiences, *With the Russian Pilgrims to Jerusalem*, was instrumental in bringing Graham to far greater public attention than any of his previous works (it was serialised in the *English Review* and the American *Harper's Magazine*). Graham told his readers in the Prologue to the book that he had, for many years, wished to undertake a pilgrimage:

> Whoever has wished to go has already started on the pilgrimage. And once you have started, every step upon the road is a step toward Jerusalem. Even steps which seem to have no meaning are taking you by byways and lanes to the high-road. For the heart guides the steps, and has intentions too deep for the mind to grasp at once. The true Christian is necessarily he who has the wishing heart. Therein is the Christian discerned, that he seeks a city. Once we have consciously known ourselves as pilgrims on the way, then all the people and the scenes about us have a new significance. They are seen in their right perspective. Upon the pilgrim's road our imperfect eyes come into focus for all earthly phenomena.[55]

He went on to recall how even as a child he had looked "wistfully" at religious processions, seeing in them an echo of a longer journey, adding that for years his heart had responded more readily to "march music" than to "all the other melodies in the world". Although Graham did not spell it out explicitly, he had begun to acknowledge that his years of tramping in the wilderness had themselves been a kind of pilgrimage, a restless search for some form of epiphany capable of resolving the sense of dissonance and longing that had first led him to Russia. The journey to Jerusalem seemed to him to bring together the two main elements in his life: his love of Russia and his sense of the incompleteness of human life when lived purely in the material world:

> That it should be with the Russian peasants that I came to Jerusalem is also symbolically true. In the larger pilgrimage of life it is with these simple

---

[55] Stephen Graham, *With the Russian Pilgrims to Jerusalem* (London: Macmillan, 1913), p. 3, version available at http://archive.org/details/withrussianpilgr00grahuoft.

people that I have been journeying. It was the wish of the heart, the genius of seeking, that taught me to seek Jerusalem through Russia, that brought me to her simple people living in the great open spaces, lighting their candles in the little cottages and temples. At Jerusalem were hundreds of Englishmen and Americans, and the English language was as frequent in my ears as Turkish. I stood next to rich tourists from my own land; they hadn't the remotest idea that I was other than a Russian peasant, and I thought, "What luck that I didn't come with these!" But really it was not luck, but destiny.[56]

Although the Prologue echoed many of the themes that ran through Graham's earlier work, the main text of *With the Russian Pilgrims* was very different in character from much of his previous work. Whilst he was still anxious to persuade his readers of the virtues of Holy Russia, the book's tone was comparatively restrained, at least once the intensely personal *confession de coeur* of the Prologue was out of the way. He was instead content to use simple pen-portraits to illuminate the religious passion and individual idiosyncrasies of his companions on the journey to Jerusalem. It is for this reason that *With the Russian Pilgrims* is more satisfying as an example of *travel literature* than any of his previous books. Graham was anxious that his earlier books were marred by a certain immaturity of theme and over-blown style. Many years later he noted that "all description is art" and that even the most mundane "thumb-nail sketch" could be used to hint at something broader and more significant.[57] He made a deliberate effort when writing *With the Russian Pilgrims* to treat his material in a more under-stated manner.

The Russian-crewed boat that Graham boarded at Constantinople already had 500 pilgrims on board, who had joined the vessel at Odessa or Batumi, hundreds of miles to the east. The vessel was headed to Jaffa, a journey that should normally have taken a few days, but in fact lasted more than two weeks. The delays were partly due to the itinerary of the boat, which made a number of stops along the way, including one at the Holy Mountain of Athos. It also stopped at Smyrna (modern-day Izmir), as well as at Alexandrettia (today Iskenderun), where it took on twenty-nine cows for transport to Port Said! The slow journey was also due to bad weather, including one storm so violent that the captain felt impelled to call on his passengers to pray for the ship's safe arrival at port. The living conditions were dreadful and the smell in the hold

---

56 Ibid, pp. 11-12.
57 Graham, *Gentle Art of Tramping*, p. 231.

appalling. Graham slept each night on a carpenter's bench, whilst others lay down on provision chests or the sooty roof of the engine room.

There was despite these privations a strong feeling of camaraderie amongst the pilgrims, most of whom were comparatively elderly, like the seventy-six year old who had walked thousands of miles across Russia in order to join the boat headed for Jerusalem. The younger pilgrims usually made the journey in thanksgiving for some particular deliverance, such as the twenty year old boy from the Urals, who had pledged to go to Jerusalem when he was dangerously ill, and now, having recovered, was determined to redeem his promise. There were many women amongst the pilgrims too, but Graham seldom spoke to them, a result perhaps of some half-defined convention that frowned upon overly-friendly relations between travellers of different sexes. Many of the company joined in nightly services led by a Russian priest, himself making the pilgrimage, whilst the rest of the time was passed in desultory conversation or in reading and discussing the Bible. A strange reminder of developments in the outside world intruded from time-to-time into this insular ship-borne world. Many crew members were sympathetic to one or other of the various revolutionary groups back in Russia, and they tried to convert the pilgrims by telling them that the monks and priests they would meet in Jerusalem were simply robbers and bandits, interested only in lining their own pockets. Although they met with little success, the dialogue of the deaf between the earnestly pious peasants and the radically-minded crew was a stark reminder of the tensions bubbling up in a country that was, within five years, to descend into revolution.

Graham provided readers of *With the Russian Pilgrims* with a number of detailed descriptions of his companions which, although usually affectionate and respectful, made no attempt to idealise his fellow travellers. There was for example Philip, a peasant from a Ukrainian village close to the Austro-Hungarian border, who was making his fourteenth trip to Jerusalem. The extent of his piety was called into question by the fact that he made a good deal of money by acting as "a tout for ecclesiastical shop-keepers" on arrival in the Holy Land.[58] Typical of his victims was another pilgrim, to whom Graham gave the name Liubomudrof (a play on the Russian for "lover of wisdom"),

---

58 Graham, *With the Russian Pilgrims*, p. 152.

a man whose simple piety could not be doubted, even though he cheerfully acknowledged that he was earlier in his life an alcoholic and an adulterer. Graham also wrote at length of a priest travelling with the pilgrims, Father Evgeny, who, although honest and pious, could also be imperious and dismissive of those around him. Graham made no effort to hide the human frailty of those he travelled with. Nor did he try to sentimentalise his description of the Holy Land itself. He admitted that on arrival in Jerusalem he found the city to be little more than "a pleasure-ground for wealthy sight-seers", and "a place where every stone has been commercialised either by tourist agencies or by greedy monks". He nevertheless continued to believe in Jerusalem as an idea, an "existence independent of material appearance",[59] and was convinced that the idea could not be tainted by the omnipresent corruption and dilapidation. This same principle ran through his description of many of his fellow-pilgrims. Whilst Graham openly acknowledged their faults, he also believed that the instinct to pilgrimage was driven by a deep spiritual hunger, powerful enough to bring the pilgrims to Jerusalem, even if not always strong enough to transform their behaviour.

Graham played a full part in the celebrations and rituals of the Russian pilgrims (a kind of participant-observer to use modern sociological jargon). He went to the Church of the Sepulchre in Jerusalem, "not to look but to pray", and was profoundly moved by the experience of entering the burial chamber. He travelled to Nazareth with dozens of other pilgrims, passing through the Moslem town of Nablus, before arriving at the "shabby" birth place of Christ. Graham also joined thousands of other pilgrims for a journey to the River Jordan, staying en route at a hostelry managed by the Imperial Russian Palestine Society, before taking part in a mass celebration of ritual re-baptism:

> In a great miscellaneous crowd the peasants began to undress and to step into their white shrouds, the women into long robes like nightdresses, the men into full white shirts and pantaloons. Those who came unprovided stood quite naked on the banks. Then the priest, when he had given the pilgrims time to prepare, began taking the service for the sanctification of the water. The ikons and the cross were ranged around a wooden platform over the water.[60]

---

59 Ibid, p. 6.
60 Ibid, p. 190.

The priest supervising the ceremony then dipped the cross into the water and the pilgrims plunged in "crossing themselves and shivering". Graham subsequently took part in the Holy Week celebrations in Jerusalem, including a Palm Sunday service at the Church of the Sepulchre, and a visit to the Garden of Gethsemane on Holy Thursday, which followed the path taken by Jesus as he was taken to the house of the High Priest Annas. On Good Friday he joined the procession to Golgotha, re-enacting the last journey of Christ, whilst on Easter Day itself he went to the Russian Cathedral with the thousands of other pilgrims visiting the city. Although he had been present at Orthodox Easter celebrations before, he was still thrilled by the intensity of the experience, which far exceeded anything he had known growing up in the more sedate atmosphere of the Church of England:

> Then at one in the morning we passed [...] into the Russian cathedral, now joyously illuminated with coloured lights, and we heard the service in familiar church Slavonic. And we all kissed one another again. What embracing and kissing there were this night; smacking of hearty lips and tangling of beards and whiskers! The Russian men kiss one another with far more heartiness than they kiss their women. In the hostelry I watched a couple of ecstatical old greybeards who grasped one another tightly by the shoulders, and kissed at least a score of times, and wouldn't leave off.[61]

When *Russian Pilgrims* was finally published in 1913, part of its appeal rested on the thirty eight black-and-white photographs (more than in any of Graham's previous books). Graham seldom wrote much about his photography, but he kept prints of some of his best photos for many decades, blown up and mounted to ensure their preservation. Although only equipped with a basic Kodak camera, he proved adept at identifying possible subjects, and took numerous shots of individuals and street scenes. Formal photographs of men like Liubomudrov and Father Evgeny were interspersed with others that were snapped spontaneously, like one of an elderly grandmother caught in confusion on the banks of the River Jordan, as she searched for the clothes she had taken off during the service of ritual rebaptism.

---

61 Ibid, p. 296.

74 Beyond Holy Russia

Figure 4: Photograph taken by Stephen Graham of elderly Russian peasant woman on the banks of the Jordan, published by Stephen Graham, *With the Russian Pilgrims to Jerusalem* (London: Macmillan, 1913), p. 194.

Other photos in the book ranged from a shot of the funeral of a pilgrim who died on his way back from the Jordan, to ones showing crowds of pilgrims in the various cathedrals and shrines. Graham also captured more mundane scenes like the washing of shirts in the courtyard of the hostel where many pilgrims stayed in Jerusalem. These photographs gave readers of *Russian*

Pilgrims a visual sense of the rituals of pilgrimage that they could never have obtained from words alone. The shots of Orthodox priests dressed in ornate robes, blessing hordes of pilgrims clothed in the traditional costume of European Russia, conveyed brilliantly a world unknown to almost all of Graham's British and American readers.

Graham returned directly to Russia from Jerusalem in the spring of 1912, before heading eastwards to pass the summer in the borderlands of Siberia, where he hoped to "spend some months idling pleasantly amongst the Ural lakes and writing my book". After a long and tortuous train journey he finally arrived at Lake Turgoiak, situated on the eastern slope of the Ural Mountains, close to the town of Miass. He was enthralled by the natural beauty of the region, describing how the forest was "fresh with an unspotted loveliness", whilst the air was "clear and brilliant".[62] A few weeks after he moved there, the woods filled with local children harvesting the strawberries and other wild fruit that grew in abundance. Graham nevertheless began to encounter a dark side to an area that at first struck him as a place where "the scenery of the fairy tale has become actual". He visited some of the gold-mining towns that littered the Urals, finding amidst the grim surroundings "a more drunken, murderous, brother-hating population" than any he had ever seen in Russia. He also went to some of the industrial towns, where "the air was filled with choking sulphurous fumes, and the whole forest side was withered".[63] Graham later recalled how within a world of "untrodden forests, pure lakes [...] and silence" lurked "misery, dirt and despair", sensing once again that his Russian Eden faced desecration at the hands of the modern world.[64]

Graham returned to Britain in the autumn of 1912 to finish the manuscript of *Russian Pilgrims*. When the book finally appeared the following year it quickly garnered positive reviews and good sales. The *Athenaeum* praised Graham for "throwing off the bonds of society" so that he could report "with a clear-eyed simplicity the story of a pilgrimage".[65] The *New York Times* praised him as "the best modern writer of the saga of vagabondage".[66] Such fulsome praise was particularly welcome to Graham. Although he had received some positive reviews for *Tramp's Sketches* and

---

62 Graham, *Changing Russia* p. 255.
63 Ibid, pp. 265, 276.
64 Ibid, p. 270.
65 *Athenaeum*, 20 September 1913.
66 *New York Times*, 9 November 1913.

Changing Russia, both books also faced considerable criticism for their over-blown style and whimsy.[67] Reviewers applauded *With the Russian Pilgrims* precisely because it offered a series of acute sketches rather than more general ruminations on the nature of Holy Russia and the meaning of landscape. Graham's understanding of the role played by pilgrimage in Russia's religious life was, in reality, less acute than some of his reviewers realised. His suggestion that "Russian culture has rather despised the peasant and the pilgrim" was straightforwardly fantastic.[68] Both Tolstoy and Dostoevsky – amongst many others – devoted enormous attention to the subject. His account of his time with the Russian pilgrims was nevertheless genuinely original, and his book helped to establish Graham's profile in a way that his previous work never managed to achieve. It is still read today by scholars interested in learning more about the nature of popular piety in Tsarist Russia during the years before 1917.[69]

The serialisation rights of *With the Russian Pilgrims* in *Harper's Magazine* earned Graham more money than he had earned from his first two books. For all his idealism he was very hard-headed when considering the potential financial benefits of his work (the book also appeared in an unauthorised translation in Russian from which he earned nothing). The growing audience for Graham's work across the Atlantic certainly helps to explain his decision in the spring of 1913 to head westwards to the USA, in the company of a boat-load of emigrants who, like so many millions of others, hoped to establish new lives for themselves in the New World. The whole question of immigration was the subject of huge controversy in the United States at this time, as the policy of the "open door" came under increasing pressure in the face of anxiety that the sheer number of arrivals would change the character of American society. Graham was confident that a book on the subject would find a wide readership, whilst *Harper's Magazine* was once again keen to serialise his work, as was a Russian literary journal whose interest was prompted by the fact that so many of those leaving for the New World were subjects of the Tsar. In March, Graham found himself standing at a wharf on Tooley Street, near London

---

67 See, for example, *Athenaeum*, 26 October 1912; *Times Literary Supplement*, 4 October 1913.
68 Graham, *With the Russian Pilgrims*, p. 215.
69 Simon Sebag Montefiore, *Jerusalem: The Biography* (London: Phoenix, 2011), pp. 367, 387-88; Marc D. Steinberg and Heather Coleman, *Sacred Stories: Religion and Spirituality in Modern Russia* (Bloomington, IN: Indiana University Press, 2007), p. 42.

Bridge, watching a long procession of Russian peasants disembark from the steamship *Perm* in transit to a new life in America. There were also many Jews from Poland and the western provinces of the Russian Empire. The arrivals were dressed in a motley array of sheepskins and shawls, carrying their meagre possessions in wooden boxes and sacks, all looking anxious as they faced scrutiny from the customs officers on the shore. Once they had completed these formalities they were shepherded by representatives of the shipping agent to St Pancras railway station, in order to catch a train to Liverpool, where they were to join one of the Cunard liners that crossed back and forth across the Atlantic.

When the ship finally departed from Liverpool, it was carrying some 1,500 emigrants in steerage – "a strange gathering of seekers, despairers, wanderers, pioneers, criminals, scapegoats" – drawn from more than a dozen nationalities.[70] Before they boarded they were scrutinised for scabies and other diseases, after which they were shown to their quarters, which, although not luxurious, were infinitely better than the ones Graham had endured on the tramp steamer that had taken him to Jaffa the previous year. Most of the emigrants were housed in cabins which had no more than six beds, and were given soap and a towel, as well as a life-preserver (it was just a year since the loss of the Titanic). They took their meals in a huge mess-room filled with four enormous tables. Whilst the food was hardly first-class, it was plentiful and of reasonable quality. Most of the emigrants kept to their own ethnic groups, although some of the younger ones flirted and fraternised with other nationalities, as their elders played cards or walked aimlessly around the deck. Graham spent most of his time with the emigrants from Russia, who assumed that because he knew English he would be able to answer their questions about what they should do when they got to America. For a week the boat became a microcosm of pre-First World War Europe, bringing together thousands of people from across the continent, all of them nervous and excited about the lives that lay ahead of them.

The docking of the ship in New York was followed by the rituals of immigration at Ellis Island that had become so familiar to millions of new arrivals over the previous few decades. The huge crowd waited in the vast hall, with varying degrees of patience, for processing by customs officials and medical staff. Graham's description of himself as "a tramp" did little to

---

70 Stephen Graham, *With Poor Immigrants to America* (New York, 1914), p. 14, version available at http://archive.org/details/cihm_991708.

please the immigration officials, but they were mollified by his assurances that he was not an anarchist, and had no particular desire to subvert the laws of the United States. After hours of treatment as "a hurrying, bumping, wandering piece of coal being mechanically guided to the sacks of its type and size", he found himself in the streets of New York, heading to a restaurant with a number of other immigrants who were ravenous after the delays and minor torments of Ellis Island. He was in the afternoon offered work at two dollars a day, which he declined, before heading on to a lodging house on Third Avenue which sold rooms by the night.

Graham did not find it easy to adjust to the rhythms of New York. He took an instant dislike to the skyscrapers that so awed his fellow-immigrants when they first saw them from the deck of the ship, although for some reason he was favourably struck by the gothic-inspired fifty-seven storey Woolworth Building, which had opened for business just a few weeks earlier. Nor was he impressed by the views expressed to him by "an American literary man" he met at one of the city's clubs, who insisted that the United States represented the country of the future, boasting of how "there's nothing in modern America more than fifty years old. Think of what we've done in the time – clearing, building, engineering; think of the bridges we've built, the harbours, the canals, the great factories, the schools".[71] Graham found little to appeal to him in a city where "a hustling, mannerless crowd" passed along streets full of "trolley-cars dashing along at life-careless speed".[72] He was, however, more reserved when expressing his opinions in a lengthy interview for the *New York Times*, praising the city for its "free, fresh atmosphere that makes for a real creativeness", although he was brutal in his judgement of the slums on the East Side, which were "worse than any city I have ever been in".[73] In the book he subsequently published on his experiences, he recalled how "The houses are so high [...] that you get into ten streets of New York what we get into a hundred streets in London. The New York slums are slums at the intensest".[74] The United States became, in Graham's mind, the apogee of the kind of industrial society he had come to deplore so strongly over the previous few years.

Graham was appalled by the way in which the collective psyche of modern American society was being shaped by the process of economic

---

71 Ibid, p. 57.
72 Ibid, p. 57.
73 *New York Times*, 6 April 1913.
74 Graham, *With Poor Immigrants*, pp. 76-77.

development. He noted in his book *With Poor Immigrants to America* how "the influence of a great machinery gets to the heart of a people [...] Each man is drilled to act like a machine, and the drilling enters into the fibre of his being to such an extent that when work is over his muscles move habitually in certain directions, and the rhythm of his day's labour controls his language and thoughts".[75] He was also depressed by the speed with which immigrants from around the world abandoned their identities once they passed through Ellis Island. When Graham attended the Russian Cathedral on East Ninety-Fifth Street on Easter Eve, he went in traditional Russian peasant attire, admittedly because he had been invited to a fancy-dress party, and was stunned to find that the rest of the congregation wore waistcoats and ties. Although many Russian immigrants maintained their Orthodox faith, they quickly became immersed in the rituals of the host society, adopting both the habits and dress of the New World. Graham was not entirely dismissive of the idea of the melting pot (he was impressed by the way in which members of the different Slavic nations got on much better in America than they did back home in Europe). He was nevertheless perturbed that becoming an American meant shedding an older identity, sanctified by generations of history, in favour of one that was forged by the needs of the modern industrial economy. The result of this process meant that young Americans felt in their very souls "every throb of the engines" and allowed even their leisure hours to become mechanised by "shop-soiled [...] commercialism".[76]

After a few weeks in New York, Graham began a series of tramps across the north-eastern quarter of the United States, bound for Chicago, which he reached after two months on a day so hot it cost fifty three people their lives. Although he did not think that life in the city was as bleak as portrayed by Upton Sinclair in his novel *The Jungle*, Graham was still appalled by the slums, as well as "the clamour of the Chicago crowd [...] ignorant, cocksure, mocking".[77] He was also upset by the environmental degradation he witnessed en route in mining towns like Scranton, Pennsylvania. There he met a young newspaper reporter who took him up a ridge in order to get a better view of the city's "numberless chimneys" and "black chutes and shafts and mountains of slag". The sight disgusted Graham, but thrilled his guide, who noted proudly that Americans had the confidence

---

75 Ibid, p. 116.
76 Ibid, p. 122.
77 Ibid, p. 277.

"to smash up Nature in the hope of getting something better". "A revolt against Eden", Graham noted with anger, "the children's infatuation for playing with the dirt".[78]

The situation was not entirely grim. In large parts of the Northeast he found a rural world of great beauty, where "the maples were all red [and] ... in the woods the American dogwood tree was covered with white blossoms like thousands of little dolls' nightcaps".[79] Whilst most of the photographs that appeared in *Poor Immigrants* depicted urban street scenes, Graham also included some that showed views of windmills in Indiana and apple orchards in the Catskills, for he was astute enough to realise that many readers would still be interested in his descriptions of life in the remote countryside. He was nevertheless most fascinated by the rhythm of life in the large cities. Graham was convinced that Russia and America together symbolised the future of humanity, representing as they did "the Eastern and Western poles of thought", noting in *Poor Immigrants* that "Russia is evolving as the greatest artistic philosophical and mystical nation of the world" whilst "America is showing itself as the site of the New Jerusalem, the place where a nation is really in earnest in its attempt to realise the great dream of human progress".[80] For all his reservations, the United States made a powerful impact on Graham. Six years later, after the trauma of war and revolution had separated him from his beloved Russia, it was to America that he turned in his search for a new land of lost content.

Graham's long trips abroad meant that he was away from Britain for much of the period leading up to the First World War. He nevertheless worked hard during his forays back home to establish the contacts he needed to develop his career. His publisher, John Lane, was instrumental in introducing Graham to numerous figures in the literary *beau monde*, including the writer and anti-vivisectionist Stephen Coleridge, the novelist Joseph Pennell and the humorist William Caine. Lane also introduced his young author to the formidable Olga Novikov, the Russian *grande dame* and sometime confidante of William Gladstone, who had since the 1870s devoted her life to promoting cordial Anglo-Russian relations.[81] Graham

---

78 Ibid, pp. 139-40.
79 Ibid, p. 85.
80 Ibid, p. xi.
81 On Novikov see W.T. Stead, *The M.P. for Russia*, 2 vols. (London: Melrose, 1909). Graham himself later provided a preface to Novikov's own *Russian Memories* (London: Herbert Jenkins, 1917).

was a regular visitor to her house in London, particularly during the Balkan Wars of 1912-13, when it became a meeting-place for representatives from the countries of southeast Europe. He also occasionally found himself on the fringes of the celebrated Belloc-Chesterton circle, to which he was introduced by his fellow Russophile Maurice Baring, although he does not seem to have been an habitué of the restaurants and clubs where they met (he regarded Baring with awe, describing him as "ambassadorial" in his memoirs, a term that applied as much to Baring's patrician quality as to his past service in the British Diplomatic Service).

Graham's closest friend in Britain was the writer Algernon Blackwood, who had reviewed *Vagabond* so favourably in the pages of *The Tramp*. Blackwood had already made a name for himself as an author of popular ghost stories with collections such as *The Listener* (1907), which was written following a period in which he tried, unsuccessfully, to establish himself as a farmer in Canada, giving up when it became clear that he lacked the skill to make a living from the land. Blackwood had since his youth been fascinated by eastern philosophy, and was greatly influenced by Theosophy in all its various guises, as well as being involved in a number of esoteric cults, including the secretive Hermetic Order of the Golden Dawn, which included the poet W.B. Yeats amongst its devotees. A good deal of his work exhibited a kind of nature-mysticism which at times came close to ascribing a living personality to the natural world.[82] Graham and Blackwood first met in 1910, when the former was working on the *Evening Times* in London, and the two men quickly established a close friendship. Blackwood became a regular visitor to 60 Frith Street, and was staying there when a long period of writer's-block was brought to a close by the sound of a beggar playing a penny-whistle in the London fog, a moment that for some reason stirred his imagination and led to one of the most fertile phases of his literary career (he even published a short story based on the episode in the *Westminster Gazette*).[83] The two men continued to correspond regularly even when Blackwood returned to Switzerland where he chose to spend much of his time.

Blackwood was a keen admirer of Graham's early work, which he tellingly praised for its tales of "strange gospels" and "ancient superstitions", seeing in his friend's books an echo of his own mysticism and sense of

---

82 See, for example, Algernon Blackwood, *Pan's Garden: A Volume of Nature Stories* (London: Macmillan, 1912).
83 Ashley, *Starlight Man*, p. 161.

estrangement from the familiar world. Graham, for his part, was drawn to Blackwood by his "strange and elusive" personality and his belief in "a sixth sense which some of us were on the verge of using".[84] When Blackwood visited Frith Street, he often arrived in the company of the mercurial Maya, the beautiful wife of a "jealous and morose" Russian baron, who almost certainly had a good deal to be jealous about. Maya boasted a life that was as exotic as anything that appeared in Blackwood's fiction, having been born plain Mabel Stuart-King, before running away from home as a young woman to earn her living as a member of a string quartet in Vienna. She seems to have met Blackwood on a Nile cruiser owned by her husband, and the two rapidly became inseparable, appearing at parties and literary dinners across London. The friendship between Graham and Blackwood was rooted in a common love of the outdoors – Blackwood had walked extensively both in North America and Europe – as well as in a shared sense of the porosity of the material world. It only ended as a result of a quarrel between Blackwood and Rosa Graham, in the early 1920s, when the latter, for some reason, refused to allow her husband's friend to stay at their cottage in Sussex. Graham himself continued on good terms with Maya, even after she remarried in 1922, visiting her on numerous occasions at her large country house near Sandwich in Kent.

Graham's list of contacts during these years was not limited to members of the literary world. One "unlikely reader" of his work was Sir George Riddell, managing director of the *News of the World*, and a close political ally and confidante of David Lloyd George (Riddell also published *Country Life* which was of course edited by Graham's father). It was through Riddell that Graham first met David Lloyd George at Walton Heath Golf Club in Surrey, where the future Prime Minister quizzed his lunch companion about Russia, and suggested that he should turn his attention to writing about conditions in his own country. Also present at this meeting was Charles Masterman, the future director of Britain's propaganda operations during the First World War, in which Graham played some part.[85] Both politicians "smelt a Tory", recognising that Graham did not share their political views, but the meeting seems to have been a cordial one.[86] Lloyd George subsequently consulted Graham about Russia on a number of occasions when he served

---

84 Graham, *Wonderful Scene*, p. 40.
85 Michael Hughes, 'Searching for the Soul of Russia: British Perceptions of Russia during the First World War', *Twentieth Century British History*, 20, 2 (2009), pp. 198-226.
86 Graham, *Wonderful Scene*, p. 39

in the War Cabinet as Minister of Munitions and, later, as Prime Minister. Another influential acquaintance made by Graham during this time was John St Loe Strachey, owner and editor of the *Spectator*, who had for some years been involved in efforts to improve Anglo-Russian relations. It was through Strachey that Graham came to the attention of Lord Northcliffe, the autocratic proprietor of *The Times* and the *Daily Mail,* who in November 1913 sent a typically imperious telegram to 60 Frith Street asking to meet later the same day.

Graham had by this time returned from America, and although he had not yet completed the final manuscript of *With Poor Immigrants*, he was already planning a new excursion to the wilds of Central Asia. At their first meeting Northcliffe announced in characteristically abrupt style that he wanted Graham to write for his newspapers, telling him to "go where you like and write what you like", a commission that would have been hard for any writer or journalist to resist. The two men met again the following day at Printing House Square, when Northcliffe handed Graham a contract for twenty-six articles for *The Times*, all of them to be published over his name (the first time the paper had departed from its usual convention of anonymity). Over the next few weeks, Graham was invited to dinner at Northcliffe's home in St James's Place, whilst a luncheon was also held in his honour, at which he was introduced to many of the leading journalists and editors who worked for Northcliffe, including Geoffrey Dawson and Evelyn Wrench. Northcliffe was one of the principal architects of the "new" journalism that developed in Britain during the early years of the twentieth century, characterised by an emphasis on lively articles written in an accessible style with short sentences and paragraphs. He had read Graham's *With the Russian Pilgrims*, along with some of his journalism, and was convinced that his new protégé had the talent to produce the sort of material calculated to appeal to readers of his papers. Graham, for his part, had succeeded in attracting a sponsor who could give him access to the heart of Britain's most important journalistic empire. He seized the opportunity with enthusiasm.

Graham was not yet thirty when Northcliffe asked him to contribute to *The Times* and the *Daily Mail*. It is perhaps tempting to imagine that their meeting marked a turning-point in Graham's life, as the youthful wanderer began his transition into hard-headed journalist. The previous pages have shown that such a view would be too simplistic. There were always two aspects to Graham's outlook on life during the years before the

First World War. His long meditations on the meaning of nature and the loss of spirituality in the modern world were heart-felt and genuine, but, even as a young journalist on the *Evening Times*, Graham proved adept at producing a very different kind of work, one that used his gift for "lurid realism" to describe the seamier side of London life. Graham often felt perfectly at home in the modern world that he attacked so vehemently in his writings. This is not to suggest he was a hypocrite. Nor is it to argue that his early work was inspired simply by a desire to transform the worlds of Nature and Spirit into a marketable commodity designed to appeal to a large readership. It is instead to recognise that there were two different facets to his character which, together, shaped the kind of writer he had become. Both aspects of Graham's personality continued to shine through his work over the next four years, a time when war and revolution ripped apart Russia, providing him with new challenges in advancing his career and articulating his personal philosophy to a wider audience.

3. The Slow Death of Holy Russia

Graham returned to Russia at the end of 1913, armed with Northcliffe's commission to "go where you like and write what you like", travelling by train through Paris and Warsaw, before heading on to Kiev, a city he had first visited the previous year on his way back from Jerusalem.[1] Here he called on a number of old friends, including a spirited young woman called Katia, who had as a child made an unlikely attempt to run away to South Africa to help the Boers in their fight against the British. On her advice he went to a production of *Jealousy* by the novelist and playwright Mikhail Artsybashev, a play derided by Graham as "the voice of the bourgeois", a harsh judgement that probably said more about his distaste for the author's earlier novel, *Sanin,* which had explored themes of sexual perversion and spiritual anomie. Nor was Graham impressed by the audience, largely drawn from the city's philistine "new commercial middle class", who flocked to the theatre through city streets crowded with Christmas traffic. He was by contrast enthralled by "another Kieff, a quiet radiant city, silent but for the footfalls of monks or pilgrims on the snow", which stood high on the cliffs above the River Dneiper. It was here, among the "bright gilded domes" of the churches, that Graham once again encountered his beloved Holy Russia, a place where pilgrims travelled to the old hermitages housed in caves that lay honeycombed beneath the foundations of the upper town. He visited some of the massive hostelries that catered for the pilgrims, and attended a number of Christmas services, where "you hear the music of the herald-angels and see at the same time in the likeness of the listening

---

1   *The Times*, 5 February 1914.

http://dx.doi.org/10.11647/OBP.0040.03

Russian peasants the shepherds who heard the angels sing".[2] The two faces of Kiev – the modern commercial city and the ancient city of churches and monasteries – neatly symbolised for Graham the changing character of contemporary Russia.

Graham left Kiev after a few days to head for Vladikavkaz in the Caucasus, the town where he had stayed four years earlier during his first visit to the southern provinces of the Tsarist Empire. He travelled by train with an old friend, Vavara Ilinitchina, and together they watched the passing landscape of "snowy hamlets" and forests. On the second day they changed trains at Beslan, destined to become infamous more than ninety years later for the slaughter of hundreds of children by Chechen terrorists, but which in early January 1914 lay "serene and beautiful" on the Caucasian steppe. Graham returned to the old mill where he had first stayed when tramping through the region in 1909, only to find that change had come to the small village in the Terek valley. The Baptist minister who had rented rooms to him was away on a preaching tour, having previously been to America with a number of other Protestant pastors. His wife was at home, though, and astonished to see her former tenant when she answered the knock at the door. The old chapel had been replaced by a new building – evidence of the extent to which the various Nonconformist sects were increasingly free to worship openly – financed in part by donations from across the Atlantic. Graham was once again impressed by the piety of the small Baptist congregation, and whilst he lamented its growth as evidence of the declining hold of Orthodoxy on the emotions of ordinary Russians, he acknowledged that "the power and character of a Church is not dependent on its dogmas and rituals so much as on the character and spirit of its members".[3]

Graham decided that the best way to provide the kind of articles wanted by Northcliffe was to offer sketches of the places and people he knew from his earlier trips to Russia. He also sent *The Times* some more general pieces, including one on 'The Struggle against Drunkenness', in which he argued unconvincingly that the problem of alcohol-fuelled violence in Russia was largely an urban problem that was seldom encountered in "the remoter agricultural villages".[4] After several weeks in the Caucasus he headed back north to Moscow, spending his first evening there with his old friend

---
2 Ibid, 12 February 1914.
3 Ibid, 14 February 1914; 19 February 1914.
4 Ibid, 21 February 1914.

Vasily Perepletchikov, at his house on Sadovaia Street. Perepletchikov was organising an exhibition of pictures by the Samoyede painter Ilya Vilka, who was born on the remote northern island of Novaia Zemlia, and had been "discovered" a few years earlier by members of a geographical expedition surveying in the area. Some of his pictures had been sent to Tsar Nicholas in St Petersburg, who greatly admired them, with the result that the artist was brought to Moscow by well-wishers to develop his painting technique. Perepletchikov regaled Graham with tales about how difficult Vilka had found it to adjust to city life, spending much of his time hunting for birds on the Sparrow Hills above the Moscow River, before eventually returning home to the wilderness of Novoe Zemlia. Graham's admiration for such a figure shone through the account which he wrote for *The Times*, presenting Vilka as an authentic product of the Russian north, whose talent was native-born, rather than an artificial product of formal training in city salons.[5]

Graham spent most of March 1914 in Moscow, finding time to visit the Gordon Craig production of Hamlet at the Art Theatre, as well as going to a ballet at the private theatre of Prince Gagarin (one of the city's most celebrated patrons of the arts). He also visited Astapovo railway station, in Riazan province, where Tolstoy had died four years earlier following his final melancholy flight from his estate at Yasnaia Poliana.[6] Graham was convinced that the national spirit of Russian culture was becoming stronger than ever. He wrote a piece for *The Times* suggesting that the radical writer Maxim Gorky, who had recently returned to Russia from exile abroad, had become so detached from his homeland that he was fated to produce "stories and dramas which fall flatter and flatter on the ears of Russia".[7]

Graham continued his efforts to promote interest in Russian culture back in Britain, contributing a series of anonymous articles to *The Times Literary Supplement*. In January a piece appeared in the *TLS* on 'Russian Journals and Readers', describing in detail some of the publications available to subscribers, ranging from the *Universal Panorama* (offering "an extraordinary farrago [...] of fact and fantasy") through to *The Russian Pilgrim* (which gave away a free copy of the works of St John Chrysostom

---

5 Ibid, 5 March 1916; 16 March 1916. See, too, Stephen Graham, 'Ilya Vilka', in *Strange Assembly*, ed. by John Gawsworth (London: Unicorn Press, 1932), pp. 171-84.
6 *Daily Mail*, 24 February 1914.
7 *The Times*, 31 March 1914.

with every subscription).[8] A few weeks later he reviewed a collection of Russian language fairy tales by Aleksei Remizov, whom he praised as one of the small group of writers who were "leading the intelligentsia back to the truly national, the black earth, the *izba*, the peasant, and the simple fresh mystical mind of the unspoiled Slav".[9] Graham's words once again cast doubt on the depth of his understanding of Russian cultural life. Remizov's intricate work, which rested broadly within the tradition of Russian Symbolism, represented something far more subtle than a simple programmatic attempt to reassert the half-imagined traditions of Holy Russia. Graham nevertheless continued to find something deeply compelling in the cultural motifs of Russia's Silver Age.

The clue to Graham's interest in Russian Symbolism lies, as the previous chapters have shown, in his sense that carefully-crafted words and paintings could provide an insight into what William James called the "ineffable". Graham was in 1914 still interested in Theosophy, attending several meetings of the Moscow Theosophical Society, to which he was taken by Nina Rabinovich, an acquaintance of Vera Merkurieva, who had befriended him four years earlier in Vladikavkaz (Merkiureva herself had a long-standing interest in Theosophy). The Moscow Theosophical Society commanded a good deal of popular attention during this period, and its meetings were often packed affairs, crowded with people whom Graham later noted "had become dissatisfied with Christianity and imagined that India would rejuvenate their souls". He also attended a meeting at the home of Viacheslav Ivanov, at which two visiting Indian philosophers were invited to discuss their views, which seemed to consist of a rather incoherent sense that the world had fallen away from unity towards division, and that the only solution lay in humanity striving "towards being One" and ridding itself of "the assumption that we are Many".[10] The ensuing discussion was predictably a rather confused affair. Recalling this moment many years later, Graham wrote that "All wisdom is said to come from the East. It may be so, but at that time I believed that Russia was the living East, whereas mystic India was an East which had for millennia been dead".[11] His memories of his views during this time were not altogether

---

8 *Times Literary Supplement*, 8 January 1914.
9 Ibid, 9 April 1914. The collection is presumably the one published under the title *Dokuka i balagurie* (St Petersburg: Sirin, 1914).
10 Stephen Graham, *Part of the Wonderful Scene* (London: Collins, 1964), p. 90.
11 Ibid, p. 90

accurate. In an unpublished article written early in 1914, on 'Christian Missions in India', Graham noted that whilst he supported efforts to spread the Christian faith in the East, he also believed that "we, most of us, need once more the renewal of the message from the East". He went on to suggest that "We need the life of the East circulating in our body politic and spiritualizing it". Graham concluded his article with a kind of *credo* on matters spiritual:

> I believe that in the course of time all humanity must become Christian and that Christianity will be as diverse in its human expression as men themselves are diverse. Love will accommodate an infinite diversity in the unity of one Church. But for modern Christianity as practised in the West I see and wish no future except that it is vivified by the spirit. The thought that Western civilization as it now stands is the crown of Christian expression is fatuous in the extreme.[12]

The poetic insights of esoteric forms of thought continued to appeal to him, even if he was sometimes sceptical of the intellectual ruminations in which they were wrapped.

Graham had returned to Russia at the end of 1913 determined to press ahead with his original plans for a journey to central Asia. In April 1914 he headed south once again towards the Caucasus, in order to begin a trip "into the depths of the Russian East", designed to help "continue my study of Easternism and Westernism in the Tsar's Empire". He told readers of *The Times* somewhat breathlessly that "This is a long, new journey – new for English experience – because, until our entente with Russia, mutual jealousy about the Indian frontier made it extremely difficult for the Russian Government to permit observant and adventurous Englishmen to wander about as I intend to do". He noted that he had "official permission" for the journey, although this only seems to have been granted after some hesitation, since the Russian authorities were still wary of letting a foreigner travel through areas of military sensitivity.[13]

Graham was keen to deepen his acquaintance with Russia's orient, once again abandoning the heartland of Holy Russia, in order to find places that were still more exotic and perhaps better able to meet his restless search for new experiences. In the days following his departure from Vladikavkaz, he

---

12 T.I.F. Armstrong (Gawsworth) Papers (HRC), Misc. (Unpublished article by Graham on 'Christian Missionaries in India').
13 *The Times*, 23 May 1914.

revisited some of the places he had known five years before, including the ruin of Queen Tamara's castle standing high on a rock above the Terek gorge, before taking a train towards Baku on the western shore of the Caspian Sea. Baku was, as he noted ruefully, a city to which people normally came to "make money", in the burgeoning oil industry, and the only charm he found was in its "eastern quarter", where the visitor could see "camels loping up the steep streets" taking goods to a bazaar that was "wholly Eastern" in character. The porters who offered to carry his goods were, in Graham's words, "straight out of the pages" of the Arabian Nights. He only had a short time in the city, though, before heading to the harbour to board the steamer *Skobolev* for passage across the Caspian Sea. The voyage served for Graham as a symbolic passage from West to East. As the boat left Baku in the evening he stood on deck, watching the "fading lights of Europe" dim into invisibility in a "very dark and starless" night.[14]

The *Skobolev* was headed for the port of Krasnovodsk on the south-eastern shore of the Caspian Sea, which Graham quickly judged to be "one of the hottest [...] and most miserable places in the world" (when the journalist Giles Whittell followed in his footsteps, eighty years later, he described the town as "a potentially miserable place" that had only been improved since Graham's day by the arrival of piped water).[15] Although Graham had contacts amongst the Georgian community in Krasnovodsk, he headed rapidly for the station and the express train to Ashkhabad, 400 miles to the east near the Persian frontier. His train stopped at Ashkhabad for less than an hour, but he was quickly enthralled by the exotic mixture of nationalities milling around the platform, many of them holding bunches of roses which scented the air. Graham walked out of the station for a few minutes, to take the night air in a town where "densely foliaged streets cast shadow between you and the night sky", before returning to take his seat again for the onward journey.[16] The lush oriental promise of Askhabad faded as the express rolled eastwards through an area "of tumbled desert and loose sand". The landscape did however brighten up as the train headed towards Bokhara (Bukhara), thanks to the extensive irrigation system fed by the legendary Oxus River, which allowed the local peasantry to cultivate large stretches of land that would otherwise have been infertile. Graham was by now travelling through territory that had been colonised

---

14 Ibid, 23 May 1914.
15 Giles Whittel, *Extreme Continental* (London: Indigo, 1995), p. 42.
16 *The Times*, 30 May 1914.

by the Russians as recently as the second half of the nineteenth century, an advance that fuelled perennial British anxieties about a possible threat to the security of India, which, in the fevered imagination of politicians and officials in London, looked vulnerable to a land-based assault from the north and west. Bokhara itself had been a chess piece in the Great Game for many years, but by the time Graham visited the city it was firmly within the Russian orbit, although retaining a notional independence under its ruling Emir. Graham was quickly enthralled by the place, writing a lengthy article about it for *The Times* under the telling heading 'A Walled City of Romance'.[17]

Graham told his readers that at Bokhara "we were nearer China than Russia" – a claim that said as much about his orientalist construction of the city as it did about mere geography. He was impressed by the cobbled streets of the walled old town, home to "150,000 Mahomedans", which were lined with "handsome mosques" and stairways leading down to the reservoirs that held the city's water supply. The fifty or so bazaars were full of stalls selling "lustrous silks and carpets", manned by "gorgeous vendors" dressed in unfamiliar costumes, whose appearance made them seem like illustrations in books rather than characters in real life. Graham was convinced that "the Bokharas are a gentle people", who lived in a city that represented a kind of "Musulman perfection", where the natives observed "the forms of its religion and its ethical laws". He was also impressed by the fact – or the supposed fact – that "civilization and mechanical progress do not tempt them". The city itself struck him as "much more wonderful than Jerusalem […] for it seemed to me much more untouched, much more remote".[18] It was perhaps inevitable that Graham should fall in love with Bokhara at a time when he feared that European Russia was sacrificing its national traditions in favour of an unthinking Occidentalism.

The allure of the East was not, though, a universal phenomenon for Graham. After leaving Bokhara he travelled by train to Samarkand, where he visited the grave of the legendary Mongol warrior Tamurlane, before heading on to the oasis city of Tashkent. He was once again struck by the elaborate system of irrigation that allowed "wonderful vegetation" to thrive across the city, providing water for the "lofty poplars" that lined the main streets, which Graham found, to his surprise, were filled with "truly fine

---
17 Ibid, 8 June 1914.
18 Stephen Graham, 'Impressions of Seven Rivers Land and Russian Central Asia', *Journal of the Royal Central Asian Society*, 2, 3 (1915), pp. 113-26.

shops" patronised by the large Russian population. The oriental side of the city attracted him far less than in Bokhara, however, and he was convinced that "the native population" was "very dirty and disorderly". He also believed that the natives were indolent in character, preferring to spend their time lounging about on "carpets or divans", rather than repairing their homes or earning a living. Tashkent was originally a major garrison town for the Russian army which had, in time, spawned the construction of a European city of "fine cathedrals" and elaborate public gardens. Graham was convinced that the old Muslim quarter was becoming something of an anachronism.[19] He was also willing to accept that Russian colonial rule in cities like Samarkand and Tashkent represented a progressive development, even if it tended to undermine the colour and character of the indigenous society.[20] Although Graham had for years been enthralled by the colour and vibrancy of life on the periphery of Europe, he never seriously doubted that European rule in these areas represented a form of civilising mission, bringing with it the benefits of good government and civilisation. The irony in the light of his views about the threat posed by modernity to the spiritual character of the nations of Europe themselves hardly needs to be spelt out.

Graham had until now been travelling by rail rather than on foot, but after a short train ride to the out-of-the-way station at Kabul Sei, north of Tashkent, he had to begin walking towards the town of Chimkent (the rail link was completed little more than a year after his visit). He tramped through vast areas without any villages, since the region was home to Kirghiz nomads, who travelled with their flocks according to the rhythms of the seasons. Graham found the weather far hotter than he had expected, telling a meeting of the Royal Central Asian Society the following year that he "had never experienced such heat" in all his previous travels.[21] He was carrying a sleeping bag and mosquito net, which meant that he could spend the nights under the stars, although he had to beg provisions from the Kirghiz encampments he passed from time to time. At one point Graham virtually lived on *kumiss*, the drink made from fermented mare's milk, which had for centuries formed a staple part of the diet of nomadic

---

19 *The Times*, 23 June 1914.
20 For a superb analysis of Russian imperial rule in Samarkand see Alexander Morrison, *Russian Rule in Samarkand, 1868-1910: A Comparison with* British India (Oxford: Oxford University Press, 2008). See, too, Jeff Sahedo, *Russian Colonial Society in Tashkent, 1865-1923* (Bloomington, IN: Indiana University Press, 2007).
21 Graham, 'Seven Rivers Land', p. 115.

people living in the arc from present-day Kazakhstan through to Mongolia. He also ate a great deal of *lepeshka*, a kind of unleavened bread, which on one occasion was so lumpy that it stuck in his throat causing him to choke.

Graham was much taken by the Kirghiz people, believing that they lacked the "warlike spirit" of the Moslem tribes of the Caucasus. He was acutely sensitive to the pressures they faced from the growing number of Russian immigrants who lived in villages "running the whole way from the railway terminus to the frontiers of China".[22] Although the reports he had planned to write for *The Times* about this part of the journey never appeared, crowded out by news of the outbreak of war, he devoted a good deal of attention to the subject in his book *Through Russian Central Asia*, which finally appeared in 1916. Graham was struck by the care taken by the Russian Government to promote the process of colonisation, laying down which areas could be settled, and providing subsidies for those willing to move there from European Russia.[23] He was not convinced that the new settlers would find their "El Dorado" on the steppes of Central Asia, telling members of the Royal Central Asian Society that "wherever they go there is a certain feeling of discontent because their dreams are not realised".[24] He was, indeed, somewhat ambivalent about the way colonisation was being carried out. Graham accepted that Russian expansion into Central Asia represented a kind of manifest destiny, a consequence both of geographical propinquity *and* a moral duty to civilise the backward regions of the Empire, but he was acutely sensitive to the impact of the process on the indigenous people crowded out by the newcomers.

Graham's journey by foot and cart took him on to the small town of Kopal, on the Chinese border, "a place you could run round in a quarter of an hour, and yet having jurisdiction over an immense tract of territory along the Russian frontier of China".[25] The town was despite its remoteness a crossroads of the world, full of travellers from China and European Russia, as well as the adjacent central Asian provinces. There was also (rather bizarrely) a Chinese circus in town, which Graham visited, watching acts ranging from musicians and jugglers to trick-cyclists and conjurors. His stay in the town was only a short one, though,

---

22 Ibid, p. 115.
23 Stephen Graham, *Through Russian Central Asia* (London: Cassell, 1916), pp. 134-55, version available at http://archive.org/details/throughrussiance00grahuoft.
24 Graham, 'Seven Rivers Land', p. 117.
25 Graham, *Through Central Asia*, p. 175.

since he was determined to push on towards the Altai Mountains on the borders of China, Russia and Mongolia. The landscape through which he first passed on leaving Kopal – often known by the name of Seven Rivers Land – was famous for its natural beauty. Graham was suitably awestruck by such sights as the Gorge of Abakum, even though it was defaced by visitors chipping their names into the rocks, but he paused only briefly before heading on into Siberia.

He made first for the town of Semipalatinsk, first established as a military settlement by the Russians in the early eighteenth century, but better-known in the early twentieth century as the site of Dostoevsky's exile during the 1840s. It was also a major trading centre, boasting a number of department stores, although it still lacked such "graces" as streetlamps and a proper drainage system. Graham took a boat upstream from Semipalatnisk to Malo-Krasnoiarsk, where he first heard news of the murder of Archduke Ferdinand by Serbian terrorists, thousands of miles away in Sarajevo. Although the Russian papers made much more of the murder than their British counterparts, given Russia's close ties with Serbia, Graham decided to continue his journey towards the Altai range. He later acknowledged that there was something ironic about continuing his journey "away from the interest of the world", but he was hardly alone in believing that Britain could still avoid being drawn into the Balkan imbroglio.

Graham's journey into the Altai mountains took him to some of the remotest areas of Asia.[26] He planned to stay for several weeks in Altaisky, near the foot of Mount Belukha, which struck him as a kind of earthly paradise, where the valleys were full of "blue sage, mauve cranesbills […] saffron poppies, grass of Parnassus, campanula, pink moss flowers and giant thistle-heads, gentian [and] Siberian iris".[27] His idyllic stay in a Cossack village, marred only by the repetitive nature of the food, was cut short on 31 July when "tidings of war" filtered through by telegram even to this remote corner of the Russian Empire. Nobody in the village could decide who the enemy was (at first rumours went round the village that the war was with China or England). It took several days for a more accurate sense of what had happened to percolate through the community, and still

---

26 Graham was not, however, the first Briton to visit the area and write about his experiences there. See Samuel Turner, *Siberia: A Record of Travel, Climbing and Exploration* (London: Unwin, 1905). For a helpful article putting Turner's trip in perspective see David Collins, 'Anglophone Travellers in the Russian Altai, 1848-1904', *Sibirica* 2, 1 (2002), pp. 43-68.

27 Graham, *Through Central Asia*, p. 229.

more time for mobilisation orders to arrive, requiring all the men of the village who were young enough for military service to report for duty.[28] Graham decided to follow in their footsteps, leaving his Altai idyll to return to the chaos of Europe. He travelled by steamer back to Semipalatinsk, where he transferred to a larger boat that took him on to Omsk. From here he returned by railway to western Russia, although only by a slow and circuitous route, since mobilisation placed massive constraints on the movement of goods and people not needed for the war effort.[29] He arrived back to Moscow in September 1914, more than a month after the outbreak of hostilities, and more than two months since he first heard news of the assassination of Franz Ferdinand.

The war was already going badly for the Russians. The defeat at the hands of German forces in the Battle of Tannenberg in late August provided a stark insight into the problems that were destined to confront the Russian war effort throughout the following years. Although the victory of the German Eighth Army owed a good deal to the tactical *nous* of Hindenburg and Ludendorff – along with more junior officers like Colonel Max Hoffmann – the Russian defeat highlighted serious defects in military planning and execution.[30] Graham was still contracted to write for *The Times*, and his first piece after his return from Central Asia appeared on 12 September, followed twelve days later by a second article that appeared under the unlikely heading of 'The Beauty of War'. Graham described how Russian troops had engaged the enemy whilst singing hymns, much to the unease of the Germans, "who seem distressed by the songs of the Russians as they fight". The surreal account was compounded by talk of large-scale Russian advances and German retreats. Graham's subsequent articles maintained an equally positive tone. In October he published a piece arguing that Russia's "holy war" had mobilised the spiritual energies of the Russian people behind a common struggle to defend their homeland against German aggression.[31] Two weeks later he characterised the conflict between Russia and German as one between "imagination" and "will", suggesting that the Russian soldier would in time prevail, since he "has his

---

28 Stephen Graham, *Russia and the World* (London: Cassell, 1915), pp. 3-9.
29 For details of the journey see Graham, *Russia and the World*, pp. 10-14.
30 For a classic account of Russia in the First World War see Norman Stone, *The Eastern Front, 1914-1917* (London: Hodder and Stoughton, 1975). For a more recent account providing a useful focus on the domestic impact of the war see Peter Gatrell, *Russia's First World War: A Social and Economic History* (Harlow: Longman Pearson, 2005).
31 *The Times*, 13 October 1914.

eyes set on an unearthly prize [...] and goes forward in a state of rapture".[32] In November he described "suffering Poland" as "a Belgium of the East", suggesting that Britain and Russia were both fighting for the rights of the small European nations, a dubious argument given the chequered history of Russo-Polish relations.[33] The war that Graham presented to his readers was a battle between two different kinds of civilisation – one spiritual and one material – and he left his readers in no doubt that there could only be one winner in such a conflict.

At least some of Graham's dispatches were written close to the Front Line, where he "listened to the chatter of the machine-guns [and] witnessed the explosion of bombs falling from the little Taube aeroplanes, took part in a panic stampede, observed the Siberian regiments being brought up to stem the enemy's advance to Warsaw".[34] He was also briefly detained by the military authorities, who were only mollified when he produced a four-year old letter from the Governor of Archangel testifying to his *bona fides*. Graham spent just a short time behind the lines, though, and at the end of October he had travelled to Petrograd, the new war-time name for St Petersburg, in order to interview the Russian Foreign Minister Sergei Sazonov. Sazonov was a professional diplomat and a strong Anglophile, who had been posted to Britain earlier in his career, and he hoped to cultivate Graham in order to secure positive coverage of Russia's war effort in *The Times*.[35] The two men met at a flat above the Foreign Ministry, accessed by a rickety old-fashioned lift, where they discussed "the prospects for continued Anglo-Russian friendship and co-operation after the war". Graham was impressed by his courteous host, who provided an "English lunch" of lamb chops and mineral water,[36] but the interview was destined to cause considerable controversy a few weeks later, when he wrote in *The Sunday Times* that Sazonov had spoken dismissively of the contribution made to the Russian war effort by its Jewish population. The antisemitic character of Sazonov's words – which Graham may or may not have reported accurately – created furore in Britain and America.[37] The article

---
32 Ibid, 31 October 1914.
33 Ibid, 21 November 1914.
34 Graham, *Wonderful Scene*, p. 94.
35 For full details of the interview by Graham with Sazonov written some months later, see his article 'The Russians and the War', *Atlantic Monthly*, 115 (March 1915).
36 Graham, *Wonderful Scene*, p. 94.
37 For a valuable discussion of the attitude of British Jews towards Eastern Europe see, Sam Johnson, 'Breaking or Making the Silence: British Jews and East European Relief, 1914-1917', *Modern Judaism*, 30, 1 (2010), pp. 95-119.

also caused intense embarrassment for the Government in Petrograd at a time when ministers wanted to avoid doing anything that might damage their country's reputation as a key member of the coalition fighting against German militarism. The Russian Foreign Ministry quickly released a statement denying "in the most emphatic manner statements attributed to Mr Sazonoff [...] with reference to the future treatment of the Jews in Russia".[38] The incident caused lasting damage to Graham's reputation with the Russian Government. It also made him an object of suspicion amongst many liberals back home in Britain.

Following his interview with Sazonov, Graham returned to Moscow, renting a tiny room at the Hotel Europe (the indomitable Olga Novikov was staying in much more impressive accommodation in the same establishment). It was only a brief visit. Graham had not been home since the end of 1913, and although the war made travel dangerous, he was by early December back in Petrograd where he took a boat bound for Stockholm. From there he went to Oslo and across the North Sea to Britain.[39] The country at first struck him as steeped in depression, but his natural optimism soon reasserted itself, as he came to identify "a renewed national vigour" among his fellow-countrymen.[40] Graham's return to Britain may have been impelled by a vague sense that he should "join up", but his journalistic instincts soon reasserted themselves, as he decided that his war work should focus on promoting closer relations between Britain and Russia. He was also anxious not to abandon his "true line" of expressing new "creative ideas" to his readers.[41] Graham was determined to persuade his fellow countrymen that Russia was important as a source of spiritual inspiration as well as a valuable military ally in the war against Germany and Austro-Hungary.

Graham was not alone in believing that the success of the Anglo-Russian relationship depended on fostering more positive attitudes towards a country that was still regarded with suspicion by many Britons. Russia was an awkward ally in a war that was supposedly being fought for liberty and the rights of small nations. *The Times* argued on the day after hostilities broke out that Britain was joining a coalition acting as "defenders of the

---

38 *New York Times*, 23 January 1915.
39 For details of the journey see Graham, *Russia and the World*, p. 247 ff; *Daily Mail*, 1 December, 1914.
40 Graham, *Russia and the World*, p. 256.
41 Graham Papers (HRC), *Wonderful Scene* (typescript), p. 82.

weak and champions of the liberties of Europe".[42] Other papers like the *Daily Mail* also sought to harness popular patriotism to the cause of freedom, a position echoed by Government ministers in the weeks that followed. The alliance with France was easy to accommodate within this broad rhetoric of justification, given the country's well-established liberal credentials, but the position of Russia was, for obvious reasons, more complex.

The British Government made a sustained effort to foster a positive image of Britain in Russia, setting up an Anglo-Russian Propaganda Bureau in Petrograd to help win the hearts and minds of the Russian public,[43] but ministers made less effort to shape the way that Russia was viewed in Britain. A number of semi-official books and articles nevertheless appeared claiming that there was a natural affinity between the two nations.[44] Many of these pieces argued that Russia possessed a distinctive "soul", which meant that western forms of government were not necessarily appropriate for (or even desired by) the Russian people. Books with titles like *Allies in Art* and *The Soul of Russia* went to great lengths to argue that Russia was far from the barbarian nation that some in Britain still imagined it to be.[45] There was also a large increase in the publication of books about the Russian Church, including one by Bishop Herbert Bury, responsible for Anglican congregations in Eastern Europe, which challenged the notion that Russian Orthodoxy was mired in superstition and corruption.[46] These were, of course, exactly the themes that Graham had been articulating for many years in his own work. The idea of the Russian soul had, before 1914, largely been a matter of cultural and aesthetic interest in Britain. The outbreak of hostilities meant that it became central to the image held by many Britons of their new and still largely unknown ally.

Graham remained perhaps *the* pre-eminent British authority on the elusive intricacies of the Russian soul during the early years of the War (particularly after Maurice Baring left for France on attachment to the Royal Flying Corps). He was certainly in demand as a public speaker during the months he spent back in Britain during the winter of 1914-15,

---

42 *The Times*, 5 August 1914.
43 Keith Neilson, 'Joyrides? British Intelligence and Propaganda in Russia, 1914-1917', *Historical Journal*, 24, 4 (1981), pp. 885-906.
44 Michael Hughes, 'Searching for the Soul of Russia: British Perceptions of Russia during the First World War', *Twentieth Century British History*, 20, 2 (2009), pp. 198-226.
45 *Allies in Art: A Collection of Works in Modern Art by Artists of the Allied Nations* (London: Colour, 1917); Winifred Stevens, *The Soul of Russia* (London: Macmillan, 1916).
46 Right Revd Herbert Bury, *Russian Life Today* (London: Mowbray, 1915).

giving one lecture to an audience of five thousand people in Manchester, as well as talks at smaller venues such as the Ethical Church in Bayswater and Kingsway Hall in Holborn. Although most of his lectures were uncontroversial, combining reflections on recent events in Russia with a patriotic insistence that the defeat of the Central Powers was simply a matter of time, one of them raised a good deal of public furore. Graham recalled many years later how his talk on 'The Future of Russia' at the National Liberal Club, in January 1915, created "a storm" as a group "of radicals denounced Russia and myself together".[47] His critics were incensed above all by the speaker's attitude towards the treatment of Jews living in the Tsarist Empire (something that had for some time made him an object of suspicion amongst a section of British public opinion).[48] Their concern was only heightened by the uproar that followed the publication of his interview with Sazonov. The accounts of what Graham actually said at the Liberal Club were confused and contradictory, but many of those present certainly believed that he had expressed support for the Russian Government in taking harsh measures against its Jewish population. The tone became so raucous at one point that the chairman – the novelist Silas Hocking – was forced to restore order against a series of "rude interruptions".[49] Graham fuelled the controversy still further a few weeks later with an article in the *English Review*, in which he claimed that the Jews were by instinct a "western nation", adding for good measure that "All good Russians must wish the Jews God's speed when they see them embarking for America at Libau, not because they are an evil people or accursed, but because with their genius and their assumed humility they have ever been a great danger to the Russians".[50] Graham later argued that such words were intended to show his support for an independent Jewish state – a claim that does not hold much water given the paucity of any evidence in his writings.[51] It is, in any case, hardly surprising that so many members of Britain's Jewish community reacted to his views with fury, given the long history of *pogroms* suffered by Russia's Jews, which, as often as not, enjoyed a degree of patronage from leading figures in the tsarist military and bureaucracy.[52]

---

47 Graham, *Wonderful Scene*, p. 98.
48 See, for example, *Jewish Chronicle*, 28 November 1913; *Jewish Chronicle*, 13 November 1914.
49 *The Manchester Guardian*, 19 January 1915.
50 Stephen Graham, 'Russia and the Jews', *English Review*, February 1915, pp. 324-33.
51 Graham Papers (HRC), Works File, *Wonderful Scene* (autograph).
52 Amongst the large literature on Tsarist Russia's Jewish population see Zvi Y. Gitelman, *A Century of Ambivalence: The Jews of Russia and the Soviet Union, 1881 to the Present*

One member of the audience who heard Graham's speech at the National Liberal Club suggested that his words should be seen as evidence of an impractical and "poetical nature" rather than vicious ethnic or religious prejudice.[53] Not all his critics were so generous. Both the *Jewish Chronicle* and the *Jewish World* regularly attacked Graham's views on Russia.[54] The writer Israel Zangwill contributed two letters to *The Nation* early in 1915, accusing Graham of "literary mine-sowing", and condemned him for resuscitating the "monstrous medieval Myth" of the blood-libel, that is the idea that Jews regularly engaged in ritual sacrifice of Christian victims. He also accused Graham of routinely misquoting or misrepresenting people he interviewed, including Sazonov, and of spewing out an "incessant output of books and articles" designed to "prepare the world for England's abandonment of the Russian Jews at the end of this war of freedom". Zangwill concluded by complaining that "a journalist with such a code should be given such prominence in *The Times*", adding a lament "that a writer with so much engaging enthusiasm and literary charm and so precious a sense of Russian mysticism and brotherhood, a writer who might really help Russia and England to help each other, should have gone so hopelessly astray in the dreary bogs of reactionary politics".[55] Nor was this an isolated attack. In February 1915, Percy Cohen published an 'Open Letter to Stephen Graham' in *The New Age*, attacking his "despicable anti-Jewish propaganda". He went on to accuse Graham of peddling "solemn avowals of illiberalism, strongly flavoured with medieval ignorance", concluding that "the Russia of the dawn cannot be a country which perpetuates the monstrous infamies with which Jews are at present saddled".[56] Other writers weighed in with accusations that Graham had a "medieval soul".[57]

No biographer can ignore the existence of powerful anti-semitic motifs in much of Graham's writing during this period – even if such sentiments were hardly unusual within the early twentieth-century

---

(Bloomington, IN: Indiana University Press, 2001); John Doyle Klier and Shlomo Lambrozo (eds), *Pogroms: Anti-Jewish Violence in Modern Russian History* (Cambridge: Cambridge University Press, 2004).

53 *The Globe*, 30 January 1915.
54 See, for example *Jewish World*, 10 February 1915; *Jewish Chronicle*, 28 November 1913.
55 The letters are reproduced in Israel Zangwill, *Works of Israel Zangwill: The War for the World* (New York: American Jewish Book Company, 1921), pp. 405-13.
56 *The New Age*, 25 February 1915.
57 Alfred George Gardiner, *The War Lords* (London: J.M. Dent, 1915), p. 95. See, too, the attack on Graham at a Fabian meeting held in London in February 1915 reported in the *Manchester Guardian*, 13 February 1915.

British Establishment (Graham himself noted towards the end of his life that he should have "kept off the Jewish problem").[58] Nor is it possible to ignore the stark fact that the Holy Russia he admired so greatly was a place where anti-semitism was rife. Graham's attitude towards Russia's Jewish population was shaped, above all, by his suspicion of modern society. The Russian Jew served in his imagination as a symbol of the urban industrialised world that he believed was ripping apart the delicate fabric of traditional Russia. His critics in the British press spoke truthfully when they reminded their readers that another, less appealing country lurked beneath the glittering camouflage of Holy Russia. The golden cupolas that so enthralled Graham were symbols not only of spiritual depth and mystery, but also of a Church that ostracised outsiders, and condemned important sections of the population to a marginal place within society.

Many of the lectures Graham gave during the first few weeks of 1915 were on the less controversial subject of "the new and living Christianity emerging from Russia".[59] In talk after talk he criticised the formalism of Christian observance in Britain, where "religion is for the most part imprisoned in [...] the churches", comparing it unfavourably with the more vibrant Orthodox tradition. He also gave a Lenten address at St Margaret's Church in Westminster, dressed in a borrowed black cassock, on the subject of 'Dostoevsky and the Russian Church': "I spoke from the heart [...] I contrasted a Church of praise with a Church of miserable sinners, love of man with a gloating over villains, intuitive action with obedience to the 'rule' of Christian ethics".[60]

Graham's calls for an intuitive and living Christianity attracted considerable attention amongst a section of London society, particularly at a time when the horrors of total war were fostering a new interest in ethical and spiritual questions, to which the established churches seemed to have no convincing response.[61] He became a frequent visitor to a number

---

58 For an example of such anti-semitism within the context of Anglo-Russian relations, see Eliyahu Feldman, 'British Diplomats and British Diplomacy and the 1905 Pogroms in Russia', *Slavonic and East European Review*, 65, 4 (1987), pp. 579-608. Graham Papers (FSU), Box 577, 8 (Occasional notes).
59 Graham, *Wonderful Scene*, p. 99.
60 Graham Papers (HRC), *Wonderful Scene* (typescript), p. 89.
61 On the growing interest in spiritualism see Jay Winter, *Sites of Memory, Sites of Mourning: the Great War in European Cultural History* (Cambridge: Cambridge University Press, 1998), pp. 54-77. On the response of churches to the war see for example Alan Wilkinson, *The Church of England and the First World War* (London: SPCK, 1978); Keith Robbins, *England, Ireland, Scotland, Wales: The Christian Church, 1900-2000* (Oxford: Oxford University Press,

of aristocratic homes, including that of Lady St Helier, the sometime confidante of Thomas Hardy, who played an important role in fostering interest in literary matters in London society during the early years of the twentieth century. He was also taken up by Adeline Duchess of Bedford, another blue-stocking aristocrat, and a deeply-religious woman who had many friendships amongst senior clerics in the Church of England. Nor were Graham's contacts limited to the world of the literary-aristocratic *beau monde*. He also met a number of senior figures in the British political establishment – although he did not always find the experience rewarding. At one dinner party attended by Lloyd George, along with Lord Reading and Reginald Mckenna, Graham's ideas about how to deal with the Russians made little impact on the assembled company. The politicians were concerned with such practical questions as the provision of credit. Graham preferred to reflect in more general terms on how best to negotiate with the Russians, telling the company that "if you treat a Russian generously he will try to outdo you in generosity", a policy that was unlikely to have much appeal for the cash-starved Treasury.[62] He was nevertheless able, when occasion demanded, to write about contemporary events with an acuity that meant his opinion was still regularly sought by politicians and newspaper publishers. Lloyd George himself consulted Graham about Russian affairs on a number of occasions during the War. One of Graham's frustrations during this period was, indeed, that he found it easier to be taken seriously as a journalist rather than as a visionary promoting a new understanding of religion. He nevertheless remained determined to encourage his readers to think seriously about the shortcomings of modern industrial society and the shallow materialism that he believed shaped its religious and philosophical outlook.

Graham left Britain once again in the spring of 1915, bound this time not for Russia but for the Egyptian desert. He went there to learn more about the life of the early Church and its impact on the development of Eastern Christianity. He travelled via Paris and Marseilles, where he boarded a ship for Egypt, and, after spending a few days in Alexandria, he went on to Cairo where he visited the Pyramids and the Sphinx. The city had been transformed by the War, and its streets thronged with troops from across the Empire, including a large number of Indian soldiers who seemed "happier

---

2008), pp. 96-151; Michael Hughes, *Conscience and Conflict: Methodism, Peace and War in the Twentieth Century* (Peterborough: Epworth, 2008), pp. 46-78.
62 Graham, *Wonderful Scene*, p. 100.

in the glare of the desert" than their Western counterparts. Graham felt deeply sympathetic towards the troops forced to parade in the blistering heat, and even more so for the thousands of wounded who had been sent to Egypt to recuperate from injuries received during the first few weeks of the disastrous Dardanelles Campaign. He bought a large box of oranges and numerous cartons of cigarettes to take to the hospital at Heliopolis, where he spoke to the soldiers about their experiences on the battlefield, reassuring readers of *The Times* that they remained cheerful and committed to the allied cause despite their injuries.[63]

During his time in Cairo, Graham also succeeded in obtaining a letter of introduction from the "well-fed debonair" leader of the Coptic community,[64] Marcus bey Simaika, authorising his access to the monastery at the desert shrine of Makarios, where a number of Patriarchs of the Coptic Church lay embalmed. After a long journey on horseback from the desert town of Bir Hooker, he arrived at the remote place, where he was welcomed by the elderly Abbot with "thimblefuls of thick sweet coffee prepared in the Armenian way".[65] Graham also spoke with a number of other monks – there were only a handful in total – quizzing them about their solitary life far from the crowded Nile Delta. He was impressed by their detachment from the cares of the world, including the Great War being fought only a few hundred miles away, sensing that they were in spirit heirs to the "eccentric" hermits and "world-deniers" who had flocked to the desert in the sixth century.[66] He was also touched by the hospitality that he received, even though the monks were desperately poor, writing gratefully of their warmth and kindness.

Graham's visit to the Egyptian desert was prompted by his search for material for his book on *The Way of Martha and the Way of Mary* which, when published at the end of 1915, provided its readers with a highly stylised comparison of Eastern and Western Christianity, albeit one which insisted that reconciliation between the two understandings of Christianity remained possible. Graham's knowledge of the history and theology of the Eastern Church was always decidedly sketchy, and he was never clear in his own mind whether the distinctive nature of Holy Russia was a peculiarly *Russian* phenomenon, or was instead rooted in the fact that

---

63 *The Times*, 14 July 1915.
64 Graham Papers (FSU), Box 577, 13b (Graham's notes on his 1915 trip to Egypt).
65 Graham, *Wonderful Scene*, p. 107.
66 *The Times*, 21 July 1915.

the country received its Christian heritage from the East. His journey into the Egyptian desert in 1915 provided him with insights into a world about which he knew very little, but it did not give him much sense that the character of Russian Christianity could be explained simply by its Eastern heritage. Graham remained, as ever, a believer in a particularly *Russian* exceptionalism that was expressed in the innate spirituality of its people.

Graham left Egypt in June 1915, making his way via Athens to Sofia, passing "almost near enough to Gallipoli to hear the guns".[67] His journey was delayed on the Greek frontier, where he was forced to live for a week in a tent, since the Bulgarian authorities were imposing strict quarantine to prevent the spread of the plague that they believed was endemic in areas around Salonika.[68] After leaving Sofia, Graham headed on to Bucharest, before travelling eastwards to Odessa. The port was at a virtual standstill, the warehouses full of wheat that could not be exported to western Europe, given the difficulties faced by merchant shipping in navigating the straits at Constantinople. Anti-Government feeling was growing rapidly in Russia by the summer of 1915, as poor management of the war was blamed for defeats like the one suffered against the Austrian army at Gorlice. Graham saw first-hand how recent riots had led shopkeepers to barricade their windows against looting. The picture was similar in Moscow, where Graham travelled after a short stay by the Black Sea, arriving there shortly after the suppression of street disorders which had resulted in the widespread pillaging of businesses owned by individuals unlucky enough to bear German-sounding names.

The chaos proved to be the start of a major political crisis. In June 1915, a Conference of the liberal Cadet Party called for the establishment of a government commanding public support. The mood in the factories was also growing bleak, driven both by resentment against longer working days and rising food prices, as well as a fear about the possibility of conscription to the Front. Nicholas II was dimly aware that concessions might be necessary to regain popular support, and in July he appointed a new Minister of War to replace the discredited V.A. Sukhominov, who was widely if unfairly blamed for the defeats suffered by the Russian army during the previous year. The Tsar also recalled the Duma in a gesture designed to show that he was ready to listen to public opinion. The

---

67 Graham, *Wonderful Scene*, p. 110.
68 Stephen Graham, 'The Truth About the Bulgars', *English Review*, November 1915, pp. 405-10.

opening sessions quickly revealed the gulf that had emerged between the Government and its critics. A number of deputies made speeches that were, in the words of the British ambassador Sir George Buchanan, "far more outspoken than has ever been the case previously".[69] Nicholas's response was both decisive and disastrous. Within a few weeks he prorogued the Duma, dismissing popular ministers, and appointing the conservative A.N. Khvostov as Interior Minister. The Tsar also announced that he would take personal command at the *stavka* – the army headquarters behind the Front Line – even though he had no significant military experience. The diplomatic representatives of Russia's allies were appalled, fearing that such actions might foster political instability, and make Russia still less reliable as an ally in the war against the central powers.

Graham was in an excellent position to follow the political crisis, since he was in Moscow and Petrograd for most of the summer of 1915, but he was less than enthusiastic about the prospect of political reform. From the time he first arrived in Russia, he believed that the country's distinctive identity rested on the maintenance of a semi-autocratic system of government that was indelibly bound up with the whole fabric of Holy Russia. Although Graham was astute enough to realise that Nicholas and his ministers had proved ineffective at managing the war, he still found it hard to warm to members of the opposition, including the Cadet leader Paul Miliukov. When the two men met in Petrograd they quickly realised they had nothing in common. Graham recalled that Miliukov was hostile to religion and believed that it was "better to go to cinemas than to Church". Miliukov believed that Graham was "inclined to exaggerate and to extol the good qualities of the [...] plain peasants".[70] Although the meeting of the two men was friendly enough, it does not seem to have been repeated. The reports Graham published in *The Times* during this period developed the themes of his earlier articles. He acknowledged that the Russian army had suffered major setbacks at the Front, but maintained that the people were still animated by "the spirit of 1812", when Napoleon had been repulsed at the gates of Moscow. He continued to write in this vein after returning to Britain in the middle of October 1915. In a piece that appeared in the *Sunday*

---

69 Michael Hughes, *Inside the Enigma: British Officials in Russia, 1900-1930* (London: Hambledon, 1997), p. 65.
70 For Graham's views of Milukov, see Graham, *Wonderful Scene*, pp. 113-14; for Miliukov's views of Graham, see Paul Miliukov, *Russia Today and Tomorrow* (New York: Macmillan, 1922), p. 276.

Pictorial, Graham wrote that "The millions of the Russians are brave and patient soldiers, seeing visions, wearing crosses under their khaki tunics [...] courageous individually to an extraordinary degree, strong as lions, merciless in anger but tender in a moment if something touches them; the most sociable men, the most affectionate relations man to man, crazily fond of music".[71] A few days earlier, he joined the novelist John Buchan on the platform at a public meeting in London, where he told the audience that, despite recent defeats, Russia was already recuperating and would soon put millions of fresh troops into the field.[72] The optimistic tone was *de rigueur* at a time when many authors and journalists believed they had a duty to help maintain public morale, but Graham's language suggests that the growing political tensions in Russia had not fundamentally changed his view of the country. He was still convinced that the spirit of Holy Russia lived on and would unite the country and inspire its people to victory.

Graham once again gave numerous lectures during his trip back to Britain in 1915-16, including one to the Anglo-Russian Literary Society, where the chairman hailed him as "a living medium of communication between the souls of these two peoples".[73] Graham's opinions about Russia were also canvassed by members of the British political establishment. The departure of Nicholas II for the *stavka* had left something of a political vacuum back in Petrograd, leading to rumours that the Empress was playing a role in making important decisions, whilst the reports of British diplomats and journalists in Russia were already beginning to talk about the influence supposedly wielded at Court by the shamanic Rasputin and other "dark forces". Graham was invited to the Reform Club by George Riddell, who somewhat mischievously wrote up their lunchtime conversation as a column in *The News of the World,* sending in return a cheque attached to a compliment slip noting that the paper "is always glad to receive original news items". Riddell also introduced Graham to Robertson Nicoll, editor of the leading Nonconformist paper *The British Weekly,* which still enjoyed considerable influence at this time. "A more important meeting" took place with Lloyd George, who quizzed his visitor about the political attitudes of leading Russian figures and the state of popular morale.[74] Although Lloyd George had access to detailed Foreign

---

71 *Sunday Pictorial,* 14 November 1915.
72 *The Times,* 11 November 1915.
73 Stephen Graham, 'Anglo-Russian Literature', *Proceedings of the Anglo-Russian Literary Society,* 74 (1915), p. 42.
74 Graham, *Wonderful Scene,* pp. 118-19.

Office reports on Russia, he distrusted professional diplomats, and was anxious to obtain alternative sources of information. He was less interested in religious questions, although he did accept a copy of Graham's recent translation of the Russian journalist V.M. Doroshevich's *Way of the Cross*, which contained "terribly poignant" descriptions of the privations faced by refugees fleeing from the German advance.[75] Graham also left a copy of his recently published book *The Way of Martha and The Way of Mary* with Mrs Lloyd George, although she was, like many Britons of a Nonconformist background, decidedly unsympathetic to the Eastern Church, believing it to be a hot-bed of superstition and idolatry. Her visitor was realistic enough to realise that he was unlikely to change her mind.

Graham had been working on *The Way of Martha and the Way of Mary* since 1914, finding it "the hardest of all my books to write". He was convinced that the final version was something more than a "medley of impressions and stories", and was confident that the text was unified by a single "object and quest running through the whole of it", a claim that might not convince every reader.[76] The book took as its inspiration the biblical story of Mary and Martha, the two sisters who welcomed Jesus to their house at Bethany, where Mary sat at Jesus's feet to listen whilst Martha bustled around preparing food for the guests. The sisters have, throughout history, often been seen as representatives of two different aspects of Christianity: the contemplative (with an emphasis on prayer and devotion) and the active (with an emphasis on good works and love of neighbour). Graham argued that the difference between the two sisters served as a kind of metaphor for the difference between the Eastern and Western churches – a claim that ignored, in rather cavalier fashion, the manifest divisions *within* both eastern and western Christendom. In the preface to *Martha and Mary* he wrote that the two sisters represented a "touchstone for Christianity [...] and in their reconciliation is a great beauty".[77] Most of the book was, though, based on an implicit belief that the devotional-contemplative aspect of Christianity represented the highest expression of Christian faith. Graham did not hide his belief that the Russian Church was "the fairest child of the early Church",[78] although he made no real effort to explain why this should be so, given that Russia had received its faith

---

75 V. Doroshevitch, *The Way of the Cross* (London: Constable, 1916).
76 Stephen Graham, *The Way of Martha and the Way of Mary* (London, 1915), p. viii, version available at http://archive.org/details/waymarthaandway02grahgoog.
77 Ibid, p. v.
78 Ibid, p. 93.

from Byzantium many hundreds of years after it had been established in other parts of Europe. He did however hint at a possible explanation when he suggested that there was something in the Russian psyche that made it particularly receptive to Christianity, allowing it to absorb the faith and re-make it in a distinctive fashion, characterised by a readiness to reach out to the marginalized and dispossessed. Russia was above all for Graham still *the* place where Christianity extended beyond the Church and into the theatre of life.

> In such a form is the Russian notion of the world and his conception of life. It is such a church, such a theatre, such a mystery play. It has its liturgies of beauty, its many processions, its sacrifices, its ecstasies; it is a great phantasmagoria of emblems. Nothing is without significance; every man has his part; by his life he divines it and fulfils it. Every common sight and sound is charged with mystery. Everything is praising, everything is choric, everything triumphant.[79]

Graham made much in *Martha and Mary* of the central role of *podvig* in Russian Christianity – that is the supposed emphasis on "denial of this mortal life as real life" – in favour of a conception which emphasised the central importance of spiritual struggle and purification. He described a pilgrimage to the hermitage of Father Seraphim, one of the best-known mystics of the nineteenth-century Russian church, whose vow of silence and constant devotion to others marked him out in Graham's view as a saint whose life had been defined by a pursuit of the principle of denial: of self; of personal comfort; and of materialism. Such behaviour, in turn, echoed the supreme case of denial represented by the death of Christ on the cross, which was followed by the Resurrection, and its symbolic triumph of everlasting life over both mortality and material necessity. Graham discussed at some length in *Martha and Mary* the question of miracles, arguing that, despite their importance in signalling Christ's power and identity, they were essentially secondary to his spiritual mission on earth (a position which, although he did not know it, closely echoed the views of many Liberal Protestants of the period). He even suggested that some of the gospels were written by men "of the early Church who could not understand the mystic story", and therefore invented stories of miracles in an effort to convey the power and importance of Christ to their readers, in the process inadvertently placing too much emphasis on the material rather than the spiritual. Graham made it clear that he was sceptical about the story of Lazarus's rising from the dead – Lazarus was of course the

---

79 Ibid, p. 102.

brother of Mary and Martha – instead suggesting that what Jesus had meant to convey was that Lazarus was alive in the presence of God rather than in the flesh:

> Most explanations of the miracles are true, but inadequate. They often lead to confusion of thought and the emphasis on the material facts and outward manifestation rather than on the spiritual facts and inner reality. It is true that Christ "went about the world doing good," and that He is to us "an example of godly life," but the good that He did was spiritual good.[80]

Graham did not claim that the whole of Russian Christianity was shaped by the principle of contemplation and prayer, describing how even at the Convent of St Martha and St Mary, located on the south side of the Moscow river, "the idea of Martha and service stands first in their minds". Graham was also hopeful that the ideals of contemplation and spiritual quest had, in recent years, become stronger in Britain, even though the country had for many decades been a place where "thoughts about one's soul were considered rather ignoble".[81] Graham made much of the contrast between what he called the "ecclesiastical church" and the "living church", an idea that had been implicit in his thought for many years, once more returning to the notion that the true Church should be like a theatre engaging the whole emotional life of its members. A truly living Church, whether in Britain or Russia, would not be defined by dogma but instead:

> have to come into alliance with what may be called the right side of the theatre. For occasionally in the theatre people worship as much as others do in the Church. Many young people whose families have lapsed from the Church find their religious life functionised in the book, the drama, the opera, the symphony. They are not communicants in the literal sense, they are outside the church walls and the shut church doors, but they are inside the living Church. They have a common word with people inside church walls. Their chorus of praise swells from the other side of the walls, and in some countries the secular chorus of praise to God has considerably more volume than the official ecclesiastical chorus.[82]

The real task of the Christian Church was to help people develop a richer understanding of the material world and the spiritual universe of which it formed a part:

> You enter a church, such a temple, for instance, as the Cathedral of the Assumption in Moscow. At a step you are in the precincts of a different world. You have overstepped a frontier line, and the language has changed, just as

---

80 Ibid, p. 180.
81 Ibid, p. 182.
82 Ibid, pp. 183, 191-94.

when in Europe you cross a boundary and the language changes, say from German to Russian. The people are looking a different way, not Westward as to the Emperor but Eastward as to God. You are in a new kingdom; but as your thoughts go back to the street you left you realise that the kingdom is not from thence.[83]

Although Graham believed that the boundary between the spiritual and material worlds was drawn less starkly in Russia than in the countries of the West, he was certain that every nation had the potential to slough off the dead weight of materialism, and re-define its character in a way that would engage the energies of its people in a new and more profound manner.

Graham's interest in the potential for some form of national spiritual renewal in Britain, which he touched on in *Martha and Mary*, had been developing since the early days of the War. It was indeed present in many of his earlier books, which were at least partly inspired by a desire to show a western audience the full depth of Russia's spiritual traditions, in the hope of inspiring new reflections about how best to overcome the anomie of modern industrial society. During the final weeks of 1915, Graham attended a "pot-luck" lunch hosted by the Rector of St Margaret's Church in Westminster, where he met a mysterious young Serbian émigré named Dimitrije Mitrinović, who stood out from the assembled crowd with his "black longish hair and melancholy eyes".[84] Mitrinović was, like Graham, deeply committed to overcoming the divisions within Christianity, by fostering a new understanding of faith that rejected formal dogmas and creeds, and over the following weeks the two men discussed the possible establishment of a "secret society" designed to "operate from the invisible to the visible [and] from an initiated few to the many who were as yet unaware of the movement".[85] They were joined in this curious enterprise by Father Nikolai Velimirović, a Serbian Orthodox priest and author of several important philosophical and theological works,[86] who had, like so

---

83 Ibid, p. 203.
84 Graham Papers (HRC), *Wonderful Scene* (autograph). For an account of these pot-luck lunches see, too, Graham Papers (FSU), Box 581, 23a, ('Nikolai Velimirović in London'). On Mitrinović see Andrew Rigby, *Dimitrije Mitrinović: A Biography* (York: William Sessions, 2006); Predrag Palavestra, *Dogma i utopija Dmitrija Mitrinovića* (Belgrade: Slovo ljubve, 1977).
85 Graham, *Wonderful Scene*, p. 121.
86 For works dating from Velimirović's time in Britain see, for example, Nikolai Velimirović, *Serbia in Light and Darkness* (London: Longmans, 1916); Nikolai Velimirović, *The Agony of the Church* (London: Student Christian Movement, 1917); Nikolai Velimirović, *Christianity*

many of his fellow-countrymen, been driven to Britain by the exigencies of war.[87] Both Graham and Velimirović were ready to follow Mitrinović's proposal that they "cautiously seek allies and persuade them to join us and form a Christianly conscious nucleus. All in secret, all below ground. The more secret we are, the greater the spiritual strength we draw, till we are ready to break surface and grow to be a mighty tree".[88] The three men planned to pursue this grandiloquent goal by searching for sympathetic individuals who would be willing to join the society and work for the re-spiritualisation of Britain.

In Graham's 1918 book *The Quest of the Face*, which provided a thinly-veiled account of this curious enterprise, the fictionalised Mitrinović (under the name of Dushan) was quoted as saying that:

> You believe in the unity of all in Him. Well, then, let us work for that unity, for the consciousness of it throughout the world. That is Christianity itself. If we can find ten who believe as you believe, then in ten years all Europe will realise Christ, and within our life-time China and India will come in. Let us begin to-day and endeavour to realise universal consciousness of unity in Christ.[89]

Back in 1915, Graham sought to launch the project by approaching the Earl of Sandwich, well-known for his interest in various forms of Christian idealism, but the prospective candidate failed to hit it off personally with Mitrinović. A second potential candidate, Professor L.P. Jacks, the Unitarian editor of the *Hibbert Journal*, seemed unable or unwilling to grasp what Graham and Mitrinović were trying to achieve. The two men then considered approaching G.R.S. Mead, a leading British Theosophist and editor of the journal *Quest*, but after discussion they decided that he was too cerebral to understand how an essentially emotional "regeneration of Christian belief" might come about. The whole episode of the secret society sounds distinctly bizarre, although it is worth remembering that the First World War saw a growing interest in such cults as Spiritualism and Theosophy, stimulated in large part by horror at the carnage of mechanised

---

    and War (London: Faith Press, 1918).
87 For details of action by the Church of England to help train Serbian theological students in London, a process in which Velimirović was closely involved, see G.K.A. Bell, *Randall Davidson: Archbishop of Canterbury* (London: Oxford University Press, 1939), pp. 844-46.
88 Graham, *Wonderful Scene*, p. 121.
89 Stephen Graham, *Quest of the Face* (London: Macmillan, 1918), p. 78.

warfare.⁹⁰ It certainly shows the depth of Graham's determination to move beyond the role of a mere writer in order to become an agent of a new kind of spiritual evangelism in his own homeland. Both Graham and Mitrinović intuitively believed that the chaos and brutality of war had undermined traditional patterns of ethical belief and behaviour, with the result that a new form of society needed to emerge from the wreckage, one that would reject the materialism of the pre-War world in favour of a more profound understanding of the meaning of human existence.

Dimitrije Mitrinović was – and was not – a natural partner for Graham in the quest to establish a society designed to foster national spiritual renewal. He was born in Herzegovina in 1887, later attending Zagreb University, before becoming a regular contributor to a number of literary journals in the Balkans (during the pre-War years he was particularly interested in the Symbolist movement). He was also active in the Bosnian independence movement, and although he opposed the use of violence, he moved for a time in the same circles as those later responsible for murdering Archduke Ferdinand, heir to the Austrian throne, in the infamous assassination at Sarajevo in June 1914.⁹¹ He attended Munich University, where he got to know the painter Vasily Kandinsky, before fleeing to Britain when war broke out, where he was given a sinecure post by the Serbian Embassy.

It was during the war that he developed his distinctive personal philosophy, which in later years rested on the notion that there was "no Being, no principle, no force" that was higher than human reason, with the result that "the human race is the container of truth".⁹² When stripped of some of the more abstruse language, Mitrinović seems to have believed that God was best found "within" rather than "outside" the individual person, or, in the stilted language he came to favour, that "existence itself is aware of itself in humans".⁹³ Even when still living in Serbia, before 1914, he was inclined to use verse as the most appropriate way of articulating his philosophical and aesthetic view of the world, believing that a formal rational language could not alone convey his meaning satisfactorily. In one

---

90 Winter, *Sites of Memory*, pp. 54-77. For a classic and highly personal contemporary account of the issue by a leading scholar of the time see Oliver Lodge, *Raymond, or Life and Death: With Examples of the Survival of Memory and Affection after Death* (London: Methuen, 1916).

91 Vladimir Dedijer, *The Road to Sarajevo* (London, Macgibbon and Kee, 1967), p. 175 ff.

92 H.C. Rutherford, *The Religion of Logos and Sophia: From the Writings of Dimitrije Mitrinović on Christianity* (London: New Atlantis Foundation, 1966), p. 2.

93 Ibid, p. 10.

1913 poem he wrote tellingly that "Art is Magic / Magic is Life / Life is Divinity / Divinity is Humanity / Humanity is Myself".[94]

Mitrinović believed from an early age that his ideas would, if they were to have any effect, require the establishment of some form of quasi-conspiratorial organisation. He was constantly looking for suitable candidates, cultivating individuals such as the critic and writer Philip Mairet, who later recalled that being asked to become a participant was much "like conversion to a religion".[95] It may indeed be that Graham overstated his role as a co-author of the secret society, for he was almost certainly seen by Mitrinović less as an equal and more as a follower. Graham for his part was attracted to Mitrinović by his rejection of materialism as "an unworthy superstition", as well as his sense that God was to be found in personal experience, rather than in the elaborate formulae of Church doctrine. There was in Graham's emotional make-up a deep love of the esoteric, whilst the idea of a secret society doubtless also appealed to a somewhat theatrical element of his character. His war-time friendship with Mitrinović was, in any case, destined to have a lasting effect on his future. His wife became a close collaborator of Mitrinović in the 1920s and 1930s, whilst Graham himself spent the second half of his life with Dimitrije's sister, Vera, finally marrying her after Rosa's death in 1956.

Graham's hopes for fostering some form of spiritual renewal in Britain were not limited to his involvement with Mitrinović's secret society. At some point in late 1915 he also conceived the idea of writing a novel exploring the whole subject. In the final weeks of 1915, he went on a preparatory "pilgrimage" in search of "the real England",[96] seeking out places that were "in a national sense holy ground", such as Glastonbury Tor and York Minster. Amongst the places he visited was Stoke Poges graveyard, famous as the setting for Gray's "Elegy Written in an English Country Church-Yard", a poem which Graham believed showed a "great faith in the human being, above all, in the English human being". In places like Stoke Poges, he told readers of *The Times*, it became clear that "Whatever be the noisy exterior of England, the cosmopolitan clangour of its audible voice, the shames of its commercial rampages, there is another and more real being behind, and

---

94 H.G. Rutherford (ed.), *Certainly, Future: Selected Writings by Dmitrije Mitrinović* (New York: Columbia University Press, 1987), p. 45.
95 For Mairet's reminiscences of these events see Philip Mairet, *Autobiographical and Other Papers* (Manchester: Carcanet, 1981), pp. 103-6.
96 Graham, *Wonderful Scene*, pp. 143-45; *The Times*, 23 November 1915.

that is anonymous England, the quiet fount of the true English people". Graham argued that the "Elegy" itself was a great work, not because it was "beautiful", but because it captured in its understated description of an English landscape something that was "national", and "written by England for England". The picture painted by Gray of a rural world in which "The ploughman homeward plods his weary way" represented for Graham a more authentic England than the England of cities and "society gossip" and "self-advertisement". The idea of a timeless world of unchanging rituals, set against a background of pastoral beauty, must have been beguiling to his readers at a time when so many thousands of lives were being lost in the slaughter taking place just a few hundred miles away in the mud of Flanders.

The "pilgrimage" Graham took through Britain in the closing weeks of 1915 provided much of the inspiration for his novel *Priest of the Ideal*, which did not finally appear until just after the February 1917 Revolution, although he was working on the book throughout 1916. The novel represented an attempt to relocate many of the themes that had run throughout his writings about Russia to a new setting: Britain itself. It sought to mythologise, or in Graham's view reveal, the essence of Englishness (for someone who was fitfully proud of his Scottish background Graham was astonishingly inclined to shift between the terms Britain and England). The book tells the story of Richard Hampden, an Englishman in his early thirties, who in the view of his friends "knows more about England and [its] spiritual values than any man we have".[97] The first half of the book describes a tour taken through the holy places of Britain by Hampden and an American visitor named Washington King, who was hoping to buy up "historical monuments, buildings, manuscripts, paintings, furniture [that have] ceased to have any particular significance of value for [the English]".[98] Hampden's chosen mission was to convince King that the supposedly lifeless relics of an ancient way of life were still full of significance for the British people, despite their apparent obsession with science and commerce, since the country retained a potent spiritual identity rooted in its long Christian heritage. Each chapter of the book was headed by an "emblem" designed to be "part of the expression of the book and not merely an ornament".

---

97 Stephen Graham, *Priest of the Idea* (London, 1916), p. 19, version available at http://archive.org/details/priestofideal00grahiala.
98 Ibid, p. 15.

Figure 5: Two of the pictorial emblems appearing in Stephen Graham, *Priest of the Ideal* (London: Macmillan, 1917), pp. 151 and 165.

Graham sought to articulate his sense of the importance of the drawings by quoting the preface to Francis Quarles 1635 book *Emblems*: "Before the knowledge of letters, God was known by hieroglyphics. And indeed, what are the Heavens, the earth, nay, every creature, but Hieroglyphics and Emblems of his glory?" It was a sentiment calculated to appeal to Graham's instinctive symbolic reading of the world.

Hampden himself was at least in part an idealised self-portrait of Graham (something immediately recognised by Algernon Blackwood when he first read the book).[99] He was described as being thirty two years of age – Graham's own age in 1916 – and above average height with "a brown moustache and long flexible lips". He was also loved by a woman some fifteen years older than himself, in a relationship that was based as much on shared spiritual identity as on strong physical attraction, a description that has strong echoes of Graham's own relations with Rosa. The novel not only records Hampden's attempts to persuade King of his folly in seeking to appropriate cultural artefacts that retained a contemporary meaning for the British people; it goes on to describe his almost messianic attempt to convert his fellow-Britons to his vision of a country reborn into a renewed awareness of its cultural and spiritual roots. *Priest of the Ideal* is without doubt a failure as a work of fiction, but as a source for understanding Graham's view of the world during these years it remains invaluable.

The fictional tour taken by Hampden and King through the holy places of Britain was clearly based on the itinerary of Graham's 1915 pilgrimage. The two men travelled first to Glastonbury Tor – "a place of epic loveliness" – before visiting the town itself, which Hampden argued was the cradle of the British Church and proof that "the ancient Britons were ready for

---

99 Graham Papers (HRC), Letters, Blackwood to Graham, 9 October 1917.

Christianity. No race received it more humbly, more simply and more readily than they". Later on Hampden told King that Christianity had shaped the whole of British history and "was the first common ground on which our nation grew". Hampden was anxious, though, to show his companion that Glastonbury's significance was not simply historic, telling him that although "our John Bull of today does not like to call himself a pilgrim […] he has true yearnings all the same".[100]

The two men then moved on to Iona, where Hampden gave a "lay-sermon" on Columba, describing in highly stylised fashion how the saint had come there from Ireland in order to bring Christianity to Scotland. The Celtic saints figured large in the mythological history Hampden constructed for King – whether at Glastonbury, Iona or Lindisfarne – forming part of a narrative that tacitly assumed the early Celtic Church was superior in wisdom and spirituality to the Roman Church brought to Britain by St Augustine in the sixth century. Hampden's *credo*, or rather the *credo* put into his lips by Graham, rested on the assumption that it was possible to discern in history an essential England whose spirit still shaped the course of the country's development. The glorified antique collector King was by contrast blind in believing that the places and artefacts of its history were of little more than antiquarian interest in the modern world – material relics without significance. The future regeneration of England depended for Hampden, as it did for Graham, on once more connecting the British people with the spiritual reality of their island history.

Priest of the Ideal is not short of examples of "the cosmopolitan clamour" that in Graham's view drowned out the presence of the real England. Washington King himself represents a somewhat ambiguous figure, blind to the true character of England's history, but also sensitive to the perception that his own country lacked a sense of tradition. Graham gave a far more negative portrayal of the press baron Poldu, who was happy to use his newspapers to manipulate public opinion, in effect selling editorial space to the highest bidder (it is hard to avoid the impression that Graham intended Poldu to represent a "cosmopolitan" Jew). Other characters who cross Hampden's path feel themselves torn between two worlds, like Celia Cosmo, a modern young woman of twenty two, who, despite driving a car and lacking any knowledge of "what shyness was", finds herself uneasily aware of the emptiness of the privileged life she lives at home

---

100   Graham, *Priest*, pp. 51, 101.

with her wealthy parents. As the book progresses, Hampden increasingly defines his role as one of mobilising those weary of the clamour and noise produced by the representatives of "the negative side". The second half of *Priest of the Ideal* consists almost entirely of chapter after chapter of his lay sermons, designed to provide his audience with an insight into the ideal England, whose spirit was to be found in the "holy places" and in a literary tradition that ran from Chaucer through Shakespeare to Gray. Hampden's audience drinks in his words and press up "to see him more nearly or to touch him",[101] a description that seems to echo biblical descriptions of the way in which crowds thronged around Jesus almost two thousand years before (and perhaps hints at a certain messianic instinct in Graham himself).

The ideas expressed by Hampden in his talks and sermons were very much those that Graham had expressed down the years, verging at times on a mysticism in which the language served as little more than a kind of poetry hinting at the speaker's ideas which, by their very nature, defied the terms of a neatly-delineated argument. Hampden, as the Priest of the Ideal, becomes a kind of saintly figure in the final pages, embodying a transcendence that allowed him both to discern and articulate the "other" England, whilst inspiring his listeners to a form of spiritual reawakening in the material world: "We are passing from the notion that everything has an explanation to the understanding that nothing has. Science betrayed us to self-satisfaction, but life has forced us to rebellion, and out of rebellion has come the new birth – wonder".[102] At the heart of Hampden's philosophy, like that of Graham, was a strong sense that the world of the spirit could not be reduced to a system of doctrine guarded by powerful institutions:

> The visible Church stands in the way of the spiritual consciousness just as stone idols of the heathen stand in the way of the apprehension of God [...] the love which Christ started is wider and deeper and freer than all Churches whose limits are defined. And the spirit of Truth, coming like a Dove, is not a bird which has been kept and caught. It is invisible and quick as thought, and whispers to the ear of the loving heart here, there, and everywhere at once.[103]

Hampden (again like Graham) finds that such an elusive and intuitive language faced criticism from those who were unable to grasp the inner truth of what was being said. The response of Hampden-Graham was

---

101   Ibid, p. 312.
102   Ibid, p. 326.
103   Ibid, p. 399.

predictable in its claim that "The same objection was made to the teaching of the Master. It is not possible to speak explicitly. That is why teaching is given in metaphors, parables and emblematic stories".[104]

The national awakening sought by Hampden was of course exactly the kind of development that Graham and Mitrinović hoped to set in motion when they tried to establish their secret society in the final weeks of 1915. They too wanted to find individuals who would work with them to show others how to find the "prompting of God" in their own hearts. *Priest of the Ideal* therefore represented for Graham a fantasy of national spiritual renewal that had proved so elusive in the mundane setting of everyday life. He acknowledged in the Preface that the book was "difficult to classify, being a novel with emblems and at the same time an account of a pilgrimage to sacred and national places, a new survey of the progress of our Christianity and of the English idea".[105] It is certainly an elusive and, at times, tedious read. The fantastic elements in the book nevertheless become more explicable when it is remembered that so much of Graham's work before 1917, even his travel writing, was driven by a sense that the fabric of the material world was indelibly shaped by deeper organic forces. There was doubtless something comforting about such a philosophy at a time when Europe was tearing itself apart. The notion that there was an unchanging "English idea", surviving beneath the flux of history, must have been beguiling for many readers at a time of massive dislocation and change. *Priest of the Ideal* represented yet another attempt by Stephen Graham to identify and eulogise ideas and ideals immune from the forces of time and change.

Graham's search for Holy England in 1916 was prompted in part by his unease that Holy Russia was being submerged by the turbulent changes taking place in the Tsarist Empire during the months leading up to the February 1917 Revolution. Although rumours about the dark forces surrounding Nicholas II were exaggerated, the sense that the Government was both corrupt and incompetent became increasingly pervasive throughout Russian society. In November 1916, Paul Miliukov and other leading Cadet politicians used a session of the Duma to express their fears that ministers were ready to undermine the war effort in order to make a separate peace with Germany. The mood in the factories grew increasingly

---

104   Ibid, p. 332.
105   Ibid, p. v.

radical, creating a febrile atmosphere in which massive social and political change seemed not only feasible but imminent. British diplomats posted to Russia were by the end of 1916 even hearing rumours that some of those close to the heart of Government were considering a military coup, which would sideline the Emperor, and introduce a new administration capable of prosecuting the war more effectively.[106] By the end of 1916, the symbols of old Russia – the Tsar and the Orthodox Church – were no longer capable of serving as unifying symbols for the whole nation. When a series of street protests got out of hand a few weeks later, in February 1917, the Government found it impossible to restore order when sections of the army refused to fire on the crowd. The abdication of Nicholas II just a few days later was an almost inevitable outcome of developments that had been taking place over many years.

Graham spent several months in Russia during the second half of 1916, arriving in early summer at Ekaterina in the far north of the country, where he spent a few days witnessing at first hand the construction of a new harbour and railway line to support the country's war effort. He then travelled on to Archangel, where he found that the "dreamy lifeless" town he had first visited six years earlier had become a bustling port, visited by five thousand ships each year. Graham wandered along the new wharfs loaded with military supplies shipped from Britain, and visited restaurants and cafes full of sailors and local residents reaping the benefits of "unheard of wages", as well as attending as guest-of-honour at a ceremony celebrating the opening of the town's new tram system.[107] He remained in the area for several weeks, staying with some old friends, before setting off by rail to visit an estate in Voronezh province several hundred miles south-west of Moscow.

The estate was the home of the Ertel' family, whose oldest daughter Natasha had been a student in London, and under her married name of Duddington was establishing a reputation for herself as a leading translator of Russian texts into English (amongst other things she translated Vladimir Solov'ev's *Justification of the Good* for the Constable Russian Library edited by Graham). Natasha's father was a minor author who had known Leo Tolstoy, whilst her mother was "half a Tolstoyan", who "lived for the villagers, dosed them with herbal remedies, and wrote letters for illiterate

---

106 Hughes, *Inside the Enigma*, p. 78.
107 On the opening of the tramway see *The Times*, 11 October 1916.

wives whose husbands were away at war".[108] Natasha's equally erudite sister, Lola, had translated Graham's *Martha and Mary* into Russian, and already persuaded the distinguished *litterateur* and journalist Peter Struve to publish an extract from it in his journal *Russkaia Mysl'*, one of the best-known publications of the day. Graham quickly fell in love with the Ertel' family, whose cultivated lifestyle seemed to echo the vanished world depicted by Ivan Turgenev in his novels and short stories, and photographs he took of the family dining on the wooden veranda of their old house could have dated from fifty years earlier. There was nevertheless even here a stark reminder of the chaos of the war raging a few hundred miles to the west, in the guise of a party of Hungarian Prisoners of War, who worked on the estate by day, and by night congregated outside their quarters playing "wistful folk tunes" to remind themselves of home.

After leaving Ertelevo, Graham travelled back to Moscow to meet the wealthy publisher Ivan Sytin, who gave him five hundred rubles for the right to publish a Russian language edition of *Martha and Mary*.[109] The two men also discussed publishing translations of some of his other books. Although Graham's work was thoroughly disliked by many Russian liberals, he had a considerable following amongst more conservative and religiously-minded readers, who were delighted to find a western writer who saw in Russia something more than a bastion of reaction and superstition. *Undiscovered Russia* had been translated into Russian as early as 1913 under the title *An Englishman on the Russian North* (*Anglichanin o Russkom Severe*). An unauthorised translation of *With the Russian Pilgrims* was in circulation within a few months of the appearance of the English original, whilst authorised extracts from *With Poor Immigrants to America* and *Martha and Mary* appeared in literary journals before the end of 1916. Sytin was a shrewd judge of the literary market in Russia – he had become immensely rich over the previous forty years – and he believed that there was a market for Graham's particular brand of conservative Slavophilism. Graham was for his part keen to build his reputation in Russia beyond a readership who knew English, but the onset of revolution meant that the proposed translations of his works came to nothing. Whether Graham

---

108   Graham, *Wonderful Scene*, p. 131. For a longer account of Graham's visit to Ertelovo see Graham, *Russia in 1916* (London: Cassell, 1917), pp. 44-53, version available at http://archive.org/details/cu31924010358244.

109   On Ivan Sytin, see Charles Ruud, *Russian Entrepreneur: Publisher Ivan Sytin of Moscow* (Montreal: McGill University Press, 1990).

would have found a significant audience amongst a broad Russian readership must remain a matter for speculation.

Following his meeting with Sytin, Graham headed south again to Orël Province, where he stayed with Countess Olga Benningsen, whose husband was in a German Prisoner-of-War camp, where he spent his time translating *With the Russian Pilgrims to Jerusalem* into Russian. Although the Countess was very welcoming, she did not share her husband's religious idealism, and found it hard to deal both with "her quiet tragedy" and her growing deafness (she was however an admirer of her visitor's books, which she later told him had taught her how "little value is most of what I believed" before reading them).[110] The two of them sat on the veranda in the July sunshine, looking out onto the garden, where bird hawk moths hovered over the delphiniums, but Graham's attempts to ease the melancholy of his hostess proved unavailing. After a few days he went south to the Caucasus, staying first at Rostov-on-Don, before heading to the resort of Kislovodsk, situated in a picturesque spot in the mountains between the Black and Caspian seas. Graham loved the countryside around the town, but loathed Kislovodsk itself, finding "its streets heavy with the odour of decay and dirt". The real source for his distaste was, though, the character of the clientele who filled the hotels and apartments. Graham believed that many of these people had made their fortunes "out of the war […] and the emptiness of their gay life is an unpleasant contrast to the realities of the time". He was, as ever, depressed by the rise of "commercial parvenus", full of "boundless vanity and self-importance", who had replaced "the noble and wise [who] really are the nation".[111] Whilst Kislovodsk had once provided a summer watering hole for members of the Russian aristocracy, it had now become a playground for people who were "profiting by death and destruction and calamity and sorrow".[112] Graham stayed there just long enough to complete his manuscript of *Priest of the Ideal*.

Graham's visit to Russia in 1916 was designed to reacquaint him with the people and places that had become so dear to him over the previous ten years. He was by now no longer writing regularly for *The Times*. Nor does he seem to have contributed much to other newspapers. His literary activities were instead focused on finishing his novel and sketching out a book about contemporary developments in Russia (which subsequently appeared

---

110   Graham Papers (HRC), Letters, Countess Benningsen to Graham, 19 October 1916.
111   Graham, *Russia in 1916*, pp. 119-20.
112   Ibid, p. 121.

just before the February Revolution under the title *Russia in 1916*). In his autobiography, written many years later, he spoke of the "atmosphere of suppressed foreboding" that hung over Moscow. He also recalled the awful financial circumstances facing the country, describing how he overheard a conversation in which the British consul, Robert Bruce Lockhart, told a dinner companion that Moscow was effectively bankrupt.[113] Such bleakness was less visible in his contemporary writings. In *Russia in 1916*, which was largely written from notes he took whilst still in the country, he described how Moscow had been "patched up" since the riots of the previous year. He also suggested that popular morale was generally good, despite rising prices and concern about the military situation, and in a piece published in *The Times* in November 1916 he argued that "Russia is altogether in the war and for the war [...] her spirit is good".[114] Graham was certainly aware of the problems facing Russia in 1916. Nor was he blind to the shortcomings of the Russian Government. He nevertheless underestimated the severity of the crisis that was about to sweep away the old Russia.

Graham's views on Russia were by 1916 increasingly seen as eccentric by members of the British political and literary establishments. Lloyd George still met him from time to time, but the furore that erupted over Graham's anti-semitism in 1915 caused lasting damage to his reputation in progressive circles, and he was seen as out of touch by many politicians and editors. His portrayal of Holy Russia was also beginning to grate on the nerves of critics. The *Athenaeum* suggested that Graham's determination to focus on "Russia at prayer and pilgrimage" led to a "misrepresentation" of the country "at which the average Russian simply scoffs".[115] The author of the 'Russian Letter' in *The New Age*, C.E. Bechöfer, had previously dismissed Graham as a "mock mujik" [peasant] and a "sentimental innocent".[116] The *Times Literary Supplement* criticised *Martha and Mary* for providing readers with a picture of "dreamy and delicate emotions" rather than a realistic portrait of the contemporary Russian Church. The reviewer went on to add that "It would be a pity [if] we remained content to think of [Russia] simply as a country of nobly simple peasants and archaic ikons".[117] Other writers accused Graham of painting a picture of Russia that was "sicklied o'er

---

113   Graham, *Wonderful Scene*, p. 139.
114   *The Times*, 7 November 1916.
115   *Athenaeum*, January 1916.
116   *New Age*, 15 April, 1915; 25 November 1915.
117   *Times Literary Supplement*, 16 December 1915.

with sentimentality".[118] Although the outbreak of hostilities had stimulated interest in the "soul" of Britain's new ally, as the war progressed such language was increasingly seen as a distraction from the more urgent task of understanding how the country was changing. Graham seemed to have little to say about the practical issues shaping Russia's contribution to the war effort.

The Tsarist Government's failure to prosecute the war effectively raised concern in London more or less from the moment war began in 1914. Although diplomatic protocol placed limits on the extent to which the British Government could interfere in the internal affairs of its ally, there was by the start of 1916 widespread acknowledgement within the Foreign Office that political reform in Russia was vital to improve the country's war effort. The British ambassador in Petrograd, Sir George Buchanan, warned the Foreign Office as early as October 1915 that the country was "almost ripe for revolution", and asked for permission to speak to the tsar about his anxieties,[119] seizing an opportunity two weeks later when Nicholas made a brief visit to Petrograd from military headquarters. He repeated his warnings a number of times in the year that followed.

Graham was perturbed by the negative view of the Tsarist Government that was becoming more and more widespread in Britain by the end of 1916. He met Lloyd George for a "prodigious breakfast" shortly before the Welshman replaced Asquith at Number 10, but it was clear that the soon-to-be Prime Minister was convinced that the political situation in St Petersburg was chaotic, and that Rasputin and others were working for a separate peace with Germany. Graham also discussed the situation in Russia with Andrew Bonar Law, the first Chancellor of the Exchequer in Lloyd George's coalition Government, who still had lingering hopes of a military breakthrough by the Russians in the east. Wherever he went in London, though, Graham found little support for the idea that Holy Russia could yet emerge victorious on the battlefield. The novelist John Buchan, who was already closely involved in efforts to promote British propaganda abroad, advised Graham early in 1917 to stop worrying about "Russia the God-bearer and all that", urging him to work instead for "a common-sense reasonable state with which the West could wholeheartedly cooperate".[120]

---

118 T. Lothrop Stoddard, *Present-Day Europe: Its National States of Mind* (New York: Century, 1917), p. 33.
119 The National Archives (Kew), FO 371/2455, Buchanan to Grey, 16 October 1915.
120 Graham, *Wonderful Scene*, p. 148.

It was a view echoed by *The Times*, which published several pieces implying that the Tsar would never make the kind of ministerial changes capable of improving trust in the Russian Government.[121] Graham demanded a meeting with the paper's editor, Geoffrey Robinson, but he only offered an unconvincing apology. Lord Northcliffe was even more evasive. The idea that a new Government could help to improve Russia's contribution to the war was becoming widespread in Britain by the end of 1916.

When Graham came to write his autobiography, almost fifty years after the events of 1917, he still gave some credence to the idea that elements in the British establishment had been complicit in a plot to undermine the tsarist regime. Although he believed that politicians like Bonar Law and Lloyd George had no "wind of the coming revolution", he was convinced that others like Henry Wickham Steed, Foreign Editor of *The Times*, had "been forewarned of the coming palace revolution".[122] Graham's private diary shows that in 1918 he was still convinced that Nicholas II had been a victim of "cowardice, treachery and deceit".[123] There is little serious evidence to support such a view, although it has been suggested that British intelligence may have been involved in the plot to kill Rasputin, in the hope of restoring order at the heart of Russia's Government.[124] The revolution that erupted in Russia in February 1917 was driven, above all, by events on the streets. The abdication of Nicholas II was nevertheless widely welcomed in Britain. The *Daily Mail* described the February Revolution as a "benign revolution" that would rid Russia of "the pro-German and reactionary elements".[125] *The Times* suggested that the Tsar had been deposed by representatives of a "Win the War Movement".[126] Such views were echoed by Sir George Buchanan in Petrograd, who praised the new Provisional Government for its commitment to the "vigorous continuation of the war".[127] His view was shared by many of his colleagues at the Foreign Office in London and by ministers in Lloyd George's War Cabinet.

Graham's relationship with members of the British diplomatic establishment had become very strained by the end of 1916. It had never

---

121   See, for example, *The Times*, 16 January 1917.
122   Graham, *Wonderful Scene*, pp. 142, 146.
123   Graham Papers (FSU), Box 579, 49 (Diary for *Private in the Guards*).
124   Andrew Cook, *To Kill Rasputin: The Life and Death of Grigori Rasputin* (London: the History Press, 2006).
125   *Daily Mail*, 16 March 1917.
126   *The Times*, 16 March 1917.
127   Hughes, *Inside the Enigma*, p. 87.

been close. George Buchanan was concerned as early as 1915 that Graham's activities might complicate Anglo-Russian relations (he was particularly angry at the way Graham quoted, or perhaps misquoted, Sazonov's views about Russia's Jews in his article in the *Sunday Times*). Buchanan warned the Foreign Office towards the end of the year that "it is certainly regrettable that the task of interpreting the Russian people to the British Public should have been assumed by a writer whose interpretation appears to give deep offence to many of our best friends in this country. I would suggest that it might be advisable, privately and confidentially, to call the attention of the Editor [of] *The Times* to the effect produced in Russia by Mr Graham's articles".[128]

It is not entirely clear which "friends" Buchanan was referring to. Maxim Gorky certainly had no time for any spiritual-mystical interpretation of the Russian soul, lampooning such conceptions on the pages of the journal *Letopis'*, including one attack that took the form of a spoof letter by a certain William Simpleton, whose ideas bore more than a striking resemblance to those of Graham.[129] Simpleton's *bons mots*, at least as presented by Gorky, included such sweepingly banal observations as "in Russia there is nothing simple" and in Moscow life was "full of philosophy". Nor did Graham's views go down well even amongst those like the Symbolist religious poet, Dmitri Merezhkovsky, who might have been expected to be more sympathetic. Buchanan was not, though, really worried about the attitude of writers and artists. He was more concerned that members of the moderate reform movement, like Paul Miliukov and other leading Cadets, would assume that Graham's platform in *The Times* meant that his words had some kind of official *imprimatur*.

Although these fears were probably groundless, the much-vaunted Russian soul had little appeal to members of the liberal-reform movement in Russia, who instead wanted their country to become more like the countries of the West (the Cadet newspaper *Rech'* printed sharply critical accounts of Graham's views on a number of occasions). Graham for his part felt little warmth for Buchanan, whose subtle mixture of arrogance and *hauteur* was disliked by many visitors to the Embassy, including the writer Somerset Maugham, who in one story provided a thinly-veiled portrait of

---

128 The National Archives (Kew), FO 371/2455, Buchanan to Foreign Office, 8 November 1915.

129 *Pis'ma znatnogo inostrantsa*, Letopis' (April 1916), pp. 288-99. For Graham's criticisms of Gorky, see Graham, *Russia in 1916*, pp. 80-84.

the ambassador as a man possessing "a politeness to which no exception could be taken but with a frigidity that would have sent a shiver down the spine of a polar bear".[130] In a review of Buchanan's memoirs, published a few years later, Graham accused the ambassador of being "as weak as the men he called weak". He also condemned him for failing to understand "the particularities of the situation" in Russia.[131] Nor, in his memoirs written almost fifty years after the Revolution, could he refrain from some sarcastic remarks about Buchanan's "limp handshake" and "languid voice".[132]

Graham first heard about the abdication of the Tsar from a copy of the *Daily Mail*. He was asked the same day to contribute a piece to *The Times* about events in Petrograd which duly appeared under the heading 'Causes of the Revolution', in which Graham wrote that "British public opinion has helped a very great deal to bring about the success of the movement". He praised the Tsar for acting "nobly" in abdicating power, thereby avoiding a civil war that would have "shed the blood of thousands and devastat[ed] his own country".[133] Graham was moderately complimentary about the Provisional Government set up following Nicholas's abdication, but warned that "we are only at the beginning of a very long chapter", adding that the political struggle would continue with potentially damaging consequences for the Russian war effort. Such cautious words were not well-received. When he spoke a few days later at the Writers' Club in London, the audience was packed with "critics out for my blood".[134] Lloyd George agreed to a brief meeting at which the Prime Minister was sympathetic, but made it clear that he did not share Graham's views, instead expressing hope that the emergence of a more liberal system of government in Russia would strengthen the Anglo-Russian alliance. Nor were Graham's reservations simply about narrow questions of politics and diplomacy. He later recalled that "the atmosphere receptive to Russian spirituality disappeared almost overnight" in Britain, as people began to focus on the practical question of how the Revolution would impact on the war, rather than more profound questions about the nature of Russian culture and identity.[135] In a speech at the Royal Institution at the end of March, Graham told his audience of his

---

130   W. Somerset Maugham, *Collected Short Stories*, vol. 3 (London: Pan, 1976), p. 147.
131   *Evening News*, 14 June 1923.
132   Graham, *Wonderful Scene*, p. 140.
133   *The Times*, 17 March 1917.
134   Graham, *Wonderful Scene*, p. 150.
135   Ibid, p. 151.

fear that Russia would soon become a business empire "and a great many of the most beautiful institutions might be swept away".[136]

Graham acknowledged that his distance from Russia made it difficult to understand what was happening in the country, and he resolved to return there as soon as possible, in order to see developments with his own eyes (he had already been asked by a group of businessmen to go back there a few weeks earlier, to negotiate a contract for raw materials, but declined on the grounds that "I had no experience of commercial activity").[137] He was however frustrated in his intention by the Foreign Office, which refused to give permission for the trip, apparently fearing that Graham's close association with the tsarist *ancien régime* might in some way damage Britain's relations with the new Provisional Government. Graham later claimed that he was also prevented from accepting an invitation to visit America to discuss events in Russia since his "view of the Russian revolution [was] unhelpful".[138] It is difficult to untangle the rights and wrongs of some of Graham's claims (it is not, for example, clear what would have been the legal basis for stopping him travelling to the United States). It was however true that official Britain was determined to work closely with the new democratic Government in Russia, and ministers and officials in London were ready to go to considerable lengths to reassure Russian public opinion that their allies had no desire to see the Tsar restored. Graham's warning that revolution was unlikely to bring stability or democracy to Russia did of course prove prescient. The Provisional Government only survived nine months before it was swept aside by Lenin and the Bolsheviks in October 1917. Graham cannot have gained much comfort from his foresight. He spent the last fifty eight years of his life exiled from the country which had, since his teenage years, been the focus of his hopes and dreams.

The weeks and months following the February Revolution were a period of considerable uncertainty for Graham. He had for some time edited the Constable Russian Library, which published translations of short stories by contemporary authors such as Alexander Kuprin and Fyodor Sologub, a series praised by the *Saturday Review* for introducing lesser-known Russian writers to a British audience (Graham himself translated the Kuprin stories with Rosa).[139] It also published *Dead Souls* by Nikolai Gogol (another writer

---

136   *Observer*, 25 March 1917.
137   Graham Papers (HRC), *Wonderful Scene* (typescript), p. 117.
138   Graham, *Wonderful Scene*, p. 153.
139   *Saturday Review*, 19 September 1916.

who was comparatively neglected in Britain at the time). The Constable series in addition included Natasha Duddington's translation of Vladimir Solov'ev's *Justification of the Good*, complete with an introduction by Graham, who described it as "a classic work of the utmost importance in Russian studies" that elucidated "the laws of the higher idealism".[140] Graham also contributed a lengthy essay on Solov'ev to the theosophical journal *Quest*, praising the philosopher for providing "a very valuable service to the Church of Russia by breaking up its superficial formalism, orientating its traditions and genius with regard to Christian culture, thereby making it the Church of the cultured as well as of the peasant-pilgrim and the monks and priests".[141] Although it is possible to take issue with some of Graham's interpretations, the *Quest* article displayed a good deal of analytical acuity, and serves as a salutary reminder that its author was capable of producing work that did much more than convey a sense of "dreamy and delicate emotions".

Graham also spent the months following the February Revolution completing his manuscript of *Quest of the Face*, mentioned earlier – a dense quasi-novel written to inspire its readers "to become builders of the city in which Dushan (Dimitrije Mitrinović) and I have been active spiritual masons".[142] The book begins with Graham – as the barely-fictionalised narrator – wandering the streets of London searching for the face of Christ in the human beings who passed him on the streets:

> We are all seeking a face. It may be the dream face of the ideal, our own face as it ought to be, as we could wish it to be, or the face that we could love, or a face we once caught a glimpse of and then lost in the crowds and the cares. We seek a face of such celestial loveliness that it would be possible to fall down before it in the devotion of utter sacrifice. Some seek it desperately, others seek it ever hopefully, some forget and remember and then forget again and remember again. Others live their life in the consciousness of a promise that they shall see the face at some definite time by and by [...] Each has his separate vision of the face. And as there is an infinite number and diversity of mankind, so the faces of the ideal are infinitely numerous and diverse. Yet as in truth we are all one, so all these faces are one, and all the loveliness is one loveliness.[143]

---

140 Vladimir Solovyof, *The Justification of the Good*, trans. N. Duddington (London, 1918), p. vi.
141 Stephen Graham, 'Vladimir Solovyof', *Quest*, 9 (1917-18), pp. 219-39.
142 Graham, *Quest of the Face*, Preface.
143 Ibid, p. 2.

Graham's description of this odyssey, which leads in time to the meeting with Dushan, is peppered with reflections on numerous cultural and religious topics. It also reveals a kind of religious philosophy, clearly influenced by Mitrinović, that Christ is best-encountered within even though this means that "to tell of Him is to turn into an egoist".[144] The recognition of this interior presence of Christ in turn leads to a transfiguration of the individual personality:

> So it was in the after years of first working for a living. The ideal personality obtained more sway in me, and I began to live in daily consciousness that I, the true ego of me, was a celestial being, one higher than any one dreamed or than I could openly assume. I grew in spiritual stature and watched myself changing. I marvelled at the new life. My direct centre of consciousness began to move from the lower towards the higher ego, and as it did so I became vocal and wrote poetry, read poetry, lived in poetry. I walked with feet on the earth and head in the sky. From then till now I have been conscious of a spiritual truth, in the atmosphere of which I have lived, so that all the negative values of earth-living have become positive values of absolute-living. And I have grown to identify myself with the ideal personality within.[145]

The decidedly messianic tone of *Quest of the Face* comes from its description of how Graham joined with Mitrinović / Dushan to form a secret society to help the process of transfiguration move from the personal to the collective level. The fictional Dushan suggests to his friend that they should work together with others to realise "the universal consciousness of unity in Christ".[146] This consciousness in turn contains a general truth since "no one true way of expression contradicts any other true way". The implication for the various religions of the world is clear since "all the sects and churches [...] are waiting in the darkness; but it is just before dawn. The connections between them will soon be seen: all will see them".[147] This unity will in turn extend beyond the purely spiritual world and lead to a transformation of the international system, since:

> what we apply to human society around us we apply also to Europe at large and to the world. The nations are a school hitherto run on old-fashioned lines with endless condemnation and bitterness and strife and little learning. Now Europe itself might be a sort of Montessori school where the nations

---

144 Ibid, p. 66.
145 Ibid, p. 69.
146 Ibid, p. 78.
147 Ibid, p. 88.

are the children. If that is too childish a conception, remember the Christ's saying about children – of such is the Kingdom of Heaven.[148]

The search for European unity, albeit from a characteristically eccentric perspective, was to become one of the defining hallmarks of Mitrinović's intellectual quest between the two world wars.

There are certain sections of *Quest of the Face* that display an esoteric tone that smacks clearly of Theosophy. At one point the narrator-Graham suggests that:

> There are possibly several mortals living, several men who though they were born thousands of years ago have never died. Not that their immortality is more real than ours. It is different, that is all. We pass through the gate of death, pass perhaps often through death on our long way. They simply never die. By now probably they have become invisible to ordinary human gaze, completely transparent, translucent, and it is in vain that pilgrims having the clue to their existence still seek them on the remote peaks of Hindu Kush. I have the story of Celeus, or Cilfa as he was called by another generation, who discovered the infinitely rare drug which alters the psychic state and liberates the partial human soul from the chain of death.[149]

The final section of the book then fades away into a series of short stories, some clearly drawn from real life, including an account of a semi-fictional writer who, like Graham, abandons the "substance" of work and respectable society in order to pursue the "shadow" of self-fulfilment and authenticity. Such stories sit uneasily with the rest of the book, which, despite its elusive tone and indigestible style, was clearly inspired by a desire to impart a kind of poetic-religious vision to readers. It is perhaps no great wonder that reviewers struggled to know what to make of *Quest of the Face*. The reviewer in *The Bookman* praised Graham's "delicacy of touch", but found his philosophy "unconvincing", adding that he hoped the author would in time develop his powers and avoid "the overstrained idealism which has hitherto characterised his work".[150] The book certainly represented the apogee of what might be termed Graham's mystical-theosophical phase. Although it will be seen in later chapters that many of the book's motifs recrudesced in his later writings, he was by the time it was published fighting in the trenches of France, a brutal experience that inevitably influenced and changed his view of the world. The intense spiritualism of *Quest of the*

---

148   Ibid, p. 118.
149   Ibid, p. 131.
150   *The Bookman*, September 1918.

Face was diluted in Graham's inter-war work as he struggled to revise and articulate his esoteric vision within a more traditional vocabulary of fiction and travel-writing.

Graham not only spent the months after the February Revolution completing the manuscript of *Quest of the Face*, but also contributed articles on the Revolution to journals in Britain and America. One in *The Century Magazine* discussed developments 'Inside Russia', fretting that the country would now become "free for commercial exploitation". He nevertheless hoped that Russia could resolve her problems and remain "the hope of Europe".[151] When Graham was not writing he continued to give lectures up and down Britain, including some in factories, and was also invited to tour some of the Navy's warships. The turbulence of war that Graham had written about at such length finally caught up with him in a very personal way in the second half of 1917, when the arrival of his call-up papers meant that he was "belatedly" required to join those already in khaki, consoling himself with the thought that "those who praise a war should at least taste the actual experience".[152] He refused to apply for an officers' training course, on the grounds that he wanted to see the war from the ranks, and, when given a choice of regiments, he opted to join the Scots Guards.

Graham had little opportunity to reflect on the loss of Holy Russia over the following year. He had in his voluminous writings about Russia always tended to construct the country as a semi-mythological place, whose contours owed as much to his own ideals as they did to a sober observation of the complex and contradictory character of Russian society. The cataclysmic changes of 1917 made it hard for him to maintain the myth of Holy Russia even in the privacy of his own mind. It will be seen in a later chapter that Graham was, despite his anguish at the loss, often sceptical about hopes that Holy Russia could ever be restored. He certainly had little sympathy with the numerous white émigrés who crowded the capitals of Europe, hoping that their shattered world would somehow be restored to them. Although Russia continued to preoccupy Graham in one way or another for the rest of his life, the February Revolution marked a critical change in the way he thought about the nature of the Russian soul, prompting him in time to embark on fresh odysseys in search of the meaning of life in general and his own life in particular.

---

151   Stephen Graham, 'Inside Russia', *The Century Magazine,* July 1917.
152   Graham, *Wonderful Scene*, p. 153.

4. The Pilgrim in Uniform

Graham first registered for military service in the summer of 1916, shortly before setting off on his final trip to Russia, but at that stage of the war married men of his age were still not being called up for active duty. The situation was different twelve months later, when the continuous slaughter on the Western Front created a huge demand for extra manpower. Graham was thirty-three years old when he received his call-up papers, reporting to the Caterham Depot of the 3rd (Reserve) Battalion of the Scots Guards on 11 September 1917, just a few weeks before the Bolshevik seizure of power in Petrograd. Some of his friends were aghast that a writer of such talent could be conscripted into active service. The Duchess of Bedford even intervened at the War Office in an effort to stop his draft. Graham was more sanguine at the prospect. His failure to obtain permission to visit Russia after the February Revolution had left him at something of a loose end in London. Although he continued to lecture about the progress of the War, he felt increasingly redundant, recalling many years later that he hoped life in the ranks would at least give him a chance to see "how the other half lives".[1] Graham was nevertheless concerned that military service would put an end to his campaign for religious renewal in Britain, even though friends like Nikolai Velimirović sought to reassure him that he would not become "a bayonet only", but would still have opportunities to use his "spiritual power" to promote the greater good.[2]

It is not clear why Graham chose to join the Scots Guards. He was of course born in Edinburgh, but it was only later in life that he took much real interest in his family's Scottish heritage (although he had described himself to newspaper reporters as a "Scotchman" during his first visit to

---
1 Stephen Graham, *Part of the Wonderful Scene* (London: Collins, 1964), p. 155.
2 Graham Papers (HRC), Letters file, Velimirović to Graham, 14 September 1917.

the USA in 1913). The Scots Guards was the third oldest regiment in the Brigade of Guards, tracing its origins back to the seventeenth century, long before the Act of Union joined England and Scotland into a single state. The regiment was involved in most major conflicts of the next 200 years, including the Napoleonic Wars and the Boer War, in the process building a reputation for its formidable *esprit de corps*. Graham was not on the face of it well-suited to serve in such an organisation. Since his departure from Somerset House many years earlier, he had enjoyed a working life that gave him the freedom to do what he wanted. Although he knew that the War had reached a critical stage by the autumn of 1917 – the Russian armies had crumbled and American troops had not yet arrived on the battlefield in great numbers – his patriotism was bound to be tested by the everyday restrictions of military discipline. Graham recognised that the thing he dreaded most was the loss of "the marks of individuality".[3] The next three months were to prove his fears well-founded. The training camp at Caterham to which he reported had long acquired the nickname of Little Sparta, a term that hinted at the harshness of the regime there, and it retained a fearsome reputation for imposing iron discipline on all new recruits. In the book he later wrote about his experiences, *A Private in the Guards*, Graham described in detail the toughness of the training to which he was exposed. He also acknowledged that it had helped transform him and countless other recruits into effective soldiers. Graham's time in the Scots Guards showed how the romantic young author of *A Vagabond in the Caucasus* was able, like so many others who experienced the horrors of the trenches, to adjust to a world that would once have seemed unimaginable in its bleakness.

    Graham spent his first day at Little Sparta in civilian clothes, following which the process began of turning him into a soldier, complete with khaki uniform and short haircut. Like all recruits he was required to carry out a host of menial duties, designed to ensure that new guardsmen were "standardised to type", including black-leading the grates and cleaning the latrines.[4] Graham's fellow-recruits were, in his own words, "the gleanings of British manhood", men of an age or physical condition who once would not have been considered fit for military service, but now could not be

---

3 Stephen Graham, *A Private in the Guards* (London: William Heinemann, 1928), p. 22, version available at http://archive.org/details/cu31924027819956. The book was first published in 1919 by Macmillan.
4 Ibid, p. 21.

spared given the gaps in the Front Line. Many were in their thirties or early forties, like his barrack-room neighbour, a metal-worker from Newcastle, who was distraught at leaving behind a wife and four children. Others had worked on the land or the railways. A number of recruits had, like Graham, been engaged in one of the more cerebral or artistic profession. These included the composer York Bowen, a man of "charming personality and a temperament unsuited to army life",[5] who feared that the rigours of training would damage his hands and make it impossible for him to play the piano again. Another of Graham's fellow recruits was the nephew of a peer, an accountant in civilian life, who was redeployed as a clerk when his health broke down following weeks of parades and route marches. Although the conscription process made no effort to spare those who were unsuited for the rigours of military life, the regime at Little Sparta tacitly provided opportunities for some to find a less demanding niche. Graham was determined to survive the training and receive a posting for France.

The life of new recruits at Little Sparta was shaped less by the officers and more by the Non-Commissioned-Officers (NCOs) who oversaw their day-to-day training. The brigade sergeant-major was "a very great personage" to all those who passed through the camp, but despite his best efforts to monitor the way the men were treated, many of the sergeants and corporals still believed that harsh treatment was needed to make real guardsmen out of raw civilians. Graham's description of the men who dominated his life at Little Sparta was not flattering. One sergeant "had a natural malice against educated men".[6] Another insisted on sharing the food parcels sent from home to the men under his command. A third was an alcoholic, a fourth almost entirely illiterate. Almost all of them repeatedly used foul language towards the men in their charge. Some used physical violence as well. Graham later wrote in *Private in the Guards* that "the men had no greater grievance than that of being struck on parade, and it made the blood boil to be struck oneself, or to see men near forty years of age struck by corporals or sergeants of twenty three or twenty four without the possibility of striking back".[7] Nor had the memory of these humiliations faded almost fifty years later when he came to write his autobiography. Although Graham's fitness meant that he had few difficulties in coping with the demands of training, he was by his own admission clumsy on

---

5 Ibid, p. 33.
6 Ibid, p. 27.
7 Ibid, p. 24.

parade, and presented a ready target for abuse. It was indeed the whole atmosphere of coarseness, laced with an undercurrent of violence, that Graham found most repellent about his time at Caterham:

> The defects in the Little Sparta system are the humiliation of recruits by words or blows, the use of glaringly indecent language, the possibility of squaring punishments, the use by N.C.O.'s, even by lance-corporals, of recruits as batmen. I believe these were recognised as defects in peacetime, and some of them had been eradicated, others endured in secret. But in war-time the problem of breaking in those who were never intended by Nature to be soldiers was so difficult that some of these ugly things became useful. Constant humiliation and the use of indecent phrases took down the recruit's pride, and reduced him to a condition when he was amenable to any command.[8]

Although Graham loathed much of the training he received at Little Sparta, he acknowledged that it helped to build the character of recruits, and he warmly praised the cleanliness and order of the camp. He also exhibited an unexpected skill in the use of the bayonet, finding the thought of hand-to-hand combat less repugnant than killing at a distance via rifle shot, a perspective strangely at odds with most modern reflections on war.[9] Graham was intensely aware of how quickly the rituals of army life came to seem normal. During the bus journey back to Soho for his first weekend of leave, he was exhilarated at "the common sights I saw, and drank them in like wine, loved every civilian, grudged no other young man his black attire and precious liberty".[10] Within a few weeks, though, he realised that his "soul" as well as his body was now in uniform. He came to relish his weekends off less than before, and became more and more detached from his civilian friends, who were appalled by the whole idea of army life. Algernon Blackwood visited him at Caterham, and fretted that the routines must be "utterly soul-deadening for you" (Blackwood himself soon returned to Switzerland where he worked in intelligence for the British government). Dimitrije Mitrinović was so appalled at the sights and sounds of Little Sparta that he fled away at the first opportunity. Only Rosa seemed hopeful that "everything that happened made for good", even as

---

8 Ibid, p. 50.
9 For some reflections on this theme see Jonathan Glover, *Humanity: A Moral History of the Twentieth* Century (London: Jonathan Cape, 1999), pp. 64-116. See, too, Joanna Bourke, *An Intimate History of Killing: Face-to-Face Killing in Twentieth-Century Warfare* (London: Granta, 1999).
10 Graham, *Private*, p. 73.

her husband went through a "queer metamorphosis", in which "it was not the grub that became a butterfly but the butterfly that became a grub".[11]

Graham was acutely aware of how deeply his fellow-conscripts were affected by the separation from their families. The strain was made worse by the fact that the character of the men who went through military training was often transformed beyond recognition:

> A man's first meeting with his wife after being taken for a soldier is one of strange pathos. Pleasure and pain and surprise are mingled, and I think pain is sometimes the most. She has not seen him in uniform before, and it makes a great difference in his appearance […] She is robbed. And the man she meets is clearly not the same man as went away from her. Something of his personality has been shorn away from him, something of that which made him lovable to her.[12]

There was almost certainly some personal resonance behind Graham's words that, when soldiers met their wives, they often found that whilst they loved them as much as ever "yet you have nothing to say to her, and somehow you feel distant". His words were written eighteen months after his experiences at Little Sparta, at a time when he had already been through a period of fighting at the Front, but it is clear that his three months in the camp were a defining moment for him. There was no room for a free-spirited "tramp" in the Scots Guards. Nor did the coarseness of barrack-room life provide much refuge for a man who had spent his life in search of an elusive insight into new spiritual truths. The fact that Graham survived in such an environment is testimony to his physical and mental toughness.

On Christmas Eve 1917, Graham was transferred from Little Sparta to Wellington Barracks in central London. The three months that he spent in London prior to his departure for France were amongst the strangest in his life. The barracks were situated only twenty minutes' walk from Graham's flat at 60 Frith Street, and when he was not on duty he was allowed to return home, where he could revel in the sight of "familiar panels and pictures" before retiring to his own bed. It also meant that he could revel in such unexpected luxuries as shaving with warm water. The regime at Wellington Barracks was much more relaxed than at Little Sparta – Graham was at times even irritated by the lack of order and cleanliness – which allowed the men to put behind them some of the more brutal experiences of the parade ground. Along with other guardsmen Graham was charged

---

11 Graham, *Wonderful Scene*, p. 154.
12 Graham, *Private*, p. 64.

from time-to-time with carrying out guard duty at Buckingham Palace – protecting the monarch was of course historically the *raison d'être* of the guards regiments – a duty that he relished as "the crown of training" but also his greatest "ordeal".[13] The preparations for guard duty involved hours of polishing equipment, as well as careful attention to dress uniform, followed by four sets of two-hour "sentry-go" in a particular twenty-four hour period. Although Graham relished his spells on duty at Buckingham Palace, he was well-aware that most of his fellow guardsmen were not instinctive royalists, and from time to time he saw graffiti on walls near his barracks calling for an overthrow of the monarchy.[14] He later recalled in *A Private in the Guards* that many of his fellow-guardsmen were even reluctant to sing 'God Save the King'. Graham's concern was doubtless shaped by his experiences in Russia, where he had seen the impact of the growth of anti-royalist sentiment at first hand, and he was concerned enough to wonder "whether the great ferment in the ranks meant a revolution after the war".[15]

Graham's duties at Wellington Barracks were relaxed enough to allow him to attend various social and literary functions across London, but his status as a lowly guardsman did sometimes make for awkwardness. Although he was convinced that his humble position gave him a unique vantage point for understanding British society, some of his old friends and acquaintances seemed embarrassed by his lack of officer's epaulettes. One senior official who had known Graham as a writer insisted on keeping him standing-to-attention "and treated me so formally that I felt almost chilled". More common, though, were those who "shook hands and smiled, treating me as an equal".[16] Graham met numerous people at the dinners and receptions he attended, including a morose armaments manufacturer, anguished by the knowledge that the weapons produced in his factories were responsible for so many deaths. He also met Lord Ruthven, Major-General of the Brigade of Guards, who suggested to Graham that he should write about his experiences in the ranks (a meeting that may have served as the genesis of *Private in the Guards*).[17] He attended a dinner at the house of Lady St Helier, one of his long-standing patrons, at which he met Princess Marie-Louise (a grand-daughter of Queen Victoria). The

---

13 Ibid, p. 84.
14 Graham Papers (FSU), Box 579, 49 (Diary for *Private in the Guards*).
15 Graham, *Private*, p. 81.
16 Ibid, p. 79.
17 Graham, *Wonderful Scene*, pp. 159-60.

conversation turned to the future of Russia, a subject on which Graham was very gloomy given the recent seizure of power by the Bolsheviks, whilst the Princess herself was preoccupied with the safety of the Russian Royal Family who were being held in exile in Siberia. The contrast between the drawing rooms of the finest West End houses and the sometimes "squalid" Wellington Barracks was inevitably disorientating to Graham. He was nevertheless in his own words always "a good mixer".[18] It was a talent that proved invaluable throughout his time in the army.

Graham received a number of invitations to lecture whilst he was in London, but he had to refuse most of them, since "it was against the army regulations for a private to appear on a platform in the King's uniform".[19] He was nevertheless able to give a weekly Lenten address at Christ Church by the simple expedient of wearing a cassock over his tunic. The invitation to speak came from R.J. Campbell, who had taken Anglican orders in 1916, following many years as a Congregationalist minister, when he had for a time occupied the pulpit at the City Temple in London (Graham had as a teenager heard Campbell preach). During his years as a Nonconformist minister, Campbell had articulated a "Panentheistic" theology which asserted that God was best encountered through his creation.[20] In books like *The New Theology* (1907), he argued for an immanentism that claimed "we know nothing and can know nothing of the Infinite Cause whence all things proceed except as we read Him in His Universe and in our own souls".[21] Although Campbell had moved towards a more orthodox theological position by the time he became an Anglican priest, he had greatly admired Graham's *Priest of the Ideal*, and hoped that his visitor's sermons on Christian idealism would foster a religious renewal amongst the congregation at Christ Church. Graham's readiness to accept such an invitation in turn suggests that the tough times he had endured at Little Sparta had not shaken his distinctive spiritual vision. The following months were to provide an even greater test for his faith. In the final weeks of March, rumours began to circulate that his unit was about to be

---

18 Ibid, p. 158.
19 Graham, *Private*, p. 78.
20 On Campbell's intellectual development see Horton Davies, *Worship and Theology in England: The Ecumenical Century, 1900 to the Present* (Cambridge: Erdmans, 1996), p. 125 ff.
21 R.J. Campbell, *The New Theology* (London: Chapman and Hall, 1907), p. 5. For Graham's comments on the whole issue see Graham Papers (FSU), Box 580, 13c ('In the Days of My Youth').

sent to the Front. When the men were issued with new steel helmets and identification disks, it became clear that the rumours were true, evoking a mixture of fatalism and despair amongst Graham's fellow-guardsmen. On Good Friday 1918 his unit marched from Wellington Barracks to Waterloo Station, followed by tearful wives and families, and cheered by passers-by still grimly determined to support the troops headed for the Front. After a brief pause at the station to allow for final goodbyes, the men were herded onto a train headed for Southampton, where they were loaded onto a "somnolent old hulk" bound for Le Havre.[22]

Graham arrived in France on 30 March 1918, a critical moment in the history of the Great War. A week earlier the German army had begun a major offensive to smash its way through enemy lines towards Paris. Rudyard Kipling later suggested that there was a danger of "a collapse such as had never befallen British arms in the history of her people".[23] During the first few days following the attack, British and French troops were forced to retreat along huge swathes of the Front, despite their desperate efforts to prevent the German advance. It seemed for a time that the Allies might be about to lose the war in the west. It is not surprising that the troops who landed with Graham at Le Havre were only given a couple of days to rest at the Base Camp at Harfleur. On 1 April they were marched back into port and loaded into a series of rickety third-class carriages headed eastwards towards the battlefield. Although they did not know it, the train was headed for Arras in north-western France, which had already suffered appalling damage earlier in the war. The town was once again threatened with capture, and heavy fighting had taken place over the previous few days to keep it out of German hands. Despite the urgency, Graham's train crawled along at snail's pace, taking thirty six hours to reach a way-station behind the lines, where the men were de-trained and prepared for advance along the reserve trenches. The whole process was inevitably unnerving. The march through the reserve lines was undertaken in "darkness and rain, a more or less silent trudge through the mud", punctuated by the sounds of shells exploding and gas-shells going off "like wet fireworks". Although the men all had gas-masks, one of them failed to put it on in time when the

---

22 Graham, *Wonderful Scene*, p. 163. For a description of this journey to Le Havre by another member of the Scots Guards, see Wilfrid Ewart, *Scots Guard on the Western Front, 1915-1918* (Stevenage: Strong and Oak Press, 2001), pp. 9-15.
23 Rudyard Kipling, *The Irish Guards in the Great War: the First Battalion* (Staplehurst: Spellmount, 1997), p. 233.

alert was sounded, forcing him to fall out and go back ("the first casualty among my friends"). Close to the Front Line, the new troops passed the men they were being sent to relieve – "silently, heavily, steadily they march down and past" – and within ten minutes Graham found himself in the section of the reserve trench that led directly to the Front.[24] The training that he had received during the previous few months was about to be put to the test.

The sights and sounds that appeared so surreal to Graham had become all too familiar to millions of soldiers over the previous few years. The 2nd Battalion of the Scots Guard, to which Graham was transferred when he went on active service, had first arrived in France in October 1914. The Battalion's War Diary, along with the Regimental history, together give some insight into its activities over the following three years. The Scots Guards were often in the thick of the heaviest fighting. The 1st Battalion played a major role in the First Battle of Ypres in the autumn of 1914. Both battalions then endured the harsh winter of 1914-15 in the trenches – a long account of the famous Christmas truce appears in the War Diary of the 2nd Battalion – whilst the Second Battalion took part in the great offensive of 1915 that included the brutal battles of Neuve Chapelle and Festubert.[25] They also took part in the Battle of Loos, the engagement in which Rudyard Kipling lost his young son John, a member of the Irish Guards.[26] Both battalions of the Scots Guards fought in the Battle of the Somme in the summer of 1916, suffering heavy casualties, whilst the following year they took part in the Third Battle of Ypres and the Battle of Cambrai. A brief glance at the War Diaries and other records show the customary mixture of heroism and chaos so familiar to anyone with even the most cursory knowledge of the history of the Great War. Although it is not easy to reconstruct the figures in detail, it seems that by the time Graham arrived in France in 1918, some one in five of those who had seen service with the Scots Guards had been killed in action.

Graham dryly noted in a book published in the early 1920s that the Scots Guard was not by tradition "a literary regiment" (it is hard to think of a regiment that would qualify for such an accolade).[27] He was nevertheless

---

24 Graham, *Private*, pp. 127-28.
25 For a memory of the Christmas truce by a member of the Scots Guards see Wilfrid Ewart, 'Two Christmas Mornings of the Great War', *Harper's Magazine*, December 1920.
26 For details see Tonie and Valmai Holt, *My Boy Jack* (Barnsley: Pen and Sword, 2008).
27 Stephen Graham, *Life and Last Words of Wilfrid Ewart* (London: Putnam, 1924), p. 5.

given permission to record some of the stories told to him by men who had served with the 2nd Battalion in the years before he joined. A number of these appeared *A Private in the Guards*, including an account of the execution for cowardice of a young conscript, even though he was clearly suffering from shell-shock (the incident seems to have created anger and irritation in equal measure amongst his fellow guardsmen). Graham also recorded an astonishing account of an incident that took place in the spring of 1917, at the town of Cartigny south-east of Amiens, when members of the 2nd Battalion took advantage of a lull in the fighting to dig gardens in which they grew flowers and vegetables. The Battalion's Commanding Officer even held a competition to see which unit could produce the best display, the prize going to a floral clock, which was judged to be just ahead of another display consisting of a border of boxwood shaped like a heart, containing "the crimson of many blossoms [designed] to give a suggestion of passion and loyalty and suffering".[28]

Despite the vivid character of these accounts, though, Graham's descriptions of events during the years before he joined the Battalion was inevitably weakened by the fact that he could not write from first-hand experience. The same was not true of another member of the Scots Guards. Wilfrid Ewart is best-remembered today – to the extent he is remembered at all – for two very different things.[29] The first is as author of the novel *Way of Revelation* (1921), which he wrote at Graham's prompting following his discharge from the army, a book intended to provide an almost Tolstoyan panorama of the way in which war shaped human lives both on the battlefield and back home in Britain. The second is for the bizarre circumstances of his death, when he was accidentally shot through the eye by New Year revellers on the first day of 1923, whilst visiting Mexico City with Graham and his wife. All these events lay ahead, though, when Graham first arrived in France in 1918.

Ewart had received a commission in the Scots Guards shortly after the war broke out, despite being blind in one eye, and an army career seemed entirely fitting for a young man of twenty two who had been born into a minor aristocratic family that boasted a strong military tradition. His teenage years had also shown an unlikely talent for publishing articles on

---

28 Graham, *Private*, p. 154.
29 For a useful account of Ewart see, in addition to Graham's book, Hugh Cecil, *The Flower of Battle: British Fiction Writers of the First World War* (London: Secker and Warburg, 1995), pp. 119-53.

raising poultry,[30] a subject about which he knew a good deal, and he was determined not to allow service at the Front to destroy his embryonic career as a writer. Ewart was certainly no model soldier (he tried on a number of occasions to obtain a post away from the battlefield). He could also come over as snobbish and aloof. The articles which he published anonymously in periodicals such as *Cornhill Magazine* and *The Spectator* nevertheless provide a far more powerful insight into daily life in the Scots Guards than the better-known regimental histories and war diaries. One of his most powerful pieces appeared in the *English Review*, describing the Battle at Neuve Chapelle in March 1915, at which Ewart was himself badly injured.[31] He described how he had led his men in an advance across a ploughed field, deep in mud, barely conscious of what he was doing as "men fall right and left" and "prostrate khaki figures dot the ground in all directions". When Ewart himself was hit in the leg, the sensation was "outside any ever felt before", as a "sharp stab of pain" led to "the collapse of the limb, and you roll over as a shot rabbit might do. Like a rabbit, too, you squirm and kick as you lie on your back". Ewart was lucky, at least in one respect, for he was rescued and taken back to Britain where he spent months recuperating from his wounds. Before he returned to France, he wrote more articles, a number of which described life behind the lines, a useful reminder that many units spent as long waiting to go into battle as they did at the Front itself. In one of Ewart's most memorable pieces, which appeared in *Cornhill Magazine*, he described how following the First Battle of Ypres his unit was posted to Picardy, where the officers were housed in a quiet chateau which, despite the depredations of war, still boasted a beautiful parquet floor and a grand piano. In the evenings Ewart was able to ride along the "grassy rides, Arcadian by-paths and roads [which] traversed the forest", and in the evening return through "the gathering dusk of leafy lanes and the twilight of the rolling plains", to sleep for once in a soft bed made up with sheets and blankets.[32] Ewart, like Graham, had a deep if idealised love of the English countryside.[33] The contrast between life in the city and life

---

30 See, for example, Stephen J. Hicks, and Wilfrid H.G. Ewart, *Practical Poultry Keeping for Small-Holders* (London: James Stephen, 1912).
31 Wilfrid Ewart (anon), 'At Neuve Chapelle', *English Review*, June, 1915.
32 Wilfrid Ewart (anon), 'After Ypres: the Record of a Southern Journey', *Cornhill Magazine*, September 1915.
33 For a useful exploration of the growth of Arcadian motifs in literature during and immediately after the First World War, see Paul Fussell, *The Great War and Modern Memory* (New York: Oxford University Press, 1975), pp. 231-69. For an example of such motifs in the work of Graham himself, see Stephen Graham, 'England's Most Lovely Island', *Living Age*, 25 October 1919.

in the countryside was later to become one of the central themes of *Way of Revelation*.

It is not clear exactly when Graham and Ewart first met, although they were certainly introduced by Colonel J.A. Stirling of 2nd Battalion Scots Guards, a man sufficiently open-minded to recognise that the two writers were likely to have a good deal in common despite their difference in rank (Graham described Stirling as "a fine soldier with a hidden river of poetry and music in his soul").[34] Ewart at first failed to realise that Graham was not only the well-known writer on Russia, but also author of the recently-published *Priest of the Ideal*, a book that he had read and admired as "an extraordinary thing".[35] The two men became friends, spending long periods of time "talking of life and literature", conversations in which they were sometimes joined by Stirling. Graham wrote several years later that he had been responsible for advising Ewart to become a full-time writer after the war, and even suggested the basic themes of *Way of Revelation*, much of which was written in the garden of Graham's cottage in Sussex. Ewart was absent on leave when Graham arrived in France, and when he returned at the end of April 1918 he only served with his unit for a few weeks, before taking a liaison post with the French army in Paris. In July and August, Ewart was ill and sent to Normandy to convalesce. Graham served as his batman during the final weeks of the war, when Ewart was working as a temporary Transport Officer,[36] organising the dispatch of rations and ammunition to the Front Line during the British advance towards the Canal du Nord. It therefore seems likely that the two men first met in May, but only really had the chance to cement their friendship during the closing weeks of the war, when their Battalion was following the retreating German army back through Flanders.

Graham's arrival at the Front in early April came about at a fortunate juncture: the fierce fighting of the previous few days had begun to ease. The author of the 2nd Battalion's War Diary noted at the end of March that the last week had been "very strenuous", and added that the men were "very tired", if still "full of heart", following operations to prevent a German advance south of Arras.[37] The arrival of 240 "fine" new troops, including

---

34 Graham, *Life and Last Words of Ewart*, p. 4.
35 Ibid, pp. 6-7.
36 Ewart, *Scots Guard on the Western Front*, p. 171.
37 The National Archives (Kew), WO 95/1223 (2nd Battalion Scots Guards War Diary, entry for 31 March 1918).

The Pilgrim in Uniform 145

Graham, came as a welcome relief. April proved to be a quiet month for the Battalion, although the calm was broken by the occasional sound of shells and sniper fire. The troops remained in the trenches until the middle of the month, when they were withdrawn to "uncomfortable" billets in the village of Barly, a few miles behind the lines. The greatest threat facing Graham and the other men during this time was probably the threat of fever, with around thirty men a day reporting sick, perhaps an early sign of the Spanish flu pandemic that was about to sweep Europe. May was also fairly calm, although by the middle of the month the Battalion was on alert for a possible German attack, whilst artillery exchanges led to a small number of casualties.[38] In June the 2nd Battalion moved to new positions near the village of Somerin, just a few miles away, where time in the trenches was punctuated by periods of rest spent training or in organised sport. Another move in early July to Berles-au-Bois changed the scenery but not the routine, although a band competition in the middle of the month provided some variety, at which the pipers of the Scots Guard acquitted themselves "very well".[39]

Although Graham's life during these months can hardly have been pleasant, given the grim conditions both in the trenches and the reserve areas behind the lines, he still had enough time to keep a detailed if episodic diary. He sketched out possible books he hoped to write, including a love story that would explore relations between the sexes, and mused on the possibility of undertaking a long tramp through France when the war was over. He pondered too about how the war would impact on the spiritual development of the various countries caught up in it. Graham found time to read extensively, devouring authors including Jack London and Lytton Strachey, as well as jotting down his thoughts on subjects ranging from army discipline through to the ribald songs recited by his fellow-guardsmen. His diary of the period is also full of the kind of maxims and reflections that had long preoccupied him ("We are on the threshold of a new era of Christianity").[40] Graham even responded to correspondents who wrote asking about his religious views, sending one letter in June to a Mr Browne in America, noting that he was an Anglican who had "great reverence" for Orthodoxy and Roman Catholicism, but was sceptical about any church

---

38 Ibid (2nd Battalion Scots Guards War Diary, various entries for May 1918).
39 Ibid (2nd Battalion Scots Guards War Diary, entry for 10 July 1918).
40 Graham Papers (FSU), Box 579, 49 (Diary for *Private in the Guards*).

that claimed a monopoly of truth.[41] The tedium of war in the early summer of 1918 at least gave him a chance to ponder some of the ideas that had concerned him so intensely during the years before he became a soldier.

Graham's Battalion began to see more active service in August, following the start of the Hundred Days Offensive, which led in due course to the collapse of the German armies and the Armistice of 11 November. In late August, the 2nd Battalion of the Scots Guards was involved in heavy fighting around the village of St Leger. In September its members took part in the fierce battles which led to the crossing of the unfinished Canal du Nord and the breaking of the Hindenburg Line.[42] Wilfrid Ewart later wrote a powerful piece about the battle, describing how the area round the canal appeared as a desolate landscape "devoid of pity or hope", littered with German and British casualties lying dead and dying in "the most perfect picture of human loneliness that eye of man ever looked upon".[43] Ewart was by now serving as a transport officer, and was not directly involved in the fighting, but his letters home show that he often went up to the Front Line.[44] The same was true of Graham himself (who was by now acting as Ewart's orderly). It is hard to judge the extent of Graham's involvement in the various battles in which the Scots Guards were engaged between April and November 1918 (his own diary casts surprisingly little light on his experiences). A careful reading of the evidence suggests that he probably missed the worst of the fighting but was certainly not altogether spared from danger. When he came to write *Private in the Guards*, early in 1919, he was able to draw on first-hand experience in describing the horrors of the Front.

The life of a soldier, with its alternating periods of frenetic activity and boredom, provided Graham with plenty of opportunity to reflect on the strange new world into which he had been plunged. He was impressed at the way his fellow-recruits adapted to the demands of war, stoically resigning themselves to terrors and privations they could once hardly have imagined, although the sights and sounds they encountered inevitably created a "terrible impression [...] in each man's eyes was the sign of shock and strain".[45] Graham was horrified at the way the fighting had destroyed

---

41 Browne Papers (Indiana University, Lilly Library), Graham to Browne, 3 June 1918.
42 For a description of this phase of the war see Wilfrid Ewart *et al*, *The Scots Guards in the Great War* (London, 1925), pp. 288-306.
43 Wilfrid Ewart, *When Armageddon Came* (London: Rich and Cowan, 1933), pp. 137, 141.
44 Ewart Papers (HRC), Letters, Ewart to Father, 1 September 1918.
45 Graham, *Private*, p. 176.

the landscape of eastern France, in which ruined villages and churches were interspersed with muddy fields and "sinister gas-stricken woodland". He was also appalled at the way the war had ripped apart French society, leading to floods of refugees and a break-down in traditional Catholic morality, as "every mother who possessed a pretty girl seemed to use her to sell bad coffee or wine to the soldiers who crowded in to flirt with her".[46] There were nevertheless moments when Graham, like Ewart, caught glimpses of a natural beauty quite at odds with the prevailing destruction. On Ascension Day he was able to sit for a time on a "daisy-covered bank" shaded by hawthorn bushes, listening to birdsong, relishing a beauty that "was infinitely high and broad above and infinitely deep within".[47] The vision was fleeting, though, soon marred by the sight of "sulphurous flashes of smoke" breaking from a battery, camouflaged in the valley below. The war sometimes seemed to produce its own eerie sense of beauty, such as the scene at Bourlon Wood near the Canal du Nord, where Graham saw how the ruined "enigmatical" church provided a curious contrast with the nearby village "with its long red chateau like a palace".[48] The sense of unease created by such a sight must have been heightened by the knowledge that his own Battalion had been involved in a terrible battle there the previous year, in which German machine-gunners mowed down dozens of troops.[49] It was a scene that Wilfrid Ewart was later to re-create with brutal vividness in *Way of Revelation*:

> Two men had fallen across each other one dead, the other mortally wounded. Every few minutes the latter would make fruitless efforts to rise and crawl. For these two the worst was reserved. Through the air sailed a little silent spot of light. Adrian recognised it as a phosphorous bomb; he held his breath. Descending upon the topmost of the two prostrate figures, it slowly flared up. At once the dead man was burning; the other, his clothes alight, dragged himself painfully a few yards, then lay still, face downwards.[50]

Although Graham was spared the worst fighting suffered by veterans like Ewart, he saw plenty of horrific sights to remind him of the brutality of war. When *Private in the Guards* was first published, many readers were shocked by its author's frank acknowledgement that British troops had

---
46 Ibid, p. 181.
47 Ibid, p. 182.
48 Ibid, p. 239.
49 Ewart *et al*, *Scots Guards in the Great War*, pp. 222-28. Cecil, *Flower of Battle*, pp. 142-44.
50 Wilfrid Ewart, *Way of Revelation* (London: G.P. Putnam, 1921), p. 477.

mistreated and executed prisoners, something that Graham and Ewart both noted in their private diaries and letters:

> The regimental tone absolutely forbade admiration of anything in connection with Germans. 'Killing Huns' was our cheerful task as one of our leaders once told us. The idea of taking prisoners had become very unpopular among the men. A good soldier was one who would not take a prisoner. If called on to escort prisoners to the cage, it could always be justifiable to kill them on the way and say they tried to escape. Did not so-and-so get a D.C.M. for shooting prisoners? "Thank God, this battalion's always been blessed with a C.O. who didn't believe in taking prisoners," says a sergeant. Captain C, who at Festubert shot two German officer-prisoners with whom he had an altercation, was always a hero, and when one man told the story, "That's the stuff to gi' 'em," said the delighted listeners.[51]

Graham condemned such acts, not least because of the likely consequences for British soldiers taken prisoner by the Germans, but he recognised that he was not immune to the way in which war suppressed human sympathy. He recalled how on one occasion he went out to see the body of a German sniper, supposedly shot dead by members of the Welsh Guards, only to find that the man was still alive, though badly wounded:

> There he was on a dunghill in the squared yard of the farm-house [...] He had apparently been wounded the day before, for his right arm was swathed in linen and had been in a sling. His face was pink and white, very white and livid pink, and his little waxy eyes stared at us without expression. His white breast heaved up and down. So we looked at him and pitied, and went away. And he lay on the dunghill and the rain washed down, and I suppose he died in a few hours [...] "Can he stand on his spindles?" asked the kindest man at our Red Cross post. "No? Then let him lie where he is. The Taffies ought to have carried him in; he's not our case."[52]

Readers of *Private in the Guards* were also told how the bodies of the dead were often treated with callous disregard, their bodies ransacked for money or jewellery, whilst the pilferers in their haste to obtain booty threw away family letters and photographs that fluttered around forlornly in the wind.

Following the crossing of the Canal du Nord and the breaching of the Hindenburg Line, in September 1918, German resistance began to weaken quickly, allowing British forces to move eastwards far more easily than before. The War Diary of the 2nd Battalion Scots Guards describes in some detail how its members were able to advance rapidly across the

---

51 Graham, *Private*, p. 191.
52 Ibid, p. 195.

flat countryside south of Cambrai towards the Belgian frontier. By early November, the Battalion had reached the town of Maubeuge, which was taken by British forces without a fight, as the defending German forces retreated and headed for home. Recent military defeats had by now provoked enormous political unrest back in Germany, leading the Kaiser to prepare to abdicate and seek refuge in Holland, whilst informal peace-talks had in any case been taking place for some time ahead of the formal armistice declared on 11 November. Graham later claimed to be one of the first in the Battalion to hear the news, since he took receipt of the message brought by the brigade-runner, and quickly relayed details to his colleagues. Their reactions echoed those felt by men up and down the Front Line: a mixture of relief and disbelief laced with uncertainty about what the immediate future held. The senior officers in the Scots Guards, as in other British regiments, were anxious to disabuse their men of any thoughts of rapid demobilisation (Graham noted in his diary that many soldiers felt they had "done their bit" and should be shipped home immediately).[53] The members of the 2nd Battalion were therefore kept busy drilling and marching in the week following the armistice. They were also issued with new kit for an advance into Germany itself. The terms of the armistice set down that a number of major towns in the west of the country were to be occupied by Allied troops. Although the other ranks were not at first aware of the situation, the 2nd Battalion Scots Guards was one of those given the task of occupying Cologne. In late November they left Maubeuge to begin the long march to the Rhine.

The members of the Scots Guards soon witnessed the graphic consequences of war. They passed emaciated British Prisoners-of-War heading westwards, and overtook French civilians returning home, pushing their few meagre possessions in wheelbarrows. They were hailed as liberating heroes in Belgium, and feted by the local population in towns like Marchiennes, where they were treated to drinks by people whose lives had been shattered by four years of occupation and war. The Battalion then headed southwards through the Belgian Ardennes, across a landscape littered with the grizzly carcasses of slaughtered cows, killed by the retreating Germans, either for food or simply in an act of mindless destruction. Although the men of the 2nd Battalion were at first fuelled with bitter anti-Germanism, when they crossed into Germany their sentiments

---

53 Graham Papers, Box 579, 49 (Diary for *Private in the Guards*).

began to change, as they realised how much the local population had suffered in the war. Graham later recalled how the "roaring lions" who had demanded vengeance were transformed into "doves", ready to look sympathetically at faded family photographs of young German men, dead or missing at the Front.[54] The universality of suffering created new and unlikely bonds. Graham himself quickly came to loathe the nationalism of the British press and its attempts to stoke up hatred of Germany. By the time he published the final draft of *Private in the Guards*, he already doubted the morality of the Treaty of Versailles signed in June 1919, which imposed harsh terms on the defeated Germans:

> Whilst we were at Cologne the British General Election, which practically left the soldier without a voice in the State, accomplished itself in all its dishonouring vulgarity, with its cries of "Make the German pay!" and "Hang the Kaiser!" Thanks to that election, Great Britain came to the Conference Table at Paris with no moral voice, no ideals – only with a notion of bargaining and of sheltering herself from responsibility behind either Clemenceau or President Wilson. Was it not a disgrace to our political and governmental system – to come to Paris without Christian principle or national dignity, after all the sufferings, all the deaths for the cause?[55]

The 2nd Battalion arrived in Cologne at the end of December 1918, where the men continued to carry out route marches and bayonet drills, as well as parades for the numerous foreign dignitaries who passed through the city. Graham himself did not spend long in Cologne. His official war record states that he fell ill with bronchitis and "disordered action of the heart" early in 1919, and was discharged in February with a 30% disability pension, to be reviewed after one year. He was also awarded the British War Medal and the Victory Medal (which were awarded to all those who saw service during the Great War). Graham had, however, in November written to Lord Ruthven – the Commanding Officer of the Scots Guards – requesting permission for an early discharge so that he could return to London and write up his book describing his experience in the ranks. Ruthven gave his enthusiastic support, noting that he looked forward to learning about "the life and thoughts of a private soldier on active service", with the result that Graham was able to return home earlier than his less fortunate comrades-in-arms.[56] Once back in Frith Street, he gratefully wrote 'A Litany for a Discharged Solider', never published, designed to remind himself and

---

54 Graham, *Private*, p. 286.
55 Ibid, p. 300.
56 Graham Papers (HRC), Letters file, Hore-Ruthven to Graham, 13 December 1918.

others who returned unscathed from the trenches to be thankful for their good fortune and victory:

> Whereas you might have been dead you are alive – Praise God!
>
> Whereas you might have become a slave you are free – Praise God!
>
> Whereas your country might have fallen she stands – Praise God!
>
> Whereas your children might have been starved they are fed – Praise God![57]

Graham must have been an unusual member of the Scots Guards, but he seems to have got on well with his fellow-guardsmen, subsequently providing a number of them with temporary accommodation at Frith Street when they had nowhere else to stay. He certainly left a deep impression on Wilfrid Ewart, who painted a vivid portrait of his orderly in a letter to his sister, written just a few weeks before the end of the war. His words suggest that Graham still retained at least some of the outlook he had developed in the years before joining the army:

> You must meet Graham one of these days and have him autograph your book [*Priest of the Ideal*] ... You would find him a most curious fellow but I think he is a very fine man as well as a very clever one. His talk is even more difficult to understand than his books but there seems to be a breadth, strength and "humanity" about him which I have never know[n] approached in our limited intensely mediocre circle. I can't imagine him going down at, say Knightsbridge or 8 Eaton Place. But does it matter? I have an idea that I should like to accompany him on one of his wanderings after the war.[58]

Graham seems to have come through his experiences remarkably unscathed in both body and soul. He wrote many years later that his time in the trenches had made him "more critical and objective". Many of the books he wrote during the first half of the 1920s were certainly very different in tone from *Quest of the Face* and *Priest of the Ideal*, yet the change in his outlook was not as great as he later claimed. There had always been two sides to Graham's personality – one practical and the other visionary – and his time in khaki did not resolve the tension between them.

Graham was back in London by the end of February 1919, where he spent the next few months working on the manuscript of *A Private in the Guards*, although it was not published until the end of the year when he had already left for a long trip to America. The success of the book was important

---

57 T.I.F. Armstrong (Gawsworth) Papers (HRC), Misc. (Stephen Graham, 'Litany for a Discharged Soldier').
58 Wilfrid Ewart Papers (HRC), Letters, Ewart to Angela (sister), 1 August 1918.

to him, as he was determined to prove to himself and the world "that my literary gift, such as it was, did not depend on Russia and was not shattered by Revolution".[59] Graham was apprehensive that he might face criticism for his unflattering account of the training regime at Little Sparta but, in the event, the reviews were quite positive.[60] He also received praise from some of his old colleagues in the Scots Guards. Colonel Stirling described it as "the best war book I have read so far".[61] Lord Ruthven believed that Graham's depiction of Little Sparta was "absolutely correct", and confessed himself appalled upon hearing of the depth of the gulf between officers and men.[62] Graham also received letters of congratulation from well-known public figures including Conan Doyle and Lord Northcliffe.[63]

The press coverage was mixed. The *Morning Leader* noted that "the whole country has been shocked and astounded by the revelations".[64] The *Daily Express* observed that *A Private in the Guards* had raised a "great commotion".[65] Some readers were furious that the publication of the book had encouraged newspapers to open their columns to former guardsmen wanting to complain about their treatment at Caterham. One retired medical officer in the Guards wrote to *The Times* condemning Graham for casting "a very cruel aspersion" on the NCOs charged with enforcing discipline. He added that the process of forging a "squad of recruits into shape" could hardly be carried out by men "in whose mouths butter would not melt".[66] The controversy even reached Parliament, where calls were made for an inquiry into the allegations raised by Graham. Winston Churchill as War Minister rejected the demands, suggesting that the claims were of "a vague and very general character", a view supported by many other members of the House of Commons, who fretted about the "injury to the Navy and Army" caused by *Private in the Guards*.[67] Graham was in New York when *Private* was published, and seemed quietly satisfied with the sensation it made, telling a friend that the book "has simply taken the country like a

---

59 Graham Papers (HRC), Works File, *Wonderful Scene* (autograph).
60 See, for example, *Manchester Guardian*, 5 November 1919.
61 Graham, *Wonderful Scene*, p. 180.
62 Graham Papers (HRC), Letters file, Hore-Ruthven to Graham, 22 December 1919.
63 Ibid, Conan Doyle to Graham, 30 November 1919; Northcliffe to Graham, 18 May 1920.
64 *Morning Leader*, 24 March 1920.
65 *Daily Express*, 8 November 1919.
66 *The Times*, 6 November 1919.
67 *Parliamentary Debates (Commons)*, 4 November 1919, cols. 1307-8.

storm [...] Every man who served in the Guards seems to be writing to the press to corroborate what I have said".[68]

All this furore lay ahead in the spring and summer of 1919, as Graham tried to re-establish his life in London. He discussed religious questions on a number of occasions with H.G. Wells, who had for some years been familiar with Graham's work, but the two men predictably found they had little in common. He also renewed his acquaintance with Hugh Walpole, the novelist who headed the Anglo-Russian Propaganda Bureau in wartime Petrograd, but the two men had never got on, and Graham remained convinced that the author of *The Dark Forest* and *The Secret City* was "not creative or idealist".[69] The same could hardly be said of Algernon Blackwood, who had returned from Switzerland on one of his periodic sojourns in London, and, like Graham was earning money by contributing stories to publications such as the *Saturday Westminster*. Blackwood was a frequent visitor to 60 Frith Street, where he sometimes read out loud early drafts of his ghost-stories, as the gas lamps flickered and "made darkness visible" against the dark-green walls of the flat. Graham also renewed his friendship with Wilfrid Ewart, who was still serving in the Scots Guards in the spring of 1919, although he had already decided to leave the military to pursue his writing career.

Graham was marking time during these months as he considered his future. Whilst he discussed the situation in Russia with many of his friends, he had little hope that the situation there would improve in the coming years. He was sharply critical of Britain's role in the controversial Allied military intervention that took place during 1918-20, believing that it was inspired by a desire to defend British economic and financial interests, rather than to liberate Russians from Bolshevik tyranny.[70] Nor did he make any effort to cooperate with émigré organisations like the Russian Liberation Committee, which sought to mobilise foreign opinion against the Soviet government in Moscow.[71] He did however continue to pen articles with titles like 'The Hope for Russia', lamenting the fate of religion in areas controlled by the Bolsheviks, and attacking Bolshevism itself as

---

68 Vachel Lindsay Papers (Abraham Lincoln Presidential Library), SC926A, Folder 1, Graham to Charlotte Hallowell, 6 December 1919.
69 Graham, *Wonderful Scene*, p. 176.
70 See, for example, his remarks in Stephen Graham, 'Where is Holy Russia Now', *London Quarterly Review*, October, 1920.
71 On the Russian Liberation Committee, see Charlotte Alston, *Russia's Greatest Enemy: Harold Williams and the Russian Revolutions* (London: I.B. Tauris, 2007), pp. 150-53.

"a slave movement" dominated by Jews.[72] It will be seen in the following chapter that Graham's decision to pick up "a new thread at random", by going to America to study the position of the black population there, was designed above all to find a fresh outlet for his energies now that "Russia was out". In July 1919 he sub-let his flat in London, and headed off with Rosa to "very well-built and clean" Copenhagen,[73] where they boarded a ship bound for the United States. Graham's decision to spend time in the New World did not however mean that he had abandoned his interest in the old. When he returned from his trip to the United States, in the spring of 1920, he had already decided to spend much of the next year examining how the legacies of war were shaping developments in the Old World.

The question of how best to honour the sacrifices of 1914-18 provoked enormous debate in Britain during the early years of peace. The design of Sir Edwin Lutyens' Whitehall Cenotaph, submitted in the final weeks of 1919, created a good deal of controversy when it was made public. The simple slab-like structure attracted fierce opposition, both from those who wanted a memorial that was overtly religious in design, and others who wanted a more avowedly nationalistic monument.[74] Graham discussed the design with Lutyens, "a boisterous and facetious" man he had met through his father, and heartily approved the architect's view that the Cenotaph should celebrate the "memory of the dead of all creeds" (Lutyens had a long-standing interest in Theosophy and believed like his visitor that "all religions have some truth in them").[75]

Graham was also determined to use his pen to confront readers with the harsh realities of the slaughter that had so recently taken place on the continent. In August 1920 he set off on a three-month visit to the First World War battlefields, subsequently recounting his experiences in *The Challenge of the Dead*, which provided readers with a "collection of word pictures" describing Flanders and the Somme two years after the fighting stopped. The journey was also prompted by more personal motives. Although the final text of *Challenge of the Dead* said almost nothing about Graham's wartime experiences, his travels took him to the area south of Arras where he had first seen active service with the Scots Guards, giving him a chance

---

72 Stephen Graham, 'The Hope for Russia', *The Living Age*, 15 November 1919, pp. 395-99.
73 Graham Papers (FSU), Box 577, 10 (Various notes from 1921).
74 On the design and building of the Cenotaph, see Jay Winter, *Sites of Memory, Sites of Mourning: the Great War in European Cultural History* (Cambridge: Cambridge University Press 1998), pp. 102-5.
75 Graham, *Wonderful* Scene, pp. 217-18; Winter, *Sites of Memory*, p. 103.

to return in a time of peace to places he had first seen as battlefields. He was accompanied by Rosa, who was presumably anxious to see the places where her husband had fought,[76] although she was, as so often, entirely absent from the published account of his trip. A reader of *Challenge of the Dead* would have assumed that its author had travelled alone.

There was no shortage of British visitors to the First World War battlefields in the years after 1918. Graham bitterly described how some wealthy tourists liked to visit the worst places of slaughter for an hour or so, before moving on to "some French hotel where hot lunch and foaming beer [can] persuade the living that life is still worthwhile".[77] Other visitors were by contrast travelling to see the places where their loved ones had fallen. Graham's old friend Wilfrid Ewart went to the Somme in 1919 with his sister Angela, in the hope of finding the grave of her husband, who had been killed in the fierce fighting of 1916. The two roamed through the detritus that still littered the battlefield, picking their way among enamel sinks and bully-beef tins, searching for evidence of the place where Jack lay buried.[78] It was a sight that Graham was to see replicated time and again during his own visit a year later, describing how at one cemetery he saw an Englishwoman going "from grave to grave diligently examining the aluminium ribbons on which the names are fixed to the wooden crosses".[79] The cemetery was sited outside Ypres, a city which Graham described as "a terrible place still", its huge Cloth Hall destroyed, and its streets deserted in a city where "death and the ruins completely outweigh the living".[80] Outside the city he roamed through a devastated landscape, sometimes coming across the remains of bodies which had escaped the burial parties, or been exposed to the air by shifting earth. Many of the trees were still denuded of leaves, killed by the ravages of poisonous gas, providing stark evidence of the horrors that had taken place beneath their branches. Graham also went to Bourlon Wood near Arras, which he had first seen in September 1918, and found a place where "reality has become remote, remote as the last songs and shouts of the men who went through. Sadness

---

76 Vachel Lindsay Papers (Abraham Lincoln Presidential Library), SC926A, Folder 1, Rosa Graham to Charlotte Hallowell, 16 September 1919, in which Rosa refers to seeing the battlefields in "a very special way".
77 Stephen Graham, *The Challenge of the Dead* (London: Cassell 1921), p. 94, version available at http://archive.org/details/challengeofdead00grah.
78 Wilfrid Ewart, 'Pilgrimage', in *Scots Guard on the Western Front*, pp. 174-80.
79 Graham, *Challenge of the Dead*, p. 24.
80 Ibid, p. 36.

has covered the earth."⁸¹ The redemptive power of nature that had been so important to Graham throughout his whole life seemed to have fled the battlefields of France.

The scenes of devastation were repeated wherever Graham went. In the town of Albert in the Somme region he saw buildings,

> with gutted entrails half congealed and terrible to behold. There is a house that died simply of shock. But its neighbour vis-a-vis was hit by some striding giant with iron fist. Rows of houses are seen cowering, as if they had had their hands up trying to ward off the dreadful fate which stalked above them. Houses lie killed as it were in the action of flight, veritably in the act of treading on one another's heels in a frenzy to get away.⁸²

The town seemed dead and abandoned, as though it could never again provide a setting for the mundane rituals of ordinary human life. Graham was perhaps paradoxically also perturbed by other places where life seemed to be returning to normal too quickly, the past forgotten, its lessons unlearnt:

> The babies are rising, the younger men are growing, growing to hide all and everything. The nakedness of reality which we see to-day will be hidden in the shade by and by. These brand-new cemeteries, looking often so fresh and rich in their masses of brownstained wood, will pass. They will first be re-set-up in stone. 1921 will see them rolling out in new stone crosses, at first startlingly pallid and virginal, but as the months go on, getting gradually greyened and darkened, rain-washed, wind-blown, then falling a little from the straight. Flowers will bloom as new summers shine o'er the dead. Visitors will come. There will be a greater time of visiting the cemeteries and the battlefields than there yet has been. Gardeners will be conscientious, and then some less conscientious as the years roll by and visitors become less. Most of the cemeteries in the more obscure places will be half-forgotten and gone desolate. There must come a time when no more visit the burial-places of the great war than visit now the cemeteries in Crimea.⁸³

When he headed towards Paris at the end of his tour, presumably with Rosa, Graham seemed almost disheartened by the extent to which the population now sought only "gaiety", as though it somehow diminished the suffering of so many millions just a few years before. It was for this reason that he placed such emphasis on the need for both commemoration and reconciliation. Graham had long become uncomfortable with some of

---

81 Ibid, p. 132.
82 Ibid, p. 91.
83 Ibid, p. 96.

the more violent expressions of national hatred that were spewed out by British newspapers. He noted rather gnomically in an epilogue to *Challenge of the Dead* that "even Germans had to die that Europe might be free", and finished the book with a serious of aphorisms calling for the nations of the world to learn to act in the interests of humanity rather than their own selfish ends.

> It hath been said: "He liveth best who is always ready to die". It can be put in a new way: "He liveth best who is always ready to put all upon the Altar". Humanity is well served when nations are ready to sacrifice themselves for her good. She is worst served by the nations who still preserve the tribal instinct to fight and destroy their neighbours. She is worst served by the nations who are enslaving other nations. And that nation is most alive which has most people ready to sacrifice themselves and their estate. That nation liveth worst which contains the most selfish.[84]

Graham was instinctively sceptical about the formal mechanisms that were established after 1919 to prevent the world from ever again plunging into war, placing little hope in organisations such as the League of Nations, believing instead that real peace could only come about via an almost existential transformation of the human spirit.

A few months after returning to Britain from the battlefields, Graham set out once again on his travels, this time on a more ambitious trip of Europe, designed to gauge how the continent was adapting to the realities of the post-Versailles world. Rosa accompanied him, but once again remained invisible in the sketches Graham submitted on each of the countries he visited to *Country Life* (which subsequently appeared in 1922 in book form, under the somewhat convoluted title *Europe Whither-Bound or Europa Qua Vadis?*). He began his trip convinced that Europe was facing a crisis, in which the social and economic dislocations of the recent war might yet provide the conditions for Bolshevism to spread westwards, and consign "the pride of Christian culture" to "dissolution and death".[85] He spent most of his time in Central Europe, touring the new states that had emerged from the collapse of the Austrian and Ottoman empires, although he also visited Greece as the symbolic home of European culture. Graham's published account of his itinerary did not reflect his actual movements. His private

---

84 Ibid, p. 174.
85 Stephen Graham, *Europe Whither-Bound? (Quo Vadis Europa?): Being Letters of Travel from the Capitals of Europe* (New York: Appleton, 1922), p. 11, version available at http://archive.org/details/europewhitherbou00grah. The book was first published in Britain 1921 by Butterworth.

diary shows that he began his journey in Rome, before travelling to Greece, after which he headed across Yugoslavia and Bulgaria to Constantinople, and then went northwards through central Europe into Germany. In *Europe Whither-Bound?* he implied that he began his trip in Athens and only then travelled up through central Europe, by way of Constantinople, before heading south again towards Rome. Graham's decision to write up his journey in this way was prompted by a mixture of aesthetic and thematic concerns, since it allowed him to start his book with some general reflections about the challenges facing European civilisation in the symbolic setting of Athens, before providing readers with an account of his travels that was more ordered than the somewhat chaotic reality. It was an approach that became a marked feature of his travel writings in the 1920s.

Graham and Rosa arrived in Rome at the start of February 1921, where they visited St Peter's Cathedral and the Vatican, before travelling eastwards by boat from Brindisi to Athens via Corfu. Graham himself seems to have been somewhat underwhelmed by the experience, although Rosa was enthralled by the chance to wander through Rome and Athens, finding the cities "fragrant with memories of the past".[86] Graham and his wife arrived in Athens at a time when Greece was involved in a bitter dispute with Turkey, which periodically erupted into war, but he was already convinced that the Turks represented a barbaric civilisation, whilst the Greeks belonged to the mainstream of European culture. He was nevertheless perturbed to discover that many Greeks defined themselves by contempt for their Balkan neighbours, a phenomenon that he was to find time and again on his travels in Central and South Eastern Europe, an almost inevitable result of the recent creation of a series of new nation-states in a region that had for centuries formed a complex ethnic mosaic.

After leaving Athens, the Grahams travelled through Greek Macedonia and Albania, and on into the territory of the new state of Yugoslavia.[87] They stayed in Belgrade in rooms owned by their old friend Father Nikolai Velimirović, who had by now been appointed Bishop of Zicca. Graham quickly developed a series of friendships amongst members of the local Serbian intelligentsia. He and Rosa also travelled through the war-torn Serbian countryside, passing villages filled with "barefooted war-waifs,

---

86 Vachel Lindsay Papers (Abraham Lincoln Presidential Library), SC926A, Folder 1, Rosa Graham to Charlotte Hallowell, 10 May 1921.
87 For details of Graham's actual itinerary see Graham Papers, Box 578, 33 (1921 Journal).

skulking about in bits of old ruins".[88] Graham was under no illusions about the difficulties facing the new Yugoslavia, divided as it was between different ethnic and religious groups. He was particularly struck by the contrast between the "advanced" Croatian and Slovenian provinces of the north and the more backward Serbian lands to the south and east. It was nevertheless in Serbia that Graham felt most at home, not least because so many of the local population were Orthodox by confession, and used a Cyrillic alphabet similar to that of Russia. His war-time friendship with Velimirović and Dimitrije Mitrinović doubtless also meant that he was instinctively inclined to take a positive view of the Serbs. Graham found in Serbia many of the things that he once loved about Russia. He believed the peasantry to be instinctively religious, and was convinced that the character of the whole Serbian nation was shaped by its peasant roots, with the result that even Belgrade was for all its modern buildings populated by "the peasant come to town". He was certain that the Serbian people were "potentially gifted for literature, art, and thought", adding approvingly that "they are sincere and real in temperament, but despite their efforts probably not gifted for modern civilization as we know it".[89] Whilst Graham does not appear to have returned to the country for another nine years, the seeds of his passion for Serbia were sewn during his visit there in 1921.

From Yugoslavia Graham made his way alone to Sofia before travelling to Constantinople (Rosa stayed behind in Belgrade). The city was still in a political limbo, geographically situated in the territory of Ataturk's Turkey, but largely controlled by the British and French military. It was also home to tens of thousands of Russian refugees, who had fled the fighting in the Russian Civil War. By 1921 the remains of the White forces of General Wrangel were housed in a rag-bag series of camps a few hours from the city. Graham's time in Constantinople brought home to him with brutal clarity the fate of Holy Russia. Large parts of the city had been turned into a virtual Russian quarter, complete with shops and restaurants, along with offices staffed by Russian lawyers and accountants. There were also numerous pawnshops where refugees could obtain cash in return for the few meagre possessions with which they had managed to flee. Many of the women who worked in menial positions were from noble families, reduced to virtual destitution, and their presence helped create a strange world "where elegance mixes with melancholy". Graham was appalled to

---

88 Graham, *Europe Whither-Bound?*, p. 73.
89 Ibid, p. 77.

see the poverty and squalor faced by people who had once lived lives of great privilege, and were now forced to confront unaided "the elemental realities of life". He was even more horrified by the dark side of the city – "the hideous underworld of the Levant" – which absorbed countless young Russian women into a world of prostitution and "night-halls of low amusement". He recorded sadly how "a part of old Russia has come to Constantinople – to die".[90] Many of the refugees still clung to the desperate hope that Wrangel's armies might yet rebuild themselves with the help of the British and French, and return to Russia to drive out the Bolsheviks, but Graham did not share their faith. He met Wrangel at his base near Gallipoli, describing him as a "fine character" with "a strong military voice",[91] but was realistic enough to realise that the white émigrés who dreamed of restoring old Russia were living in a fantasy world. The huge changes that had swept through their homeland over the previous few years were too far-reaching to be reversed.

Graham left Constantinople at the end of March 1921. After collecting Rosa in Belgrade, the two of them headed north towards Budapest and Vienna, the twin administrative pillars of the old Austro-Hungarian empire, which had now lost their former imperial *raison d'être* in the post-war world. Graham was delighted to find himself once again "in Europe", rejoicing in the shops and cafes that flourished in both cities, although he feared that the desperate economic situation facing both Austria and Hungary might yet lead to unrest (Hungary had indeed had a short-lived Communist government in the summer of 1919). After leaving Vienna, the Grahams travelled on to Prague where Graham was predictably impressed by the efforts being made by the new government to establish Czechoslovakia's identity as a Slavic state, not least through the determined elimination of the German language from public life. He had the opportunity to interview Eduard Beneš, the Foreign Minister, who, seventeen years later, was luckless enough to be the Czechoslovak President at the time of the Munich Crisis. Graham also met members of the large Russian colony in Prague, who had fled there after the Revolution, in the process establishing one of the most important centres of Russian émigré intellectual life.

From Prague the Grahams took the train to Warsaw, a city Stephen had known well when it formed part of the Russian Empire, finding

---
90 Ibid, pp. 38-39
91 Graham Papers, Box 578, 33 (1921 Journal); Vachel Lindsay Papers (Abraham Lincoln Presidential Library), SC926A, Folder 1, Rosa Graham to Charlotte Hallowell, 10 May 1921.

it over-crowded and unappealing in its guise as capital of a newly-independent Poland. Graham was delighted by the recent Polish success in defeating an attack by the Soviet Red Army, but he remained enough of a Russophile to share the distrust of Poland that had been felt by many Russian nationalists before 1914. He was also convinced that the country was feared by its neighbours – something which Beneš had told him in Prague – and was particular critical of the way in which France was trying to develop its relationship with the Polish government in order to increase its influence across eastern Europe. There was indeed something almost apocalyptic about Graham's conclusion to his chapter on Warsaw in *Europe Whither-Bound?*:

> The Poles are showing that there is yet national tragedy ahead for them. They will be deceived by some nations and slaughtered by others. What have we raised her from the dead for but to live again, to live and let live. All have rejoiced in the risen Poland, even the old destroyers of Poland – Germany, Russia, and Austria, all rejoiced until they realized the nature of the phantom. The beautiful white eagle that leapt from the tomb is a more sinister bird to-day, blood-ravenous, and scanning far horizons.[92]

The Grahams left Warsaw for Munich, subsequently travelling on to Berlin, where the once "prim" and "orderly" Prussian capital had been replaced by a disorderly city where shabby people thronged to cheap cinemas showing low-quality films (Rosa found the city "sick, dumb, disillusioned").[93] Graham's main interest was in seeing how the Germans viewed the world in light of their recent defeat on the battlefield. He was struck by the numbers of people he met who did not accept that Germany was responsible for the war (a principle that had been set down in the much-resented War Guilt clause of the Treaty of Versailles). He was also horrified to realise that there was still widespread support for the idea that the provinces of Alsace-Lorraine, returned to France under the terms of Versailles, should form part of a united Germany. Graham was not convinced that the German people were naturally bellicose (although one publisher later rejected his book on the ground that it was too "John Bull" in its language). If anything he belonged with those who considered that the victor powers should have done more to prevent the German people from feeling "resentful", though he could not rid himself of a sense that:

---

92 Graham, *Europe Whither-Bound?*, p. 140.
93 Ibid, p. 151.

> In our reckonings and prognostications we should keep in mind that the German is the centre body of the Teutonic race. He is down, but he is not finally beaten. His mind is resentful, and indeed full of the revenge instinct. He has not learned the lesson of humility and obedience in the great war. Who has? He believes he is meant to be master in the vast European plain which he has fitly named "Mittel Europa," and identified with himself.[94]

The atmosphere of unease and anxiety that Graham detected in most of the counties he visited was bolstered in Berlin by a brooding sense of resentment that Germany was a victim rather than the architect of its misfortunes.

The Grahams left Berlin for Paris, and then headed back home to London, where Graham found himself still further perturbed by developments. Although he welcomed the widening of the franchise that had taken place in 1918, he still fretted about the creation of "a democracy which languishes in ignorance", where voters did not understand the issues, and candidates were content to make "sentimental appeals to various popular prejudices". He was scathing about the quality of government ministers, along with commercialisation of more and more aspects of daily-life, including the press from which he largely derived his income, although he retained some hope that "the spirit of England will overcome the vulgarity of the age".[95] Paris was by contrast a far more self-confident city, where the streets were better-kept than in London, although even here all was not well. Graham was deeply perturbed at the foreign policy pursued by the *Quai d'Orsay*, which, he believed, was based on the old-fashioned principle of promoting national interest to the exclusion of all else, a policy that he feared would in time foster the same kinds of tensions that erupted in 1914:

> France wishes to run this new Europe which has come into being, on the old lines, playing with hatreds and jealousies and conflicting interests as a chessplayer with his pieces. The idealists of England and America want to eradicate the jealousies and hatreds and run the same new Europe on principles of pure love. France says human nature never changes. Britain and America say human nature has progressed with them and it must progress similarly in Europe. France's final answer is laughter. So constant is France's amusement at the expense of the Anglo-Saxon that she has adopted the *sourire ironique* as something necessary to typical beauty in a Frenchman.[96]

---

94 Ibid, p. 174.
95 Ibid, pp. 201, 205.
96 Ibid, p. 214.

Graham's trip across Europe had convinced him that politics, both at home and abroad, had to be based on a new footing if the disasters of 1914-18 were not to repeat themselves in the near future. A few months after he returned he wrote to a friend in the USA fretting that without major changes Europe was heading "toward complete catastrophe".[97]

Graham was not alone in believing that a lasting international peace demanded something more than a new system of collective security of the kind institutionalised by the League of Nations. One of the most elaborate attempts to consider the whole question came from his old friend Dimitrije Mitrinović who, in 1920-21, contributed several dozen columns on 'World Affairs' to the periodical *New Age*, still edited at this time by the literary critic A.R. Orage.[98] Many of these articles were extraordinarily complex, weaving together a host of economic and psychological issues. At their heart was an attempt to think through the metaphysical foundations of international life, in order to show how a genuinely peaceful global order needed to rest on something more than mere paper agreements between governments. Mitrinović was determined to take issue with the prevailing view that international conflict was simply the result of a struggle for economic advantage. He instead suggested that "there remains a residue of desire, after the economic need has been satisfied, which, unless it be sublimated in a higher satisfaction than war can provide, would impel nations to war long after the economic necessity ceased to exist". He went on to argue that:

> The assertion that Mankind is a single species needs to be supplemented by the assertion that Mankind is One Man; and this again must be particularised in the assertion that every man is that man. It may be said that there is something mystical in this; but the truth is, as has often been said elsewhere, that Mysticism is common sense; and it is in this sense that the assertion is made and can be verified – that every man is at one and the same time individual and universal, both Man and Mankind.[99]

Many readers of *The New Age*, along with a number of its sponsors, were not impressed by the abstruse language used by Mitrinović to articulate his vision of international order. He was however at this stage of his life

---
97 Van Wyck Brook Papers (University of Pennsylvania, Rare Book and Manuscript Library), MS Coll. 650, Box 17, Folder 1149, Graham to Brooks, 12 January 1922.
98 The articles were in fact often jointly authored between Orage and Mitrinović. For details see Philip Mairet, *Autobiographical and Other Papers* (Manchester: Carcanet, 1981), pp. 181-83.
99 *The New Age*, 27, 16 (19 August 1920).

enormously influential on Orage, whose mind was well-attuned to "the transcendental idealism" articulated by the Serb, responding eagerly to "a gospel of world salvation inspired by the perennial philosophy and the Christian revelation".[100] Orage himself had long been interested in esoteric thought in all its various guises, and in 1922 he headed off to Fontainbleau where he worked for a number of years with the elusive Russian-Greek sage G.I. Gurdjieff. Nor was there anything unique about the attempt by Mitrinović and Orage to interpret the contemporary situation through a prism that emphasised the spiritual realities concealed by the material world. In 1921, a new publication appeared in London, under the title *The Beacon*, whose opening editorial suggested that the world was "figuratively in something like Stygian darkness at this new epoch in the world's history". It went on to promise that future contributors to the journal would seek "to clear the path of conventionalities" and "stand definitely against materialism". The editorial also declared that although some believed that the churches had failed, "it must be remembered that Christianity [...] has always shown adaptability to new surroundings".[101] The articles in *The Beacon* were very wide-ranging, touching on subjects ranging from politics to aesthetics, but many of them spoke of the importance of fostering "vital religion" and "spiritual truths", rather than "ready-made systems [that] are of little use to anyone who has emerged from the nursery stage of life".[102] A large number also focused on the international situation, arguing that "after the terrible experience through which the world has passed, there can surely be little need of emphasising the necessity for Spiritual Regeneration as the Basis of World Reconstruction".[103] It was a view that Stephen Graham had long come to accept.

Much of Graham's published work during the immediate post-war period appears at first glance to be less esoteric in tone than his earlier works. The language he used in *Private in the Guards* and *Europe Whither-Bound?* was more prosaic than the youthful metaphysical speculations that filled books like *Vagabond in the Caucasus* and *A Tramp's Sketches*. Graham himself hinted on occasion that this was a result of his experiences in the trenches, but, as was seen earlier, the reality may have been more

---

100 Mairet, *Autobiographical Papers*, p. 177.
101   *The Beacon*, 1 (1921-22).
102   G.R. Dennis, 'Hidden Treasures', *The Beacon*, 1 (1921-22); L.W. Fearn, 'Creative Christianity', *The Beacon*, 1 (1921-22).
103   Sydney T. Klein, 'Spiritual Regeneration as the Basis of World Reconstruction', *The Beacon*, 1 (1921-22).

complex, reflecting above all a deliberate effort to produce a new kind of commercially-viable work capable of appealing to a wide readership. The *private* diaries and journals he kept throughout the post-war years contained countless jottings about religious and spiritual matters, as well as more mundane notes about the places he had seen and visited. Graham frequently noted down such aphorisms as "Believe in the hidden hand which is working for good". Even when he served in the trenches, he still believed that the world was on "a new threshold of Christianity", and that he himself had a "splendid destiny" fuelled by "an infinite love to Lord the Father".[104] The very first issue of *The Beacon* contained the opening words of Graham's *Credo*, a lengthy document that eventually ran to twenty-three chapters, serialised over a number of issues. Graham himself described it many years later as a kind of prose-poem "written in rhythm". It is in reality almost impossible to classify the *Credo*, but it can perhaps best be described as a series of aphorisms, loosely connected by a conviction that there was a need for a new domestic and world order rooted in an individual and collective spiritual renewal. It began with a rousing declaration that:

> The old order of life in the world is dying and a new order of life is rising to take its place. Nothing can stop it. It grows out of the collective human heart and the hidden forces. It is not advanced by thought; it is not brought about by propaganda – it grows. It does not arise from one man's action or one man's prominence, but comes of all men.

The *Credo* went on to demand the abandonment of all forms of egoism, calling on nations to learn "to act not for their own sake alone but for humanity's sake", just as at a lower level families had to learn to live for the nation and "men to live for their families". This ladder of affinities would, in turn, ensure that "patriotism has had its day" and "soon it will be the morning of world-patriotism". Graham argued that as this new spirit permeated humanity, so "nations shall not hold other nations in thrall". Economic peace would reign in a world without tariffs or customs-barriers. Graham was no clearer about the foundation of this new consciousness than Mitrinović had been in his *New Age* articles. As so often before, he was critical of the churches, suggesting that "Christianity flows around and about church doors and will not or cannot go in", with the result that "something that is not Christianity sits in most of the churches". It was of course the supposedly authentic spiritual form of Christianity that Graham

---

104   FSU (Graham Papers), 579, 49 (Diary for *Private in the Guards*).

believed had the potential to spread and reveal its message that "material wealth [is] dust and ashes". The salvation of humanity depended above all on a rejection of the materialism of the world.

The *Credo* is perhaps best read as a form of poetry, rather than a formal analytical critique of the human condition, relying above all on its evocation of a new form of spirituality that could alone transform the world. The portentous tone inevitably infuriated some readers ("a deliquiscence of undisciplined emotion"),[105] although it was in tune with many of the other articles that appeared in *The Beacon*, albeit articulated in a form that was unusually elusive and opaque even for that publication. Graham's *Credo* was written at a time when he was in something of a state of emotional and intellectual flux. Despite (or perhaps because of) his experiences in the trenches he was still deeply interested in struggling against "the New Materialism". The very nature of the *Credo* meant that it touched on everything from art to philosophy. Graham's reflections on the need for new forms of international unity, based on a conception of the common foundations of humanity, were echoed by his emphasis on the organic character of all aspects of human life (a position he had of course sketched out many years before in his youthful *Ygdrasil*). The language he used makes it difficult to relate the *Credo* in any straightforward way to Graham's own experience of the trenches or his subsequent witness to the problems faced by post-war Europe. It was nevertheless fuelled by a powerful sense that human conflict in all its forms was the product of egoism and materialism, which could only be overcome via a spiritual revolution across the whole world, a vision that he had sketched out in previous works like *Priest of the Ideal* and *Quest of the Face*. Its quasi-poetic form was designed to provide readers with insights and ideas of a kind that they were unlikely to receive from their daily newspaper.

Graham's dislike of the New Materialism was still strong enough for him to devote a chapter of his memoirs to the subject more than forty years after his *Credo* appeared in *The Beacon*. During 1922 he attended a number of lectures at the Aristotelian society, including one by the celebrated Marxist biologist J.B.S. Haldane, who sharply attacked any trace of an idealist philosophy that "depends on the mind of man". Graham was predictably not impressed by a philosophy that had "no room for the hypothesis called God", and feared that the widespread acceptance of such views would

---

105   *New Age*, 10 November 1921.

The Pilgrim in Uniform 167

reduce idealism to little more than a blue-print for progress, rather than a particular way of experiencing the world.[106] Nor however was he much more impressed by the Russian philosopher-guru P.D. Uspensky, who spent time in London during the early 1920s, where his obscure teachings on "the Fourth Way" attracted interest from several members of the British aristocratic elite.[107] He was equally sceptical about the ideas of G.I. Gurdjieff, who gave a number of lectures in Britain during this time, before setting up his celebrated institute at Fontainbleau.

Graham was always suspicious of those who set themselves up as gurus whose self-appointed task was to enlighten their disciples (it was one of the reasons why his relationship with Dimitrije Mitrinović became increasingly strained in later years). Nor did he have much sympathy for the abstruse language favoured by both Gurdjieff and Uspensky. Although Graham had himself acquired something of a cult following over the previous few years, largely as a result of *Priest of the Ideal*, he insisted (not altogether accurately) that his starting point was "the world as I found it" rather than any elaborate metaphysical insight.[108] When the novelist Allen Upward tried to insist that he should devote all his energy to showing the world "how to revive something of the spiritual life in our frightful den of thieves",[109] Graham demurred from such a task, rightly concluding that his elderly friend was suffering from a despair that had distorted his judgement (Upward later committed suicide). Graham was, for all his continuing idealism, as sceptical of many of the idiosyncratic lunacies of the Higher Thought as he was of the banalities of the New Materialism.

The themes articulated in the *Credo* had of course been visible in Graham's work from the time he first went to Russia. His focus on the spiritual rather than the institutional dimension of religion had been a feature of his books since he published *A Vagabond in the Caucasus* ten years earlier. So too was his emphasis on the ephemeral character of the material world. And, of course, the idea that real social and political change required a revolution in the hearts and minds of individuals had underpinned his collaboration with Mitrinović in 1915-16 over the proposed secret society. Although it would be futile to look to Graham's work at this time for

---

106 Graham, *Wonderful Scene*, p. 249.
107 For a lively biography of Uspensky see Gary Lachman, *In Search of P.D. Ouspensky: The Genius in the Shadow of Gurdjieff* (Wheaton, IL: Quest, 2004).
108 Graham, *Wonderful Scene*, p. 250.
109 Graham Papers (HRC), Letters file, Upward to Graham, 9 December 1920.

anything approaching a coherent political or aesthetic philosophy, it is possible to identify a consistent series of insights and perceptions, which together helped to shape his understanding of the world. His experience in the trenches had removed some of the emotional exuberance and diffuse pantheism that had been a hallmark of much of his pre-1914 work. The brutal realities of death and destruction could hardly be dismissed as things of secondary importance. The *Credo* nevertheless revealed that Graham's self-proclaimed idealism had deep roots. The next three chapters will explore the development of the tension between his idealism and realism during the inter-war years, examining how the latter increasingly came to hold sway in determining the character of his fiction and travel-writing.

5. Searching for America

Graham's travels throughout Europe in the early 1920s were interspersed with a series of lengthy trips across the Atlantic. From 1919 to 1923 he travelled extensively throughout North America, from the East Coast to the Rockies, and Canada to Mexico, revelling in the sights and sounds of a continent that seemed, at least for a time, to offer the "wide open spaces" that helped to inspire his love of Russia so many years before. When Graham first encountered the United States during his 1913 trip, he was appalled at the social consequences of the country's rapid industrialisation. The grandeur of the landscape he saw on his long tramp through the rural parts of the North East did not compensate for the memory of the slums of New York and Chicago. Graham acknowledged that the United States represented the apogee of humanity's quest for material and scientific advance, but he made no secret of his belief that such progress had been purchased at the cost of huge spiritual disfigurement and human misery. The country nevertheless made a deep enough impression for him to return there six years later following the turmoil of war and revolution. The "other America" that Graham had glimpsed in the rural areas of the northeast persuaded him that the USA could not simply be dismissed as the apotheosis of rapacious commercialism. He expected to find this new America – a place both geographical and spiritual – beyond the great cities of the East Coast and the Midwest. In the post-war period Graham was searching for a new idyll, somewhere that could replace Russia in his imagination, and he hoped for a time that America could come to fill this void. His decision to return there had a kind of logic, even if at first glance it seems surprising that a man consumed by a fear of modernity should immerse himself in a country rapidly coming to define the world's understanding of the modern.

http://dx.doi.org/10.11647/OBP.0040.05

Graham wrote in his autobiography that his experiences of the trenches in 1918 meant that "I was no longer visionary and imaginative [and had become] less concerned with religion and more with social problems". As was seen in the previous chapter, this shift in focus was less clear-cut than he later claimed, although it helps to explain why he returned to the United States in 1919 with the intention of studying "the colour question".[1] Graham had been struck during his time in the trenches by the poor treatment of black troops in US divisions posted to France, and he was intrigued to see how they would be affected by their experiences once they returned home. His first trip to the United States in 1913 made him intensely aware of the country's racial divisions, even in the North, and he was repeatedly struck by the tension between the egalitarian rhetoric and grim reality of life in modern America. His new voyage across the Atlantic in 1919 proved difficult to organise, since civilian passengers were still a low priority at a time when US soldiers were being shipped back home. Graham eventually had to take passage via Denmark, arriving in New York in late summer. He was accompanied by Rose – for some reason the name 'Rosa' was by now giving way to 'Rose' – who was determined to see the New World with her own eyes. There are also hints that she may have been increasingly unwilling to continue playing the role of Solveig, content to remain at home in Frith Street whilst her husband travelled the world. She went with Graham on most of his trips during the first half of the 1920s – illness forced her to remain at home when he hiked in the Rockies in 1921 – only parting from him when he headed out into the countryside on lengthy tramps which would have been too exhausting for her. Although the strains in their marriage only erupted fully a few years later, there were signs of tension between the Grahams as early as 1918.

Graham planned to use his 1919 trip across the Atlantic to follow in the footsteps of the journalist and landscape architect Frederick Law Olmsted, whose book, *A Journey in the Seaboard Slave States*, aroused enormous interest and controversy when it was first published a few years before the Civil War.[2] Graham's *modus operandi* varied from the one he had previously used in his travels, since he could hardly pass unnoticed amongst the

---

1 Stephen Graham, *Part of the Wonderful Scene* (London: Collins, 1964), p. 173. For a useful overview of Graham's views on the United States after the war see, too, Stephen Graham, 'The Spirit of America after the War', *Fortnightly Review*, June 1920.
2 Frederick Law Olmsted, *A Journey in the Seaboard Slave States with Remarks on their Economy*, 2 vols. (New York: Dix and Edwards, 1856).

people he planned to write about, as had been possible in his encounters with pilgrims and peasants during his long tramps across Russia. He was systematic when sketching out his journey through the southern United States. Graham planned to start with a brief stay north of the Mason-Dixon line, before going south to Virginia and the Carolinas, after which he intended to head for Georgia and Louisiana. He also planned to make most of the journey by train rather than foot, not surprisingly given that he was for much of the time with Rose, although the Grahams did separate at one point so that Stephen could tramp through Georgia, following the path taken by General Sherman and his troops to the coast following the burning of Atlanta. Once he arrived in America, Graham covered the ground comparatively slowly, stopping in some places for two weeks or more, which provided him with an opportunity to conduct numerous interviews with both black and white Americans. He also visited black schools and churches, answering questions from audiences about his trip, and giving his reactions to the things he had seen and heard. Graham also made detailed notes in his journal, in order to make sure he had the material he needed to write his book.[3]

Graham began his book *Children of the Slaves* by highlighting the familiar paradox that a country committed to "the development of free democracy" had tolerated slavery for so long and, since abolition, had struggled to manage the bitter divisions that it fostered in American society. In his introduction he made no effort to hide the horrors of the slave era, which he believed provided a graphic manifestation of "the devil in man", and proved that "no man is good enough to have complete control over any other man".[4] His principal focus was not, though, on the moral and material character of slavery as it existed in the years before the Civil War. Graham instead provided his readers with a picture of black America at the start of the third decade of the twentieth century. The discussion in the first few pages showed Graham's penchant for an essentialism that was both patronising and banal (attitudes that can be seen even more strongly in his journal of the time). He suggested that most black Americans had arrived in the United States "more morally pure than they are today", but had since "learned more about sin, and sin is written in most of their bodies". He also believed that many blacks wanted "revenge" for the wrongs that had

---

3 Graham Papers (FSU), Box 578, 18-19 (Journal of trip to USA 1919).
4 Stephen Graham, *Children of the Slaves* (London: Macmillan, 1920), p. 11, version available at http://archive.org/details/childrenofslaves00grah.

been done to their race (in the unpublished version of his memoirs, written many years later, he was sharply critical of those who campaigned for civil rights).[5] Graham was nevertheless insistent that most of the failings that supposedly characterised black Americans could be traced back to the evils of slavery rather than to colour. This somewhat reductionist approach ran through his book and, at times, sat unhappily with its numerous anecdotes and vignettes, which taken together appeared to show precisely how difficult it was to generalise about the experience of the people he wrote about. Graham was never entirely successful in *The Children of the Slaves* at reconciling his twin roles of artist and sociologist, a flaw that had been evident in many of his earlier writings on Russia.

Graham was well aware that the legacy of slavery was intimately bound up with the identity of the American South. Whilst he did not address the whole question directly, the phenomenon posed a particular challenge for him given that he was, like so many travellers, bewitched by the region's subtle blend of culture and climate. He recalled how as he made his journey southward:

> Crossing the Mason-Dixon line was rather a magical and wonderful event for me. After all, the North, with its mighty cities and industrialised populations, is merely prose to one who comes from England. Pennsylvania is a projection of Lancashire and Yorkshire, New York is a projection of London, and massive Washington has something of the oppressiveness of English park drives and Wellingtonias. But Southward one divines another and a better country. It has a glamour; it lures.

Graham went on to remember how:

> I journeyed on a white-painted steamer in the evening down the Potomac to Old Point Comfort, leaving behind me the noise and glare of Washington and the hustle of Northern American civilisation. It was the crossing of a frontier without show of passports or examination of trunks – the passing to a new country, with a different language and different ways. The utter silence of the river was a great contrast to the clangour of the streets of Philadelphia and Baltimore and the string of towns I had been passing through on my way South. Sunset was reflected deep in the stream, and mists crept over the surface of the water. Then the moon silvered down on our course; my cabin-window was full open and the moon looked in. I lay in a capacious sort of cottage bed and was enchanted by the idea of going to "Dixie".[6]

---

5 Ibid, p. 22; Graham Papers (HRC), Works File, *Wonderful Scene* (typescript), p. 167; FSU Graham Papers, 578, 19 (Journal of trip to USA 1919).
6 Graham, *Children of the Slaves*, pp. 26-27.

Graham skirted round the obvious paradox that it was precisely the soulless North which had fought for the end of slavery during the Civil War, and, even in the 1920s, provided a far more congenial home for the 'Children of the Slaves' than the former slave states. He did not, however, make any attempt to minimise the problems faced by the black population in the Southern states. Some of these were comparatively petty but still imposed harsh indignities on those who suffered them. Graham recalled how in Virginia some car dealers would not sell their more expensive models to black customers for fear that it would contaminate the brand. Nor did he shrink from discussing darker aspects of Southern culture, including the whole question of lynching. Graham also recalled that whilst staying in Georgia there were three reported lynchings in the state, including that of Paul Brooker, who was accused of sexually molesting a white woman. Brooker was attacked by a large crowd, who threw him to the ground, where he lay "maltreated but living; gasoline was poured over him, a lighted match was applied, and he was burned to death".[7] In a letter to a friend in New York, Graham noted how he feared "mob violence" was likely to grow still worse in the future.[8] He spoke to many Southern whites throughout his long journey, making no effort to hide their vitriolic racism from his readers, even though he acknowledged that most of the people he spoke to were polite if deeply suspicious of outsiders. Nor could Graham understand the mentality of whites "who boasted of having taken part in a lynching", adding that he had met "those who possessed gruesome mementoes in the shape of charred bones and grey dry Negro skin".[9]

Graham's attitude towards black Americans in the South exhibited many of the contradictions and prejudices typical of a British traveller of the period. He was happy to speak without any awkwardness of "the terrible odour of the blacks" that he first encountered in Norfolk Virginia. He also wrote about the black population in patronising terms as "a friendly, easy-going fond-to-foolish folk by nature", suggesting at one point that it was not yet clear whether most had sufficient education to justify receiving the vote.[10] Graham offered countless sweeping generalisations, such as his claim that black culture became more "stagnant" the further south he

---

7 Ibid, p. 161.
8 Vachel Lindsay Papers (Abraham Lincoln Presidential Library), SC926A, Folder 1, Graham to Charlotte Hallowell, 26 November 1919.
9 Graham, *Children of the Slaves*, p. 209.
10 Ibid, pp. 30, 210.

went (he was particularly disappointed by New Orleans, which he found a ramshackle and run-down place, rather than the city he had imagined of "wide open streets" and men dressed "all in white").[11] His portrayal of many of the individuals he met was, though, both sympathetic and vivid. He wrote movingly of a sermon given by a black woman in a chapel in Virginia that was "so rousing [...] that I had to do everything in my power to avoid breaking down under the influence and sobbing like a child".[12] He was also repeatedly struck by the intelligence and intellectual curiosity of the students he met in black schools and colleges, as well as the energy of a new class of black entrepreneurs who were determined to use their businesses to promote the welfare of the black community. Graham's journal notes also show that he was impressed by the civil rights leader William Dubois whom he interviewed at some length (Dubois provided him with introductions to many of the people he interviewed).

Although *Children of the Slaves* undoubtedly perpetuated many stereotypes, it made a genuine attempt to provide readers with an understanding of the complex situation faced by black Americans in the South in the years after the First World War, recording with sympathy their efforts to develop richer personal and community lives in the face of immense historic prejudice. The reviewer in the *Times Literary Supplement* even suggested that Graham was, if anything, "over-tender to the weaknesses of the negro".[13] The anonymous reviewer in the *Athenaeum* took a rather different line, suggesting that "Mr Graham's observations are more valuable than his reflections",[14] in effect suggesting that his gifts as a writer lay in reportage and anecdote rather than in his more formal reflections on the things he had seen and done. Graham's ideas also found an American audience through the pages of *Harper's Magazine*, which serialised at length his account of his tramp across Georgia following the footsteps of General Sherman, although the US edition of his book received surprisingly few reviews.[15] It may be that the whole question of race remained a deeply sensitive one even for the denizens of the East Coast literary establishment. Graham recalled many years later that *Harper's* had stopped running his articles following threats of a boycott by Southern advertisers.[16] His book

---

11 Graham Papers (FSU), Box 578, 18 (Journal of trip to USA 1919).
12 Graham, *Children of the Slaves*, pp. 82-3.
13 *Times Literary Supplement*, 11 November 1920.
14 *Athenaeum*, 5 November 1920.
15 Stephen Graham, 'Marching Through Georgia', *Harper's Magazine*, April 1920, May 1920.
16 Graham Papers (FSU), Box 573, 7, Graham to Hay, 18 November 1950.

was by contrast widely advertised in the black press (including *The Crisis*, the journal produced by the National Association for the Advancement of Colored People).

Although Graham never again wrote at length on the treatment of black Americans, his interest in the subject continued for some time to come, and he gave several lectures on the topic following his return to Britain in March 1920. He also offered help and support to the young black singer Roland Hayes during his first visit to London.[17] Despite Graham's claim that the war had changed his outlook on life, by making him more "critical and objective", his journey through the Southern states provided him with an opportunity to return to some of the questions that had preoccupied him in the years before 1917: the potential for the natural world to provide insights into the nature of existence; the devastating effect of industrialisation on traditional communities; and so forth. Whilst Graham was ambivalent about the "spiritual atmosphere" which he found in black chapels and churches, he believed that the black population was, like his beloved Russian peasantry, "very thirsty for religion".[18] He was also deeply sensitive to the charms of the Southern landscape, finding in it "an assurance of some new refreshment of spirit",[19] although the exuberantly pantheistic ethos of his earlier work had by now begun to fade. Much of Graham's interest in the South rested above all on his awareness that it provided a contrast to the commercial and industrial society of the North. Although he was far too aware of the harsh character of Southern culture to suggest that the Civil War had resulted in the wrong outcome – such an argument would have run counter to the whole tenet of *The Children of the Slaves* – he was still determined to show his readers that cities like New York and Chicago did not represent the best aspect of modern America. *The New York Times* journalist who suggested in 1913 that Graham was captivated by the wide open spaces of America precisely because they reminded him of Russia was, in a very real sense, correct. Graham's fascination with the United States was conditioned in large part by his desire to find a new place where he could feel at home.

Graham left New Orleans with his wife late in 1919, heading up the eastern seaboard by boat to New York, where they spent the following weeks in an apartment located across the street from Grand Central Station.

---

17 Graham, *Wonderful Scene*, pp. 233-34.
18 Graham, *Children of the Slaves,* p. 15.
19 Ibid, p. 27.

Graham was not at first enamoured by the city's literary scene, writing many years later that everyone he met was obsessed with politics rather than "the religious idealism in which I was most interested".[20] He did, however, meet a number of people who were interested in Theosophy, spending time in the Catskill Mountains at the home of one wealthy devotee, who surprised him with her eccentric insistence that the Holy Grail could be found in a New York church where it had been taken from its original home in Antioch.[21] He met the American Slavic scholar Charles Crane, whose daughter was married to Jan Masaryk, son of the new President of Czechoslovakia, and gave numerous lectures including one to an audience of 3,000 women at Carnegie Hall (a striking testimony to Graham's growing reputation in the USA). Graham also travelled to Boston and Philadelphia, speaking both on Russia and his recent trip through the South, in some cases displaying an entrepreneurial spirit by organising the hire of the hall himself.[22] Despite his initial dislike of the New York literary scene, he was extremely successful in meeting some of the city's most influential editors and publishers. Graham stayed with Ellery Sedgwick, editor of the *Atlantic Monthly*, and through him met the architect Ralph Cram, who had played an enormous role in the American gothic revival ("a fine architect, placing beautiful edifices among the wildernesses of the commercial buildings in modern America").[23] He also made the acquaintance of younger writers and journalists, including Christopher ('Kit') Morley, who were later to become prominent figures in their own right. Graham came to like New York, despite his periodic diatribes against the city's lack of soul. Its literary elite provided him with a welcome that he could only dream about back in London, whilst his lectures there and in other cities on the eastern seaboard provided him with a useful additional income. When his personal life began to disintegrate during the second half of the 1920s, it was to New York that Graham travelled, secure in the knowledge that he had as many friends there as he did back home in Britain.

Although Graham was delighted to find in the Southern states of America a lifestyle that seemed largely free from the taint of materialism, the bleak legacy of slavery made it impossible for him to celebrate the region as the

---

20 Graham, *Wonderful Scene*, p. 198.
21 Graham Papers (HRC), *Wonderful Scene* (typescript), pp. 175-76.
22 For an account of Graham's almost frantic activities in this period, see Vachel Lindsay Letters (Abraham Lincoln Presidential Library), SC926A, Folder 1, Rosa Graham to Charlotte Hallowell, 10 February 1920.
23 Graham Papers (HRC), *Wonderful Scene* (typescript), p. 182.

'real' America, spared from the commercialism that dominated life in the great cities of the North. He was nevertheless reluctant to give up entirely on the idea of finding a place in the United States free from the scars of racism and commercialism. Graham was confirmed in his view by the unlikely figure of the self-proclaimed 'Prairie Troubador', Vachel Lindsay, whom he first saw perform in New York at the home of the political reformer Charles Burlingham, before welcoming him a few months later in Britain when Lindsay visited London and Oxford on a recital tour.[24] Lindsay had in his youth made a number of tramps across America as a kind of eccentric vagabond-poet, earning his food and lodging by giving impromptu recitals of his poems ('Rhymes Traded for Bread'), whilst promoting his idiosyncratic Gospel of Beauty to the bemused farmers of the Mid West. He subsequently acquired considerable fame with poems such as *The Congo* and *General William Booth Enters the Kingdom of Heaven*, which were composed to be read (or sung) aloud, and toured widely throughout the United States reciting his work to audiences that sometimes numbered in the thousands.[25]

By the time the First World War ended, Lindsay had established himself as a central figure in the Chicago literary renaissance, along with his fellow Illinois poets Edgar Lee Masters and Carl Sandburg.[26] It is not surprising that he quickly struck up a *rapport* with Graham, for Lindsay's *credo*, which he had previously set down in such books as *A Handy Guide for Beggars* (1916), closely resembled that of his new friend. Lindsay was sharply critical of the commercial and industrial character of America's great cities, describing himself as a "peddler of dreams" and "Troubador", who toured his country seeking "lodging in exchange for repeating verses and fairy tales".[27] He also shared Graham's instinctive nature-mysticism, describing

---

24 On Lindsay see Edgar Lee Masters, *Vachel Lindsay: A Poet in America* (New York: Scribners, 1935); Eleanor Ruggles, *The West-Going Heart: A Life of Vachel Lindsay* (New York: Norton,1959); Dennis Camp, *Uncle-Boy* (unfinished biography available at http://www.vachellindsayhome.org/#!uncle-boy). For details of Lindsay's tour in Britain, see the notebook by his mother in Abraham Lincoln Presidential Library (Springfield), Catherine Blair Collection, Box 2, Folder 1.

25 See, for example, Paul H. Gray, 'Performance and the Bardic Ambition of Vachel Lindsay', *Text and Performance Quarterly*, 9, 3 (1989), pp. 216-23.

26 On this subject see Dale Kramer, *Chicago Renaissance: The Literary Life of the Midwest, 1900-1930* (New York: Appleton-Century, 1966). For useful reminiscences of Lindsay see Eunice Tietjens, *The World at My Shoulder* (New York: Macmillan, 1938), pp. 48-57; Louis Untermeyer, *From Another World: the Autobiography of Louis Untermeyer* (New York: Harcourt Brace and Co, 1939), pp. 175-79, 182-83;

27 Vachel Lindsay, *A Handy Guide for Beggars* (New York: Macmillan, 1916), p. 5.

in his book how, when bathing in the Falls of Tallulah in North Georgia, the water flowed "like a sacerdotal robe [...] over my shoulders and I thought myself the priest of solitude". Lindsay believed that Nature could serve as a kind of balm "to those crushed by the inventions of cities", providing them with a sense of the ineffable that had been lost in the rhythms of industrial society.[28] Whilst Lindsay was, like Graham, a practising Christian – he belonged to The Disciples of Christ sect – he was convinced that a sense of the Divine presence was best sought not "in temples made with man's hands" but, rather, in the by-ways of "the infinite earth".[29] He also believed, like Graham, that beauty in both the natural world and in art represented a way of knowing God ("Let me give thanks to God for my artist friends, those who have given their hearts to the Christ of beauty, though they may not call on his name").[30] And, again like Graham, Lindsay believed that the visible world was in some sense merely a series of signs pointing towards another invisible universe (he was fascinated by Egyptian hieroglyphics, which he interpreted as symbolic texts, capable of yielding up their meaning only to those initiated in their mysteries).[31] Lindsay proclaimed his ideas with an extravagance and missionary zeal bordering on eccentricity: "For good or ill I have eaten of the flower of the Holy Spirit, the most dangerous bloom of the Universe. There are days when visions come in cataracts. With these pictures burning heart and conscience away, I would compass Heaven and Earth to make one proselytise. I would go through smoke and flame to prove that these my visitations come to me".[32]

Lindsay was not only interested in these questions from a narrowly aesthetic point of view. He also believed that he was destined to play a role in transforming America by encouraging the revival of local communities where art and education would be valued more than money and industry. In *Adventures Whilst Preaching The Gospel of Beauty* (1914), he described his conviction that:

> The things most worthwhile are one's own hearth and neighbourhood. We should make our own home and neighbourhood the most democratic, the most beautiful and the holiest in the world. The children now growing up

---

28 Ibid, pp. 39, 45.
29 Ibid, p. 132.
30 Dennis Camp (ed.), *The Prose of Vachel Lindsay* (Peoria, IL: Spoon River Press, 1988), p. 107.
31 Masters, *Vachel Lindsay*, p. 273; Camp, *Prose of Vachel Lindsay*, p. 109. Lindsay's longest statement about his attitudes towards hieroglyphics can be found in Vachel Lindsay, *The Art of the Moving Picture* (New York: Macmillan, 1922), pp. 171-88.
32 Quoted in Camp, *Prose of Vachel Lindsay*, p. 107.

should become devout gardeners or architects or park architects or teachers of dancing in the Greek spirit or musicians or novelists or poets or story-writers or craftsmen or wood-carvers or dramatists or actors or singers.[33]

In his fantasy *The Golden Book of Springfield* (1920), Lindsay imagined how his home town in Illinois might look in a hundred years' time, describing how the utopian Springfield of 2018 would boast a vibrant artists' colony but few bankers or businessmen. The town of his vision was also a place that prompted a passionate loyalty amongst its citizens (Lindsay had from a young age proclaimed the value of what he called "The New Localism").[34] The book represented a kind of sustained critique of East Coast America. Lindsay was increasingly convinced that the United States was a country of regions – and that the regions had to assert themselves in order not to be swamped by the tide of materialism flowing out from cities like New York and Chicago. The real America, for Lindsay, was to be found in the farms and small towns rather than the urban conglomerations. It was a philosophy guaranteed to appeal to Stephen Graham.

When Lindsay met Graham during his trip to London in 1920, the two men spent a good deal of time planning a long tramp together through some of the remotest areas of America. Graham was at first somewhat cautious about the prospect (he usually preferred to tramp alone).[35] Lindsay was increasingly tired of reciting his poems to large audiences, even though it brought him considerable popular acclaim, telling his fellow poet Sara Teasdale that he "would give almost anything to escape forever from the reciting and chanting Vachel [...] My whole heart is *set* on escaping my old self".[36] He was also increasingly disillusioned by his failure to persuade his fellow Americans about the value of his idiosyncratic vision of their country's future (*The Golden Book of Springfield* made almost no impression when it appeared in 1920). Lindsay was therefore ready to embark upon a new adventure which, he hoped, would provide a catalyst for transforming his life. He discussed with Graham the possibility of walking the US-Canadian border from east to west, or crossing the ice-bound Bering Straits that separated America and Russia, although his friend was not sure

---

33 Vachel Lindsay, *Adventures while Preaching the Gospel of Beauty* (New York: Mitchell Kennerley, 1914), p. 16.
34 Vachel Lindsay, 'The New Localism', *Vision: A Quarterly Journal of Aesthetic Appreciation of Life*, 4 (1912).
35 Vachel Lindsay Papers (Abraham Lincoln Presidential Library), SC926A, Folder 1, Graham to Charlotte Hallowell, 31 December 1920.
36 Ruggles, *Lindsay*, pp. 249-50.

"if it could be done".³⁷ The two men were joined on occasion by Wilfrid Ewart, who also hoped to travel to the United States, a country he had never visited before. The three men wandered through the grim streets of the East End, making travel plans, and imagining vast and remote landscapes against the backdrop of urban noise and squalor.

Both Lindsay and Graham were determined that their putative American tramp should be something more than a simple hike. Lindsay was entranced by the prospect that "a great English writer" like Graham would be able to describe "the America I see [which] never gets written down by anyone, least of all by me".³⁸ He was also convinced that he shared a particular vision of the world with his new friend, writing to Graham that "You and I are the only two men writing I know of who have the same general habits and moods of obedience [...] we are destined to see chunks of the world together".³⁹ The prospect of the tramp became for Lindsay something like a pilgrimage, particularly in the early months of 1921, when in a flurry of correspondence it was agreed that he and Graham should meet in Springfield in the summer before heading west to tramp through Glacier Park in the Rocky Mountains. Lindsay was, in all respects, a thoroughly other-worldly character given to fits of rapture and excess. Graham shared much of his friend's enthusiasm – he was eager to see the American West with his own eyes – but he was also much more attuned to the commercial possibilities of his forthcoming tramp. On his arrival in New York, equipped with little more than a capacious knapsack and a tweed hat, accoutrements that made him look decidedly eccentric in the heat of summer, he went to see Christopher Morley at the *New York Evening Post*. Morley, in turn, persuaded the paper's editor to commission a series of sketches from Graham detailing his experiences in Glacier Park. Graham was "thrilled" to imagine that he would "be read by the New York crowds streaming homeward on elevated trains" (he hoped his column would win new readers for his books).⁴⁰ Lindsay and Graham's trip also attracted coverage in the pages of American provincial papers ranging from the *Miami Herald* to *The Oregonian*.⁴¹

---

37 Graham Papers (HRC), *Wonderful Scene* (typescript), p. 210.
38 Vachel Lindsay Papers (HRC), Letters file, Lindsay to Graham, 9 February 1921.
39 Ibid, Lindsay to Graham, 11 February 1921.
40 Graham Papers (HRC), *Wonderful Scene* (typescript), p. 212.
41 *Miami Herald*, 26 July 1921; *The Oregonian*, 9 October 1921.

Both Graham and Lindsay published books about their tramp through Glacier National Park in the late summer of 1921. Graham's contribution took the form of a travelogue, published under the less-than-original title of *Tramping with a Poet in the Rockies*,[42] which contained a series of striking illustrations by the sculptor and illustrator Vernon Hill, who was paid a princely £25 for his work.

Figure 6: Two of the illustrations by Vernon Hill in Stephen Graham, *Tramping with a Poet in the Rockies* (London: Macmillan, 1922), pp. 1 and 201.

Lindsay, for his part, published a long poem cycle, *Going-to-the-Sun*, named after one of the peaks in the area. The six-week hike was valued by both men as much for the chance it gave them to discuss topics ranging from politics to literature as for the opportunity to engage with the wilderness first-hand. Lindsay ruefully noted that his friend was much fitter than he was, which meant that he spent much of his time "trying to keep Graham in sight when he was a quarter of a mile ahead of me climbing mountains absolute perpendicular".[43] He was nevertheless exhilarated at the beauty and isolation of the mountains.

Graham's published account of his experiences was, as so often, a fusion of the descriptive and the philosophical. He praised Lindsay as a man "who is something more than an entertainer. He has a spiritual message to the world and is deeply in earnest [...] I have rarely met such a rebel against vulgarity, materialism and the modern way of life". He went on to note that he had undertaken the trip with his friend to escape for a time from the world of European cities and instead be able:

---

42 For a review complaining that Graham should in fact have made his book less of a travelogue and more a literary biography of Lindsay, see *Times Literary Supplement*, 6 January 1922.
43 Vachel Lindsay, *Going-to-the-Sun* (New York: Appleton, 1923), p. 2.

> To sleep under the stars, to live with the river that sings as it flows, to sit by the embers of morning or evening fire and just dream away time and earnestness, to gather sticks to keep the old pot aboiling, to laze into the company of strangers and slip out of their company in time, to make friends with bird and beast, and watch insects and grubs – to relax and to be; that's my idea of tramping.[44]

Although both men were disappointed to discover when they arrived at Glacier Park station that the local hotel was full of tourists, interested only in pleasant views and gentle walks, within an hour of leaving they found themselves "in the deep silence of the mountains encompassed on both sides by exuberant pink larkspurs and blanket flowers and red paint-brush".[45] Lindsay was as ever wildly enthusiastic about their adventure, "roaring hurrah and making the mountains echo with his roar", whilst the more restrained Graham looked forward to nights spent relishing "the stars and moon and stillness". As the two men hiked on into the wilderness they felt like "Wagnerian pilgrims, toiling upwards in the ecstasy of mystical opera".[46] They walked by compass, leaving the trails behind, scrambling instead up the mountain-sides and through dense forests that filled the valleys below.[47]

Graham was deeply impressed by the sheer scale of Glacier National Park, which was in turn just one of a number of national parks in the American West, together making up tens of thousands of square miles of wilderness. Although *Tramping with a Poet* was surprisingly sparse in its description of the Park, Graham left his readers in no doubt of the importance of wild landscapes to humanity, looking forward to a time "when national wildernesses will have an acknowledged significance in our public life, when men and women of all classes of life will naturally retire to them for recreation – as naturally as people used to go to church on Sundays and for a similar reason".[48] Nor did he believe that mountains and wild landscape existed only in the far reaches of countries like Russia and America:

> The spiritual background of Great Britain is in the mountains of the North, among the Cumberland lakes and on the wild border. Or it is in the obscure grandeur of the Sussex Downs or on Dartmoor, or on the Welsh hills. Small

---

44 Stephen Graham, *Tramping with a Poet in the Rockies* (London: Macmillan, 1922), p. 11, version available at http://archive.org/details/trampingwithapoe002652mbp.
45 Ibid, p. 17.
46 Graham Papers (FSU), 578, 33 (Journal for 1921, entry dated 28 July 1921).
47 Catherine Blair Collection (Abraham Lincoln Presidential Library), Box 3, Folder 13, Lindsay to Mother, 3 July 1921.
48 Graham, *Tramping with a Poet*, p. 73.

though the mountains may be, they are continually in the minds of the English people. The way of escape is clear. And many of the bright spirits of England and Scotland have derived their strength direct from the hills.[49]

Lindsay and Graham both believed that the real heart of America was to be found in places like Glacier Park, away from the urban centres of the East. In their fireside conversations, "discussing everything",[50] Lindsay expressed his belief in "the war of the mountains and the desert against the town. Only the deserts and mountains of America can break the business-hardened skulls of the West". He also raged against "the praise of dollars and the implication that everything in the world has a commercial value or it has no value".[51] Graham, for his part, revelled in a world where "American and European civilisation ceased to fill the mind". He also made clear his belief – albeit in rather cod-religious terms – that life in the mountains offered insights into the mysteries of the universe that could seldom be found in the cities. The wilderness acquired for both men a distinctive status as a place of authenticity, a natural world in which it was possible to understand humanity's place in a world alive with religious and metaphysical meanings.

Graham's book was not only given over to rarefied reflections on the significance of landscape. It also contained humorous accounts of Lindsay's strong stone-ground coffee, with "a kick like a mule",[52] and the constant challenges involved in ensuring that the local bear population did not steal their food supplies. Graham also provided a series of rather arch (if affectionate) pen-pictures of his friend, with his "curious old-man of the woods appearance".[53] The presence of these lighter elements in the book was partly rooted in the commercial realities of publishing. Graham kept up a surprisingly detailed correspondence with Christopher Morley during his time out-west, sending him numerous pieces for the *Evening Post*. In order to appeal to the paper's readership he had to make sure his sketches were light and humorous.[54] When he came to write his book, though, he was still determined to regale his audience with his distinctive

---

49 Ibid, p. 72.
50 Christopher Morley Papers (Haverford College), Collection 810, Graham to Morley, August 1921.
51 Graham, *Tramping with a Poet*, p. 129. Lindsay noted in his introduction in *Going-to-the-Sun* that he did not always recognise himself in the portrait painted by Graham, although in this case the views ascribed to him are consistent with everything else he believed.
52 Graham, *Tramping with a Poet*, p. 112.
53 Ibid, p. 47.
54 For details see the various letters from Graham to Morley in Christopher Morley Papers (Haverford College).

life-philosophy. The more reflective passages in *Tramping with a Poet* were not only designed to persuade his readers that the American West was in some sense superior to the urban conglomerations of the East Coast; they were also designed to show how modern industrial civilisation invariably made it difficult to live what a later generation would call an authentic existence.

Graham was nevertheless still determined to portray the American West in a realistic manner, as one distinctive aspect of the manifold complexity of the modern United States, rather than a semi-mythical place detached from the challenges of the modern world. Lindsay repeatedly sought to persuade his friend to "disassociate America from the dollar, from the noisy business rampage, and from all that was unworthy". Graham was reluctant to do so, both because he feared that it would make people suspicious of the accuracy of his work, and because he recognised that the ethos of modern America was increasingly governed by the *mores* and practices of the East Coast.[55] Despite these disagreements, Lindsay believed that he and Graham were "natural allies" in the fight for a spiritual vision of life against the materialism of the modern age.[56] He also believed that he was himself beginning to shed the "dust and ashes" of his old life and establish a "great overhauling" that would in time allow him to return refreshed and invigorated to his work.[57]

One subject that preoccupied both Lindsay and Graham during their tramp was the relationship between the USA and the British Empire. In the early 1920s, following the return of US troops from the battlefields of Europe, many Americans viewed Britain with distrust as an imperial nation that had helped to drag the world into war. Lindsay was not one of them. Although his trip to London had not been an altogether happy experience, despite his warm reception at recitals in London and Oxford, England was to him "something that forever was – beautiful, the substance of poetry, the evidence of things not seen". Whilst he was ill-disposed to the idea of monarchy, as something radically at odds with his instinctively democratic outlook on life, he was convinced that the United States and Britain were united by ties that went beyond mere politics. When he walked with Graham to the Canadian border, north of Glacier Park, both men rejoiced

---

55 Graham, *Tramping with a Poet*, p. 244.
56 Catherine Blair Papers (Abraham Lincoln Presidential Library), Box 3, Folder 13, Lindsay to Mother, 3 July 1921.
57 Harriet Moody Papers (University of Chicago Library), Box 1, Folder 19, Lindsay to Moody, 7 August, 1921; Catherine Blair Papers (Abraham Lincoln Presidential Library), Box 3, Folder 13, Lindsay to Mother, 7 August 1921.

at finding "an unguarded line" where there were "no patrols, no excise or passport officers". They stood either side of one of the posts that marked the frontier and "put our wrists together on the top [...] As we two had become friends and learned to live together without quarrelling, so might our nations".[58] After this brief moment of stylised Anglo-American bonding – which seems characteristic of both men – they walked northwards into the Alberta plains which Graham found "much wilder than the Wild West". He was delighted to find living in one valley a group of Dukhobors, a primitive Christian sect, whose members had emigrated from Russia in the late nineteenth century. Graham was instinctively sympathetic to a religious group that believed in the principle of universal brotherhood, but he was overjoyed above all to find "a bit of old Russia" living on in the unexpected setting of the foothills of the Rocky Mountains.

In his introduction to *Going-to-the-Sun*, Lindsay described Graham as a "lifetime friend", even though they had only first met eighteen months or so before venturing into the mountains, evidence of his belief that the Briton was a true fellow spirit. Whilst they were still in Glacier Park, he wrote to the poet Alice Corbin Henderson, telling her that his tramping partner was "permanently enthused over the Western idea", adding that he believed his friend could become an important figure in persuading Americans to develop a new vision of their homeland.[59] Graham also appears in person in some of Lindsay's poems in *Going-to-the-Sun*, which began with a piece 'We Start West to the Waterfalls', and combined a longing for the wilderness with a sense that the natural world was able to provide an insight into the numinous. Some of Lindsay's poems were set, imaginatively at least, in Glacier Park. 'The Mystic Unicorn of the Montana Sunset' tells how "the Unicorn-No-Storm-Can-Tame" materialised on the mountainside above "Stephen's campfire in the rocks", and sat down to discuss the Himalayas with him, an image designed like so many of Lindsay's poems in *Going-to-the-Sun* to show the porosity of the boundary between the real and the imaginary. Lindsay's poems were accompanied by dozens of illustrations that he penned himself, echoing his interest in the symbolism of hieroglyphics, for they were designed to convey meanings that even the elaborate metaphors of the poems could not achieve. *Going-to-the-Sun* mountain is depicted in the opening illustration as a hollow rock with fairy-like creatures flying about inside. The Mystic Unicorn is

---

58 Graham, *Tramping with a Poet*, pp. 226-27.
59 Alice Corbin Henderson Papers (Harry Ransom Center), Box 4, Folder 13, Lindsay to Henderson, 18 August 1921.

embedded in a background of leaves. The bird described in the poem 'The Pheasant Speaks of his Birthdays' is shown sitting by a branch set against the background of a mountain illuminated by the rays of the sun. Both poems and illustrations were inspired by their author's desire to import fantasy into the everyday world, to shake up settled ideas of landscape, and hint at ideas that Lindsay found difficult to articulate in discursive language. Reviewers did not altogether know what to make of the book. The critic in the *New York Times* described Lindsay as "the modern Mark Twain" whose best friends were the Mad Hatter and the March Hare. The review ended with a shrewd observation that the poet wanted to show how "beauty, humour and truth are one".[60] The critic for *Time* assured his readers that Lindsay was not "crazy", although they acknowledged there was a kind of madness in "the very excited intensity of his sanity".[61] Even the most generous critics nevertheless failed to get to the heart of the poet's elusive and allusive "message".

Figure 7: Press photograph of Vachel Lindsay and Stephen Graham (on the right) in 1921.

Graham was in private unimpressed by *Going-to-the-Sun* when it first appeared at the start of 1923, believing that the talent which had distinguished its author's earlier verse was beginning to fade, although he only expressed such a view long after Lindsay's suicide in 1931.[62] He was

---
60 *New York Times*, 25 February 1923.
61 *Time*, 3 October 1923.
62 Margaret Haley Carpenter Papers (University of Virginia), 10, 18, Graham to Carpenter,

nevertheless inspired enough by their hike through Glacier Park to discuss the possibility of repeating the experience the following year, and although the project was scuppered by the death of Lindsay's mother, the prospect of a new tramp became a staple of the two men's correspondence. Vachel returned to Glacier Park on a number of occasions by himself, as well as travelling there with his new wife in 1925, showing her the places that he had visited with Graham.[63] He also moved for a time to Spokane to be closer to the Rocky Mountains (the city for a time replaced Springfield in his imagination as a Holy City capable of serving as the foundation for an American aesthetic and spiritual renaissance).

There was in truth always a marked difference between Lindsay's view of the world and that of his friend. Graham's interest in "vagabondage" was never rooted so much in a radical rejection of civilised society as in a belief that an outsider was best-placed to understand the world in which he found himself. There was, by contrast, something more hobo about Lindsay's view of the world (although one columnist in *The Oregonian* did question whether "such a pleasant-mannered youth could really be kin to society's derelicts").[64] Although less of an outsider than he sometimes painted himself, Lindsay was an uneasy figure when he found himself in the world of polite society, at least as it existed in the major cities and university campuses where he sometimes lectured or recited. Graham was by contrast always comfortable in the literary and social world of London and New York. For all his undoubted love of travel and tramping, he looked at the landscape with the eyes of a writer, ruminating on how he might make use of it in his books and articles. Lindsay was by contrast more of a true poet, who was like "all poets [...] mad, or, to be gentler, estranged, alienated, perceiving too much, feeling too much, ranging too far, lingering too long at the poles of exaltation and morbidity".[65]

After finishing their tramp through Glacier Park, Lindsay returned with Graham to Springfield, where they gave lectures to local schoolchildren and church groups about their adventures. The two of them then went on to Chicago, where Lindsay introduced Graham to Harriet Moody, a leading figure in the city's cultural scene (by the early 1920s Chicago had become a rival to New York for the title of America's leading literary centre). He

---

1 February 1961.
63 Vachel Lindsay, *Going-to-the-Stars* (New York: Appleton, 1926), p. 8.
64 *The Oregonian*, 9 October 1921.
65 Mark Harris, *City of Discontent* (New York: Boobs Merril, 1952), Preface.

remained there for a week where, in Moody's words, "he endeared himself to us all",⁶⁶ before heading home to Britain via New York in the middle of October on the White Star Line's 'Olympic'.⁶⁷ Graham's enthusiasm for America meant that he was determined to return there as soon as possible, writing to Moody early in 1922 that he hoped to be back in North America within a few months, in order to climb the Peak of Darien in Panama, before heading northwards again to the United States. He was in the event delayed in London for a number of reasons (it was during this period that he wrote his esoteric *Credo* for *The Beacon* and attended Haldane's lectures on biological materialism). He also used the time to make a brief visit back to the Essex suburbs where he was brought up, in order to provide inspiration for his autobiographical novel *Under-London*. Graham also seems to have hoped that he might be given a visa by the Soviet authorities to visit the country,⁶⁸ noting many years later that it was blocked by the personal intervention of Trotsky, although it is not clear how he could have known this was the case.⁶⁹

In early April Graham and Rose finally closed up Frith Street, and departed for central America via Spain, with just a couple of rucksacks, hoping to find there "fun and adventure and poetry and sunburn".⁷⁰ Graham took a strong dislike to Spain more or less from the moment he arrived there – his first visit to the country – freely acknowledging his dislike of the "bull-like heads" and "sombre eyes" of the Spaniards he met in Madrid.⁷¹ He was also appalled at the cruelty he witnessed at a bullfight in the city. The Spanish themselves lacked "discipline and order".⁷² From Madrid he travelled southwards via Cordoba to Cadiz, one of the few places he liked, praising its "solidly-built houses" and "beautiful iron work gates".⁷³ He was not, however, smitten by the Spanish ship that he boarded for Puerto Rico, which reeked of onions and was infested by rats, although

---

66 Olivia Hoard Dunbar, *A House in Chicago* (Chicago: University of Chicago Press, 1947), p. 186.
67 See, too, Harriet Moody Papers (University of Chicago Library), Box 1, Folder 14, Graham to Moody 14 October 1921.
68 Ibid, Graham to Moody, 31 December 1921.
69 *Montreal Gazette*, 1 December 1930.
70 Harriet Moody Papers (University of Chicago Library), Box 1, Folder 14, Graham to Moody, 23 March 1922.
71 Stephen Graham, *In Quest of El Dorado* (London: Macmillan, 1924), p. 5, version available at http://archive.org/details/inquestofeldorad00grah.
72 Graham Papers (FSU), 578, 34 (Journal for 1922, entry dated 10 April).
73 Ibid (Journal for 1922, entry dated 20 April).

the journey itself passed smoothly enough. By the time the ship approached the New World, Graham and Rose were starting to adjust to the rhythms of the tropical climate, sleeping in the hottest part of the day, before going up on deck to enjoy "the freshness of afternoon breezes". On their arrival at San Juan they were met by US immigration officers – Puerto Rico was a US possession – who subjected them to the usual barrage of absurd questions including "are you a polygamist" and "do you believe in subverting an existing government by force"? Graham resisted the temptation to reply in the affirmative.[74]

Graham had a number of objectives in making his third trip to North America in as many years. He was in the first place planning to follow in the footsteps of the Spanish *conquistadores* of the sixteenth century – men such as Herman Cortes and Francesco Vásquez de Coronado – who had travelled to the New World in search of gold and other riches. He also wanted to trace the route taken by the explorer Vasco Nunez de Balboa, who had in 1513 led an expedition to the Pacific from the eastern seaboard of America, catching his first glimpse of the ocean from the Peak of Darien, which rises out of the jungle of modern-day Panama. Graham also planned to spend some months in Santa Fé, in New Mexico, where he had been advised to go the previous year by Vachel Lindsay, who himself had numerous contacts with members of the burgeoning artists' colony that had grown up there over the previous few years. Lindsay hoped that Graham's residence in the town would make him still more enthusiastic over "the Western idea". He wrote to Alice Corbin Henderson, a member of the literary colony, expressing his hope that Graham would confirm Lindsay's own (as ever eccentrically enthusiastic) view that "Santa Fé is [...] the psychic centre of America [...] Stephen is just the man I want to go there and confirm my suspicion".[75] To Graham, Lindsay described Santa Fé as "a holy city to me".[76] In another letter he told his friend that "with a horse and a house you have every chance to build a city of the soul and I have every hope you will build it [...] you can make Santa Fé a Mecca for many believers". He went on to add that "I think it possible to maintain all the richness of medieval times, and yet burn every book on Theology

---

74 Graham, *In Quest of El Dorado* p. 38.
75 Alice Corbin Henderson Papers (HRC), Box 4, Folder 13, Lindsay to Henderson, 18 August 1921.
76 Vachel Lindsay Papers (HRC), Letters file, Lindsay to Stephen and Rose Graham, 11 July 1922.

and Dogma, burn every creed, abolish every priesthood and every caste".⁷⁷ Graham was for his part curious to see parts of America that he had never seen before. Whilst he was not convinced by Lindsay's enthusiasm about the possibility of creating a "holy city", capable of serving as a beacon for a new vision of life, he still had hopes of finding a place spared the materialism and commercialism of the East Coast. He also had plans to write a book about his experiences in the New World, encouraged by the success of *Tramping with a Poet in the Rockies*, which had reassured him that he could establish himself in the public mind as something more than a propagandist for the old Russia.

Graham used the opening section of *In Quest of El Dorado* to describe the first stages of his journey from Puerto Rico via Haiti to Cuba (the chapters were, as was the case with *Tramping with a Poet*, originally serialised by Christopher Morley in the *New York Evening Post*). He not only regaled his readers with descriptions of the people and places he encountered *en route*, but also described the history of the region, including the legacies of conquest and slavery that had shaped the area's racial composition (he always had a keen, and to modern eyes somewhat unhealthy, interest in the nuances of colour and race). Graham devoted a good deal of space to discussing the impact of the influence of the United States in the region in the wake of the 1898 US-Spanish war (which, amongst other things, led to the end of Spanish rule in Cuba and Puerto Rico). He regarded the extension of the US presence with a marked degree of ambivalence. Graham seems to have accepted as inevitable a process in which "The dominant spirit of the Anglo-Saxon has overcome the gentle, sluggish conservatism of the old Spain", tacitly recognising the legitimacy of imperial expansion by a more "advanced" race at the cost of one that was less energetic.⁷⁸ He was nevertheless distinctly grudging in his description of the way in which US business and businessmen operated in the area. His perplexity echoed the contradiction that characterised his views on Russian imperialism in the years before 1917. Whilst he acknowledged the right of more advanced countries to extend their power over the "backward", he was not convinced that such a development was always of benefit to the recipients, who faced the prospect of losing important aspects of their heritage. The virtues of imperialism were, for Graham, at best ambiguous.

---

77 Ibid, Lindsay to Stephen and Rose Graham, 14 July 1922.
78 Graham, *In Quest of El Dorado*, p. 49.

Graham had originally intended to head to Mexico from his tour of the Caribbean islands, in order to follow Balboa's footsteps across the isthmus to the Pacific, but the weather by the end of May was so hot that he decided to postpone the trip. He and Rose took a boat to New Orleans, which they had visited three years earlier during their trip through the South, and from there travelled by train to Houston, El Paso and on to the desert city of Santa Fé, located seven thousand feet up in the Sangre de Cristo mountains. The city had over the previous twenty years become a focus for writers and artists, who were drawn there not only by the magnificent scenery, but also by distaste for "a modern world [...] marred by excessive materialism, greed, corruption, and mechanization". They hoped, in the words of one of the recent chroniclers of the Santa Fé colony, to find in the remote countryside of northern New Mexico "an antidote to America's focus on urbanization, industrialization and preoccupation with military power".[79] Many of the writers and artists who flocked to the region were also attracted by the dry climate, ideal for those who suffered from tuberculosis and could find no relief for their condition in the polluted cities of the north. Others relished the prospect of living close to the Pueblo Indians, studying their folk-lore and myths, which attributed an almost divine significance to the local landscape and the creatures that populated it. The artistic colony at Santa Fé was certainly not unique in America – others were formed in places like Woodstock in New York and Carmel in California – but it was, by the 1920s, the best-known. It is easy to understand why Graham was happy to respond to Lindsay's advice to visit the town. The love of nature and suspicion of urban civilisation that was a hallmark of many members of the colony, along with a somewhat diffuse emphasis on the importance of a spirituality that transcended any particular doctrine or church, had clear similarities to his long-established vision of life.

After a few days in Santa Fé, Stephen and Rose arranged to rent a small mud-built house of three rooms, complete with a porch and a large corral.[80] They also bought two horses, 'Billy' and 'Buckskin', for use on their expeditions through the nearby desert (Graham told Christopher Morley in New York that they planned "to ride far and wide across the mountains").[81]

---

79 Lynn Cline, *Literary Pilgrims: The Santa Fe and Taos Writers' Colonies, 1917-1950* (Albuquerque: University of New Mexico Press, 2007), p. 1.
80 For Graham's first impressions of Santa Fé see Harriet Moody Papers (University of Chicago), Box 1, Folder 14, Graham to Moody, 15 June 1922.
81 Christopher Morley Papers (Haverford College), Graham to Morley, n.d.

Vachel Lindsay had provided the Grahams with an introduction to Alice Corbin Henderson, who had previously worked with Harriet Monroe at *Poetry Magazine* in Chicago, before moving to Santa Fé, where she spent much of her time collecting material about the folklore and poetry of New Mexico.[82] They also met the writer Elizabeth Sergeant, the politician-journalist William Allen White, and the cowboy-poet Jack Thorp,[83] whose poems such as 'Little Joe the Wrangler' had already played a significant role in shaping popular images of the West. Graham renewed his acquaintance with the poet Witter Bynner whom he had first met in New York, although he had little time for Bynner's friend D.H. Lawrence, "a wicked fellow" in Graham's view, who was at the time living across the mountains in Taos with his wife Frieda.[84] Bynner himself was a great admirer of Graham, and had previously written a short poem about his travels through Russia, which appeared in his 1920 collection *A Canticle of Pan*.[85]

Graham found the literary milieu of Santa Fé congenial, although he got into trouble amongst some of his neighbours for supposedly describing the place itself as "a shabby little town". He was in reality both enthralled and disappointed by his first encounter with a part of America situated so far from the soulless cities of the North, writing in *El Dorado* that Santa Fé's:

> sun and air, its mountains, its horses, give it a marvellous possibility. The shabbiness lies in certain little things such as the mean commercialisation of the shops and the absence of a popular market for dairy products, fruit and vegetables. This is an Americanisation of life ... [the population] lives on canned milk, canned tomatoes, dried fruit, storage meat, coffee ground years ago in Chicago, eggs of uncertain age and origin. Fruit falls to the ground and rots because they are plenty and stores do not want the price reduced. There is something artificial and unpleasant in living in New Mexico on rations from Chicago. It militates against simple living, and it should be the essence of a literary colony in the mountains to live simply. And it raises a problem for Americans – how to escape from the American standardisation of life.[86]

Graham had come to accept – even in the face of protests from Vachel Lindsay – that the pattern of life in the United States was largely moulded

---

82 See, for example, A.C. Henderson (ed.), *The Turquoise Trail: An Anthology of New Mexico Poetry* (Boston: Houghton Mifflin, 1928).
83 On the tradition of cowboy poetry see David Stanley and Elaine Fletcher (eds.), *Cowboy Poets and Cowboy Poetry* (Urbana, IL: University of Illinois Press, 1999).
84 Christopher Morley Papers (HRC), Graham to Morley, 18 October 1922.
85 'Russians' in Witter Bynner, *A Canticle of Pan* (New York: Alfred Knopf, 1920).
86 Graham, *In Quest of El Dorado*, p. 93.

by the conventions and culture of the industrial North and East. Its tentacles spread far from the great urban centres to influence life even in the remote vastness of New Mexico. Whilst Graham relished the dramatic scenery of New Mexico, he never for a moment shared Lindsay's hope that it could become the new spiritual heart of an alternative America.

During the summer of 1922, Graham sat in the shade in the front of his adobe house working on the manuscript of his novel *Under-London*, as well as preparing articles for the unlikely setting of the *American Legion Weekly*. He and Rose also spent a good deal of time exploring the deserts and mountains of the South-West. Graham was introduced to the world of the cowboy by Jack Thorp, accompanying him on some of his rides into "the greener heights of the mountains", when he took horses up to pasture there. He was convinced that the figure of the cowboy retained a vital place in the American imagination, since "A great nation entirely composed of clerks is unthinkable. It must have peasants, or high-landers, or cowboys, behind it; something of the wild and primitive, something of romance. Therefore it is that America clings to her conception of a glorious Wild West behind her drab clerical East".[87]

Graham's views may have partly been shaped by the romanticised view of the West that ran through Thorp's songs and poems, although he travelled extensively himself in order to gain a deeper understanding of cowboy life, including a trip to the annual Las Vegas Reunion. In *El Dorado* he described for his readers the carnival atmosphere of the rodeo, where cowboys competed with each other at breaking-in horses. He provided a vivid account of the chuck-wagon races in which competitors vied with one another to steer their vehicles through a complex obstacle course in the shortest possible time. Silent western films were just becoming popular in Britain around the time Graham wrote his book, and he seems to have portrayed cowboy life in a way calculated to correspond to the expectations of his readers, but there is no doubt that he was genuinely enthralled by Western culture. His descriptions of the Native American settlements he visited were also rather stylised, complete with descriptions of tent settlements and ritual dances, in which the men were "all painted" and the women were "beautiful […] with long hair hanging down their backs".[88] Graham's discussion of the plight of the Indians was nevertheless more subtle than such simple stereotyping might suggest. He acknowledged the

---

87 Ibid, p. 98.
88 Ibid, p. 110.

brutality with which the native population had been treated in the past, attacking those who had crushed their way of life in the name of progress, and suggested that the recent tendency to romanticise Indian culture was a sign that it was now regarded as little more than a quaint souvenir of a vanished past. Although Graham valued the world of Cowboys and Indians, he was painfully aware that the rituals and customs of the Wild West were becoming a form of ritualised museum theatre, rather than evidence of a living culture strong enough to resist the increasingly homogenised life of the contemporary United States.

At the end of July, Graham headed south once again, leaving Rose behind in Santa Fé, in order to tramp across Panama and see the Pacific from the Peak of Darien, as Balboa had done some 400 years before. He took a boat from New Orleans to Colon, which was filled with Americans heading back to Panama from their vacations back home (the Canal Zone had some years earlier become US territory, and thousands of engineers and other workers subsequently moved there to help develop the region). The trek from the east of the isthmus to Darien proved tiring even to a seasoned walker like Graham. He and his two guides – one carried his pack and gun, whilst the other used a machete to hack through the jungle growth – made slow progress through a "dank and steaming" world where the ground was covered with "mud and slime". They spent their nights in villages where the impoverished locals provided them with meals of "oil and rice and bits of fat pork", or under "the scantiest shelter", surrounded by "thousands of flaming fire flies [that] lit the floating mists which along the edge of a jungle clearing looked like phantoms living in dark houses". The days were spent trekking under a canopy of trees filled with howling monkeys and squawking parrots. The going became a little easier when Graham and his companions were able to follow the *Camino Real*, a rough track carved out through the jungle centuries before, which led them to "the scarp of a commanding" ridge where the Pacific could be glimpsed "far away [...] beyond the hills and forests and the ridges". Graham was exhilarated by his first sight of the Pacific Ocean, and he later recalled in *El Dorado* how "a warm current ran through my veins and something seemed to lighten heavy boots". His guides barely paused at the sight and could not understand his excitement ("Grande Oceano" muttered one of them reflectively). Together they marched on for many hours to the shoreline, where like Balboa they stared through the twilight at "the many colours of glory sinking towards oblivion".[89]

---

[89] Ibid, pp. 152-53, 155, 159, 161.

Graham began the description of his trek to the Peak of Darien with for him an unusually detailed meditation on travel and place. He told his readers that:

> Religious geography is part of the art of living. To come to each new place on the chart called Earth, not in a spirit of mere jollity but with some reverence, gives a richness to life. Whilst some seek gold, others seek spiritual gold, the soul's possession, which is neither sentimental nor unreal but is indeed the one *substance* out of which in the beginning all things were made.

He went on to add (rather ungrammatically) that:

> The apology of a world-traveller that he did not see the Pacific before, from the heights of Tehuantepec, from the Golden Gate of San Francisco, from the stone eminence of the new city of Panama – he preferred to see it with Balboa's eyes, climbing a peak out of the jungle and looking also and in like manner for the first time, in that way to perform a geographical rite in the world-temple.[90]

Such words sat rather oddly with the tone of the rest of *El Dorado*, which consisted mostly of a mixture of anecdote and narrative history, echoing instead the pilgrim motifs that had run through so much of his earlier writing. Graham's 1922 journal certainly shows that many of his esoteric concerns continued to preoccupy him. Although many of his earliest meditations on landscape had concerned the *Russian* landscape, he still believed that the natural world could offer insights into alternative forms of reality. In his writings on America, throughout the early 1920s, he displayed an on-going interest in what would today be called sacred geography. Whilst his main task in *El Dorado* was to show his readers how the past continued to shape the present in central America, he had not altogether lost his desire to hint at the metaphysical foundations of the material world, suggesting that it could still be interrogated to provide a richer set of meanings than a more cursory examination might at first suggest.

After spending a few days in Panama City, where he praised the US administration for turning "one of the most pestilential swamps in the world [into] something like a health resort",[91] Graham headed by boat from Colon up the east coast to New York. He arrived there at the end of September, planning to meet his old friend Wilfrid Ewart, who was travelling to America in the hope of recovering from a severe mental and physical collapse that had followed his completion of *The Way of Revelation*. Graham also planned to meet Vachel Lindsay, who was in New York at the time, although Lindsay

---
90 Ibid, p. 152.
91 Ibid, p. 173.

too had fallen victim to a nervous breakdown following the death of his mother a few months earlier. Lindsay and Graham wandered the New York streets together, finding themselves both repelled and fascinated by the city. Although they were appalled by the power of Wall Street, dismissing its denizens as so many "Babbits", the two men were mesmerised by New York's raw energy and power. They immersed themselves once again in the city's literary scene, and were amongst those who signed the door to Frank Shay's bookshop in Greenwich Village, adding their signatures to a list which included names ranging from Christopher Morley and Sherwood Anderson to Upton Sinclair and Sinclair Lewis.[92] Graham was impressed by the decline in poverty since he first visited the city ten years earlier, later writing that the majority of its residents, like most Americans, had come to regard themselves as middle class. He offered a paean of praise for Prohibition, suggesting that the city had improved greatly since his first visit, when he had been appalled by "the huge gin-palaces" and the night-courts that met to process the large number of prostitutes arrested on the streets. Lindsay and Graham toured some of the old bars of New York, finding that many had been converted into shops or restaurants, whilst others remained surreptitiously in business, posting look-outs to warn of a possible raid by the police. They were joined on some of their expeditions by Ewart, although he preferred to spend his time touring Broadway or walking through Central Park, sketching out in his head a new novel that was partly to be set in the city.[93] Although Lindsay and Ewart seem to have got on reasonably well, both in New York and during their earlier meeting in London, the exuberant Prairie Troubador and the reserved British army officer always found one another distinctly enigmatic. Graham himself acknowledged that his friendship with the two men was the only thing they had in common.

Ewart had come to North America hoping that his trip would provide new material for his writing, and he was eager to see both the big cities of the East and the remote deserts of the South West. After a few days in New York, he travelled with Graham to Chicago (Lindsay remained in New York before travelling south to Gulf Port College in Mississippi where he taught

---

92 On the literary scene in Greenwich Village in the 1920s, see Carolyn F. Ware, *Greenwich Village: 1920-1930* (New York: Houghton Mifflin, 1935). The original bookshop door signed by Graham and Lindsay is held by the Harry Ransom Centre (University of Texas).

93 Stephen Graham, *Life and Last Words of Wilfrid Ewart* (London: Putnam, 1924), pp. 185-86.

English for a time). In Chicago, Graham and Ewart visited Marshall Fields Department Store, and sampled the local hot dogs, before taking a train southwards to Kansas. From there they travelled to Santa Fé, arriving in a dust storm in the second half of October. Ewart rented a small adobe house from the artist Gerald Cassidy,[94] located a few yards from the Grahams' home, and bought a horse from a member of the literary colony who was heading back East to finish their University degree.[95] The horse was too small for Ewart – who was well over six-feet tall – and proved remarkably stubborn. "George" nevertheless proved sturdy enough to allow his new owner to ride out into the desert, either on his own, or in the company of the Grahams.

Ewart was quickly riveted by the landscape of the Southwest, writing in awe how "the spirit of the mountain and desert, its sorrow and majesty, its profound mystery and unhappiness, steals out again, as if, before the year should die or before we two should part for ever, it pleaded to be known, to be understood".[96] In December he and Graham drove by car to the Grand Canyon in Arizona, a five-day trip, much of it through a "blinding snowstorm", but the experience proved worthwhile "for the sake of seeing what is unique in the world".[97] The two scrambled down the side of the Canyon, almost falling at one point, following an old Indian trail that had been widened to make it safer for visitors. Nor was Ewart only enthralled by the natural landscape. He accompanied Graham on a 150 mile round trip to watch the celebrated ritual dance of the Jemez Indians, a sight that made a huge impression on him, although the Mexican and Indian houses in which the two men stayed were "infernally cold and uncomfortable".[98]

Ewart made a considerable impression on the Santa Fé colony.[99] Although he was, in Graham's words, a "reserved [and] almost inarticulate Guards officer", whose fastidiousness at times blended into a snobbish disdain for others,[100] he proudly sent back home to his parents various

---

94 Christopher Morley Papers (HRC), Graham to Morley, 18 October 1922.
95 For Ewart's memories of this period, see Wilfrid Ewart, *Scots Guard* (London: Rich and Cowan, 1934), pp. 260-86.
96 Ibid, p. 286.
97 Ewart Papers (HRC), Letters, Ewart to Father, 3 December 1922.
98 Ibid, Ewart to Father, 19 November 1922. For Graham's account of the trip see *In Quest of El Dorado*, pp. 216-36. Ewart's account of the trip is reproduced in Graham, *Life and Last Words of Ewart*, pp. 197-240.
99 Graham, *Life and Last Words of Ewart*, p. 193.
100 Graham, *In Quest of El Dorado*, p. 186.

newspaper cuttings showing "how fashionable I am here".[101] Ewart had spent the post-war years determined to become a successful writer – and he had made a real impression with *Way of Revelation* – but there was always something rather tortured about him. There is a sad irony in the fact that, within a few weeks of boasting about how "fashionable" he had become, he was laid to rest in a cemetery in Mexico City, the victim of a bizarre shooting incident in the early hours of the first day of 1923.

Ewart had originally intended to stay in Santa Fé until January, in order to finish a history of the Scots Guards he had been commissioned to write, the notes for which were contained in a large metal trunk that followed him around America. His plans changed in December, though, in part because he found it difficult to tolerate the bitter cold of the desert in winter. He may also have been influenced by the Grahams' decision to leave Santa Fé, in order to head southwards to Mexico, so that Stephen could continue his journey in the footsteps of the *conquistadores*. Ewart's original intention was, by contrast, to head eastwards to New Orleans, a city he had never visited, but which had long grabbed his imagination. Graham and Rose left Santa Fé on 17 December heading for El Paso on the Texas-Mexico border, a city that made a surprisingly positive impression on them, at least when compared with the poverty of La Ciudad de Juarez on the opposite side of the Rio Grande. A few days later, on 21 December, they were in Chihuahua, where Stephen was by now feeling "relief" that "America is off my back".[102]

The Grahams had learned the surprising news from a journalist in El Paso that Ewart had abandoned his original plan to head to New Orleans, and was now bound for Mexico City, and they half-expected to meet him *en route*. Wilfrid was, however, several days ahead of them, and he arrived in the Mexican capital before Christmas, celebrating the festive season by feasting on "strawberries and cream every day". His private correspondence does not cast much light on why he abandoned his earlier plans to go direct to New Orleans from Santa Fé (a postcard sent to his parents in the middle of December said that he definitely planned to go to Louisiana *before* heading on for "old Mexico").[103] His decision is all the more surprising given that he had already sent his metal trunk – complete with his treasured notes – on to New Orleans. What is clear is that Ewart had

---

101   Ewart Papers (HRC), Letters, Ewart to Father, 19 November 1922.
102   Graham Papers (FSU), Box 578, 34 (Journal for 1922, entry dated 21 December 1922).
103   Ewart Papers (HRC), Letters, Ewart to parents, 12 December 1922.

quickly fallen in love with Mexico, even though Graham had previously warned him that he would find life there difficult, given both his lack of Spanish and the perennial instability of a country that had a well-earned reputation for violence. Ewart was by 27 December eulogising the city in a postcard to his parents as a place of "oranges, apricots, figs, bananas, roses, geraniums – gardens and suburbs marvellous". He was also enthralled by the views of the surrounding mountains. Nevertheless, at this stage he told his family that he planned to head on to New Orleans by 31 December "as my baggage and mail are there"[104] – even though on the *same* day he had written to the carriers asking them to forward his possessions *from* America *to* Mexico.[105] Whatever his intentions, he was never reunited with his baggage. Nor did he ever leave the city with which he had so quickly fallen in love.

The Grahams seem to have arrived in Mexico City on the 27 December, checking into the Hotel Cosmos for a night, before transferring to the Hotel Iturbide, "a fine old structure built round stone courts and a garden of palm trees and flowering shrubs".[106] It also had the added advantage of being a "moderate price" (both Graham and Ewart commented in their letters and diaries about the high cost of living in Mexico). The Grahams toured the major hotels of the capital trying to find out where Ewart was staying, in between visiting the magnificent cathedral of Our Lady of Guadeloupe, where they admired the grand series of pictures depicting the Revelation of the Virgin. Stephen and Rose eventually ran across Ewart on 30 December. He was, as usual, cutting a somewhat incongruous figure, standing "in riding breeches and puttees" on the street corner of St John of Latran, staring up into the sky. The three of them headed for a nearby restaurant, where Ewart enthused about Mexico, telling his friends that he had "been looking for a place like this all my life". Graham could not understand this fascination for a place "without culture and without comfort",[107] but Ewart had fallen in love with the climate and the parks, which he seemed to prefer even to the wild grandeur of the New Mexico desert. The company parted after dinner, meeting up again the following day around noon in order to take a tram out to San Angel, a distant suburb

---

104   Ibid, Ewart to parents, 27 December 1922
105   Ibid, Ewart to Messrs Camphuis and Co, 27 December 1922.
106   Graham, *In Quest of El Dorado*, p. 291.
107   Graham, *Life and Last Words of Ewart*, p. 247.

which Ewart had already visited, admiring it for its stunning views of the two great volcanoes that dominated the horizon. They had lunch on the patio of an old inn, where Ewart discussed his plans for the future, telling Graham that he was considering whether to abandon fiction in order to try to establish himself as a foreign correspondent.

A few hours later the Grahams and Ewart returned to the city centre, arriving around tea-time, and that evening the three of them attended a revue at the *Teatro Lirico* celebrating the end of the old year. They then went on to the Hotel Cosmos for supper, pushing their way through streets filled with New Year revellers, some of whom were already firing guns indiscriminately into the air. In his published accounts of these events, Graham described how he and Rose said good night to Ewart around 11.30pm, before heading off through the crowds to the Hotel Iturbide. In his journal he recorded their parting rather differently, noting that he and Ewart would have liked to stay out on the street to soak up the atmosphere, but abandoned their plan when Rose "nudged" her husband and asked to be taken home: "she was tired of the noise and a little nervous of the incessant firing of guns, and the scene did not mean as much to her as it did to us". Graham also noted that his wife was "perhaps [...] a little possessive".[108] His words suggest that Rose did not always find Ewart such good company as her husband did. What is certain – or at least seems certain – is that an hour or so after their parting, Ewart was shot through the eye by a stray bullet whilst standing on his hotel balcony, surveying the New Year celebrations below. According to a Mexican newspaper that reported his death, Ewart's body was found late on the morning of 1 January by a hotel chambermaid, who went into the bedroom and saw his corpse on the balcony covered in coagulated blood.

In his novel *The Dark Back of Time*, which weaves Ewart's last hours in Mexico City into a dense tapestry of historical narrative and meditation on the fragility of human experience, the Spanish novelist Javier Marias reflects at length on the random circumstances that led up to Ewart's death. Ewart had only come to Mexico on a whim – and he only decided on a whim to stay in the country rather than head back north in pursuit of his missing luggage. The hotel he was staying in was located some distance from the main tourist areas, and he only found it as a result of a chance

---

108   Graham Papers (FSU), Box 578, 34 (Journal for 1922, entry dated 31 December 1922).

recommendation by a passing stranger. Ewart had also for some reason changed accommodation twice at his hotel, and the night of 31 December was the first time he had entered the room where he met his death (he never even had the chance to turn down the bed sheets). And, as Graham's journal shows, if Rose had not wanted to return back to the Hotel Iturbide, then he and Ewart would have remained on the streets, and his friend would not have been on his hotel balcony at the time the fatal shot was fired.

The bizarre nature of Ewart's death inevitably aroused a brief flurry of interest in both the Mexican and British press (the reporting in some cases became confused with accounts of the death of another Briton who was shot a few days later when caught in the cross-fire between two marauding gangs). Graham identified the body together with a young British clerk named Hollands, who had befriended Ewart when he first arrived in Mexico City a few days earlier. An autopsy had been carried out, and when the two men saw the body in the hospital, it was lying exposed on the dissecting table, amongst "an incredible stench of blood and decay".[109] Graham issued a statement to the press, relating the random set of circumstances that had brought his friend to Mexico, whilst the newspaper *Excelsior* printed some words about Ewart from Rose who spoke of his "pleasant personality" and lack of enemies. Ewart was buried shortly afterwards in the British cemetery, his funeral attended by Graham and Hollands, along with a few other members of the British colony in Mexico City. His coffin was interred with a bunch of white roses dropped into the grave by Rose.

Graham's journal shows how difficult he found it coming to terms with the bizarre death of his friend. On 1 January he jotted down in his journal the dry fact that "Wilfrid Ewart was killed last night within an hour of parting from him". Two days later he wrote that he could feel Ewart's "stupefied" spirit watching events, and comforted the unseen ghost by reassuring him that although "you feel lost [...] you will find your way". On 5th January Graham noted in his diary that "Ewart has gone back to look at his grave. He feels homeless and restless and rather lonely and disconsolate".[110] Graham's sense of his friend's lingering presence was doubtless fuelled by the shocking nature of Ewart's death. Such thoughts

---

109 Graham, *Life and Last Words of Ewart*, p. 260.
110 Graham Papers (FSU), Box 578, 35 (Journal for 1923, entries dated 1 January 1923, 3 January 1923, 5 January 1923).

nevertheless came easily to a man who had since adolescence believed in the existence of a spiritual dimension that lay beyond the carapace of the material world. The obituaries in the British press contented themselves with lamenting how a "literary career of great promise" had been tragically cut short, whilst pointing to the irony that a man who had survived three years in the trenches should meet his death in such an unexpected and violent fashion.[111]

In *The Dark Back of Time*, Marias describes in some detail the investigation into Ewart's death, highlighting a number of contradictions in the statements made to the police by hotel staff. He also points out how Graham took a good deal of artistic licence when he later described Ewart's precise movements once he had returned to his hotel room. Despite speculation at the time and since, there is no real evidence that Ewart's death was anything other than what it appeared to be: a tragic accident. The police enquiries certainly threw up little of interest. Several other people were killed in shooting accidents in Mexico City on the same night. Nor is there any implication that Graham knew more than he was letting on. A close reading of his books and diaries hints that he was, on occasion, frustrated by Ewart's reluctance to settle down and complete his various writing projects (an accusation that could never be directed against Graham). There are also hints that Ewart's mixture of reserve and snobbishness occasionally grated on his friend. Graham's sadness at Ewart's death was nevertheless very deep.[112] The Grahams soon found that Mexico City was so "haunted" by his memory that they were forced to move on to complete their journey through Mexico.[113]

Graham was fascinated by Aztec civilisation, and insisted on visiting various sites of human sacrifice, which he later described at some length in *In Quest of El Dorado*. He also visited a number of cities including Vera Cruz and Jalap. When he came to write up his material, he ruminated at some length on the hopeless quest of the Spanish adventurers who had, hundreds of years earlier, incurred hardship and death in their search for gold. In words that could have reflected his own philosophy of travel – or

---

111 *The Times*, 5 January 1923; *Daily Express*, 5 February 1923.
112 Graham's despair did not however prevent him from seeking new commissions within a few days of Ewart's Death. See Van Wyck Brook Papers (University of Pennsylvania, Rare Book and Manuscript Library), MS Coll. 650, Box 17, Folder 1149, Graham to Brooks, 11 January 1923.
113 Graham, *In Quest of El Dorado*, p. 307.

indeed served as an epitaph for Wilfrid Ewart himself – he wrote that "If ever in life you find what you are seeking you have gone wrong. Finding you lose. The whole of life is balanced betwixt the aching heart and the golden dream".[114] There is a pathetic sadness in the fact that Ewart died within days of finding a place that seemed to encapsulate so many of the things for which he had been searching.

---

114   Ibid, p. 344.

6. A Rising or Setting Sun?

Graham arrived back in Southampton on the White Star Line's 'Majestic' liner at the start of April 1923, ending a hectic four-year period in which he made three extended trips to the USA and two long tours of Europe. He spent most of the next year in London, writing his biography of Wilfrid Ewart and completing the manuscript of *In Quest of El Dorado*. He also began to immerse himself in London's cultural life, casting off his rather reclusive *persona* to mix freely with the capital's *literati* at parties and gallery openings. Graham's success in the literary world of New York seems to have given him a new interest in the intellectual *beau monde* of his own country. Frith Street became a setting for gatherings of artists and writers (the Grahams held a regular Sunday evening 'at home' where the guests assembled to hear readings of new poetry and prose). By 1926 *The Bookman* was able to publish, without comment, a picture of 'A Round the Fire Party at Stephen Graham's', secure in the knowledge that most of its readers would know that the author's home had already become a recognised if minor site of literary London.[1] Graham's year-long sojourn in London during 1923-24 also provided him with a chance to immerse himself once again in the rhythms of the city's life, including its more seamy side, which had fascinated him since he worked as a journalist on the *Evening News* so many years before.

In the early summer of 1923, a few weeks after returning from the United States, Graham was approached by the chaplain at Wandsworth Prison who asked him "to come down [...] and talk about your travels or about ideals".[2] He wisely chose to speak about his travels, giving a talk to 600 prisoners on life in the 'Wild West' and Mexico, which received

---

1 *The Bookman*, April 1926.
2 Stephen Graham, *London Nights* (London: John Lane, 1929), p. 96 (first published in 1925 by Hurst and Blackwood).

"tremendous ovation" from his (literally) captive audience. A few weeks later he volunteered to become a prison visitor at Pentonville Prison, at the suggestion of a young Quaker he met at Toynbee Hall, the pioneering East London settlement established in the nineteenth century to allow undergraduates to experience first-hand the realities of urban deprivation. The Governor and Prison Chaplain enthusiastically welcomed Graham, and gave him permission to move from cell to cell unaccompanied, talking to men who were glad to see him even though he "could do so fantastically little for them".[3]

Most of the prisoners Graham met were guilty of minor offences. One was a former army general, who had passed bad cheques to fund his wife's expensive tastes. Another was a middle-aged clerk "in prison for stealing a piece of silk to get money to pay his rates", who now faced the anguish of knowing that he had lost his job, and was likely to lose his home and family as well. A third prisoner befriended by Graham was a former RAF pilot, sentenced to gaol for staying at a hotel even though he had no money to pay the bill. A fourth man had been imprisoned for "sodomy", and had since found religion in prison, where he was keen to talk about his new-found faith to anyone who would listen. A fifth man had been sent to Pentonville for attacking his wife.[4] Graham recognised that many of the men were victims of difficult personal circumstances. Some had no homes outside prison. Others were ex-soldiers who found it difficult to integrate back into civilian life after the horrors of the trenches. He was nevertheless hard-headed enough to recognise that a large number were "humbugs, conspiracy-maniacs and liars".[5] Graham spent a good deal of time meeting the families of prisoners (he even bought a car to travel around London to carry out his work). He visited a number of wives in their own homes, coming across many who lived in "curious dens" surrounded by "children, cats, old clothes and dirt".[6] He also liaised with the welfare organisations that tried to help prisoners find work when they were released from custody. It was an uphill task. Graham was often disturbed at Frith Street by ex-prisoners demanding money. The problem eventually became so serious that he had to end his association with Pentonville to avoid being

---
3   Ibid, p. 108.
4   All cases taken from Graham Papers (FSU), Box 578, 35 (Journal for 1923) or Stephen Graham, *Part of the Wonderful Scene* (London: Collins, 1964), pp. 307-11.
5   Graham, *London Nights*, p. 118.
6   Ibid, p. 110.

harassed. It might, less charitably, be suggested that he had also exhausted the novelty of his new vocation.

Graham depicted some of his prison-visiting experiences in articles later reproduced with other material in his 1925 book *London Nights*, describing the "riff-raff of cocaine-sellers, fraudulent dole-lifters, bicycle stealers, and incorrigible 'drunks' who occupied so many of the cells".[7] Some of them were fantasists who claimed to have been at top public schools. Others lay in their cells fretting about what would happen to their families whilst they were inside. There was little sentimentality in Graham's description of prisons like Pentonville as "a human zoo", where the animals were caged and cowed, their claws and talons cut to make them "harmless".[8] Other chapters in *London Nights* provided accounts of the early-morning bustle at major markets like Billingsgate, "the vast caravanserai of East London", full of porters in "gutter-brimmed hats" carting round boxes of mackerel and cod.[9] Graham also described at length his perambulations through some of the outer suburbs of the East End, as well as nocturnal street-life in his own home quarter of Soho, with its shifting population of drunks and prostitutes. He wrote of his visits to cheap music halls, where the unfortunate acts were barracked by cat-calls from the audience, and described too his trips to illegal drinking dens hidden away in the back streets of the capital. Graham also relived some of his Moscow days by spending nights in East End doss-houses, sharing a stuffy dormitory with thirty or forty other homeless men seeking shelter from the cold of the streets.

The sketches in *London Nights* conveyed all Graham's talent for "lurid realism" that had won him the approval of his superiors on the *Evening News* thirteen years earlier. The reviewer in *The Bookman* praised his "fine gifts of observation" and commended him for never descending to sensationalism "for sensationalism's sake".[10] Graham himself noted that the main aim of the sketches was to capture the "poetry" of the capital's streets at night which was missing in the glare of day. There was nevertheless a clear tension between his fascination for the rituals of the night and his moralistic distaste for the tawdry world of nightclub and music hall. His

---

7 Ibid, p. 118.
8 Ibid, p. 121.
9 Ibid, p. 65.
10 *The Bookman*, February 1926. See, too, the positive review in the *English Review*, March 1926.

vivid description of night-time cafes, where "hot-blooded men carouse with women of the carmined lip and hennaed hair", contrasted curiously with his priggish lament that "immorality has so grown upon us in London that one may say it is becoming national".[11] Graham's life as an urban vagabond, surveying the streets and squares of the city, could hardly have contrasted more sharply with his earlier sojourns as a rural tramp relishing the solitude and beauty of the countryside. Both represented authentic aspects of his personality, but by the mid-1920s the Romantic in Graham was starting to fade, as he began to exercise more systematically his talent as a kind of urban *flâneur*, chronicling the street scenes through which he wandered, involved and yet remote from the scenes he described.[12]

Graham's fascination with his native city shone through his 1923 novel *Under-London*, even though it had been written the previous year in the shade in front of his mud-walled house in Santa Fé. The book was heavily autobiographical, describing the life of a small group of boys growing up in one of the less privileged suburbs of London in the 1890s, a time when the young Graham had himself been living with his family in Chingford. It was a world in which "houses in their thousands marched outward [from London] like infantry upon a great battlefield", gradually eating up "the green fields and the trees in the country", one side looking towards "a vast urban area" and the other to "the still unspoiled" land.[13] The young Freddie Masters – modelled on Graham himself – is raised in a household where life is governed not by real poverty but "by thrift and mean circumstances".[14] Freddie, again like Graham, relishes the sights and sounds of the countryside that lie just beyond the "wilderness of brick and mortar" of the suburbs. His fascination with lepidoptera, along with his schoolboy crush on another boy, also echo the childhood experiences of his creator.

Under-London was, as several reviewers noted, less a novel and more a loose series of episodes in the fictional life of a group of boys on their journey into adulthood. It certainly captured the pathos of the fading dreams of youth, as "office life closed in on their horizons", and childish

---

11 Graham, *London Nights*, pp. 12-13.
12 Amongst the vast literature on this broad topic see, for example, David Frisby, *Cityscapes of Modernity* (Cambridge: Polity, 2001). For an early classic treatment of the subject see Walter Benjamin, *The Arcades Project* (Cambridge, MA: Harvard University Press, 1999).
13 Stephen Graham, *Under-London* (London: Macmillan, 1923), p. 4.
14 Ibid, p. 66.

hopes of being an explorer or engineer gave way to the prosaic realities of commuting to work as a clerk in the city.[15] The book finishes with an acknowledgement that "Many will ask why this chronicle has been made". The answer Graham gave was, in effect, that the petty rituals of suburban life were of great importance to those who lived them, even if they "are not to be compared with the one-mile radius from Hyde Park Corner".[16] The drafting of the final manuscript of *Under-London* must also have given Graham a chance to recall the world that he had escaped from so many years earlier, when he abandoned his post at Somerset House in favour of the uncertain prospect of life in Russia. Graham's pen-portraits of London life lacked the merit of more literary works like Ford Maddox Ford's *The Soul of London*, but books such as *Under-London* and *London Nights* still possessed "a charm and interest" that attracted a readership, both in Britain and, more surprisingly, the United States.[17]

The first half of 1924 witnessed a resurgence of Graham's interest in Russia, prompted in part by changes in the international political situation. The Labour government that came to office in February moved quickly to offer *de jure* recognition to the government in Moscow, a decision that caused considerable concern amongst many in Britain, who feared that "the party of revolution" would destroy "the very bases of civilised life".[18] Graham was deeply conscious of the loss of his personal ties with Russia over the previous few years. Although he had sent financial help to old friends there for some time after the 1917 Revolution, he was by now no longer in contact with any of them, fearing that they had died in the violence and famine of the Russian civil war. Nor could he get a visa to visit the USSR, for the authorities there knew full-well that their putative guest was unlikely to paint a positive picture of the Soviet experiment upon his return home. Most Britons who visited Russia in the 1920s came from a left-wing political background that predisposed them to look with at least a degree of sympathy on attempts to build a new workers' state. Very few of them shared Graham's nostalgic sympathy for the old Russia that had been swept away by the Revolution of 1917.

---

15 Ibid, p. 365.
16 Ibid, p. 367.
17 *The Bookman*, October 1923 (on *Under-London*); see, too, the *New York Times*, 24 October 1926 (on *London Nights*).
18 *English Review*, January 1924.

Since Graham could not visit the USSR in person, he decided to do the next best thing, and contacted Harold Williams, the Foreign Editor of *The Times*, and an expert on Russia in his own right, suggesting that the paper should commission a series of articles describing a trip down the western border of the USSR from Finland to the Black Sea.[19] The proposal was quickly approved by *The Times* editor, Geoffrey Dawson, and in early summer Graham set off from Hull bound for the Baltic. Graham went first to Finland – which had been a province of the Tsarist Empire before the Revolution – where he visited the tenth-century Orthodox monastery on the island of Valamo in Lake Ladoga. A pall of melancholy hung over the buildings. The number of monks had fallen dramatically over the previous few years as the turmoil of war and revolution had taken their toll. Those who remained spent their time staring "with sunken eyes" at the grey waters of the lake, whilst others talked "as if they felt God had let them down" by turning his face away from the collapse of the world to which they had once belonged.[20] Back on the mainland, rows of grand houses on the lake shore stood deserted and forlorn, their wealthy owners long since vanished. Graham visited the home of Ilia Repin, perhaps the most celebrated artist in pre-revolutionary Russia, famous for such pictures as 'Ivan the Terrible's Murder of his Son' and the 'Volga Boatmen'. Although over eighty, he remained "robust and vital", and, to Graham's eyes at least, retained "an unspent spiritual reserve" that had survived the upheavals of the previous few years.[21] The plight of other ethnic Russians stranded in newly-independent countries like Finland and Estonia was seldom as comfortable. Many struggled to find work, and lived in great poverty, whilst even formerly wealthy aristocrats were reduced to near-destitution. The situation was a little better in Latvia, where the Lettish authorities "allowed their Russian subjects to live in their traditions as if no revolution had occurred". Even here, though, poverty and dislocation were the fate of most of the refugees met by Graham.[22]

---

19 On Williams's life and career, see Charlotte Alston, *Russia's Greatest Enemy: Harold Williams and the Russian Revolutions* (London: I.B. Tauris, 2007). Graham's private journal suggests that he may have considered the trip as early as the summer of 1923. See Graham Papers (FSU), Box 578, 35 (Journal for 1923, entry dated 1 May).
20 *The Times*, 29 August 1924.
21 Graham, *Wonderful Scene*, p. 279.
22 Ibid, p. 282. See, too, *The Times*, 9 September 1924. For a contemporary account of problems faced by Russians living in the Balkans, albeit written from a very Russian nationalist perspective, see Baron A. Heyking, *The Main Issues Confronting the Minorities*

After leaving Latvia and Lithuania, Graham headed by train for Poland, a country he had never warmed to since first going there almost twenty years before. In Warsaw he visited the homes of numerous Russians, finding in their lodgings the "scenes of poverty" suffered by those who shared "a strange history of calamity, driven to point from point and pillar to post downward". One of the people he met was the wife of a former tsarist minister, who had tramped across Soviet Russia for two years before crossing the Polish border "completely destitute, parting with her last bundle to the women who led her across". In another house he came across a group of young Russian men living lives that seemed to be drawn straight from Gorky's *Lower Depths* "but with society people playing the parts". Graham also heard numerous stories describing how Russian refugees were thrown into prison by the Polish authorities, or taken back to the Soviet frontier and dumped there.[23] After leaving Warsaw he headed southwards through Galicia towards Rumania, arriving in Bessarabia, territory which had once formed part of the Tsarist Empire but was now a province of Rumania. Graham believed that the local Russian-speaking peasantry was worse off than in pre-revolutionary times, living under harsh conditions which included punishment by flogging for non-payment of taxes.[24] He also condemned the "war that was being waged against Russian culture" by the Rumanian authorities, ranging from savage censorship to the closure of libraries.[25] Graham doubted whether the region could ever be fully integrated with the rest of Rumania, as the peacemakers in Paris had envisaged back in 1919.

The plight of the Russian refugees who talked to Graham revived his anger at the Soviet regime, which had been curiously muted over the previous few years. Graham had never supported British intervention to crush the Bolsheviks during the Russian Civil War. Nor had he endorsed the rabid anti-Soviet views expressed by some of his fellow-countrymen in the years that followed. Witnessing at first hand the plight of old Russia in emigration hardened his views, though, and in the book he wrote about his trip, *Russia in Division*, he attacked the new Soviet culture as nothing "more than a jargon culture superimposed on the old culture. The old Russia

---

of *Latvia and Esti* (London: P.S. King, 1922).
23 *The Times*, 23 September 1924.
24 Graham, *Wonderful Scene*, p. 285.
25 *The Times*, 14 October 1924.

brought manifold great gifts to the common altar; the new one brings only death and change".[26] He also turned his anger on the Labour government for recognising the Soviet regime and receiving "the representatives of those who killed the kindred of the king".[27]

Graham's anger about the Labour Government's policy towards the USSR made him determined to play a role in the October 1924 election campaign, which took place following MacDonald's decision to seek the dissolution of Parliament. Although he claimed to have supported the Labour Party in the two previous elections,[28] he now wrote to the Conservative leader, Stanley Baldwin, offering his services as a lecturer. He was subsequently dispatched to talk to working-class audiences in constituencies as far apart as London and Tyneside, where he often faced barracking for his "scathing denunciation" of the MacDonald government's "pro-Soviet policy".[29] He also used his pen to attack MacDonald himself, writing in *The Weekly Westminster* that the Prime Minister's desire to secure a trade treaty with Russia was carried out "at the bidding of the most extreme and unrepresentative group within his own party".[30] Graham's article appeared on the same day that the *Daily Mail* published the infamous Zinov'ev Letter, a forgery concocted in Paris, which purported to contain instructions from the Comintern calling for "a successful rising in the working districts of England". Graham recalled many years later in his autobiography that it was the Zinov'ev Letter that prompted him to get involved in the election campaign. His memory was as so often at fault. It was his anger about the misery of the refugees from Soviet rule, casualties of the chaos and violence that had swept through Russia since 1917, which led him to make a rare foray into the world of party politics.

The electoral victory of Baldwin's Conservative Party allowed Graham to return to his more accustomed activities. He spent the winter of 1924-25 at Frith Street, writing up the first part of *Russia in Division*, although he also travelled to Paris to meet some of the Russian émigrés who had congregated in the city since 1917.[31] Graham had a long talk with the writer

---

26 Stephen Graham, *Russia in Division* (London: Macmillan, 1925), p. 8.
27 Ibid, p. 26.
28 *Western Morning News*, 17 October 1924.
29 *The Times*, 23 October 1924; Graham, *Wonderful Scene*, p. 287.
30 *The Weekly Westminster*, 25 October 1924.
31 For Graham's views of the émigrés in Paris see Stephen Graham, 'Russian Vignettes', *Saturday Review*, 21 February 1925.

Ivan Bunin, "a bright-faced, slightly-built man of middle years", who was best known in Britain for his short story *The Gentleman from San Francisco*. Bunin had by now become a bitter critic of the Bolshevik regime, and was intrigued to know why it still appeared so popular amongst certain sections of British society, something that Graham unconvincingly put down to the legacy of the pre-revolutionary anti-tsarist campaign waged by radical émigré writers like Peter Kropotkin and Sergei Stepniak.[32] He also met the novelist Alexander Kuprin, "sitting at a table with a bottle of wine in a bare kitchen in a house on the Avenue Mozart", where he lived with his small dog for company (Graham and Rose had translated a number of Kuprin's stories for Constable's Russian Library back in 1916).

One of Graham's most enjoyable encounters was with Aleksei Remizov, "one of the few undoubted geniuses of modern Russia", whose tales of folklore and myth he had long admired.[33] Remizov invited Graham to his studio, a curious place cluttered by books and a melée of fish-bones, seaweed, ducks feet and starfish. Although he was less critical of the Bolsheviks than some of his fellow-émigrés, and still hoped one day to return to Russia, Remizov's views were coloured by intense homesickness. His sitting room was arranged to include a "holy corner" of the kind found in most peasant houses before 1917, complete with an icon of the virgin flickering in the light of a candle, whilst in a small powder box he kept a pinch of Russian soil to remind him of home. Graham was deeply moved by these symbols of his host's love of Russia. The writers he met in Paris had been spared the worst of the destitution suffered by many of their compatriots, but the pathos of their lives served only to fuel his melancholy at the demise of old Russia. The country "still remained in my subconscious" and fuelled an inchoate longing of the kind that had first taken him to Moscow some twenty years earlier.

Graham's nostalgia for old Russia was intensified by the problems he faced in his personal life. The death of Anderson Graham at the end of October 1925 seems to have led to tension between Anderson's old and new families. If the fictionalised account that Stephen later set down in *Lost Battle* is to be believed, then he and his father had grown closer in later years, and Anderson's death was felt by his son "in the marrow of his bones", even though he once considered his father "the betrayer of his

---
32 *The Times*, 3 April 1925.
33 Ibid, 28 April 1925.

mother".³⁴ In his will, Anderson left most of his money and his Lutyens house in Hertfordshire to his second family, although he bequeathed a small number of shares to Stephen to help take care of his mother. There were some irregularities in the will, since it named no executor or residuary legatee. The High Court in London eventually appointed Stephen as executor, since he was the "son and next of kin", and Stephen faithfully carried out the provisions of the will, even though some of his siblings wanted to challenge its provisions. The fate of Graham's mother Jane – to whom he remained "bound by passionate affection" – remains unclear. Although she renounced any right to administer Anderson's estate herself, her *alter ego* in *Lost Battle* bitterly resented the exclusion of her children from her husband's will. The fictional Jeannie Macrimmon in *Lost Battle* dies within a few weeks of her husband, before the family could put into effect plans to move her to a flat in Bloomsbury. No death certificate has been found for the real Jane Graham. There is, however, strong circumstantial evidence to suggest that she died early in 1926. Whatever the exact nature of the calamities that swept through the Graham family in the winter of 1925-26, they exercised an enormous emotional toll on Stephen himself. A short trip to Paris with Rose in January restored his spirits a little, allowing him to get away from the recent "troubles" in London, but even the "light-hearted" French capital could not offer much relief from his worries.³⁵

Graham's personal life had in fact been descending into turmoil well before his father's death unleashed a whole series of new problems. He had always been inclined to jot down cryptic notes and self-motivating maxims, but the entries in his journal for 1925 are far bleaker than those of earlier years. Some of them are impenetrable and reflect the instinctive mysticism (or obscurantism) that had long characterised his outlook on life ("You are either a plus or a minus"). Others reflect a sharp deterioration in Graham's relations with Rose (hints of which can be traced back over a number of years). In the summer of 1925, he noted down an aphorism that may have been intended for a novel, but was clearly rooted in personal experience, writing that "You have many secrets but do not know yourself. Your will is weak. You are in danger of having the will of others imposed on you". A few weeks later, in September, he jotted down the words "Promise never to quarrel with me. In return: whatever you ask me to do at any time I

---

34 Stephen Graham, *Lost Battle* (London: Ivor Nicholson and Watson, 1934), p. 299.
35 Vachel Lindsay Papers (HRC), Letters, Graham to Lindsay, 18 January 1926.

will do it". The significance of the words becomes clearer from a journal entry a few weeks later, when he was in Paris on his own, and noted down that "I have three girls" and "do nothing but go to Montmartre to draw the money".[36] The marital stress must have caused Graham anguish. There had always been something of the moralist in his outlook. He was still a practising Anglican, although he periodically spoke at national meetings of the Congregational Church, and ruminated occasionally on becoming a Catholic "if they would get rid of their Pope". Graham's interest in religion had invariably focused on its spiritual rather than its ethical dimension, and his earlier sojourns into the dark sides of the cities of Europe and North America showed that he was no prude, but the presence of Rose in London had always provided him with an emotional and geographical centre to which he could return from his travels abroad. By 1925 the texture of his personal life was beginning to fall apart.

It is ironic that the two books Graham was beginning to sketch out during this period were both optimistic celebrations of life. The first of these was published in 1926 under the title *The Gentle Art of Tramping*, and became one of his most popular books, proving that there was still a steady market for his distinctive brew of vivid description and mystical philosophising. Although it was some years since Graham had undertaken any major tramp – his recent journeys had mostly been carried out by train – he was still anxious to assure his readers that "know how to tramp and you know how to live". He went on to describe tramping as "a way of approach, to Nature, to your fellow-man, to a foreign nation, to beauty, to life itself". Part of the book was concerned with providing practical advice about what kit the aspiring tramp should take with on their journeys (Graham's idealised tramp was, as ever, less a vagrant and more a noble searcher after truth). Nor was there any shortage of somewhat trite maxims denouncing materialism and the popular obsession with money. At the heart of the book, though, was the familiar nature-mysticism of his earlier work, laced with an almost metaphysical sense that a close study of the landscape could provide access to new and unfamiliar truths. For the tramp "Nature becomes your teacher, and from her you will learn what is beautiful and who you are and what is your special quest in life and whither you go". Nature itself was "trying to tell us something; she is speaking to us on

---

36 Graham Papers (FSU), Box 578, 36 (Journal for 1925).

a long-distance wave". There was also a strong hint of another familiar motif from Graham's earlier work, namely that the tramp was a kind of pilgrim, an exile from Eden wandering the earth in a quest to find the shards of a paradise long abandoned. It is not difficult to ridicule much of what Graham had to say. His tramp was in essence an idealised portrait of himself – clever, sensitive, and committed to discovering new truths about the world – and had little resemblance to the human flotsam that moved up and down the highways of Britain in the difficult economic years between the wars. There was nevertheless something touching about the wistful yearning of his book, even if the style was, as so often with Graham, overblown. "Each day nature puts her magic mirror in our hands. 'Oh child do you see yourself today'. We look, we look, and answer wistfully, not to-day, not to-day".[37]

The Gentle Art of Tramping proved to be an immediate commercial success, running through several editions, although the critical response was more lukewarm. The *Saturday Review* described it as a "masterly book",[38] but the *Times Literary Supplement* regretted the absence of more practical advice needed by walkers, and suggested that many would be put off by its "sentimentalism" and "high-brow baby talk".[39] Although few readers could have known, the elegiac tone of the book was shaped by the crisis which its author was experiencing at the time of writing. The memory of Graham's earlier trips through Russia and America, undertaken at a happier time of his life, provided the inspiration for his romanticised portrayal of a life led in the fields and mountains. At least a part of *Gentle Art of Tramping* seems to have been written when Graham was in Paris in the early autumn of 1925, immersed in the city's life, and uncertain about where his future lay. The lyrical reflections on landscape and meaning were composed at a time when he was under enormous strain and, perhaps, teetering on the edge of a breakdown. Many of the urban readers of *The Gentle Art of Tramping* were doubtless seduced by its apparent promise of a life free from conflict and strife. They could hardly have realised that Graham's words were fuelled by his own desire to recapture some of the joys and simplicities of an earlier stage of his life.

Graham started work in 1925 on a second book, a novel that subsequently appeared the following year under the title *Midsummer Music*, which tells

---

37 Stephen Graham, *The Gentle Art of Tramping* (New York: Appleton, 1926), pp. 1, 4, 5, 221.
38 *Saturday Review*, 30 April 1927.
39 *Times Literary Supplement*, 26 May 1927.

the story of a group of British writers and artists invited by an eccentric Croatian professor to spend the summer on the Dalmatian coast. The genesis of the book can probably be traced back to an invitation extended to Graham himself early in 1925 to visit the eastern coast of the Adriatic (he does not appear to have gone). The central character of the book is a middle-aged literary scholar, Felix Morrison, who travels to Dalmatia to complete his *magnum opus* on Shakespeare's *A Midsummer Night's Dream*. Although he faces enormous tribulations, living in a draughty half-ruined castle, Morrison soon finds himself enthralled by a region where "all dissolved in harmony, starlight, and pomegranate blossoms".[40] He also finds himself enchanted by the rhythms of life followed by the local peasantry, a world of song and music, in which the young people regularly meet together by the shore to sing ballads of love and mystery. Morrison himself falls in love with a local beauty, Slavitsa, who although engaged to a wealthy Jew from Zagreb prefers to remain in her childhood home of sea and music.

Graham portrayed Kastelli – the village where most of the book is set – as a dream-like place remote from the cares of the real world. Morrison is however alone amongst the English visitors in succumbing to the charm of the place. Most of his compatriots see only poverty and dirt or, as Graham drily put it in his narrator's voice, "Fairyland always becomes invisible in the presence of a dozen Englishmen".[41] In a rare example of artistic restraint, Graham refrained from making any but the most glancing parallels between the juxtaposition of fantasy and reality in *A Midsummer Night's Dream* with Morrison's experiences on the remote coast of the Adriatic. There is something profoundly melancholy in his description of the way that Morrison is finally forced to accept that he can never share his life with Slavitsa, but must instead return home to his arid bachelor life in Britain. It was a theme that came easily to Graham. The tension between dream and reality must have been particularly potent for him at a time of personal crisis. The critical reception of *Midsummer Music* was surprisingly low-key, given Graham's reputation, although the reviewer in *The Bookman* was enchanted by a novel whose characters and setting were "romantic enough to have wandered straight out of a beautiful and wonderful musical comedy".[42] Graham himself later told Vachel Lindsay

---

40 Stephen Graham, *Midsummer Music* (New York: George H. Doran, 1927), p. 63 (first published by Hurst and Blackett in 1926).
41 Ibid, p. 67.
42 *The Bookman*, February 1927.

that the book represented a deliberate attempt to strike out in a new artistic direction at a time when his outlook on life was going through a rapid process of change.[43]

If 1925 was a difficult year in Graham's life then 1926 proved to be far worse. In the winter of 1925-26 he flitted between London and Paris, managing the fall-out of his father's death, a process which placed a huge strain on his nerves. And then, at some point in late January or early February, he met at one of his Frith Street literary evenings a young writer with whom he soon fell deeply in love. Her name was Margaret Irwin – invariably referred to as Peg or Peggy in Graham's journal – and she was later to achieve fame as the author of the historical romance *Young Bess*. Graham's random use of his journal makes it difficult to chart the exact chronology of their relationship, but by February he was already fretting about his relations with Peggy, and wondering whether "I want something that is not there [...] friend, inspirer, life-giver".[44] He was nevertheless confident that "I feel I was right [...] when I adopted her as one of my little circle living and dead to whom I turn at night". By March he was confiding to his journal that "I am afraid of this life of seeking excitement". Other entries show a strong sense of self-doubt, and a fear that the success of his public self was somehow unreal and unconnected to "my real self". The precise nature of the relationship between Graham and Peggy at this time is uncertain, but Rose was deeply upset to see her husband's obsession with a woman almost twenty years younger than herself (Graham had the previous year noted in his diary the importance of having the "inspiration of a young girl in a man's life").[45] On 28 March Graham recorded in his journal that he had arranged "to take Peggy out on Tuesday. R. straightforwardly grieved, preoccupied the whole of our poetry reading". That night he felt her "sighing, trembling", before heading for the sitting room couch, only for Graham to beg her to return. By April, Graham was sure that "I love Peggy that is a gay and happy fact [...] R has the first place in my heart, but is not sure of it. She is mortified [...] We have such passionate talks in tears". Rose almost certainly had a good deal to worry about. By May Graham was confiding to his journal snippets of conversation that make it clear he had asked Peggy to travel the world with him, an offer she declined, preferring to remain in London to develop her writing career.

---

43 Graham Papers (HRC), Letters, Graham to Lindsay, 20 March 1927.
44 All the quotations in this and the following paragraphs are unless stated otherwise taken from Graham Papers (FSU), Box 578, 37 (Journal for 1926).
45 T.I.F. Armstrong (Gawsworth) Papers, Misc. (1925 Diary, entry dated 16 January).

Figure 8: Stephen Graham in 1926 (photographer unknown).
Courtesy National Portrait Gallery, © CC BY-NC-ND.

The relationship between Graham and Rose throughout their earlier life necessarily remains opaque given the absence of any substantial cache of letters or diaries to cast light on it, whilst many pages of his 1926 journal were ripped out and destroyed, probably by his second wife, making it difficult to chart with any precision the emotional turbulence of their *annus horribilis*. The thinly-veiled autobiographical references to Rose in *Priest of the Ideal* suggest that their relationship was always based on what might loosely be called spiritual affinity rather than sexual passion. Rose's own isolated journal entries for the critical months of 1926 certainly indicate that she saw her relationship with Graham in such terms. At the start of April she noted that "Love seems to me the watchword of today. Love and spiritual life – that life which is not merely to be the life of the individual, but the mysterious and mystical life in connection and union with others". A few weeks later, she wrote that "Stephen gave me a wonderfully beautiful thought about the life of the Virgin and therefore all women – She not only received the message of the Annunciation and responded at once […] She was never unmindful of the heavenly vision – all her life she heard the voice of Gabriel in her heart and knew her path of life in sorrow and joy".[46] Such moments of reconciliation and reflection could not overcome the strains in their relationship. By the end of May, Rose had left Frith Street and taken a room at a religious retreat, although she continued to see Graham, who noted mournfully that "R very serious, earnest, melancholy, wants me to talk as in a problem-play conversation". Even when she returned home at Graham's urging, he found that he could think only of Peggy, and felt "cold and guilty" at the anguish he was causing his wife, who "naturally hates to see P in her place in my heart, mind, life, society". By the start of June, Rose was blaming the decline of their marriage on the fact they had no children. Graham agreed, recalling that "we were both blind in those early married years" when neither of them could imagine the sadness that lay ahead.

By the early summer of 1926, Graham was deeply depressed at being torn "between two women". It is not clear whether Peggy felt as deeply about him as he did her. There are certainly numerous obsessive entries in his journal fretting about meetings at which she seemed cold or distracted. The hot-house atmosphere was relieved, at least for a time, when Graham was asked by *The Times* to visit Czechoslovakia and write a series of articles on his experiences there. Although it was not a country he liked, Graham welcomed the opportunity to get away from a situation that had become intolerable to him, whilst he was in any case still too much the professional writer to turn down a lucrative assignment. Prague was "hung with little flags" when he arrived, in celebration of a local festival. Graham was struck by the extent to which the city had become "more Slavic" and less German during the five years since he last visited. He met President Tomáš Masaryk, as well as his son Jan, the future Foreign Minister, who died twenty years later when he fell from a window in mysterious circumstances at a time when his country was falling under Soviet control. Neither man had much sympathy for Graham's brand of religious idealism. Jan Masaryk in particular was indignant at a speech Graham gave on the role of religion in public life, responding that the Czechoslovaks were "a practical people" whose future lay in "the building of civilization and the conquest of Nature".[47]

Graham's own heart was not really in such polemics at this stage of his life. His nights were disturbed by terrible dreams and his days

---

46 New Atlantis Foundation Archive 1/6/2/12/1 (Rose Graham notebook).
47 Graham, *Wonderful Scene*, p. 293. Also see *The Times*, 8 September 1926.

punctuated by thoughts of Peg. After leaving Prague, Graham moved on to Bratislava, the Slovak capital situated on a picturesque site by the River Danube, where he tried to lose himself in street cafes thronged in a "flood of electric light". His attempt to find solace amongst the crowds met with little success. He headed on to the remote Carpathian lands in the east of the country, arriving in the "charming" capital Uzhgorod, where the local Ukrainian-speaking people were resisting attempts to "absorb [them] into Czechoslovak culture".[48] He then left Uzhgorod behind in order to travel on to a Ruthenian village close to the Polish border, where he arrived to find the local people dressed up in national costume to celebrate the festival of St Peter and St Paul. The journey there took him through "wild and beautiful" scenery, whilst the village itself was "very picturesque", with wooden houses capped by "pyramid-like roofs".[49] Such distractions could not take Graham's mind off events back home. Ten years earlier, he would have been overcome with joy at finding himself in such a setting. Now he could only think of the situation that would confront him when he returned to London.

Graham's journal entries in the weeks following his return from Czechoslovakia show a man in the grip of both obsession and depression. Within days of arriving in London he was recording how "I love my Rose, probably I love Peg. I feel so lonely and weep and weep". He also noted how Rose had become "very bitter" and "inclined to break down and cry and I cannot bear it". By the middle of August things were close to erupting. Graham felt that the whole situation was driving him to become a recluse, as he withdrew from the normal round of literary and artistic events which had come to form an important part of his life in London in recent years. He also – tellingly – wrote with regret about how his relationship with Peg lacked "that touch of maternal tenderness". Peg herself was finding the strain of the situation too much to bear. She accused Graham during a trip to Brighton of selfishness, a charge from which he did not entirely demur, although he fretted about how the "brightness" of their relationship had faded as Peg became "indifferent" to "my life, my happiness or sufferings".

Rose grew "hysterical" under the strain of events, torn between urging her husband to give up Peggy and offering advice about how best to handle

---

48 Uzhgorod is today in the Ukraine (Uzhhorod) and Graham's treatment of its people as Russian rather than Ukrainian at least in part reflected his instinctive great Russian nationalism.
49 *The Times*, 16 September, 1926.

the situation in which he found himself (a tension, perhaps, between her uxorial and maternal instincts). Graham noted bitterly in his journal that he and Peggy would never have been in such a situation if Rose had "given me my freedom", ignoring his own doubts as to whether Peggy herself actually wanted to be with him at all. He also angrily told Rose that she would be happy if he was dead so long as she still had his books to remember him by. A few days later, Graham drove Peg out of London and the two of them went for a walk through the countryside. The outing ended in bitter arguments about the future. Peggy angrily told Graham that the "next time you have a woman see that you have finished with Rose before you start with her". Graham for his part felt "empty-hearted" as they returned to the car, which he raced back towards London, before suddenly stopping the vehicle and breaking down in uncontrollable sobs. When they resumed their journey, he was tempted to "drive the car under a motor bus", noting that he was only prevented by the thought that Peg might die whilst he survived. Although there was yet again a brief reconciliation between the two, it was clear by the middle of August that Graham had little prospect of securing a future with Peggy. It was also becoming clear that his relationship with Rose had been damaged forever, even if it was to be another three or four years before they finally drifted apart entirely.

The immediate storm was once again dampened by Graham's departure on his travels, this time for New York, where he planned to carry out research for a series of articles about the city's night life for *Harper's Magazine* and the *New Yorker*. It is astonishing that he felt able to make the trip, given the desperate state of mind visible in his journal entries, which included one on the eve of his departure that read: "Darling mother where are you now? Do you know how solitary I am? You know how foolish I have been. Terribly sad. Lonely empty day". During the journey his mind ran endlessly over the events of the past few months, whilst at night he dreamt of Peggy, including one dream in which the two of them were furnishing a flat together. His arrival in New York provided him with the usual distractions of establishing himself in a hotel and catching up with the latest literary gossip, but thoughts of Peggy continued to obsess him: "Peg does not want what I want. I have failed to inspire her and after all we have no common interests in life. I go away but her thoughts do not follow me". He tried to "school my mind" against thoughts of her, but it proved to be a "fruitless cause", and he spent evenings poring over her old letters. Peg herself still wrote to him occasionally, although she had now left with friends on an extended holiday to France, leaving Graham to write a piece of doggerel about his state of mind:

> I'm feeling very blue today,
> I do not care for song or dance,
> I haven't any heart to play,
> My Peg is eating frog in France.

Graham was gradually distracted by his forays into New York's nightlife (he also found time to broadcast on the radio and give a number of lectures). His first impression of the city after dark was that prohibition had ended all activity beyond "a little cabaret" and a few "dancing-bars". He quickly realised how wrong his judgement had been. Within a couple of weeks he was visiting speak-easies with a journalist friend, and attending various burlesque shows, as well as going to clubs where "a naked contortionist tickled her own chin with tenuous fingers of arms which were locked behind her head".[50]

Graham's tours through New York nightlife were punctuated with reflections about the way in which recent events had shaped his personality. A few weeks after his arrival he noted in his journal that he had until recently been:

> Making for a late maturity, thought I was a setting sun in fact a rising one. My mind goes back to early Moscow days, when I was vaguely in love with a young married woman, who had the reputation of being v. immoral. She said I was a quiet boy and she had swallowed me. But she had not the sense to help me and I was very quiet. I've gone through a great deal since those days – and wakened several times, but curiously enough I am stale – about to waken, about to be someone broader and in every way powerful.

His words may have reflected the fact that he found himself in what he wryly termed "an interesting situation". Graham's tours of the nightclubs of New York usually took place in the company of one of a number of young women, typically working in publishing or some part of the entertainment industry, and there is little doubt that he was seeking female company to provide him with the emotional support he always so desperately craved. By the end of October he was torn between two women, both in their mid twenties, one of them looking for love and the other very "loose […] twenty years ago I should have chosen the good girl but now it seems the other holds me". Graham was soon involved in an affair with Patrica (Pat), to

---

50 Stephen Graham, *New York Nights* (New York: George H. Doran, 1927), p. 246.

whom he eventually dedicated the book *New York Nights* when it was published the following year. Together the two of them went to exotic clubs like Samarkand, a place populated by "people in evening dress" and decorated with "oriental lamps hanging from the ceiling".[51] Graham himself was uncertain whether he was in love with Pat – he tried to change the conversation whenever the subject came up – but there is little doubt that he was searching for a new kind of relationship utterly different from the one he had with Rose. Graham had always been attracted by the hum of the streets, finding in the major cities of the world an excitement that exercised a surprising thrall over a man whose early reputation had been made by his lyrical descriptions of the Russian countryside. In more recent books, like *London Nights*, he still looked on the world of nightclubs and late-night drinking dens with the eyes of an outsider, fascinated by its decadent aura, but faintly repulsed by the lax morality and uninhibited behaviour of its habitués. In New York during the tail-end of 1926 he immersed himself far more thoroughly into this world of urban decadence than ever before.

Graham returned to London for a few months at the end of 1926, before heading off again to New York at the start of April the following year. At Christmas he saw Peggy at a party, looking "tired and drained", but the two did not talk to one another.[52] A few weeks later he wrote in his journal that "It is dangerous to fall in love with a hard unimaginative but sentimental person", and noted bitterly that he had been nothing more than "a literary experience for Peggy", a claim that must remain entirely speculative in the absence of any perspective other than his own. Graham sent flowers to her on a number of occasions, although they seem to have been rejected, leading once again to the familiar self-pitying lament that Peggy had been "very cruel to me". Despite his gloom, Graham found the time and motivation to attend the Gargoyle Club regularly, whilst the party he held in March to celebrate his birthday was "the largest party I have ever had at Frith Street lasting till three in the morning". He also used some of the time to sketch out an article on the 'Passing of the Old Russia', which appeared a few months later in a symposium published by the New York journal *Current History*.[53] Although he was generally adept at keeping his private

---

51 Ibid, p. 28.
52 The quotations in this and the following paragraph unless otherwise stated are taken from Graham Papers, Box 579, 48 (Journal for 1927 although the original erroneously labelled 1926).
53 *Current History* (New York), 27, 2 (1927), pp. 229-32.

troubles to himself, the turmoil in Graham's personal life was well-known enough to his friends to lead to speculation that he would not return home from his next trip to New York. A few days before he left London, he wrote to Vachel Lindsay telling his old friend that:

> It's been a stormy year for me, as I've been terribly torn up between a love affair and my affection for my wife. I have been restless and passionate [...] My life and outlook is changing a great deal and if I come to Spokane [where Lindsay was living] you will see a difference between the Stephen of Glacier Park days and that of today [...] I have turned a bend and there are new horizons.[54]

Graham's departure for New York in April certainly removed him for a time from the setting of his recent woes. On arrival there he wrote to Lindsay telling him that he was "so happy" to be back in America.[55] The relief proved short-lived. He found Pat "very flat as though she has lost her soul", and he alternated between convincing himself that she "still loves me dearly", and fretting that there was "nothing" between them. He also lamented that she seemed to have "no care for me", the cry of anguish of a man who always expected those he loved to devote their lives unreservedly to him in return, as Rose had done throughout their marriage. Although Graham dedicated *New York Nights* to Pat when it appeared later in 1927, by the time he returned to Britain in the summer its seems clear that their relationship was over, or at the very least that Graham had recognised it could not provide him with the emotional support he still so desperately wanted.

The personal crisis that Graham went through in 1926-27 did, for once, reduce his astonishing productivity, although he still managed to write a considerable amount, including several articles about his nocturnal ramblings in New York,[56] which were in due course reproduced in *New York Nights*. No reader of the book would have guessed at the turmoil faced by its author. The self-revelatory tone that characterised so much of Graham's early travel writing had by now long disappeared. There were a few references to Pat and a number of other "pretty women" who provided him with "the best passport to New York at night",[57] but most of

---

54 Vachel Lindsay Papers (HRC), Letters, Graham to Lindsay, 20 March 1927.
55 Ibid, Graham to Lindsay, 20 April 1927.
56 Stephen Graham, 'The Bowery under Prohibition', *Harper's Magazine*, February 1927; Stephen Graham, 'In a Flop-House', *New Yorker*, 30 July 1927; 'Transient's Impressions', *New Yorker*, 23 July 1927; 'A Rooming House in Speakeasy Street', *New Yorker*, 9 July 1927.
57 Graham, *New York Nights*, p. 53.

the chapters were designed to give pen portraits of the city, ranging from the scene at celebrated nightclubs like the one run by Texas Guinan to the human detritus thronging the Bowery. The book also contained a series of pictures by the German-born book illustrator by Kurt Wiese who had recently moved to the USA. During his first visit to New York, fourteen years earlier, Graham had condemned the city as the apotheosis of the kind of commercial and industrial society that he loathed. His views were now more nuanced, reflecting his changing outlook on the world, as he found in the city a glamour that had eluded him when his heart still lay firmly within the grasp of Holy Russia. Graham acknowledged that the modern American city was inhabited by crowds of:

> solitary people, friendless and lonely men and women, who have moped all day in wretched gloomy rooms, in homes which are mocked by the happy idea of home. At eleven o'clock at night they bethink them of the radiant shore just so many blocks away, pick themselves out of their loneliness, and make for the light, to lose themselves in the light-intoxicated throngs. Poe's man in the crowd is walking there every night, back and forth, forward and back again, his eyes lit by some dream.[58]

He now however found the experience of belonging to such a world exhilarating as well as dispiriting, relishing the anonymity of New York, and the extraordinary richness of its street scenes. Although he was unable to find "poetry" or "tenderness" in the city,[59] he was gradually seduced by its energy, sensing that for all its faults it served as "a portent of this and coming time, the towering apex of a growing pyramid of civilisation".[60]

New York Nights was not short of details of the city's *demi-monde*, including vivid descriptions of the night life in one club in Harlem, where a nearly-naked contortionist distorted her body for the gratification of the audience. Graham also visited a number of burlesque shows, as well as dance halls, where men and women could pay to secure a dancing partner, whose morals he noted pointedly "I could not vouch for". His old censorious tone also occasionally surfaced when he saw performances that he thought were "an offence against decency", but most of his writing was simply designed to capture the texture of what he saw. Some of the best passages in *New York Nights* focused on his travels along the Bowery, still at that time a by-word for flop-houses and illegal speak-easies, which Graham described as a street

---

58 Ibid, p. 14.
59 Ibid, p. 20.
60 Ibid, p. 17.

that had "not been made; it grew, and even if it be a fungoid, it is natural".[61] He explained how he used secret passwords to gain access to illegal clubs, which served drinks of such potency that many patrons collapsed on the pavement as soon as they left, as well as describing the crowds of beggars who swarmed round any faintly prosperous-looking passer-by demanding money and cigarettes. Graham acknowledged that, for all its squalor, he found the Bowery "a strange, haunting, haunted street", whose denizens had their own particular code of honour, and he was convinced that the time he spent watching its street-life gave him "a true perspective of the city, and I think I know more of New York because of the many nights I have spent there".[62] The reviewers varied in their judgements about the success of his attempts to convey his experiences. *The New York Times* praised his book for providing "an important part of the picture of New York as quite a lot of people not New Yorkers are currently seeing it".[63] The reviewer in the *Times Literary Supplement*, by contrast, found Graham's descriptions those of "a very external observer", who managed only to make his subject matter sound "dreary".[64] The *Saturday Review* found the sketches "sensitively written" but lacking the interest "to warrant publication in book form".[65] The variation in the reviews may help to explain why *New York Nights* sold better in America than in Britain. Graham was still finding greater critical and commercial success in the New World than he was back home.

Graham returned to England from America in July 1927, noting rather cryptically in his journal that he was returning home "for my soul", perhaps suggesting that he had begun to worry that his New York lifestyle was warping his personality and outlook. His chronic restlessness meant that he only stayed in London for a few days, though, almost immediately leaving the capital for a car trip to Scotland.[66] Graham stopped off to admire the medieval Romanesque architecture of Ely Cathedral, before moving on northwards up the east coast, camping out on Holbeach Marsh in Lincolnshire, where he watched bats swooping to take insects at sundown. He then visited the gothic Minister at Beverley in Yorkshire, before heading for Berwick and the border, travelling through the area

---

61 Ibid, p. 183.
62 Ibid, p. 199.
63 *New York Times*, 6 November 1927.
64 *Times Literary Supplement*, 19 April 1928.
65 *Saturday Review*, 4 February 1928.
66 Graham Papers (FSU), Box 580, 5c ('Camping out in Scotland'). For further details see Graham Papers (FSU), 579, 48 (Journal for 1927 erroneously labelled 1926).

where his father had spent his early years. By the second half of July he was at John O'Groats, "in perfect weather", after which he drove round to the west coast of Scotland through lanes full of summer flowers. Graham covered more than 2,000 miles during his seventeen-day trip, and later wrote that he found himself appalled at the emptiness of my "native land", a phrase that had considerable significance. Although his interest in his Scottish roots had previously been rather desultory, his mother was always enthralled by the songs and literature of the land of her birth, whilst Anderson Graham had, in later life, spent much of his time and energy writing about the borderlands.[67] Graham's trip to his "native land" was made at least in part in homage to his late parents. It may also have been designed to help him delay, at least for a while, his return to the city where he had recently endured so many frustrations and disappointments. His respite was only temporary. By the start of August he was back home in London, where he began collecting pieces for a collection, *The Tramp's Anthology*, which included works by authors including Vachel Lindsay and George Borrow. Graham hoped it would sell well on the back of the recent success of *Gentle Art of Tramping*.[68]

Rose Graham had by the second half of 1927 become deeply involved in the establishment of the International Society for Individual Psychology – more often known as the Adler Society – an organisation that was the brainchild of Stephen's old friend Dimitrije Mitrinović.[69] The Society was formally committed to fostering the establishment of "an organic social order based upon the understanding of human beings affected by modern psychology" (despite its nomenclature the Austrian psychologist Alfred Adler was decidedly luke-warm about the organisation that bore his name).[70] Although Mitrinović was convinced that recent developments in psychology and sociology meant that "knowledge of the soul has become an exact science", the records of the Society show that many of its members were interested, above all, in various forms of eastern and esoteric thought, even if these were clothed in a language designed to make them seen scientific and objective. Rose served as Secretary of the Adler Society from

---

67 P. Anderson Graham, *Highways and Byways in Northumbria* (London: Macmillan, 1920); P. Anderson Graham, *Lindisfarne* (London: Knight, Frank and Rutley, 1920).
68 Stephen Graham (ed.), *The Tramp's Anthology* (London: Peter Davies, 1928).
69 On the Adler Society see Andrew Rigby, *Dimitrije Mitrinović: A Biography* (York: William Sessions, 2006), pp. 95-105.
70 New Atlantis Foundation archives, NAF 3/1/2 (1928 Statement of the aims of the Adler Society).

its formation, as well as chairing one of the early meetings of the Society, and her notes record talks on subjects ranging from Zen Buddhism to Hegelian dialectic. Her husband briefly participated in the Adler Society on return from his trip to Scotland, nominally serving as Vice-President of its Sociological Group, before being replaced by the writer and critic Philip Mairet (who had like Graham known Mitrinović for many years). Although the reasons for the end of his involvement are not clear, it is hard to imagine Graham having much time for debate about such topics as 'Communism and the Zodiac', which formed the subject of one of the Sociological Group's meetings soon after he left.

Graham's brief participation in the Adler Society suggests that neither he nor Rose were convinced that the breach between them was as yet final. He nevertheless chose to spend the final months of 1927 alone in Paris, the city he had for years escaped to whenever life had become too difficult in London, spending his time rather aimlessly attending the Folies Bergères and various cabaret performances. Although Graham knew a number of artists and writers in the French capital – he had met Ernest Hemingway there a few years earlier – his visit in the autumn of 1927 seems to have been a solitary and rather lonely affair. The gradual breakdown of his relationship with Rose removed a central anchor in his life, fostering a powerful sense of anomie that he could not shake off wherever he went. There was something distinctively forlorn about Graham's last entry in his 1927 journal that "I have not lived as much this year as last". Whether he felt that the gentle air of melancholy pervading his life was preferable to the storms of emotion unleashed in 1926 by his affair with Peg is hard to say.

Graham's journal entries for the first few weeks of 1928 suggest that the scars of the previous few years were still far from healed. He reflected on the way that love was "often a mean state. One wants so much more than one gives. How preferable the innocent state of living in daily happiness, taking and giving, the joys which are possible".[71] Graham was, though, gradually regaining some of his old energy. He spent the first few months of 1928 working on his novel *The Lay Confessor*, which he regarded as his finest work of fiction right down to his death, writing 43,000 words in May alone. The experience left him drained. By the middle of June he had

---

71 Graham Papers (FSU), Box 578, 38 (Journal for 1928).

finished revising the novel – "harder work than writing" – although he was still confident that it was his "strongest book".

The setting of *The Lay Confessor* took Graham back to the turbulent days of pre-revolutionary Russia. The central character is one Epiphanov, a kind of tavern-philosopher, whose outward interest in "eating and drinking" conceals the "ascetic under-garb of a confessor", who attracts those around him precisely because they find him more approachable than the priests and deacons of the Orthodox Church.[72] Many of the sentiments uttered by Epiphanov echo those of his creator, including his attacks on the new Russian middle class as "a dangerous element", and his claim that "Peter the Great cheated Russia of her true capital" by moving the Court from Moscow to St Petersburg. Graham also used his own narrative voice to condemn Britain for its policy towards Russia before 1917, suggesting that the government in London had worked to undermine the tsarist *ancien régime* by encouraging investors to extract wealth rather than allow it "to flow freely into the communal life of the country".[73] Epiphanov himself plays a morally ambiguous role in the plot of *The Lay Confessor*, living openly with a young woman who had once been in love with a former student, Sasha, himself a leader in one of the more violent revolutionary factions. Graham made Rasputin a central character of the novel, providing a surprisingly positive portrait of the celebrated Holy Man as one who lived "very simply" in rooms "utterly devoid of luxury".[74] The denouement of *The Lay Confessor* comes when Epiphanov is thrown into prison following the revolution, and Sasha only agrees to release him if his former lover returns to him, a condition which she accepts. Epiphanov himself dies, still anguished by the fate of his beloved Russia, his character enriched by personal suffering.

It is not easy to see why Graham regarded *The Lay Confessor* as his best novel. The language is often stilted ("Let's go to Yama and have some cabbage pies and tea"). The portrayal of the historical background is extremely confused (the February and October revolutions are in effect conflated into one). The characters are, as all too often in Graham's fiction, extremely one-dimensional. The reviews were nevertheless generally positive. *The Manchester Guardian* praised the book as "genuinely realistic

---

72 Stephen Graham, *The Lay Confessor* (London: Ernest Benn, 1928), p. 43.
73 Ibid, p. 62.
74 Ibid, p. 208.

art".[75] *The Observer* praised the "superbly sharp" observation.[76] *The Bookman* was less effusive, but still believed that the "dignified competence" of the novel would enhance Graham's reputation,[77] whilst the *Times Literary Supplement* praised him for "snaring" readers with his vivid prose.[78] Some critics claimed to detect in the book an echo of the themes found in the major works of nineteenth-century Russian literature, including redemption through suffering and the co-existence of virtue and vice in the human heart. The positive reception of the book is particularly surprising given that Graham's critical reputation in British literary circles had declined over the previous few years (his fiction in particular seldom attracted favourable reviews). His reputation as an expert on Russia, albeit one who had not visited the country for many years, was still powerful enough to encourage critics to presume that he had an unusually vivid insight into the dramatic events of 1917. Graham's lectures on Russia continued to attract audiences eager to hear him talk about how Bolshevik Russia might yet change as a result of the "pent-up national spiritual forces" suppressed over the previous ten years by the Soviet leadership.[79]

Graham recovered from the strain of finishing *The Lay Confessor* with a car trip through the West Country, sleeping outside when the weather was good, in an attempt to recapture something of the free-spirited life he had relished so strongly twenty years earlier. He then headed off to Fontainbleau, the headquarters of Gurdjieff's controversial Institute, in order to visit the ever-mercurial Maya (the sometime companion of Algernon Blackwood). His trip was only a short one, though, and by the middle of August 1928 he was back home working on the publicity for *The Lay Confessor*. He also worked on the early drafts of a series of literary essays, as well as regularly visiting the British Library to carry out research for a biography of Peter the Great, which was published the following year. Graham had by now started to recover a good deal of his emotional equanimity. The *Daily Mail* published articles by him on 'London Evenings' which told of his visits to fashionable restaurants and clubs.[80] By the end of 1928 Graham was enough of a fixture on the London social scene to warrant a gently ironic (and astute) comment in the *Daily Mirror's* 'As I see Life' column that for

---

75 *The Manchester Guardian*, 2 November 1928.
76 *The Observer*, 21 October 1928.
77 *The Bookman*, November 1928.
78 *Times Literary Supplement*, 2 August 1928.
79 *Manchester Guardian*, 24 February 1928.
80 See, for example, *Daily Mail*, 12 July 1928.

"a writer of mystical books" he loved "to look at gaiety".[81] An entry in his journal a few weeks earlier noted laconically, and without comment, that "Rose goes to 6 Denmark Street to live". Rose Graham's exact whereabouts over the previous few months is in fact something of a mystery, although she certainly stayed for a time with her sister-in-law Eleanor, who lived not far away from Frith Street in Bloomsbury. Rose's own journal conveys little of her emotions at this time. She would however surely have been tempted to agree with one of her husband's journal entries dating from December 1928, when he wrote cryptically that "there's a lot of mystery about my family but I can't fathom it".

Graham's partial break with Rose provided the springboard into a new phase of his life, and the period 1929-30 saw a number of changes that were to have a profound impact on his work, as he began to concentrate on writing novels and biographies rather than travel books. His biography of Peter the Great, which appeared in 1929, was predictably unsympathetic towards a Tsar whose life had been dedicated to making his country more western and less Russian in thought and culture. Peter was portrayed as a man who "throve in an atmosphere of fear, cruelty, and burlesque mirth" and, although not personally cruel, he could be brutal in his determination to change "the appearance and style" of the lands over which he ruled.[82] Some critics praised the book for possessing the drama of Tolstoy's *War and Peace*, "set back a couple of centuries and embodied in one man",[83] but Alexander Nazaroff writing in the *New York Times* found the book accurate but "not very dramatic".[84] Professional historians were still less kind.[85]

Graham himself wrote many years later that he had never found writing historical biographies a rewarding experience, since he lacked the patience to engage in detailed historical research, preferring the art of "writing from what you see".[86] The essays of literary criticism he prepared for publication during 1928-29 were altogether more impressive. A few of the pieces that appeared in the collection *The Death of Yesterday* had been published previously. Some of the unpublished pieces dated back to 1914, whilst others were of far more recent origin, including articles on Vachel Lindsay and Rudyard Kipling. The best work combined a shrewd appraisal

---

81 *Daily Mirror*, 12 December 1928.
82 Stephen Graham, *Peter the Great* (London: Ernest Benn, 1929), p. 113.
83 *The Bookman*, October 1929.
84 *New York Times*, 22 December 1929.
85 *Journal of Modern History*, 2, 1 (1930), pp. 124-25.
86 Graham, *Wonderful Scene*, p. 299.

of individual writers and literary trends with Graham's characteristically lively, if over-coloured, prose. Nietzsche was described as "a man killed by his loneliness". The poems of Carl Sandburg "should be slowly intoned, the way one might read the Book of Job at Vespers". Robert Burns provided "a voice for the voiceless".[87] Even the most cursory reading of *The Death of Yesterday* shows how much more emotionally involved Graham was in the work than in his biography of Peter the Great. His travel writing had always been at its best when offering something more than simple descriptions of landscape and people. His best literary criticism showed a similar ability to hint at the deep textures and colours that characterised the work of his favourite writers.

Graham continued to travel a good deal in 1929-30, although the financial crisis that erupted with the collapse of the Wall Street markets cost him a good deal of money, and made it hard to find new commissions for his writing. His two longest trips were to the United States. One of Graham's main reasons for travelling to America in the spring of 1929 was to see Vachel Lindsay and his new wife Elizabeth, who had recently moved back to the old Lindsay family home in Springfield from Spokane, along with their two young children (Lindsay and Graham had corresponded regularly since their Glacier Park hike eight years earlier).[88] After staying in New York for a few weeks to discuss business with his publishers, Graham took the train to Illinois, where he was struck by the change in his old friend: "It was surprising to sit with Vachel in his home, drinking red wine and [smoking] cigarettes. He adored his wife to a point that was almost embarrassing to a guest".[89] After leaving Springfield, Graham travelled back eastwards to New York, which he found "very blank and uninteresting", and quickly "got on the first boat I could find". He arrived in London in June where he felt "in the blues for a whole month", and it was only with a short trip to France that he began to recover his spirits. He wrote to Elizabeth Lindsay that he planned to return to America in a few months if his biography of Peter the Great was a commercial success, adding mournfully that "the worst of your dear country is that for a man of my type it is very difficult to earn a decent living. I spend much and earn

---

87 Stephen Graham, *The Death of Yesterday* (London: Ernest Benn, 1930), pp. 147, 87, 101.
88 For letters between Graham and Lindsay during the 1920s, see Marc Chenetier (ed.), *Letters of Vachel Lindsay* (New York: Burt Franklin, 1979).
89 Eleanor Ruggles, *The West-Going Heart: A Life of Vachel Lindsay* (New York: Norton, 1959), p. 404.

little, so I am always seeking some success such as I might easily have with a book of this kind".[90] His hopes were not fulfilled. He was unable to return to America until the autumn of 1930, when he gave a series of lectures in the United States and Canada on subjects including such unlikely topics as 'Family Life in the USA' (the lecture circuit remained profitable for overseas speakers, although the Wall Street crash of 1929 meant that lucrative engagements were harder to come by than before).[91] Graham also once again met Vachel and his wife in New York. It was their last meeting before Lindsay took his life the following year by drinking a bottle of Lysol disinfectant, following a long struggle with depression and financial worries. Graham arrived back in London a few days before Christmas 1930. He published nothing about these two trips – unusual for a man who had always been so adept at turning his experiences into prose – and evidence perhaps both of his weariness and the collapse in the market for such work.

Vachel and his wife still addressed their letters to both Stephen and Rose right down until 1930, even though they were at least dimly aware of the problems between them. It is almost impossible to recreate in any detail the texture of the relationship between the Grahams during the final years of the 1920s. The two of them certainly went on holiday together to the Pyrenees in 1928. They also occasionally drove out from London into the countryside, where they lay side-by-side, staring at the sky, relishing the peace and quiet. The few letters that survive from Rose suggest that she was withdrawing into a private world, punctuated by her involvement in the Adler Society, and she seems to have found consolation in precisely the kind of esoteric language and outlook that her husband had increasingly abandoned. She wrote to Vachel Lindsay in 1929 that "to obey the dictates of one's spirit and create a satisfactory adjustment and vision to see through this contradictory little world of ours is no easy matter [...] Perhaps it is true that there is a recipe for solution of any problem: a measure of honesty and sincerity with one of wonder and bewilderment topped off with a puff of humour".[92] The wistful tone of the letter suggests that she had not herself found the solution. Rose's presence simply fades out of her husband's life during these years. Graham was left with the task of building a new personal and professional life to replace the one that had slowly crumbled apart.

---

90 Vachel Lindsay Papers (HRC), Misc., Graham to Elizabeth Lindsay, 29 August 1929.
91 *Montreal Gazette*, 1 December 1930; *New York Times*, 7 November 1930.
92 Vachel Lindsay Papers (HRC), Letters file, Rose Graham to Lindsay, 15 June 1929.

Even the most diligent of biographers can never hope to penetrate fully to the subtle interplay of hopes and dreams that shape the life of their subject. Nor is it possible to recreate the storms of emotion that inevitably surround the breakdown of any long-term relationship. It seems that the collapse of Graham's relationship with Rose was not so much the catalyst as the consequence of changes in his outlook on life which had been taking place over many years. The youthful Graham found in his half-imagined idyll of Holy Russia a place of order and harmony, which provided him with a sense of consolation for the deracination and estrangement he felt in the prosaic world of Edwardian Britain. Rose herself seems to have taken her place in Graham's emotional life at this time as a serene presence who provided him both with the freedom to travel and the security of having someone to return to from his sojourns across the world. Yet even Graham's early writings showed a fascination with the colour and contradictions of a "Little World" that possessed its own allure and vibrancy. Before the First World War, he was already torn between his search for the eternal and his interest in the rich texture of everyday life. His experiences in the trenches and his travels through post-war Europe made this tension even stronger, as he increasingly came to question the metaphysical musings of his youth. The breakdown of his relationship with Rose flowed from these changes. Her presence in his life had come about when he was still a very young man, hopeful of finding a place – both physical and emotional – where conflict and uncertainty could be banished to the margins. The more mature Graham intuitively understood that such an escape from the cares of the world was not possible. His break with Rose was part both of an anguished loss of old dreams and a step towards building a new life.

7. New Horizons

When Graham published his novel *The Lay Confessor* in 1928 he was already taking a renewed interest in Russian literature. The following year he edited a thousand-page collection of *Great Russian Short Stories*, including works by authors ranging from Pushkin to Tolstoy, as well as less familiar writers who had long been favourites of his such as Aleksei Remizov and Aleksander Ertel'. He also included pieces by Soviet authors such as Isaac Babel. When Graham made his tour down the western borderlands of the USSR, in 1924, he was convinced that the Soviet Government had crushed all literature and art of any value, but his views changed somewhat during the following years, as the modest cultural thaw of the 1920s led to the publication of some fictional works of high quality.[1] Graham visited Paris several times during the late 1920s, where he spent time rooting around in the second-hand book kiosks that lined the banks of the Seine. It was here that he came across a number of Russian novels that were almost unknown back in Britain. He persuaded his publisher, Ernest Benn, to commission translations of several of these books, including Panteleimon Romanov's *Three Pairs of Silk Stockings*, Valentin Kataev's *The Embezzlers* and Roman Gul's *General B.O.* (Gul', unlike the other two, was writing in emigration in Berlin). Graham paid for the works to be translated, although he carefully supervised the quality of the final text. He also provided a preface to each book introducing the writer to an English-language audience.[2] The

---

1   On the cultural dimension and artistic experimentation in Soviet Russia during the 1920s see Abbot Gleason, Peter Kenez and Richard Stites (eds.), *Bolshevik Culture: Experiment and Order in the Russian Revolution* (Bloomington, IN: Indiana University Press, 1985); Richard Stites, *Revolutionary Dreams: Utopian Visions and Experimental Life in the Russian Revolution* (New York: Oxford University Press, 1989).

2   For correspondence relating to the translations see John Gawsworth Papers (University of Reading Library), Box 10, Graham to Gawsworth, 15 October 1930, 18 November 1930, 24 November 1930.

http://dx.doi.org/10.11647/OBP.0040.07

translations were well-received by critics. The *Manchester Guardian* praised Kataev for "his fine work".³ The *Observer* told readers that Romanov's work was reminiscent of Chekhov at his best.⁴ Vita Sackville-West writing in *The Listener* praised *The Embezzlers* as "amusing".⁵ Despite the positive reception, though, the series only lasted a short time, since the sales figures were rather less glowing than the reviews.

Graham's main contact at Ernest Benn during this time was an aspiring young poet called Terrence Armstrong, who, under his *nom de plume* of John Gawsworth, soon became a long-standing if eccentric fixture in the London literary scene, before subsequently drinking himself to poverty and an early death. Gawsworth was an avid bibliophile. During the 1930s he published the unknown manuscripts of Graham's old friend, Wilfrid Ewart, as well as editing numerous collections of short stories. He later served as literary executor for the fantasy writer M.P. Shiel, the self-styled King of Redonda, a title that Shiel claimed to have inherited from his father, who asserted his unlikely right to the throne of the small rocky Caribbean island when living on nearby Montserrat. When Gawsworth received the title upon Shiel's death in 1947 – he had been heir apparent since the 1930s, when the two men cut their wrists and mingled their blood in a bizarre ceremony at a remote cottage in Sussex – he in turn conferred "dukedoms" on various friends and acquaintances.⁶ Nor was the title of King Juan of Redonda Gawsworth's only affectation. By the 1930s he had already constructed a largely imaginary genealogy for himself, claiming descent from a number of Scottish lairds who took part in the Jacobite Rebellion of 1745, as well as Mary Fytton of Gawsworth Hall in Cheshire (often identified as the dark lady of Shakespeare's sonnets). Gawsworth was, despite his eccentricities, successful in establishing a place for himself in London literary life, developing friendships with writers ranging from Rebecca West to Lawrence Durrell. Although his talent for self-promotion grated on many of his contemporaries, he had by the middle of the 1930s shown himself to possess "a brain as sharp as an awl when it came to any matter that touched on publishers or publishing".⁷ Nor did his poetry

---

3 *Manchester Guardian*, 12 July 1929.
4 *Observer*, 5 July 1931.
5 *The Listener*, 5 June 1929.
6 For memoirs of Gawsworth and details about the history of Redonda, see Paul De Fortis (ed.), *The Kingdom of Redonda, 1865-1990: A Celebration* (Wirral: Aylesford Press, 1991).
7 Lawrence Durrell, 'Some Notes on My Friend John Gawsworth' in Fortis, *Kingdom of Redonda*, p. 55.

lack its admirers; amongst those who praised his early work was Stephen Graham, who many years later received his own "dukedom" of Redonda, albeit one that lacked the more grandiloquent soubriquets that Gawsworth bestowed on some of his closest friends.

By the time Graham received his 'dukedom' in 1949, he had come to regard Gawsworth as "a crazy poet" – a verdict with which it is hard to disagree – but the two men kept up a correspondence that lasted for more than thirty years after their first meeting in 1930. Gawsworth was just eighteen at the time, having left Merchant Taylors School two years earlier, but he was already determined to pursue a literary career. Graham offered the young man a "haphazard" job at Frith Street, filing papers and dusting books, but the older man also became something of a literary mentor.[8] He gave Gawsworth detailed advice about his poetry, and wisely suggested that it would be prudent to develop a career in journalism, given the challenges of earning a living through verse alone. Gawsworth appreciated the advice, which he characteristically ignored, preferring to earn his money from proof-reading and book reviewing. He dedicated one of his earliest pieces to Graham, a cumbersome prose-poem titled *Above the River*, which described the revelation of a *manqué* poet who, when walking through the mist of the Welsh hills, sees in a brief moment of sunshine "with blinding clarity the hidden secret of his heart".[9] The sense of epiphany and the intimation of a hidden world were calculated to appeal to Graham, who saw in Gawsworth an echo of his younger self. The two men's interest in the unseen also found expression in a less elevated fascination with ghost stories. Gawsworth edited a number of collections of mystery stories throughout the 1930s, publishing several pieces by Graham, including one which described how the ghost of Lord Kitchener arrived in Archangel, following his death at sea in 1916 when his ship was torpedoed by a German U-boat *en route* to Russia.[10]

Gawsworth helped to manage Graham's affairs during the early 1930s, at a time when his friend was living for long periods in the Balkans, an area that had intrigued him ever since he first met Dimitrjie Mitrinović and Nikolai Velimirović in London in 1915. Graham never really lost the Serb

---

8 T.I.F. Armstrong (Gawsworth) Papers (HRC), Letters, Graham to Armstrong, 11 March 1930.
9 John Gawsworth, *Above the River* (London: Ulysses, 1931).
10 Stephen Graham, 'Kitchener at Archangel', in John Gawsworth (ed.), *Thrills, Crimes and Mysteries* (London: Associated Newspapers, 1936), pp. 371-76.

sympathies that had been fostered by his links with the Serbian war-time diaspora. His decision to visit Yugoslavia in 1929 was prompted by his determination not to fall into the trap of living a passive life in what was, he later told readers of the *Daily Express*, "a sitting-down age" in which even "babies are born with spectacles on".[11] It was also prompted by his long-standing friendship with Mitrinović, who had himself visited the country a few weeks earlier, apparently at the behest of King Alexander (the monarch who had recently declared a royal dictatorship, in the hope of breaking the political deadlock between Serbs and Croats that dogged Yugoslavia between the two world wars). Mitrinović had, even as a young man in Bosnia, been a staunch believer in the need for a pan-Yugoslav spirit, based on mutual toleration between the various ethnic and religious groups, and he travelled to Belgrade to discuss editing a new journal designed to promote such ideas. The project came to nothing, apparently because he made an unfavourable impression on the King's advisors, and he quickly returned to London to resume his work with the Adler Society. Graham's trip to Belgrade shortly afterwards was almost certainly linked in some way with these activities. Mitrinović certainly provided his friend with a range of political contacts, as well as an introduction to members of his own family, a gesture that was destined to have a huge impact on the rest of Graham's life.

When Graham first visited Belgrade, at the start of the 1920s, he found a place still largely populated by "the peasant come to town". The city looked very different nine years later, and despite the problems facing the country, its capital had become a construction site where "white stone facades rise from cobble stones to the sky". There were now crowds of "thoroughfares, lines of taxis, modern shops, a plenitude of bowlers and velours, [and] a great number of people who have money to spend". Graham recorded his impressions for the *Manchester Guardian*, describing how the steps leading up to the Parliament building lay "symbolically in ruins", following Alexander's abandonment of "constitutionalism" a few weeks earlier. He was nevertheless convinced that the monarch still commanded popular support, despite unease about "where he is now steering his country".[12] Graham was not able to obtain an audience with the King, but he did meet many other influential figures in Belgrade, including the Patriarch of the Serbian Church. He also spent time in the city's cafes and restaurants, many

---

11 *Daily Express*, 3 March 1930.
12 *Manchester Guardian*, 28 November 1929.

of them run by Russian émigrés, which gave him an opportunity to sample once more the dishes he knew so well from his time in the Tsarist Empire. Graham did not speak Serbo-Croat, but his fluent Russian allowed him to understand the gist of the conversations on art and politics that flourished in the bars and eateries of Belgrade. Within a few years he was fluent in the language itself.

Graham left Belgrade for London after just a few weeks, but he told Vachel Lindsay in America that he planned to return as soon as possible, in order to collect "some local details for a novel I am writing on the outbreak of the First World War in Serbia".[13] It was not only literature that pulled him back. During his time in Belgrade, Graham met various relatives of Dimitrije Mitrinović, including his younger sister Vera. Following his return to London, Graham wrote to Vera recalling how "happy" he had been during his visit. He also thanked her for the flowers she had given him, which although now "withered hang on my wall over a doorway", adding that he had bought a Serbian dictionary and was hard at work trying to learn the language.[14] By the time he was back in Belgrade, early in 1930, Graham was fretting endlessly about Vera's health, worrying that she might contract tuberculosis from her brother 'Lubo', with whom she lived in a tiny flat, conditions that he feared were "dangerous for Vera [since] she is weak and nervous and coughs a lot and I am afraid she may become infected". He also fretted that Lubo might soon die which "would be a terrible experience for a young girl". Graham gave the two of them money to take separate rooms, but Lubo spent the cash on something else, whilst his sister remained "absolutely self-sacrificing and devoted in nursing her brother".[15] Vera was a good deal younger than Graham – he was forty six years old and she was just twenty seven – and there was something almost paternal about his concern for her welfare. He was nevertheless clearly smitten by her from the time they met. Graham had been attracted to older women throughout his life, seeking an almost maternal tenderness from them, but in Vera he believed he had found someone capable of offering the kind of whole-hearted devotion he craved even though she was so much younger than himself. She was soon to become his companion and later his wife – a relationship that lasted until Graham's death in 1975.

---

13 Vachel Lindsay Papers (HRC), Letters file, Graham to Lindsay, 16 December 1929.
14 T.I.F. Armstrong (Gawsworth) Papers (HRC), Letters file, Graham to Vera, no date but probably late November 1929.
15 New Atlantis Foundation Archives, NAF 1/8/7, Graham to Mitrinović, 16 January 1930.

Graham's emotional entanglements did little to reduce his ferocious work-rate. During the summer of 1929 he had started work on an historical novel, *St Vitus Day*, which explored the motives of the young Bosnian Serbs who assassinated Archduke Franz Ferdinand at Sarajevo in June 1914. Graham told a friend many years later that the book was not so much a novel as an imaginative reconstruction that was faithful to the facts. When the book appeared the following year, the distinguished East European scholar Robert Seton-Watson praised *St Vitus Day* as a "remarkable book", noting that it was based on first-hand information provided to its author by some of those who had been close to the conspirators. Seton-Watson also commended Graham for showing how in 1914 "the younger generation in Bosnia was riddled through and through with revolutionary feeling", which fuelled the determination of Gavril Princip and his accomplices to carry out the assassination, in the hope of fomenting an insurrection that would lead in time to Bosnian independence from Austria.[16] It is unclear where Graham got all his information, particularly as he completed the manuscript after just a short time in Belgrade, but some of it certainly came from Dimitrije Mitrinović (who himself briefly appears as a character in the novel). Mitrinović had nothing to do with the murder of Franz Ferdinand, having opposed the use of violence when he was active in the Young Bosnia movement before 1914,[17] but he was able to provide his friend with access to individuals who possessed more detailed knowledge of the events in Sarajevo. Some of the material in Graham's private papers suggests he spoke to people who had been on the fringes of the conspiracy.

Seton-Watson noted in his review of *St Vitus Day* that its author had managed to avoid "appealing for sympathy with the murderers", a strange comment, for Graham made little secret of his approval of the nationalist cause espoused by Princip and his fellow-conspirators. Although one of his friends was correct in noting that Graham did not want to "whitewash" the killers,[18] his sharpest criticisms were reserved for the Austrian authorities, telling his readers that "the real reason for the assassination of Franz Ferdinand [...] lay in Austrian outrage upon the national feeling",[19] a reference to the fact that Ferdinand had insisted on visiting the Bosnian capital Sarajevo on St Vitus Day, which marked the anniversary of the

---

16 *Slavonic and East European Review*, 9, 26 (1930), pp. 494-95.
17 Vladimir Dedijer, *The Road to Sarajevo* (London, Macgibbon and Kee, 1967), p. 217 ff.
18 Bernard Newman, *Albanian Back Door* (London: H. Jenkins, 1936), p. 94.
19 Stephen Graham, *St Vitus Day* (London: Ernest Benn, 1930), p. 276.

sacrifices made by Serbian armies in 1389 in the Battle of Kosovo. The massacres that have scarred Yugoslav history throughout the twentieth century make it hard to accept Graham's suggestion that the main ethnic and religious fault-line in Bosnia in 1914 was between German ruler and Slav subject. Nor is it easy to accept his wilful decision to ignore the presence of large Croat and Moslem minorities in Bosnia-Herzegovina, many of whom looked with suspicion at their Orthodox neighbours, since to do so would have complicated a narrative that tacitly assumed Princip and his fellow assassins were nationalist heroes, commanding universal support in seeking to throw off Austrian rule.

Graham's book was serialised in translation in a number of Yugoslav newspapers, which made him something of a local hero, at least amongst the country's Serb population (Serbs dominated the leading positions in the Yugoslav government and army throughout most of the inter-war years). In 1931 its author was invited to attend the St Vitus Day celebrations in Sarajevo, standing as a guest of honour before the stone memorial to Princip with the assassin's elderly mother. A few years later he was given the Order of St Sava by the Yugoslav government, for meritorious achievements in the arts and sciences, a prize that he received alongside the novelist and travel-writer Rebecca West (who, ironically, had long been a sharp critic of Graham as "one of the more mechanical practitioners of Russian mysticism").[20] *St Vitus Day* also bolstered Graham's reputation back home. One or two reviewers in Britain and America were disturbed by Graham's attempt to "justify the deed" [i.e. the assassination],[21] but most were positive, including one in the *Manchester Guardian* that praised the book for being "so vivid that we feel ourselves taking a dismayed part in it, as we did when the actuality occurred sixteen years ago".[22] The critical and commercial success of *St Vitus Day* was instrumental in encouraging Graham to devote much of his time to writing fiction during the following years.

Graham spent a good deal of 1931-32 in Yugoslavia, although his movements are not easy to follow, given his peripatetic lifestyle. He was certainly in Belgrade early in 1931, when Lubo Mitrinović died from his

---

20 Rebecca West (ed.), *Selected Poems of Carl Sandburg* (New York: Harcourt Brace and Company, 1926), p. 23.
21 *New York Times*, 8 February 1931.
22 *Manchester Guardian* quoted in Stephen Graham, *Part of the Wonderful Scene* (London: Collins, 1964), p. 295.

tuberculosis. Vera was distraught at her brother's death, even though it had long been expected, and much to Graham's distress she sat for hours by his coffin in the apartment stroking his hair. The funeral itself took place in the late afternoon of a cold winter's day. Vera and her brother Chedomir followed the coffin, which was covered with bouquets of violets and mimosa, whilst Graham walked further back in the procession, along with a group of family friends who, for some reason, insisted on discussing the economic crisis in Britain. Vera collapsed in "a burst of hysterical weeping" as the coffin was lowered into the earth, but later in the afternoon at home became "gay and excited", "laughing and joking over everything" that was even remotely amusing.[23] When Graham's old friend Nikolai Velimirović heard about Vera's plight, he expressed a fear that it might prove difficult to "keep [her] mind in control and sanity", adding that it might be sensible to take her to Britain or at least to the Dalmatian coast for a holiday.[24] In a letter to Dimitrije Mitrinović, recounting details of the funeral, Graham assured his friend that, although the cost of the funeral had drained Vera's savings, "she has me and what I have is hers". He also criticised some other family members for not providing her with more emotional and material assistance.[25] It seems unlikely that Dimitrije Mitrinović was entirely put at ease by Graham's declaration of support. He wrote to a doctor friend in Belgrade shortly afterwards, asking him to provide Vera with help, and suggested that she should leave the city for a time to recover her strength in the peace of the countryside.

Mitrinović does not seem to have approved of the burgeoning relationship between Graham and Vera, something that probably contributed to a later falling-out between the two men, although they had been drifting apart ever since their cooperation over the proposed secret society back in 1915-16. Graham was by 1930 concerned that Mitrinović was promoting an obscurantist ideology that fostered an almost cult-like discipline amongst his followers (he may have been thinking of Rose when he noted many years later that Mitrinović's appeal had been greatest amongst middle-aged women who treated him as a veritable guru). The two men nevertheless continued to collaborate occasionally during the first half of the 1930s, at a time when Mitrinović and his followers were establishing the New Europe and New Britain movements, which were both designed to stimulate new

---

23 New Atlantis Foundation Archive, NAF 1/8/7, Graham to Mitrinović, 31 March 1931.
24 Graham Papers (HRC), Letters file, Velimirović to Graham (n.d.).
25 New Atlantis Foundation Archive, NAF 1/8/7, Graham to Mitrinović, 31 March 1931.

forms of national renewal capable of reducing international and domestic conflict. In the summer of 1934, Graham contributed a piece to the journal *New Britain* entitled 'The Way of the Young Man', which bore more than a passing resemblance to the *Credo* he had published in *The Beacon* more than ten years earlier, linking together the destinies of individuals and nations:

> There are two wisdoms: one for the mature and another for the adolescent.
> He is wrong who gives old men's wisdom to the young.
> Or who contradicts the young man's wisdom with the old man's experience.
> There is not one standard way of life for young and old.
> For the Altar requires sacrifice but it is the Moloch which requires slaughtered babes.
> The sacrifice of the immature is no gain to the Altar.
> For they sacrifice, not their true selves but only their unripeness.
> The young nation must not be allowed to sacrifice itself. It must first become what it was intended by God to be and then sacrifice itself.[26]

Although such esoteric language was no longer typical of his work, it would be unwise to dismiss the significance of such pieces altogether, for the "matter-of-fact" Graham of the 1930s retained at least some features of his earlier outlook, despite his growing focus on middle-brow fiction and historical biography.

Graham was greatly exercised throughout the early 1930s by the onset of the Great Depression that followed the Wall Street Crash of October 1929. In early 1931 he published an article in the *Manchester Guardian* warning that social unrest was likely to erupt in the United States as a result of rising unemployment in a country with little tradition of supporting for those facing poverty.[27] The economic collapse in America also had a more direct impact on him, drastically reducing his income from commissions and royalties, which he needed to fund the house in Frith Street and pay for his trips abroad. One of the reasons Graham spent so much time in Yugoslavia in the early 1930s was indeed that the cost of living, at least outside Belgrade, was much lower than in Britain. On 21 September 1931, ironically the day the British Government was forced to abandon the Gold Standard, Graham therefore once again headed back to Yugoslavia, following a short break in London, in order to spend several months in a cottage in the Julian Alps writing a new novel. Although the train journey to Ljubljana was

---
26 *New Britain*, 18 June 1934.
27 *Manchester Guardian*, 13 February 1931.

uneventful, he found to his consternation that the Yugoslav banks were unwilling to exchange British pounds for dinars, ruefully noting that it was "humiliating that a country like Yugoslavia should have doubts about the ultimate value of the pound sterling".[28] The situation improved a little in the weeks that followed, but Graham was still forced to rely heavily on the small amount of French currency he had brought with him, with the result that his lifestyle in the winter of 1931-32 was considerably impoverished.

This period was, nevertheless, a happy one. Graham rented a white-washed tumble-down cottage, suffused with the smell of drying corn and smoked pears, which was located on a lane near Lake Bohinje close to the Austrian border. He walked daily down to the lake past streams filled with "darting trout" – Graham became a keen angler whilst living at the cottage – and stared at the motionless water which reflected the numerous pine trees that rose up the steep valley sides. In the evening he ate trout washed down with a local Riesling, and talked to his one-armed landlord "on religion and immortality", or went into the village to listen to the peasant music that rang out from the houses. As autumn passed into winter the rain turned to snow, transforming the landscape, and making the views of the mountains that towered above the lake even more dramatic. Graham fed the local bird-life that flocked to the windows of the cottage, and sometimes walked up high into the mountains, passing local youths on skis and the occasional sled.[29] He also found time to pen a novel – *Everybody Pays* – which charts the unlikely romance between a tax inspector and a young woman who earned her living as a nightclub dancer.[30] The book is without doubt amongst the most lifeless of all his fictional works, perhaps because its author was so entranced by his surroundings that he found it hard to concentrate on his writing. It was certainly composed at breakneck speed. He also found the time to write a long piece for the *Manchester Guardian* describing how the global depression was affecting Yugoslavia, leading to a growth in poverty which he feared would trigger "a social eruption" if the situation did not improve.[31] Financial questions were to loom increasingly large in the second half of Graham's life, the natural obsession of a man who never had a stable source of income. His letters were increasingly full of mundane reflections

---

28 Ibid, 6 October 1921.
29 *John O'London's Weekly*, 23 January 1932.
30 Stephen Graham, *Everybody Pays* (London: Ernest Benn, 1932).
31 *Manchester Guardian*, 31 December 1931.

on questions of taxation that would never have occurred to the young man who left Britain to pursue his Russian "shadow" so many years before.

The indifferent critical response to *Everybody Pays* did not deter Graham from writing more fiction in the years that followed. The 1930s was, perhaps, the last time when a British writer could derive a reasonable income from fiction, even without producing a best-seller. Graham was convinced that his ability to write at speed meant that it was a potentially lucrative outlet for his talent. In 1931 he had already published another novel about London life, *A Modern Vanity Fair*, which traced the career of the enigmatic Xavier Riddell, a wealthy Anglo-American seeking to make his way in London High Society. Graham populated the book with numerous characters who lived their lives between the world of the aristocratic salon and the world of Bohemian nightclubs (a border-land which he had himself inhabited a good deal during the second half of the previous decade, when he was a regular at Soho's Gargoyle Club, which provided a meeting place between these two disparate settings.[32]) The characters are as so often in Graham's fiction drawn in a highly stylised fashion, complete with an array of flappers and aristocratic young men, who all seem to lack any definite occupation, relying instead on generous parental allowances to finance their life-styles. The novel's title expressed Graham's irritation at the triviality of much of what passed for London Society, but the book was written (to use Graham Greene's phrase) as an "Entertainment", rather than a serious social critique of the London *beau monde* in all its various guises. It did however focus a good deal on the nature of truth and falsehood in the presentation of self – something that was to become a marked feature of much of Graham's fiction – perhaps tellingly given his careful attempt throughout his life to conceal himself beneath a veneer of seeming candour. *A Modern Vanity Fair* ends with the revelation that Xavier Riddell is in fact the heir both to a baronetcy and a considerable fortune, something that he has kept hidden during his early days in Society, for reasons that remain obscure even to the most attentive reader. Graham had by the early 1930s become fascinated by the extent to which individuals could construct false personas persuasive enough to fool those around them, a fascination that seems to have spilled over from his own life into his fictional creations.

Graham's next novel, *One of the Ten Thousand* (1933), was once again written at the village of St Janez on the shore of Lake Bohinje "in view

---

32 Hugh David, *The Fitzrovians: A Portrait of a Bohemian Society, 1900-1950* (London: Michael Joseph, 1988), pp. 122-23.

of the lake and snow-capped mountains".[33] Despite the exotic setting of its composition, Graham drew extensively on his experience of prison-visiting during the early 1920s, telling the story of one Murray Maudant, sentenced to a year's imprisonment in Pentonville for knowingly cashing a cheque whilst having insufficient funds in his account to meet it. According to the story Maudant tells the prison chaplain, he was acting for a friend, and did not realise that he was being asked to commit a crime, although he freely admitted to having been 'inside' on two previous occasions. He also tells the padre a horrific story of how his wife had killed herself and their two children whilst he was in gaol for the second time (when he had been convicted of pawning ornaments owned by his landlady). The chaplain becomes convinced of the prisoner's innocence, not least because of his belief in Maudant's claim to have experienced a religious conversion whilst in Pentonville, and he therefore begins a campaign for his release. Maudant is also supported by his fiancée, 'Queenie' Lorrimer, one of the 'fast' young women who were a staple in Graham's fiction during this time. The campaign was in time successful. Only in the last two pages of the book does it become clear that Maudant is not who he claims to be – casting doubt on everything that he has said – including his tragic tale about the loss of his wife and children. When he is yet again convicted for minor larceny, whilst working at an aircraft factory in north London, the police discover that his real name is Ellis, a career criminal who has been in trouble with the law since his teenage years. The stories about his past life and sufferings are exposed as probable falsehoods. The prison chaplain and others who believed in Maudant seem, in the light of this revelation, to have been gullible fools. The book is nevertheless ambiguous about the extent to which Maudant had almost come to believe his own stories. Graham's account was loosely based on a number of cases he recorded ten years earlier, in the diary he kept whilst prison-visiting, a time when he was already struck by the extent to which many prisoners had lost all sense of truth and falsehood. The anonymous character of the metropolis allows Maudant to remake his identity time and again, fooling even those close to him, for in a modern city the absence of strong communal ties makes it impossible to establish the truth about the streams of people who throng the crowded streets.

---

33 T.I.F Armstrong Papers (HRC), Letters, Graham to Gawsworth, 14 May 1932.

The figure of the con-man also dominates Graham's 1934 novel *The Padre of St Jacobs*, which seems to have been written in London during one of his periodic returns home to Britain. The two central characters in the book are Edgar (Gar) Lloyd, a mysterious adventurer and 'rough diamond', who has supposedly made his fortune in America, and the Revd Mark Whyte, vicar at the (fictional) Royal Chapel of St Jacobs in London. The novel revolves around Lloyd's promise to give Whyte a million pounds, to support a revivalist campaign in London, just as soon as he can repatriate the money from America. Lloyd's own professed conversion sits uneasily throughout the book with his raffish lifestyle and rough manner of speech, but Whyte comes to believe in the reality of Lloyd's improbable fortune, and willingly provides his own savings to pay the fees needed to facilitate the transfer of the money to Britain. Lloyd encourages the Padre to develop detailed plans for the revivalist mission, and explains each delay in providing the necessary funds by reference to some obscure legal problems back in America. The art (or at least the suspense) of the novel consists precisely in Graham's success in fostering uncertainty about whether Lloyd is really a fraudster. His demeanour and scam seem so obvious that they create uncertainty in the reader's mind as to whether he can really be a con-artist. It is only in the final pages of the book, when Lloyd not only takes all of Whyte's savings, but even repeats his scam by returning to take further funds given to the padre by his loyal parishioners, that the situation becomes clear. The morality of the book does however remain profoundly ambiguous. Whyte is painted by Graham in too intricate a fashion to be condemned simply as a gullible and other-worldly priest. Lloyd, for his part, has much of the patina of the loveable rogue who almost seems to believe in the elaborate fictions he weaves. The simplistic moral vision that fuelled the youthful Graham's diatribes against the spiritual bankruptcy of modern urban society had long since faded, replaced by a more mature awareness of the moral ambiguity of the contemporary world.

Graham's 1934 novel *Lost Battle* has already been discussed on a number of previous occasions, since it provides a useful biographical source casting light on the complexity of his early family background. At the heart of the novel lies John Rae Belfort's (Anderson Graham's) decision to desert his family in Essex and establish a new family on the other side of London. The fictional Belfort goes to enormous lengths to conceal the character of his second family from his neighbours in Buckinghamshire, both by refusing to allow them to mix socially, as well as by steadfastly failing to acknowledge publicly the existence of his original household. It is only when he allows his oldest son, Mark, to visit his home of Morebattle Hall that the elaborate charade begins to fall apart. Graham's presentation of Belfort appears to represent little more than a thinly-disguised portrait of his father, and there can be little doubt that the unconventional nature of his own family background helped to fuel his interest in the authenticity of social appearance. Anderson Graham was hardly a con-man like Gar Lloyd, but he too seems to have gone to great lengths to control the way others perceived him, in order to maintain the veneer of respectability necessary for the editor of so august a publication as *Country Life*. Graham's growing awareness of the mystery of his family, which struck him so powerfully after his father's death in 1925, fuelled a fascination with appearance and reality that ran through many of his novels of the early 1930s.

The fiction and non-fiction that Graham wrote during the first part of the 1930s in a sense signalled the triumph of the realist over the idealist in his writing. The concerns of books like *A Modern Vanity Fair* and *Everybody Pays* were utterly different from those of earlier novels such as *A Priest of the Ideal*. It is indeed difficult at times to believe they could have been written by the same man. Graham's early fiction rested to a greater or lesser degree on the assumption that all social and political problems were an expression of some deeper religious or metaphysical malaise. His novels of the 1930s overwhelmingly concentrated on exploring the foibles and frailties of his characters without ever really penetrating to the heart of their identities and anxieties. It was as though, having lost his earlier intensely idealistic view of life, Graham was left adrift in a world where people appeared to him as strangely brittle and without depth. The reviews of his novels were, for the most part, unenthusiastically positive, typically praising their author for his "realistic skill" in "capturing the follies of contemporary life",[34] but pointing out that he struggled to "make plain" in his characters "that human understanding which is all great art's foundation".[35] The novelist and critic James Agate believed Graham was, "for a first-class or very nearly first class novelist [...] astonishingly little known",[36] words which his subject rightly took as a compliment, but such sentiments were not widely shared. The quality of Graham's fiction was undermined by the

---

34 *Times Literary Supplement* (Reviews of *One of the Ten Thousand*, 23 February 1933; and *A Padre of St Jacobs*, 22 March 1934).
35 *The Bookman* (Review of *Lost Battle*), October 1934.
36 *Daily Express*, 15 February 1933.

speed at which he wrote it. The sheer scale of his productivity in writing fiction in the first half of the 1930s seems even more astonishing given that he also wrote several substantial biographies and numerous articles in the London press.

Although Graham wrote several of his novels at St Janez on the shores of Lake Bohinje, he did not abandon London altogether during the first half of the 1930s, not least because his presence there was required to deal with the practical business of checking proofs and approving publicity material. His visits were also necessary to collect the material he required as a writer of non-fiction. The life of London's streets continued to fascinate him, as it had for quarter of a century, inspiring a series of vignettes that appeared in a 1933 collection *Twice Round the London Clock*. The book was illustrated by Rick Elmes, who accompanied Graham on a series of nocturnal jaunts through the city, and provided humorous pictures of life in places ranging from railway stations and pubs to suburban whist drives and theatres. Graham also chronicled life in his own "village" of Soho, which he described somewhat surprisingly as "a quiet place where one can rest at night",[37] despite the sound of clubs emptying in the early hours and the local Italian population exercising their dogs in the dim pre-dawn light.

The title of the collection was adapted from an 1858 book by the journalist George Augustus Sala, *Twice Round the Clock: Hours of the Day and Night in London,* which had contained sketches on subjects ranging from fashionable gentlemen's clubs through to Billingsgate market. Although Graham coloured the chapters in *London Clock* with his usual penchant for anecdote and description, lingering beneath them was his intense interest in the city's deeper identity, reflecting a sense that it possessed a character that could not be neatly delineated, but might be hinted at by means of episodic sketches and remarks. He was determined to show his readers that it was possible to find a poetry in the rhythms of London, writing that, in all the cities of the world he had visited, he had "never found one so satisfying, so alluring, and unfathomable in mystery and beauty as London". Whilst Moscow was "an awakener of the soul" and Constantinople offered "an enchanting window upon Asia and old time", London offered "labyrinths and lost places" that made the city strangely "unsearchable", concealing from view the "untold pathos" of millions of lives led in the privacy of "little houses, rooms, flats". Graham also suggested that, for all the bustle

---

37 Stephen Graham, *Twice Round the London Clock* (London: Ernest Benn, 1933), p. 215.

of the city's streets, "Londoners probably have more faith, more calm of the soul, than the people of any other great city of the world".[38] In a striking final paragraph he criticised John Ruskin, so long his hero, for only seeing in London "a festering wilderness of brick and mortar". Ruskin's passionate desire to live in garden cities, designed according to the credo of the Arts and Crafts movement, had led him to miss the "ever-wonderful life" of London, which for all its slums and "desecrations" remained a place of wonder, possessing a soul that was absent in more planned communities. Whilst the sketches in *London Clock* were for the most part quite light-hearted, they showed that Graham had retained his talent for finding poetry in the mundane world of city streets.

It was not only Graham's fascination with the street-life of London that tied him to Britain for long periods of time. He also needed access to the British Library, just a few minutes' walk from his home, in order to carry out the research for a series of biographies that he published in the first half of the 1930s. In 1931 he published one of the earliest biographies of Joseph Stalin, who had only recently established himself as the unchallenged leader of Soviet Russia, describing him as "a man of sagacity and will who carried the revolution to its present stage". He also stressed Stalin's "gift for organisation", as well as arguing that despite his lack of charisma he had become "a hero to red youth", evoking a distinctive mix of "admiration and dread".[39] Although Graham's biography of Stalin has not stood the test of time particularly well, its portrayal of the Soviet leader was reasonably acute given the paucity of information available to him. The book was remarkable for what one reviewer called its "kindly and sympathetic" tone,[40] evidence perhaps that Graham wanted to shed his reputation as a chronicler of old Russia, and instead establish a name for himself as a commentator on the contemporary Russian scene.

His interest nevertheless soon returned to the more traditional world of Tsarist Russia. In 1932 Graham published a biography of the sixteenth-century tsar Ivan the Terrible, famous for his brutality towards thousands of his subjects, many of whom were tortured to death in ways that still appal even today in a world inured to the most grotesque atrocities.[41] He followed this up with a biography of Boris Godunov , who ruled Russia at

---

38 Ibid, pp. 217-19.
39 Stephen Graham, *Stalin* (London: Ernest Benn, 1931), pp. viii, 43, 121.
40 *The Observer*, 22 November 1931.
41 Stephen Graham, *Ivan the Terrible* (London: Ernest Benn, 1932).

the start of the seventeenth century, and whose death in 1605 precipitated the Time of Troubles that led to the rise of the Romanov dynasty.[42] Graham worked diligently in the British Library to collect material for the two books, reading earlier Russian biographies and collections of documents, although he was uncharacteristically poor at painting a vivid sketch of either tsar. Nor were the books well-received by scholars, one of whom noted that Graham was "by temperament and training [...] a novelist rather than an historian".[43] It was a verdict with which Graham would probably have agreed.

Graham's next attempt at biography was more successful, or at least more interesting, for the light it cast on his attitude towards Holy Russia almost twenty years after the 1917 Revolution. In his book on Alexander the Second, the Tsar Liberator who ended serfdom in 1861, Graham returned to his familiar theme that no church was "identical with Christianity [...] They are human institutions, each with a glory of its own, and need not be criticised with reference to the Gospel which was addressed to the heart of man and not to a committee or a society". He was nevertheless complimentary about the Russian Orthodox Church, suggesting that it had always been a "national" church, that "embodied in a visible form the ideals and aspirations of a young nation".[44] Graham argued that Holy Russia was, in large part, a creation of the defeat of Napoleon in 1812, which helped to forge a sense of national identity that had previously been inchoate and fragmentary. As a result, the Russia over which Alexander ruled was a place where "there was no atheism, no free-thinking, but instead a superfluity of belief [...] the peasants not only believed in the Trinity but had a superfluity of beliefs, an eagerness to believe in the supernatural, even in the absurd".[45] The biography boasted an impressive set of primary and secondary sources in Russian, although Graham made little effort to pretend that it was a work of scholarship, acknowledging that the book was "a special interpretation of the drama of Alexander's life and is written with the presumption that self-expression and national development are

---

42 Stephen Graham, *Boris Godunof* (London: Ernest Benn, 1933). For a positive review of the book as "a distinguished contribution to letters", see *The Atlantic,* December 1933.
43 *Speculum*, 10, 1 (1935).
44 Stephen Graham, *Alexander II: Tsar of Russia* (London: Nicholson and Watson 1935), pp. 179, 160.
45 Ibid, p. 279.

the only justifiable aims of political movements".[46] Although it was many years since Graham had written about Holy Russia, he still believed that pre-revolutionary Russia possessed a distinctive spiritual character, which had for almost two decades been systematically submerged and repressed by the Soviet regime that seized power in 1917. It was not an argument calculated to appeal to professional historians, more familiar with the subtle complexities of tsarist Russia, which defied easy reduction into the rigid historical framework of the kind Graham offered his readers.

Graham was not really successful at concealing his lack of interest in writing biography, a task he carried out in large part simply to make money. The call of Vera in any case kept summoning him back to Yugoslavia. He was by the early 1930s a comparatively well-known figure in the country. There were unfounded rumours in Belgrade that Graham worked for British intelligence, making him an object of suspicion in some quarters, particularly towards the end of the 1930s when the Yugoslav government moved closer to the axis powers. His Serb sympathies nevertheless meant that he continued to be well-regarded by many individuals in positions of power. When the writer and journalist Bernard Newman cycled through the country, in 1935, he found that Graham's name opened doors even to senior political figures in the capital.[47]

Graham in fact avoided Belgrade as much as possible, preferring life in what Newman called the "wild and unsophisticated" countryside around Lake Bohinje, which had captivated him since his first sojourn there in 1931. He was joined in the area in 1935 by the American journalist and writer Negley Farson, who moved there with his family to finish his book *Way of a Transgressor*, an autobiographical account that became an unlikely best-seller when it was published the following year.[48] Graham had known Farson in pre-war Russia, where they both worked as journalists, and had subsequently praised the American's books in the British press. When they were reunited in the wilds of the Julian Alps – Farson too was looking for somewhere cheap to live[49] – the two men delighted in fishing for trout in the shadow of the mountains that rose above the lake shore. So struck was Farson by his experiences that he later set them down in a book, *Going Fishing*, in which he described catching trout in streams that

---

46 Ibid, p. 315.
47 Newman, *Albanian Back-Door*, p. 93.
48 Negley Farson, *Way of a Transgressor* (London: Gollanz, 1935).
49 Daniel Farson, *Never a Normal Man* (London: Harper Collins, 1997), p. 19.

flowed through "a pastoral land where the valley filled with the tinkle of cow and goat and sheep bells".⁵⁰ Farson was like Graham very much a product of urban life – he had worked for many years in Chicago before serving as foreign correspondent in a number of European cities – but he was also a natural adventurer, who relished the call of the wild, and felt "more at home in the desert and in the middle of some swamp than I ever have on Fifth Avenue".⁵¹ Throughout their lives both men needed "wide open spaces" as a counterpoise to the more confining world of the city. The Yugoslavian landscape seems to have captivated many foreign writers during the 1930s. The case of the novelist and spy-writer Bernard Newman has already been mentioned. More famous, perhaps, is Rebecca West, whose magisterial 1941 book *Black Lamb and Grey Falcon* was based on her travels through the country during the previous decade. Graham and Farson were not alone in finding in Yugoslavia a place that sat on a dense web of historical and geographical boundaries that seemed to make life there resonate with a particular richness and depth.

Graham did not spend all his time in Slovenia during the mid 1930s, for he travelled a good deal to see Vera, who spent time in Belgrade and Sarajevo trying to develop a career in journalism. In 1935 the two of them headed off, complete with tent and fishing rods, for an extended journey to the south of Yugoslavia, more specifically to the region round Lake Ochrid, located on the borders of modern-day Albania and Macedonia. It was also the region where Graham's old friend Nikolai Velimirović had by now become a bishop. Graham provided readers of the *Manchester Guardian* with a brief description of this journey through "a beautiful mountain country", where East met West, and the rivers were full "of big lusty" fish so powerful that they broke the lines of anglers who set out to catch them.⁵² A fuller account had to wait until 1939, when he published *The Moving Tent*, which contained some of Graham's best travel writing since his youthful accounts of his journeys through the Russian Empire so many years before (the manuscript itself was probably finished early in 1937).⁵³ It was a connection that he consciously tried to create in his readers' minds, by archly referring to himself throughout the text as 'The Vagabond', an

---

50 Negley Farson, *Going Fishing* (London: Country Life, 1942), p. 137.
51 Negley Farson, *A Mirror for Narcissus* (London: Gollanz, 1956), p. 17.
52 *Manchester Guardian*, 30 September 1935.
53 For Graham's later memories of this time see Graham Papers (FSU), Box 573, 12b ('War-Time Radio Broadcasts: A Visit to a Village in Yugoslavia').

allusion of course to his very first book *A Vagabond in the Caucasus*. The Preface to *The Moving Tent* contained faint echoes of some of Graham's pre-war ideas, including his claim that "Wild Nature is the heritage of every man", along with his assertion that those who chose to live in cities were like "absentee landlords" who could not even bother to "derive revenue from what is theirs".[54] The book itself was nevertheless more restrained in tone than most of Graham's early travel writing. It provided readers with a melange of vivid details and anecdotes, almost certainly derived from more than one trip, but without indulging in the exuberant philosophising of his younger self.

Graham originally visited southern Yugoslavia to collect information for a novel about Black Magic in Macedonia, but he quickly became convinced that his readers would be more interested in his efforts to "escape from the hurly-burly of war-mongering, daily newspaper sensations, cinemas and barrel-organs".[55] The book focused on providing detailed descriptions of landscapes and people in a region that was still so far from the heart of Europe that it seemed to retain a fairy-tale glint of unreality. His account of the impoverished fishing villages on the shores of Lake Ochrid, with their "low stone-houses" and "swarms of children and moulting fowls", was superb at capturing the texture of life in one of the most isolated corners of the continent.[56]

Graham visited numerous remote churches and shrines, finding places of solitary pilgrimage where it was possible to recapture something "of the glory of religion" as it had existed in "the morning of the Christian faith".[57] He was also surprisingly positive, if unduly picturesque, in his description of oriental-looking Moslem villages complete with "turbaned Dervishes and veiled women". Perhaps most surprisingly, Vera appeared repeatedly in *Moving Tent*, which included a photograph of her sitting in bathing costume on a rock above Lake Prespa with a fishing rod in her hand (in his own copy of the book, Graham noted many years later that the picture was taken on "an idyllic morning in October"). Graham's portrait of Vera bordered on the angelic, although he was understandably reticent in his description of their exact relationship, simply describing her as a

---

54 Stephen Graham, *The Moving Tent: Adventures with a Tent and Fishing-Rod in Southern Jugoslavia* (London: Cassell, 1939), p. vii.
55 Ibid, p. vi.
56 Ibid, p. 78.
57 Ibid, p. 97.

"dark handsome girl with uncut black hair [and] merry eyes and one of those aquiline noses which the ancient Romans left behind on the Balkan peninsula".[58] He told readers how she helped to heal a Moslem woman in one village where they stayed by dint of her careful nursing. He also provided a touching account of how Vera provided care to a wounded goat that crossed their path, its flesh slowly being eaten away by the wasps that plagued the region, washing the creature's wounds and finding its owners to insist that they took care of the animal. The description of Vera in *Moving Tent* was striking enough for some reviewers to see her as the heroine of the book. The sales were however badly damaged by the timing of its publication. Although Graham had been working on versions of the book since 1936, it only appeared in 1939, at a time when readers had more on their minds than the lure of far-away exotic landscapes. The delay in publication was not only a financial blow for Graham. *Moving Tent* is no classic of travel literature, but it did reflect many of his strengths as a writer, most notably his ability to evoke the lure of faraway places in a way that made them seem both familiar yet tantalisingly strange.

Moving Tent was not the only book in which Vera appeared. A few months before his 1935 trip to Lake Ochrid, Graham finished a new novel called *Balkan Monastery*, which was subsequently chosen by the *Daily Mail* as its Book of the Month (a "fine novel" that "fills in the details of an unfamiliar landscape").[59] *Balkan Monastery* tells the thinly-disguised story of Vera Mitrinović, Desa Georgevitch in the book, who is evacuated during the First World War with a number of other young Serb girls to an ancient monastery, where they are forced to scrounge in the fields for food to stay alive. Vera-Desa is subsequently handed over to a Bulgarian family, as part of a deliberate attempt by the Bulgarian authorities to undermine Serb identity, but succeeds in escaping to return home to her family. Graham presented Vera's story against the turbulent historical background of the time, including the Serb army's dramatic retreat through Albania to Scutari, in the face of a rapid Austrian and Bulgarian advance from the North and East. The horror of the forced march is told through the story of Desa's brother, Sava, attached to a unit guarding the Serbian King Peter. Sava's own suffering makes him almost indifferent to the pain of those around him, his heart unmoved even when he sees fellow-soldiers frozen

---

58 Ibid, p. 106.
59 *Daily Mail*, 5 December 1935.

to death, their bodies encased in ice besides the fires they lit in a desperate bid to keep alive. Nor did Graham conceal the pain of Desa-Vera's own experiences, as she and her fellow "orphans" struggle to survive in the face of food shortages and the threat of rape. It is as so often with Graham's novels difficult to identify the precise boundary between fact and fiction. Whilst he cannot have known at first-hand the dramas he described, he always insisted that *Balkan Monastery* represented a faithful account of Vera's experiences.[60] The vivid tone of the book certainly commended it to reviewers, who were moved by the description of the struggle of Desa and her fellow-orphans to survive in a country ripped apart by war.

Graham made no attempt to tell his readers that *Balkan Monastery* was based on a real story. Nor does the book cast much real light on the woman who inspired its central character. Graham dedicated the book to Vera, but their relationship was still a sensitive issue for members of her family, and, to the end of his life, he was evasive when describing exactly how and when they met.[61] Graham's relationship with Vera during the mid 1930s was in any case made more complicated by the fact that he remained married to Rose (a subject of particular concern to Vera's relatives). There is little doubt that Graham himself wanted a divorce. In the year following the publication of *Balkan Monastery*, he wrote a piece for the *Daily Mail* under the title 'Marriage Ruined his Life', lamenting the dangers posed by the matrimonial state for "a young man of much promise", as the routine conventionalities of life crushed his youthful enthusiasms and hopes. The situation was, he suggested, different on the continent, which remained "a man's world", where women were unable to yoke their husbands to a world of domestic routine: "John Bull with one leg tied to a leg of Mrs Bull is neither elegant nor speedy. Untied they can compete with anyone and win".[62] The piece was intended to be light-hearted, and few readers would have picked up on the under-current of bitterness beneath the whimsy, with the exception of the handful of people who knew about Graham's own situation. It is a moot point whether Graham recognised that the plight of the young man who married early was not unique in his family history. It echoed the experience of his own father, who had abandoned his wife for a woman he was never able to wed, frustrated by the constraints

---

60 Graham, *Wonderful Scene*, p. 295; Graham Papers (FSU), Box 573, 7, Graham to Marion Hay, 2 October 1950.
61 See, for example, *Evening News*, 30 June 1973.
62 *Daily Mail*, 22 October 1937.

family life placed on his career. Matrimonial complications seem to have been embedded in the genes of the Graham family.

Money remained short for Graham throughout the second half of the 1930s, and he was forced for a time to carry out translation work, then as now a distinctly unprofitable affair. He translated Professor Y.P. Frolov's *Fish Who Answer the Telephone and Other Studies in Experimental Biology* (Frolov had worked in the laboratory of Ivan Pavlov, best-known today for his work with dogs on conditioning).[63] He also, more profitably, wrote a good deal for the *Daily Express*, including a series of sketches that appeared in 1935-36 describing the national character of various countries, which were later published in book-form under the title *Characteristics* (a title inspired by Thomas Carlyle's book of the same name). Graham wrote in the Preface that he did not aim to produce "a book of theory elaborated beyond opinions. It is rather a collection of facts, impressions and curiosities of travel".[64] The sketches that appeared in the *Express* failed lamentably to provide the mixture of anecdote and observation at which Graham excelled in his best writing, instead favouring a degree of generalisation that sought to reduce the richness of particular cultures to a crude national type, more often than not in a way calculated to reinforce the prejudices of *Express* readers. The Greeks tended to be "fat and gross" since they liked sweetmeats. The Scandinavians were "the most honest" people in Europe. The Celtic nations were inclined to "melancholy", the Russians "cried easily", and the French were "a small people" with "little heads" and "small feet" (the latter were like all the "Latin races [also] more subject to panic than others").[65]

The articles in *Characteristics* all too often reflected a rather unpleasant penchant for banality and over-simplification, of the kind that had characterised Graham's descriptions of Russian Jews and American blacks in some of his earlier work. Since the articles were originally written for serialisation in a newspaper, in the form of a brief column that provided little room for nuance or subtlety, there was no space for the kinds of descriptions of people and places that were Graham's forte. The sketches instead provided a leaden series of insights unrelieved by their author's penchant for colour and detail. They were followed by a later series of

---

63 Professor Y. Frolov, *Fish Who Answer the Telephone and Other Studies in Experimental Biology* (London: Kegan Paul, 1937).
64 Stephen Graham, *Characteristics* (London: Rich and Cowan, 1936), Preface.
65 Ibid, pp. 6, 58, 72, 107.

articles in the *Sunday Express* on 'The Soul of the British Empire' – in practice the White Dominions – which appeared under such banal headings as 'Australians are Extraordinary'. Nor was Graham hindered in expressing his opinions by the fact that he had not actually visited some of the places he described. The articles assumed unequivocally the value and worth of Empire, at a time when the threatening international situation was creating a pervasive sense of unease in Britain about the country's future. Graham's columns were written to a formula designed to appeal to the paper's readers, as well as its owner, the imperially-minded Lord Beaverbook.

One of the articles which appeared in the *Sunday Express* in 1937 was about South Africa. In this case Graham spoke from personal experience, for the previous year he and Vera had set sail from Southampton headed for Cape Town. During the long sea journey he jotted down sketches of his fellow-passengers, who included an intelligent doctor searching for a wife, the editor of a leading Cape newspaper, and a middle-aged woman who annoyed her fellow passengers by invariably being late for dinner because she took so long over her preparations. He also wrote some notes about how he might write a novel populated by characters based on his travelling-companions.[66] After their arrival in Cape Town, Stephen and Vera headed northwards to Swaziland, where the two of them stayed on a remote farm owned by Neal Harman, who subsequently established a reputation as a novelist with such books as *Crown Colony* and *Death and the Archdeacon*. They quickly took to life on the *veldt*. Both were keen anglers, and they spent time fishing for the exotic species that teemed in the local rivers and ponds, taking care to avoid the crocodiles that floated in the reeds along the banks. They also drove out into the remote countryside in an ancient lorry, which periodically broke down and refused to start again, camping under the stars and listening to the shrieks and roars of the local wildlife.[67] The couple were enthralled by the sight and sounds of creatures they had previously only read about, and found no difficulty in adjusting to the rigours of life on the African plains, relishing the sense of isolation and remoteness. It was with regret that they eventually headed eastwards, to Mozambique, in order to catch a boat which took them back to London

---

66 Graham Papers (FSU), Box 581, 24a ('People on a Trip to South Africa').
67 Gawsworth Papers (University of Reading Library), Box 10, Graham to Gawsworth, incorrectly dated, but probably June 1936.

via Port Elizabeth and Tenerife. They arrived back in London at the end of August 1936.

Graham's African novel was duly published in 1937 by the London firm of Rich and Cowan under the title *African Tragedy*.[68] The book tells the story of Tom Anderson, a former soldier from Scotland, who after the war travels to the southern states of the United States where he becomes caught up in the activities of the Ku Klux Klan. He flees America after being sickened by the sight of a mob lynching a young black man accused of having sex with a white woman, and eventually finds his way via Trinidad to South Africa. Anderson relishes the freedom of his new life, working for a time as a gold miner, before using the money he saves to buy a remote farm in Swaziland, where he lives surrounded by a small number of scrawny farm animals and a handful of Zulu servants. Anderson's farm fails to become a commercial success due to its owner's lack of capital, and his life soon starts to alternate between a "serene existence" of shooting and fishing, punctuated by severe bouts of fever. This solitary existence is shattered when a telegram summons him back to Scotland to see his dying father Jock. Tom's initial sense of desolation at father's death soon fades when he meets one Lady Laura Charters, a regular at the hotel, who had for years been regaled by Jock with stories of his son's adventures. Tom is bewitched when he sees Laura for the first time, and over the next few weeks the two of them travel together across Europe, making plans to head back to Africa where Laura promises to invest money to help develop the farm.

Graham provides his readers with hints from the moment Tom and Laura first meet that there is something obsessive about Anderson's feelings. The second half of the book is characterised by a strong sense of foreboding, as the struggles in their relationship start to echo their battle to build a profitable farm in the hostile African *veldt*. Although Tom plans to build a grand house for Laura, the life they lead together falls far short of the idyllic vision that had passed before her eyes when they had been in Britain, and the tragic denouement of their life together comes when Laura decides to return home to her husband and small child. Tom remains in Swaziland where he turns into a half-crazed figure – a cross between Kurtz in *Heart of Darkness* and Tony Last in *A Handful of Dust* – and when his fever is particularly bad he becomes convinced that his farm has been cursed by

---

68 Stephen Graham, *African Tragedy* (London: Rich and Cowan, 1937).

one of the local witch-doctors. In his saner moments he recognises that the house he had built for Laura is actually being eaten away by white ants, which chew through the furniture and rafters, causing them to crumble into dust at the first attempt to make repairs. The book ends with Anderson's death in a raging storm, when the weakened house proves unable to resist the wind, and the roof falls in burying Tom beneath the rubble along with one of his pet wildcats. The book was well-received by critics. The reviewer in *The Times Literary Supplement* wrote that "Mr Graham has not shirked one item in the list of small trials that make Africa so sordid and at times so unbearable; yet he has succeeded in building up for his Tom and Laura a background of such immensity that they themselves take on heroic stature and the story of their misfortunes attains the dignity of tragedy".[69]

Although *African Tragedy* is one of Graham's best novels, anyone wanting to buy a copy today will almost certainly be disappointed, for within a few months of publication the unsold stock was pulped by Rich and Cowan. They took this decision after settling a libel action brought by Neal Harman and Margot Hilda Layton (Lady Chesham), with whom Graham and Vera had stayed during their visit to Swaziland in 1936. Harmon and Layton – like the fictional Anderson and Charters – owned adjacent farms. Layton, like Charters, stayed in the main house on her neighbour's land when visiting her property since it had no suitable accommodation. The basis of the libel action rested on the fact that Graham had drawn on recognisably "real life" people and places when writing his book, but had "added some fiction to his fact and recounted incidents which never occurred, but, if they had occurred, would have revealed Mr Harman and Lady Chesham as very undesirable characters".[70] Graham was himself named in the libel action but could not be contacted to defend it (he was back in Yugoslavia at the time). The barrister for Rich and Cowan noted that the firm had accepted *African Tragedy* in good faith as a work of fiction, given that Graham was "an author of some repute", adding that his clients were happy to accept that there was not a "vestige of foundation for the objectionable passages" in the book (which were presumably the ones relating to the relationship between the fictional Tom and Laura). Rich and Cowan agreed to pay damages to the plaintiffs as well as withdrawing the book from circulation.

---

69 *Times Literary Supplement*, 9 October 1937.
70 *The Times*, 18 November 1938.

It is no surprise that one of Graham's novels eventually led to a libel action (in another strange echo of his father's life, it is worth noting that Anderson Graham had suffered a similar fate more than forty years earlier). Much of his previous fiction had drawn closely on his own life and the lives of people he knew. *Under-London* was highly autobiographical in character. *One of the Ten Thousand* echoed Graham's experiences of prison-visiting in the early 1920s. *Last Battle* used only the thinnest of disguises when portraying the complex personal life of Anderson Graham. *Balkan Monastery* was largely based on Vera's experiences as a child in Serbia. And, as has already been seen, Graham was even on his trip out to South Africa already thinking how he might translate his fellow-passengers into fictional characters. Graham always freely acknowledged that he wrote best from life, noting in the *Daily Express* at the start of the 1930s that good writing was always rooted in personal experience and the "testing of reality through hardship".[71] His liveliest novels were based on real events, whilst his dullest books, like *Everybody Pays*, were written purely from imagination. It is possible that Graham wrote *African Tragedy* believing that no one would ever relate the central characters to their two real life protagonists. It seems more likely that his own *modus operandi* meant that he never really understood the risks of what he was doing. It was certainly, as the barrister for Harman and Chesham noted in Court, in questionable taste to "accept another's hospitality and afterwards turn him into the subject of a book". Graham never mentioned the incident in any version of his memoirs. Nor does it arise in his surviving correspondence. It is however striking that he did not publish another work of fiction for almost two decades – and when he did it was a sequel to the tediously safe *Everybody Pays* – suggesting that the whole experience of the libel action had been serious enough to scar him for years to come. It is perhaps superfluous to add that Rich and Cowan did not publish any of his later books.

The *African Tragedy* libel trial more or less coincided with the publication of another book by Graham, *Alexander of Yugoslavia: Strong Man of the Balkans*, a detailed work of documentary history which examined the controversy surrounding the murder of the Yugoslavian monarch at Marseilles four years earlier in October 1934. The "horrible crime" predictably aroused furore across Europe,[72] including Britain, where it fuelled concerns about

---

71 *Daily Express*, 3 March 1930.
72 *The Times*, 10 October 1934.

international relations at a time when fascism and communism were both on the rise. The assassination also raised questions about who was behind the attack (the actual gunman killed by police was a Bulgarian, Vlado Chernozemski, who had for years been involved in the campaign to free Macedonia from Serbian control). In the weeks that followed the shooting, newspapers across the continent were full of details of the plot. Most of those implicated in the investigation by the French authorities were Croatians, with strong links to the nationalist Ustaša organization headed by Ante Pavelić, although the government in Belgrade made clear its suspicion that the Italian and Hungarian governments were also involved in the affair (the Ustaša had training camps in both countries). The potential diplomatic consequences of the murder were considerable, given that Alexander was, at the time of his death, seeking to build a complex set of alliances with countries across Europe. The *Daily Mail* even carried a report that that the assassination was designed to bring about war.[73] Although the immediate crisis passed, in part because the French and British governments were reluctant to confront the governments behind the killing, Alexander's murder remained etched in the public consciousness. The assassination was one of the first political killings caught on film, making it possible for thousands to see the final moments of the King, as his body slumped back in his open-top car and a crowd of soldiers desperately tried to capture the assailant and protect his victim from further harm.

Graham's account of the assassination is one of his most compelling works of history. The basic premise of his argument was that Pavelić had been responsible for master-minding the assassination from Italy, with the help of Mussolini's government, since both Croatian nationalists and Italian fascists had an interest in bringing about the disintegration of the Yugoslav state. Graham told the story with his usual vigour, blending together a mixture of history and speculation, which at times makes *Alexander of Yugoslavia* read like a novel. It was, nevertheless, far more a work of history than his earlier book *St Vitus' Day*. Although Graham invented dialogue, and described incidents that he cannot possibly have known about, the book was built around a skeleton of fact, derived in part from the published accounts of the trials of the surviving conspirators that took place in France early in 1936. He was also able to rely on another less public source. The cover of *Alexander of Yugoslavia* claimed that the book had been written

---

73 *Daily Mail*, 12 October 1934.

with the cooperation and advice of members of the Serbian Royal Family. Graham's private papers contain transcripts of interviews he conducted in the autumn of 1937 with a number of people, including Prince Paul, who became Regent after the murder of his cousin.[74] The Prince warned his interviewer that he would find it difficult to write a conventional biography of Alexander. Graham responded that he had no desire to write such a book, telling Paul that, although he wished to provide an accurate account of the murder in Marseilles, he wanted his book to have a sense of "drama" designed to appeal to British readers.

Graham also interviewed Queen Maria, widow of Alexander, who told him that her late husband was often "impatient of measures taken for his own safety". She added that neither of them had any "special forebodings" about the journey to France, even though there had been rumours of a definite plot to kill the King. Graham in addition interviewed a number of senior Yugoslavian political figures, including Bogoljub Jevtić, who had been Foreign Minister in 1934. The notes he made of these interviews were detailed, although since he conducted them just a few months before his final manuscript was submitted to the publishers, they were probably used to fill gaps in the narrative rather than provide a foundation for the whole analysis. Nor did the interviews cast much light on the motives of the assassins themselves, rather providing Graham with a greater insight into the personality of the King, with the result that the chapters dealing with Alexander were more substantial than those that explored the actual details of the plot against him.

Graham's Serbian sympathies ran deeply through *Alexander of Yugoslavia*, but although he made no secret of his admiration for the King, the book was far more than a piece of simple hagiography. Whilst he praised Alexander's commitment to promoting international peace, as well as his bravery in the face of an earlier assassination attempt, he acknowledged that large numbers of Croatians felt that they were excluded from positions of power in the Yugoslavian civil service and military. He gently criticized the King for his *coup d'etat* of 1929, even though it had been intended to reduce ethnic tensions in the country, suggesting that he had "slipped into the error of paternal government which might have worked in old Montenegro but was unsuitable for a large state and a complex of jealous races". He also

---

[74] Graham Papers (HRC), Misc. (Interviews with members of Yugoslav Royal Family and Yugoslav politicians).

suggested that after 1929 Alexander had become "more aloof, more hedged in majesty", which made it harder for him to gauge the mood of his people, even though he was genuinely determined to build a federation in which all ethnic groups could flourish.[75]

Graham nevertheless placed most of the blame for Yugoslavia's problems on the post-war settlement devised at Paris in 1919, which he believed had sought to impose democracy in a region where it could only come about as the result of a slow process of evolution. The reviewers of *Alexander of Yugoslavia* were generally positive, although those of a scholarly turn of mind suggested that the more controversial material required footnotes, so that readers could see for themselves the sources for Graham's various claims.[76] This criticism was a fair one. Graham did a good deal of research for the book, and had privileged access to valuable material about Alexander and his family, but his description of the plotters and their links to the governments in Rome and Budapest was both impressionistic and speculative. The lively portrayal of Alexander and the other *dramatis personae* made *Alexander of Yugoslavia* an enthralling read. It is less clear whether it cast much new light on the assassination itself.

By the end of the 1930s, Graham had spent ten years dividing his life between Yugoslavia and Britain, largely abandoning the long journeys of his earlier years, with the striking exception of his trip to South Africa in 1936. The decade was for him a time of reorientation and reinvention. In private he focused his energy on building a new life with Vera. In public he concentrated on writing more fiction and biography in place of the travel accounts that had once been his signature piece. Graham's decision to change his literary focus was a consequence both of financial necessity and a reluctance to return to the kind of confessional work that had once been his forte. This sense of flux was echoed in his novels. Even the most cursory reading of his fiction shows the extent of his fascination with the gulf between public and private *personas* – the sense that people could present themselves to the world in ways quite unlike their true selves – or, and perhaps more tellingly, in ways that suggested they only possess a weak sense of their real identity. As Graham spent the first part of the 1930s

---

75 Stephen Graham, *Alexander of Yugoslavia: The Story of the King who was Murdered in Marseilles* (New Haven: Yale University Press, 1939), pp. 5, 153 (first published in Britain by Cassell in 1938 as *Alexander of Jugoslavia: Strong Man of the Balkans*).

76 E.C. Helmreich, *Annals of the American Academy of Political and Social Science*, 204 (July 1939), pp. 192-93.

stumbling towards a new personal and professional life, in place of the one that had fallen apart in the second half of the previous decade, his sense of the fragility of his own identity seeped out in his work. It was only in the second half of the decade that a new Graham began to emerge. Both the travel writing of *Moving Tent,* and the quasi-investigative journalism of *Alexander of Yugoslavia*, were of a higher quality than anything he produced in the first half of the 1930s. How his life and work might have developed if he had been able to develop these interests in tranquillity can only be a cause for conjecture. The outbreak of War in Europe in 1939 transformed Graham's life, as it transformed the lives of countless millions of others. London had always been important to him as the place to which he returned physically and emotionally from his travels around the world. For the next thirty five years, down to his death, the city was to become home for Graham in a far more immediate and enduring sense.

8. A Time of Strife

Graham and Vera were living together at 60 Frith Street when the British Prime Minister Neville Chamberlain made his historic broadcast in September 1939 announcing that "this country is now at war with Germany". Vera was working as London correspondent for the Belgrade newspaper *Stampa*, having previously been employed by a paper in Sarajevo, although it is not exactly clear what her position entailed. She certainly filed news stories on a routine basis during the first few months of the War, taking them in person to be approved by the British authorities, before sending them on to Yugoslavia for publication. Graham was at fifty-five too old for military service. Nor could he continue with his peripatetic lifestyle since war-time conditions made international travel impossible. He and Vera decided to stay in London at the outbreak of war, unlike some of their friends, who joined in the exodus from the city convinced that it would soon become a target for German bombers. The War created a huge change in the rhythms of London life. The streets and railway stations became crowded with young men and women in uniform. The shops began to empty of goods. More challengingly for Graham, the literary world became increasingly "comatose" in the face of paper shortages and changing tastes. He filled his time by cycling around the London streets, delivering his own letters, as well as settling down to a number of new writing projects.[1] Vera passed her days writing articles and dress-making. No air-raid shelter was installed at Frith Street, despite the threat of bombs, since the house was blessed with a sturdy cellar that its occupants hoped would provide sanctuary should the Luftwaffe appear in the skies above London.

The start of hostilities dented sales of Graham's books. Even his recent *Moving Tent* failed to find many buyers (thousands of copies were also

---

1 Graham Papers (FSU), Box 573, 6, Graham to Marion Hay, 10 October 1939.

http://dx.doi.org/10.11647/OBP.0040.08

lost when the publisher's warehouse was bombed). It was for this reason that he set out to write a number of new works designed to respond to the demand for "books about the war interest".[2] He quickly produced a book *From War to War* which provided a list of the key international developments of the previous twenty years, and was, in Graham's own words, "like those jottings one makes before going on a platform to make a speech".[3] A more substantial work – and an even more unlikely one from the pen of Graham – appeared in 1940 under the title *Liquid Victory*. This book examined the critical role played by oil in fuelling modern warfare. It was generally well-informed, reviewing the oil-producing capacities of the major world powers, including the attempts by Nazi Germany to increase its production of synthetic oil. Graham was convinced that the anticipated "war of attrition" would in effect become a war of "attrition of oil supplies". He also correctly suggested that the liberal powers were far better placed by dint of geography to secure access to major oil reserves than members of the axis coalition. Although one of the main themes of *Liquid Victory* was that "oil is on the side of the democracies", he could not resist a jibe at "so-called democratic government[s]" that were seldom "controlled by principles, but by men who usurp the authority of the principles".[4] Graham was often uneasy in the years that followed about the ethics of the diplomacy pursued by the British government in defeating Nazi Germany and its allies. He was particularly critical of the alliance established with the USSR in the summer of 1941, and angrily condemned the readiness of London to surrender Yugoslavia to communist control during the final months of the War. There were indeed times when Graham seemed more appalled by the behaviour of Britain's Soviet ally than he was by the activities of the country's actual enemies.

One of his acquaintances later suggested that Graham hoped that Britain would ally itself with Nazi Germany in order to do joint battle against Soviet Russia, adding that it was only following the German invasion of Holland and Belgium, in the spring of 1940, that he began to reassess his views. The claim, if true, is not as shocking as it may sound. Throughout the 1930s, there was no shortage of political figures in Britain who believed that Stalin posed a greater threat to Britain than Hitler (it was one of the

---

2 Gawsworth Papers (University of Reading Library), Box 10, Graham to Gawsworth, 18 September 1939.
3 Stephen Graham, *From War to War* (London: Hutchinson, 1940).
4 Stephen Graham, *Liquid Victory* (London: Hutchinson, 1940), pp. 51, 96.

reasons Lord Halifax, Foreign Secretary from 1938 to 1941, had initially supported the appeasement of Nazi Germany).[5] The Nazi-Soviet Pact of August 1939, which paved the way for the carve-up of eastern Europe, in any case diminished sympathy for Soviet Russia beyond a small core of committed communists.[6] Graham issued an updated version of his biography of Stalin shortly before the Pact was made public, and although the book was still subtitled 'An Impartial Study', its tone was more hostile than the earlier edition published in 1931. At the start of 1940, Graham also made a broadcast in the BBC's Men of the Hour series, telling his audience that "Stalin considers himself an Asiatic", adding that his attitude towards his fellow men and women was shaped by the fact that he originally came "from an area [Georgia] where life is cheap". Graham noted that the Soviet leader's decision to enter a pact with Hitler in August 1939 was evidence of his fundamental "opportunism".[7] Before Hitler turned his forces eastwards, in the summer of 1941, the status of the Soviet Union in British diplomacy and propaganda was extremely problematic. Although there were some senior figures in the British government who hoped that the two dictators would before long break with one another, opening the door for some kind of understanding between London and Moscow, there were plenty of people who believed that it was only a matter of time before war broke out between Britain and Russia.

Stephen and Vera lived in London throughout the period of the Phoney War, which lasted from September 1939 through to the spring of 1940, when the British expeditionary force was evacuated from Dunkirk.[8] Many families who had been evacuated following the declaration of war began to drift home, believing that the absence of bombing raids proved that earlier warnings about the danger of massive civilian casualties had been exaggerated, whilst the cafes and pubs filled with men and women in uniform attached to military units that had nowhere obvious to go. The

---

5   On Halifax, see Andrew Roberts, *The Holy Fox: A Life of Lord Halifax* (London: Weidenfeld and Nicolson, 1991).

6   For a valuable discussion of British attitudes towards Russia in the war years see Philip Bell, *John Bull and the Bear: British Public Opinion, Foreign Policy and the Soviet Union, 1941-1945* (London: Edward Arnold, 1990). See, too, the numerous reports commissioned during the period by Mass Observations.

7   BBC Archives (Caversham), Transcript of 'Men of the Hour: Stalin', broadcast 7 January 1940.

8   On civilian morale during the phoney war see Robert Mackay, *Half the Battle: Civilian Morale in Britain during the Second World War* (Manchester: Manchester University Press, 2002), pp. 46-58.

fall of France in May signalled the start of a new phase of the War. In July and August, the Luftwaffe carried out extensive attacks on British military targets and harbour installations, despite repeated harassment from RAF fighters in the Battle of Britain. In September, a change in German tactics led to the start of huge aerial attacks on London, heralding three months of almost daily (and nightly) raids. Tens of thousands of lives were lost and hundreds of thousands of buildings damaged in the destruction that followed. The residents of London faced months of uncertainty and fear, as the routines of everyday life were ripped apart. The emergency services learned to deal with the horrendous aftermath of attacks like the one that took place at Trafalgar Square, not far from Frith Street, when a bomb hit the nearby tube station where dozens of people were sheltering.[9] For Graham himself, the Blitz represented an assault on the physical and psychological landscape of a city that he had known and loved all his life.[10]

Graham had long been concerned about the consequences of major bombing raids on London. In 1936 he had predicted that if bombers ever appeared over the city then:

> London must come under the spell of fear because of its vast population, its quarter-educated submerged masses. The capital is one great terrible trap. What with heavy poison gases filling the obvious refuges of the underground railways, fire devastating the panelled Georgian houses and the jerry-built erections of wood and brick of the Edwardian age, the falling tenements of the slums, terror is bound to seize the city in time of aerial attack.[11]

In that same year he contributed a short story '5,000 Enemy Planes over London' to a collection edited by John Gawsworth, which described a future conflict in which Italy and France declared war on Britain (Germany remained neutral), and sent their bombers to destroy London. It told how the population fled in panic to the shelters, or headed out into the countryside, leaving factories and offices deserted as "widespread terror" gripped the country. The story concluded with a prophetic warning that "No country that is not supreme in the air can reckon winning a modern war [...] The new air war aims at an invasion of the mind".[12] The events of

---

9 William Sansom, *The Blitz: Westminster at War* (Oxford: Oxford University Press, 1990), pp. 56-57.
10 For a general discussion of Graham's attitudes toward London, see Michael Hughes, 'The Traveller's Search for Home: Stephen Graham and the Quest for London', *The London Journal*, 36, 3 (2011), pp. 211-24.
11 Graham, *Characteristics*, p. 79.
12 Stephen Graham, '5,000 Enemy Planes over London', in *Masterpiece of Thrills*, ed.by John

1940 and 1941 gave Graham the chance to see whether his grim pre-war predictions would become true. He chronicled events in the capital in a detailed 'Air Raid Diary', which was probably intended for publication, but was also prompted by his desire to record the experiences of a city at war. It provides a valuable insight into his own reaction to the Blitz, as well as a record of the impact of mass bombing on the life of the city around him.[13]

When the first major air raids took place on London, on the night of 7 September 1940, Stephen and Vera were picking fruit near Chingford in Essex, in the garden of a cottage they rented for weekend visits. Even on the borders of Epping Forest, several miles from the East End, their cottage shook as bombs fell and anti-aircraft guns fired back into the sky. The Anderson shelter at the cottage had flooded, a perennial problem with the design, and they took cover under a large pear tree, lying on the ground counting the German planes flying overhead "like storks crossing a continent". The two of them decided to return home to Frith Street, despite the risk, and on the first part of their journey by bus to Chingford Station they looked towards "the eastern sky suffused with crimson". At Chingford they boarded a train which, they were told, could travel no further than Hackney Downs. As it crawled eastwards towards the London suburbs, they could see the docks on fire, and at Stratford saw another train which had taken a direct hit ablaze on the adjacent track. A few hundred yards further on, Vera was soaked by water from a fireman's hose as they passed an explosives warehouse that had lost its roof in a blast. When Stephen and Vera finally reached central London they found that Tottenham Court Road station was closed, forcing them to make their way on to Leicester Square, where they emerged into a throng of pedestrians being marshalled by police and air raid wardens to nearby shelters. The pair trudged home to Frith Street, incongruous figures with heavy sacks of fruit over their shoulders, passing through chaotic streets of frightened Londoners confronting a new and horrific threat.

Although the East End took the brunt of the Blitz in London, the West End was also hit, and Graham had a number of near misses when out shopping or surveying the damage caused by previous raids. On one occasion he was forced to flee a Soho market, taking shelter in a nearby shop, as a bomb fell destroying the stalls and scattering the shop-keepers' money to the

---

Gawsworth (London: Associated Press, 1936), pp. 339-46.
13 The incidents in this and subsequent paragraphs are taken from Graham Papers (FSU), Box 573, 12a ('Air Raid Diary').

four winds. He was particularly saddened by the destruction of St Anne's Church in Soho, on 24 September 1940, which he mournfully described as the "mother" of the seventeenth-century houses that surrounded it. Graham also ventured eastwards from time to time to see at first hand parts of London that had been damaged more severely than his own. A few days after the start of the bombing, he went to St Paul's Cathedral, "surrounded by hosepipes coiled about as by an enormous boa constrictor". Nearby buildings lay in "smoking ruins" whilst at each side street there was "a vista of burning buildings [...] looking up Cheapside from the Bank" was an endless parade of "high ladders, water towers, and helmeted firemen in silhouette on top of them". On another occasion he walked down Oxford Street, just a few hundred yards from his home, surveying shops with smashed windows whose contents had been strewn across the pavement. Perhaps even more unsettling than the immediate sights and smells of destruction were the rumours of horrors that had supposedly happened elsewhere ("all back of Fitzroy St blown up" or "all Edgeware Road gone"). Graham was himself on occasion inclined to hyperbole, particularly when reports began to circulate of the damage suffered by provincial cities like Coventry, following the extension of the Luftwaffe's bombing campaign beyond the capital. Mostly, though, he tried to preserve a more judicious tone, writing in his diary on 17 October 1940 that "the war on London is methodical and mechanical. It is no Blitzkrieg, no mere assault, but a factory operation [...] It goes on unhasting [and] unresting till its object is achieved, and the ruins of the metropolis become uninhabitable".

Graham could not miss the misery that surrounded him as he walked through the devastated streets of the city he had known since he was a boy. A few days after the bombing started, he noted in his diary that by six o'clock in the evening there were long lines of Londoners queuing to enter the public shelters, which only opened when the siren sounded, leading to a stampede to "get the best places" where it was possible to lie down. He added forlornly that there were too few such shelters which were, in any case, little more secure than the basement of a house, since they could easily be destroyed by a direct hit. The deep shelters provided by the tube stations were little better. On one occasion, when coming back from the cottage at Chingford, Stephen and Vera passed through a station where:

> thousands of people [...] were settling to spend the night underground, children, babies, dogs, would-be smart flappers looking woebegone as they lay on the platforms and train after train passed them [...] nearly everyone

had brought something to sleep on and a pillow or cushion. The air was hot and thick, the stink appalling. For there are no WCs. In the train one's head began to throb in a splitting headache. Vera says "And this in the biggest and richest city in the world".

Graham added grimly that the onset of winter was likely to lead to more problems, as flu and other diseases took hold of a population whose health was already weakened by exhaustion.

The household at 60 Frith Street did not have to rely on tube stations for shelter, preferring to head to the basement when the siren sounded, even though its members knew that it would provide little protection against a direct hit. Nor was such a prospect unlikely. Graham diligently noted down details of the bombs that fell on Soho, including one in Great Windmill Street in November, and another in Frith Street itself just a couple of hundred yards from his home. A few weeks earlier, three houses had been gutted in Dean Street, although Graham slept through the explosion, exhausted after many nights without proper rest. His perennial fear was that he and Vera would be trapped in the basement in a firestorm that would suffocate them to death. The most frightening moment for the occupants of 60 Frith Street took place just before New Year. On 30 December 1940, following a comparative lull over the Christmas holiday, Graham faced what he believed to be "the greatest and worst raid so far". Such a judgement was partly clouded by personal experience. In the early evening there was suddenly a loud crash,

> like a collapsing china shop. Our back windows, frames and all, had gone [...] soot in bushels came out from the chimney and lay inches deep on the carpet. Cat ran up the chimney. Pictures fell. We went down to the basement to hear the clatter of many fire bombs falling. The street and workshop at back lit up like day. Old woman with canary begged to be sheltered. We did not stay long below, but returned to clear up the terrible mess. Didn't do badly, but we have a very draughty flat.

The damage was not fully repaired until the War was over, but Stephen and Vera had already become thoroughly accustomed to a life shorn of pre-war comforts. Gas and water supplies were often cut off, whilst any journey was made difficult as streets damaged by blast or fire were closed down, requiring lengthy detours to cover short distances. The constraints of rationing were also beginning to prove increasingly irksome. Graham complained bitterly throughout the War about the problem of getting adequate supplies of food and wine, with the result that he and Vera increasingly ate at one of the numerous local restaurants in Soho, in order to avoid the queues for supplies. They also feverishly bottled supplies of plums and tomatoes "as a store against winter".[14] There were nevertheless limits to what even the most determined residents of London could do to manage the soul-sapping business of daily life in a capital city at war. The challenge of obtaining new furniture for Frith Street at one point became so bad that Graham even sketched out in his head "an essay [on] the advantages for entering the second-hand furniture trade instead of literature".[15]

Graham's Air Raid Diary for 1940-41 gives an interesting insight into the way in which Londoners became accustomed to the extraordinary circumstances in which they found themselves.[16] His entries give little evidence to support the familiar myth that the Blitz created a new sense of community based on shared hardship. He noted how in some parts of London it was possible to find expensive hair-dressers that had set up business in special shelters to provide their customers with regular service even during the fiercest raids.[17] Nor did he conceal the episodes of bad temper and squabbling that broke out in shelters populated by the less fortunate. At the same time, though, Graham's diary also reflects the astonishing stoicism exhibited by many Londoners during the Blitz. Even after a night of heavy bombing, workers still travelled into the city centre to see if their offices and factories were standing, whilst the sounding of the air-raid siren was usually met as much with weary resignation as real panic.

Graham's own household at Frith Street seems to have been remarkably phlegmatic at dealing with the challenge of nightly bombardment. By February 1941, Stephen and Vera were both working at the BBC, requiring them to travel daily through the broken streets of London to Bush House, where they had to do a full day's work, despite having spent the night in the confines of their Soho basement (or sometimes, in Graham's case, fire-watching on the roofs of nearby houses). The two of them had, of course, known considerable hardship earlier in their lives, Graham in the

---

14 Gawsworth Papers (University of Reading Library), Box 10, Graham to Gawsworth, 21 September 1943.
15 Ibid, Graham to Gawsworth, 17 June 1943.
16 For details of the reaction of Londoners to the Blitz see Mackay, *Half the Battle*, pp. 68-90; Helen Bell, *London was Ours: Diaries and Memoirs of the London Blitz* (London: I.B. Tauris, 2008); Juliet Gardiner, *The Blitz: the British Under Attack* (London: Harper Press, 2011).
17 On the ability of parts of the West End to continue despite the bombing, see Matthew Sweet, *The West End Front: The Wartime Secrets of London's Great Hotels* (London: Faber and Faber, 2011).

trenches, and Vera as an "orphan" forced to survive the turmoil of war-torn Yugoslavia. Such experiences doubtless bred a certain toughness of spirit (although by the spring of 1942 Graham was fretting about Vera's fragility in the face of the stresses of daily life).[18] Like all their fellow-Londoners, though, neither had any experience of how to cope in the surreal atmosphere of a war-torn city where the routines of urban civilisation were daily under threat. And yet, within a few days of the start of the Blitz, Graham was able to note laconically in his diary that, after visiting one scene of utter destruction, he popped into a nearby store to buy a much-needed new shirt. The juxtaposition of devastation and normality had, in just a short period of time, come to seem almost normal to him.

The outbreak of the War inevitably disrupted cultural life in London, prompting E.M. Forster's grim dictum that "1939 was not a year in which to start a literary career". It would nevertheless be wrong to assume that the literary scene closed down altogether (although one cynical journalist writing for the *Daily Express* suggested that it might be no bad thing if it did so). The poet Stephen Spender recalled in his autobiography that the War created "a revival of interest in the arts. This arose spontaneously and simply, because people felt that music, the ballet, poetry and painting were concerned with a seriousness of living and dying with which they themselves had suddenly been confronted".[19] Those who were able to meet this demand found themselves in a privileged position. Whilst plans to exempt some better-known writers from conscription came to nothing, in the face of opposition from the War Office, there were always plenty of young intellectuals who, for reason of health or conscience, were not called up for military service. Many of them congregated in the area surrounding Graham's home in Frith Street. Pubs like the Highlander in Dean Street and the Marquess of Granby on Rathbone Street became the setting for alcohol-fuelled squabbles about abstruse questions of poetry and prose. The coffee bars of Soho also witnessed an influx of literary types, many of them working in the near-by BBC and Ministry of Information, both of which expanded enormously in the months following the declaration

---

18 Graham Papers (FSU), Box 573, 6, Graham to Hay, 5 March 1942.
19 Stephen Spender, *World Within a World: The Autobiography of Stephen Spender* (London: Hamish Hamilton, 1951), p. 286. On literary life in this period see Robert Hewison, *Under Siege: Literary Life in London, 1939-45* (London: Weidenfeld and Nicholson, 1977). Also see the relevant pages of Hugh David, *The Fitzrovians: A Portrait of a Bohemian Society, 1900-1950* (London: Michael Joseph, 1988).

of war. Graham chose to remain largely aloof from this world of alcohol and literature. Although 60 Frith Street had been something of a cultural salon in the 1920s, Graham had never been very interested in the quarrels that periodically transfixed a section of the capital's intelligentsia, and his surviving correspondence reflects his impatience with the petty jealousies of those who talked "day and night" but did little.

Graham's closest literary ties were with middle-brow writers who, like himself, had little in common with the *literati* who pored over *Horizon* when it appeared each month. The Australian romance writer Maysie Grieg and her husband Max Murray were frequent visitors to Frith Street. So too was Grieg's first husband, the American Delano Ames, who worked in London for military intelligence during the War, before becoming famous as author of the Dagobert Brown and Jane Hamish detective novels. Graham's sister, the publisher and writer Eleanor Graham, was also a regular visitor to Frith Street, where she took refuge from German bombs in the cellar of her brother's house (her flat in nearby Bloomsbury was not blessed with such a sturdy facility). Vera was no great lover of company, in part because she was self-conscious of her irregular marital position, whilst some who knew her felt that she was always unsure how to fit in to English society. Graham too, despite being "a good mixer", was increasingly uncomfortable in large crowds. During the thirty five years he lived with Vera in London, the two became increasingly detached from the world around them, preferring to develop a few close friendships rather than immerse themselves in "Society" in all its myriad forms.

Whilst the challenges of daily life absorbed a good deal of Graham's attention during the early years of the War, he still had to face the practical problem of earning a living. George Orwell spoke for many writers when he complained that "the money situation [was] becoming unbearable". Vera Brittain recalled how "the grim inexorability of war" had greatly reduced many "civilised forms of employment" including journalism and literary work.[20] The difficulty of making a living through writing was certainly one factor that prompted Graham's decision to begin work for the BBC at the start of 1941 – an aspect of his life discussed later in this chapter – but he also needed to find other outlets for his prodigious energy. A few months after the start of the War, he accepted a request by the Anglican and Eastern Churches Association (AECA) to edit a new publication, which

---

20 Hewison, *Under Siege*, p. 20.

subsequently appeared under the cumbersome title of *Stephen Graham's Newsletter about the Orthodox Churches in War-Time*. Graham had not previously had many dealings with the AECA, but members of its General Committee identified him as the best person to publicise the plight of the Orthodox Church, at a time when the Nazi-Soviet pact was reshaping social and political life throughout eastern Europe.[21] The Foreign Office also gave its blessing to the project, apparently hoping that the *Newsletter* would foster the perception that Germany posed a fundamental threat to religious freedom, helping to re-enforce the broader propaganda message about the horrors of Hitler's government.

The first issue of the *Newsletter* gave a clear signal that Graham did not believe that Nazi Germany posed the only, or even the principal, threat to religious freedom in Europe. His attention instead remained firmly focused on developments in the USSR. His opening editorial roundly declared that "We believe that, sooner or later, the anti-God regime in Russia will founder", adding that "a crash in Stalinism is inevitable".[22] He pursued this theme even more strongly in the second *Newsletter*, which examined the situation in the territories occupied by the USSR and Germany during the months following the Nazi-Soviet Pact. Graham argued – or at least seemed to argue – that the Nazi Government had treated the Orthodox Church less brutally than its Soviet counterpart.[23] His claims created a furore within the normally sedate world of the AECA hierarchy. The General Committee received a number of letters of complaint from its members. Their concerns were echoed by the Bishop of Lincoln, the President of the Association, who feared that Graham was "unwittingly" producing "anti-British propaganda". Graham himself went to Lambeth Palace to discuss the subject with the Archbishop of Canterbury's secretary. He was also invited to attend a meeting of the AECA's General Committee (where discussion actually showed that his views commanded a good deal of support).[24]

Whilst the immediate crisis was smoothed away, Graham's views on Russia became more controversial in the following years, once Hitler's fateful decision to invade Soviet Russia meant that the USSR and Britain

---

21 Lambeth Palace Library, MSS 4736, Minutes of the General Committee of the Anglican and Eastern Churches Association, 4 October 1939; 15 January 1940.
22 *Stephen Graham's Newsletter About the Orthodox Churches in War-Time*, No. 1, March 1940.
23 Ibid, No. 2, April 1940.
24 Lambeth Palace Library, MSS 4736, Minutes of the General Committee of the AECA, 29 April 1940.

became allies in the fight against Nazism.[25] Although the British Prime Minister Winston Churchill had for many years been as bitter a critic of Stalin as any member of the British establishment, he moved quickly to welcome Soviet Russia as a new ally in the fight against Nazism following the start of Operation Barbarossa (Hitler's attack on the USSR in June 1941).[26] In his broadcast just a few hours after Germany launched its *Blitzkrieg*, Churchill described developments in eastern Europe as "one of the climacterics of war", following this up with a resounding offer of support to "Russia and the Russian people".[27] This dramatic turn of events changed the way in which the USSR was perceived in war-time Britain. Senior figures at the BBC immediately began to discuss how they could provide more positive coverage of Soviet Russia, without provoking "hostile and cynical reactions" from an audience accustomed to viewing the country with suspicion and distaste.[28] The question of Stalin's harsh treatment of the Russian Church was of particular concern to those responsible for fostering a less negative image of the USSR amongst the British public. At the start of the War, the Ministry of Information established a Religions Division designed to harness religion to the cause of victory, by portraying Nazi Germany as the greatest threat to religious freedom across Europe.[29] It produced a publication called *Spiritual Issues of the War* that carried numerous articles attacking the axis powers, as well as other pieces encouraging readers to view the conflict as a kind of metaphysical struggle, a conflict "between light and darkness which God puts before us all".[30] The Division also produced a regular *Orthodox Church Bulletin* which, amongst other things, sought to provide a positive picture of the religious situation in the USSR.

---

25 Amongst the large literature on Barbarossa and the Eastern Front see Richard Overy, *Russia's War, 1941-1945* (Harmondsworth: Penguin, 1998); John Erickson, *The Road to Stalingrad* (London: Weidenfeld and Nicolson, 1975).
26 On Churchill's shifting attitude towards Soviet Russia in wartime, see David Carlton, *Churchill and the Soviet Union* (Manchester: Manchester University Press, 1999), pp. 70-134.
27 *The Times*, 22 June 1941.
28 BBC archives (Caversham), R51/520/1 (various letters dated June and July 1941). For the BBC's reaction to how Barbarossa should change its strategy on Russia, see Asa Briggs, *The War of Words* (London: Oxford University Press, 1970), p. 387 ff.
29 Dianne Kirby, *Church, State and Propaganda: The Archbishop of York and International Relations. A Study of Cyril Foster Garbett, 1942-55* (Hull: Hull University Press, 1999), esp. p. 27 ff. See, too, Dianne Kirby, 'The Church of England and "Religions Division" during the Second World War: Church-State Relations and the Anglo-Soviet Alliance', *Electronic Journal of International History*, 4.
30 *Spiritual Issues of the War*, 30 October 1941.

Leading figures in the Church of England played their part in efforts to build closer links between Britain and Russia. The new Archbishop of Canterbury, William Temple, supported the translation into English of a Soviet propaganda publication *The Truth about Religion in Russia*.[31] He also gave his blessing to a visit to Russia by Cyril Garbett, Archbishop of York, in the autumn of 1943. Garbett was well-received in Moscow, where he gave speeches condemning the "treacherous and unprovoked Nazi attack".[32] On his return home, he gave a press conference declaring roundly "that there can be no doubt that worship within the churches [in Russia] is fully allowed" and that "anti-religious propaganda has come to an end".[33] It was not an edifying performance, but the Archbishop was only too well-aware of the importance of the Anglo-Russian alliance to the war effort, and he hoped to play his part by persuading his fellow-countrymen that Stalin had relented in his previous harsh treatment of the Church.[34] Like many previous British visitors to the USSR, he may also have convinced himself of the absurdities which he proclaimed to the world.

The change in the military and diplomatic situation created by Operation Barbarossa had consequences for both the AECA and Graham's *Newsletter*. The Association's General Committee discussed developments at its meeting in July 1941, recognising that some of its members were likely to be perturbed at finding their country allied with a government that had for years ruthlessly attacked religion in all its guises. The minutes cautiously noted that there were "different points of view" on the subject, leading the Committee to refrain from issuing any formal pronouncements for fear of stirring up division among members.[35] The mood changed a few months later, though, when the Annual Meeting of the Association approved a motion expressing its "admiration [for] the heroic resistance with which the armies of the Russian people are opposing the onslaught of Nazi oppression". Its leaders also approved plans for a Thanksgiving Service to honour those who had died during the fighting in Russia.[36]

---

31 William Temple Papers (Lambeth Palace Library), 38, Martin to Temple, 7 December 1942.
32 *The Times*, 22 September 1943.
33 Ibid, 12 October 1943.
34 Kirby, *Church, State and Propaganda*, p. 57.
35 Lambeth Palace Library, MSS 4736, Minutes of the General Committee of the AECA, 30 July 1941.
36 Ibid, Minutes of the AGM of the AECA, 25 September 1941.

Graham found it difficult to come to terms with the more positive mood towards Russia that became a staple of British life following the outbreak of war between Moscow and Berlin. He responded by downplaying developments in Russia in his *Newsletter*, focusing instead on the situation in Yugoslavia, which had been occupied by the axis powers in the spring of 1941. When he did write about the USSR, he grudgingly acknowledged that the Russian Church was being allowed to play a greater role in the country's life, but described such a development as a cynical attempt to use religious and patriotic motifs to mobilise the population behind the War.[37] When Stalin made the decision in 1943 to re-establish the Moscow Patriarchate, Graham dryly remarked that such a "remarkable event" had only come about because it was "politically expedient", adding that the move was governed, above all, by the desire to impress Russia's allies who were now asked "to believe that Holy Russia was never murdered".[38] A number of his editorials provided a curious echo of his younger self, combining a detailed analysis of developments in Europe with a more diffuse sense that the roots of conflict were to be found in the follies of a world that had allowed its sense of the transcendent to wither and die. His readers were divided in their reaction to this approach. Some expressed their enthusiasm, whilst others found such a juxtaposition of the prosaic and the numinous distracting and unconvincing.

Some senior figures in the AECA were concerned that Graham's *Newsletter* was too negative in its portrayal of Soviet Russia at a time when the country had become an important ally for Britain. The issue came to a head at a meeting of the General Committee in December 1943, when the Association's Secretary noted that it was clear that Graham's sympathies were "with the old Russia". He went on to add that "it had been evident for some time that he finds himself unable to accept the new relationship between the Church and the State in Russia. This has for some time been a source of embarrassment, in view of the attitude of our own ecclesiastical authorities, the Archbishops of Canterbury and York being officials of the AECA and the News-Letter being published under is auspices". He added that some "strongly-worded criticism" of the *Newsletter* had come

---

37 On the way in which Stalin's treatment of the Orthodox Church in wartime was linked to diplomatic questions see Steven Merritt Miner, *Stalin's Holy War: Religion, Nationalism and Alliance Politics, 1941-45* (Chapel Hill, NC: University of North Carolina Press, 2003).
38 *Graham's Newsletter about the Orthodox Churches*, No. 37, September-October 1943.

from the Ministry of Information.[39] The precise nature of this criticism is unclear, but it seems that Graham's *Newsletter* was viewed with concern by senior figures in the Religious Division, who feared that it might undermine official attempts to promote a positive image of Britain's Soviet ally. When Graham was told of these concerns he immediately tendered his resignation. The effective dismissal of the eponymous editor of *Stephen Graham's Newsletter* was done with the discretion and dignity appropriate for an organisation that included senior figures of the British Establishment amongst its membership. Graham was effusively thanked in the first edition of the *Newsletter's* successor – *The Eastern Churches Broadsheet* – for the skill with which he had written "about current affairs *sub speciae aeternitas* against the background of an intricate network of political and ecclesiastical relations".[40] Readers were not informed that Graham had in effect been sacked for refusing to respond to the dictates of those who wanted to promote a more positive image of Uncle Joe Stalin and the country he ruled over.

The growing disquiet within the Anglican and Eastern Churches Association about Graham's response to international developments was not only focused on his attitude towards the USSR. Some senior figures in the organisation were also concerned about his attitude towards the situation in the Balkans. The intricacies of the political situation in Yugoslavia during the Second World War defy easy characterisation. The period was, in the words of one distinguished commentator, "the story of many wars piled on top of one another".[41] In the spring of 1941, the country was invaded by Italy and Germany, forcing the young King Peter to flee to London, where a Royal Yugoslav Government-in-Exile was quickly established.[42] In the months and years that followed, occupying axis troops fought with local resistance groups who in turn often fought with one another. The puppet government of Ante Pavelić, established by the Germans to rule over a nominally-independent Croatia, instituted a racial policy that led to the extermination of hundreds of thousands of Serbs luckless enough

---

39 Lambeth Palace Library, MSS 4736, Minutes of the General Committee of the AECA, 30 December 1943.
40 *The Eastern Churches Broadsheet*, January 1944.
41 Noel Malcolm, *Bosnia* (London: Papermac, 1996), p. 174.
42 For a useful summary of the Yugoslav Government-in-Exile see Stevan K. Pavlowitch, 'Out of Context: The Yugoslav Government in London, 1941-45', *Journal of Contemporary History*, 16, 1 (1981), pp. 89-118; M.A. Kay, 'The Yugoslav Government-in-Exile and the Problems of Restoration', *East European Quarterly*, 25, 1 (1991), pp. 1-19.

to be living in the territory of the new and enlarged state. The activities of this fascist regime – the *Ustaša* – in turn evoked the hatred of countless Serbs who flocked to join the Royalist and nationalist-inspired *Chetniks*. The *Chetniks* were led, at least nominally, by Draža Mihailović, who was, at the start of 1942, appointed as Minister of War by the Government-in-Exile in London. The picture was complicated by the emergence of a multinational communist-inspired partisan resistance, led by Josef Tito, which was often virtually at war with the *Chetniks* as well as the occupation forces and the *Ustaša* regime of Pavelić. The complex shifts and turns of events in Yugoslavia during these tortured years have spawned a cottage industry of memoirs and histories seeking to disentangle the rights and wrongs of the period.[43] The situation was even harder to understand during the chaos of war itself.

Yugoslavia was of vital concern to the British, since it was one of the most active sites of resistance to German rule, and likely to prove strategically important should the allied powers launch an invasion of occupied Europe from North Africa. The area was also a particular preoccupation of Winston Churchill. It was for this reason that the Special Operations Executive devoted so much attention to the region, directing various initiatives from its regional base in Cairo, as well as broadcasting propaganda from its radio stations in Palestine. The Royal Yugoslav Government in exile was, at first, feted in London, and the young King and his ministers received huge amounts of sympathetic news coverage,[44] and enjoyed regular access to leading figures in the British government. When Mihailović was appointed Minister of War, early in 1942, his *Chetnik* forces acquired a kind of patina as the official resistance group worthy of logistical support by the British.[45] The situation soon began to change, though, for reasons that remain controversial today. Detractors of Mihailović – both at the time

---

43 See, for example, Marcia Christoff Kurapovna, *Shadows on the Mountain: The Allies, the Resistance and the Rivalries that Doomed WWII Yugoslavia* (Hoboken, NJ: Wiley, 2010); Sabrina P. Ramet and Ola Listhaug (eds.), *Serbia and the Serbs in World War Two* (Basingstoke: Palgrave, 2011); Sebastian Ritchie, *Our Man in Yugoslavia: The Story of a Secret Service Operative* (London: Frank Cass, 2004); Walter R. Roberts, *Tito, Mihailović and the Allies* (Durham, NC: Duke University Press, 1973); Anne Lane, 'Perfidious Albion? Britain and the Struggle for Mastery of Yugoslavia, 1941-44: A Re-examination in the Light of "New" Evidence', *Diplomacy and Statecraft*, 7, 2 (1996), pp. 345-77. For a valuable memoir of the time, see Fitzroy Maclean, *Eastern Approaches* (London: Cape, 1949).
44 See, for example, *Manchester Guardian*, 22 January 1942.
45 For a discussion of British policy at this time see Simon C. Trew, *Britain, Mihailović and the Chetniks, 1941-2* (Basingstoke: Macmillan, 1998).

and since – argued that the General was conspiring with the occupying axis powers to prevent the communist partisans from acquiring too much power and influence. His supporters angrily denied such claims. The reality probably lies somewhere between these extremes. Mihailović was certainly determined to prevent the growth of communist influence in Yugoslavia, but his caution in confronting German and Italian troops was largely driven by his reluctance to act until he was sure that the western powers could provide him with material support. There was nevertheless a major shift in British policy during 1942-43, away from support for the *Chetniks* and towards the partisans, which was motivated, at least in part, by concern that Mihailović was not a reliable ally. It may also be the case that Mihailović was the victim of black propaganda from left-wing sympathisers within the British government and military.[46] This was certainly the view held by Stephen Graham.

Graham repeatedly used his *Newsletter* throughout 1940-43 to review developments in Yugoslavia. Even before the country's occupation, in the spring of 1941, he condemned the Roman Catholic Church for supporting "Croat separatism".[47] In his first editorial following the attack on Yugoslavia by the axis powers, he suggested that Croat ministers in the government had favoured cooperation with the invaders. He also bitterly condemned Pavelić, who had of course featured in *Alexander of Yugoslavia*, as "a bloodthirsty assassin" (a prescient judgement given that news of the scale of the *Ustaša's* barbarities was yet to reach Britain).[48] The *Newsletter* for November 1941 attacked the "violently cruel campaign" against the Serbs, and claimed that they were actively supported by the Moslem population of Bosnia and Herzegovina, as well as large sections of the Croat population. By 1942 the *Newsletter* was praising Mihailović and condemning the Pavelić regime for murdering half a million Serbs. Graham did not, by contrast, say anything about the reports that circulated of *Chetnik* atrocities against Croats and Jews. Nor did he show much sympathy for Tito's partisans, even though

---

46 For an argument along these lines see Michael Lees, *The Rape of Serbia: The British Role in Tito's Grab for Power* (San Diego, CA: Harcourt, Brace, Jovanovich, 1990). For a discussion of the role of James Klugmann – a Communist operating within SOE who had many dealings with Yugoslavia – see Roderick Bailey, 'Communist in SOE: Explaining James Klugmann's Retention and Retainment', in *The Politics of Strategy and Clandestine War: Special Operations Executive, 1940-1946*, ed. by Neville Wylie (London: Routledge, 2007), pp. 66-89.

47 *Graham's Newsletter About the Orthodox Churches*, No. 11, February 1941.

48 Ibid, No. 14, May 1941.

they played an increasingly important role as the War dragged on, instead suggesting that their animus was directed "as much against thrones and churches" as "against the Germans, the Bulgars, the belligerent Croats, etc".[49]

Graham was particularly bitter about the British government's decision to switch its support from Mihailović's *Chetniks* to the Partisans. Writing to a friend in the summer of 1943, he condemned the "poisonous intrigue" taking place against the *Chetnik* leader in London, adding that "if he ever comes to London he could collect thousands of pounds in libel actions". He also condemned members of the "German fifth column" in Britain who were anxious "for the British Government to discard Mihailović".[50] By the summer of 1944 he was railing against the "Tito intrigue" as "unspeakably dirty".[51] Graham had no doubt that Mihailović was "a champion of national honour and liberty" – although he did not say whether the nation involved was Serbia or Yugoslavia – angrily dismissing claims that the General was a Quisling who cooperated with the occupation authorities. His sympathy for the Serb nationalist cause rendered his interpretation of events very one-sided, even if it is easy to sympathise with his criticism of Britain's wartime policy in the Balkans, which played a significant part in facilitating Tito's eventual bloody rise to power.

The source of Graham's information about Yugoslavia is something of a mystery. Although there was no shortage of articles available to him in the press, some of his letters suggest that he had knowledge that could not be derived from newspapers alone. Vera was for obvious reasons unable to contact her family who were, in any case, desperate to conceal their links with Graham, fearful that any evidence of Anglophone sympathies might compromise their position in the eyes of the German Occupation authorities. The two of them probably obtained a good deal of information from their work at the BBC. When Graham first joined the Corporation, Russia was not yet at war with Germany, whilst Yugoslavia was still free from axis control. It is not clear what role he was expected to play. The BBC was certainly making plans to launch a new Russian service during the months before Operation Barbarossa,[52] and it seems likely that he was initially employed to contribute to this new initiative, which was

---

49 Ibid, No. 38, November 1943.
50 Graham Papers (FSU), Box 573, 6, Graham to Hay, 27 June 1943.
51 Gawsworth Papers (University of Reading Library), Box 10, 21, Graham to Gawsworth, 1944.
52 Briggs, *War of Words*, p. 396.

later dropped when the Soviet authorities made clear their opposition to such broadcasts. The BBC did, by contrast, play an important role after Operation Barbarossa in promoting a more positive image of Russia in Britain, broadcasting concerts of Russian music and discussions of Russian literature,[53] although Graham was not included in this process. It may be that his knowledge was considered out-of-date, for it was twenty five years since he had last been in the country. Graham always believed that the BBC regarded him as too anti-Soviet to put on the airwaves at a time when official Britain was anxious to strengthen its alliance with the USSR. It was only later in the Cold War, when Soviet Russia was once again the enemy, that he became closely involved with the BBC's newly-established Russian Service.

By 1943, the BBC Annual Review described the European Service as "a vast machine [that] broadcasts in twenty-four languages for over thirty-one hours a day". The Controller of the European Services, the diplomat Ivonne Kirkpatrick, noted that the Service was "not a propaganda service in the usual sense of the term […] it is primarily a news service".[54] Kirkpatrick was much franker in his memoirs, published many years later, when he recalled the huge problems faced by the Corporation in maintaining its reputation for objectivity whilst supporting the war effort.[55] Senior members of the BBC worked closely with the Foreign Office and the Ministry of Information in planning the content of broadcasts, a relationship that was often vexed, requiring numerous meetings to obtain even a modicum of agreement on sensitive issues.[56] Such tensions were not simply about questions of editorial control and judgement. Some of the offices of the Political Warfare Executive, which specialised amongst other things at spreading 'black propaganda' in enemy and enemy-occupied countries, were located just above the offices of the European Service at Bush House in London.[57] The boundary between the PWE and the European Services was extremely porous. Kirkpatrick recalled that, as Controller of the European Services,

---

53 BBC Archives (Caversham), R51/520/1 (various letters and memoranda relating to the reorientation of the treatment of Russia in broadcasts following Operation Barbarossa).
54 Ivonne Kirkpatrick, 'Calling Europe', *BBC Yearbook 1943*, pp. 103-7.
55 Ivonne Kirkpatrick, *The Inner Circle* (London: Macmillan, 1959), pp. 157-59.
56 Sian Nicholas, 'Partners now: Problems in the portrayal by the BBC of the Soviet Union and the United States of America, 1939-45', *Diplomacy and Statecraft*, 3, 2 (1992), pp. 243-71.
57 On the Political Warfare Executive see David Garnett, *The Secret History of PWE: The Political Warfare Executive, 1939-1945* (London: St Ermin's Press, 2002).

he was bound "to receive my political guidance from PWE",[58] although in administrative and financial matters he reported to the Board of Governors, with the result that the distinction between 'black' and 'white' propaganda was not as clear-cut as it sounded. The situation faced by the European Services was made more complicated by the need to carry coded messages in its broadcasts from the Special Operations Executive (SOE) to its agents in the field. Although the PWE maintained its own broadcasting stations in North Africa and Palestine, transmitting black propaganda to occupied Europe, it too on occasion needed access to the powerful equipment owned by the BBC.[59] Whilst the European Service maintained a degree of autonomy, its operations were embedded in a complex set of relationships that provided limits to its independence.

Graham's role in this murky world must necessarily remain speculative, but he seems to have been attached to the Serbo-Croat section of the European Service, dealing with broadcasts to Yugoslavia, although the official BBC records do not formally show his presence there. His job was probably that of language supervisor, responsible for overseeing the specialist linguistic aspects of the broadcast, a role he certainly played in the BBC Russian Service when it was established after the War. Vera worked as a translator. The issue of broadcasting in Serbo-Croat was assigned high priority by the British during the War, given the need to encourage resistance to the occupying forces in the Balkans. The PWE used its transmitters to broadcast to the country in order to undermine the authority of the Pavelić government in Zagreb, and attack any Serbs cooperating with the German occupation authorities.[60] The Serbo-Croat section of the BBC European Service was itself established just a few weeks after the start of the War, when it broadcast to south-east Europe for fifteen minutes a day (by the end of the War it was broadcasting for more than one and a half hours a day). The members of the section were inevitably caught up in the tensions that divided the Yugoslav emigration in London. The Government-in-Exile periodically called for existing staff to be dismissed in favour of replacements authorised by the King and his ministers – a demand that was always rejected by the BBC. Members of the Croat diaspora complained (probably fairly) that the Serbo-Croat section

---

58 Kirkpatrick, *Inner Circle*, p. 158.
59 For a discussion of wartime relations between the BBC and PWE see Briggs, *War of Words*, pp. 418-25.
60 Garnett, *Secret History of PWE*, pp. 204-5.

was strongly biased towards the Serbs. The question of broadcasting to Yugoslavia became still more complex as the British government gradually reduced its support for Mihailović's *Chetniks* in favour of Tito's partisans. Graham's growing anger about the "abandonment" of Mihailović in 1943 was almost certainly based on first-hand observation of what was taking place at the BBC.

The rhythm of Graham's life in war-time London continued largely unchanged throughout 1943 and 1944. He was, however, appalled by the changes that took place in Soho, lamenting how every time he went to the Post Office he had to push his way through "a guard of honour of young prostitutes", touting for trade from the soldiers who flocked to the area.[61] Graham was also dismayed by the amount of boot-leg liquor and illegal drugs that flooded the area.[62] He looked with a jaundiced eye at "the home-based journalists" who vied with one another "in lick-spittling", and lamented how "the smugly-placed civilians" gloated over news from the battlefield, secure in the knowledge that their own lives were not at risk now that mass bombing had ended.[63] Although lone bombers occasionally appeared in the skies above London, sounding like "low-flying angry wasps", it was only with the first V1 flying bomb attacks in June 1944 that Londoners once again had to confront the fear of daily bombardment. Graham began a biography of Franklin Roosevelt, but soon gave up on the idea, in part because "the tax situation forces us to write on half-pay".[64] Although it was hard to leave London, he occasionally managed to get away from the city with Vera, leaving behind the "destructive intrigues" he witnessed at the BBC for the pastoral delights of Dorset or Devon.[65] The two of them were, however, resident at Frith Street when it suffered minor damage from a bomb in the spring of 1944. More problematic for Graham were the periodic war-time interruptions to the service provided by the London Library, which forced him to trawl the capital's second-hand bookshops, searching for copies of the books he needed for his writing. Vera meanwhile fretted about the news that Yugoslavia was soon likely to be liberated by the Soviet army. Nor were the two of them spared more

---

61 Gawsworth Papers (University of Reading Library), Box 10, Graham to Gawsworth, 29 April 1943.
62 Graham Papers (FSU), Box 573, 6, Graham to Hay, 27 June 1943.
63 Gawsworth Papers (University of Reading Library), Box 10, Graham to Gawsworth, 29 April 1943.
64 Ibid, Graham to Gawsworth, 29 April 1943; 17 June 1943.
65 Ibid, Graham to Gawsworth, 10 September 1943.

humdrum concerns: they were forced throughout 1944 to struggle with a plague of rats, whose numbers in Soho rocketed thanks to the decision by local restaurants to keep chickens in their back-yards, in an effort to ensure they had a supply of meat and eggs to satisfy their diners.

Although Graham's work in the Serbo-Croat section during the final years of the War mainly consisted of behind-the-scenes production and supervision, he did make a number of broadcasts himself, usually consisting of short announcements and news reports. By the end of 1944, he was established enough in his job to be asked to broadcast a number of Radio Letters in Serbo-Croat. The international political and military situation had by now changed dramatically. The Red Army liberated Belgrade in October 1944, raising the prospect that the communist partisans would dominate the country's post-war politics, a subject that was inevitably of grave concern to the British government, even though it had long shifted its support to Tito from Mihailović. The BBC's developing strategy in such cases was to provide foreign listeners with material designed to give them insight into the British Way of Life, in the hope it would prove more appealing than the propaganda blandishments of communism. Graham's talks followed this pattern. He told a friend in the United States that his broadcasts, which went out on short wave just after 8.00pm on Wednesdays, were about "new developments here, nothing political".[66]

Graham's first Radio Letter was "devoted to the young", whose voice he believed was largely unheard in public life, since so many of those under thirty were in uniform. Graham told his listeners in the Balkans that there was a desire for change amongst British youth, predicting that when hostilities ended they would no longer be willing to "be found in long queues waiting for old gentlemen to tell them what to do next".[67] In his next broadcast, Graham spoke about the cinema in Britain, describing how even the largest theatre was full from mid-morning, more often than not showing serious films like the recent version of Henry V starring Laurence Olivier. His third broadcast described a recent visit he had made to an aircraft factory somewhere in the English Midlands, where the management made enormous efforts to promote the welfare of its workers, organising dances and employing a workers' bard who had already published a volume of his "proletarian rhymes". Such vignettes were calculated to provide an

---

66 Graham Papers (FSU), Box 576, 6, Graham to Hay, 5 April, 1945.
67 The quotes in this and the following paragraph are taken from Graham Papers (FSU), Box 573, 6 ('Wartime Radio Letters').

image of Britain as a place where war-time unity had helped to erode class divisions and foster a new sense of national unity. It was a message that the BBC was keen to get across to listeners across occupied and 'liberated' Europe.

Other Radio Letters broadcast by Graham in the first few months of 1945 included one in which he reported from a Naval Pageant held at the Albert Hall, taking the opportunity to provide his Yugoslav audience with a brief tour of English seamanship since the reign of Elizabeth I. The following week he described a visit to a production of Chekhov's *Uncle Vanya*, at which "every seat was sold out and there were many people standing both in the pit and the gallery". In line with BBC policy, Graham did not conceal the bleaker side of life in Britain, noting in one of his letters how "wide areas of desolation" across London had been colonised by a profusion of weeds and wild flowers. He criticised much of the house-building programme already under way, complaining that the new flats were too small, and arguing that the sheer scale of what was needed required much greater government intervention. Graham also regaled his listeners with a description of the devastation in his own area of Soho. BBC policy had since 1939 been predicated on the assumption that its broadcasts were most likely to be believed, whether at home or abroad, if they did not deny the obvious consequences of war. Graham's Radio Letters followed this approach, painting a positive but realistic picture of his homeland, designed to appeal to a continent still reeling from the agonies of occupation.

By the spring of 1945, it was clear that the defeat of Nazi Germany was imminent. When news of the surrender was finally announced on 8 May, huge crowds flocked onto the streets of London, thronging Trafalgar Square and stretching up the Mall to Buckingham Palace. Hourly services of Thanksgiving were held at St Paul's, whilst the surrounding streets were, in the words of *The Times*, "gay with flags" that gave "an almost oriental exuberance of decoration". Winston Churchill's car was mobbed as it drove through Whitehall, and the Prime Minister later appeared in front of a huge crowd proclaiming "the victory of the cause of freedom". The festivities extended to the poorer areas of the city, such as Stepney, where East Enders celebrated in the shadow of bombed-out houses and factories. *The Times* noted in duly patronising tones that such scenes reflected the sense of community that had allowed "the heroes and heroines of the Battle of London" to survive "the worst the enemy could do".[68]

Although the sense of popular relief was palpable, more prescient observers had predicted for some time that the end of hostilities in Europe was likely to signal the beginning of a new set of problems. Graham wrote in a letter in early April that whilst the threat from rockets and flying bombs might be over, the outlook was still "a bit queer", adding that "the political and economic situation of a dying continent baffles description".[69] His forebodings were based in part on what was taking place in Yugoslavia. Vera had recently discovered that her brother Chedomir and his family had survived the War, albeit "bombed-out and starving", but she found it impossible to send them any help since "Tito and company do not want any personal intercourse between people in Belgrade and people abroad".[70] Graham tried desperately to find ways of sending them food parcels, but to little avail, noting presciently to a friend in America that "an iron curtain comes down between 'liberated' lands and the West". His use of the words "iron curtain" pre-dated Churchill's adoption of the phrase by almost a year.

The concern at Frith Street about Vera's family would have been much greater if its occupants had known what was really going on in Yugoslavia. The victory of Tito's partisans led to mass murder, as anti-communists and other "socially-undesirable" elements were executed or sent to forced labour camps that few survived.[71] The crowds who thronged the streets of London to celebrate the Nazi surrender in the spring of 1945 had no real sense of the scale of the political and humanitarian crisis that was facing Europe. The Labour Government that was elected in the summer of 1945 moved quickly to implement its promises to nationalise industry and establish a welfare state. It also tried to work with the Soviet government over such questions as four-power control of Berlin. It was nevertheless clear within a few months of the end of the War that victory against the axis powers was not going to usher in a new age of peace and prosperity for Britain. The transition to a peace-time economy proved stubbornly difficult, leading to worsening shortages of many basic commodities, whilst the

---

68 *The Times*, 9 May 1945.
69 Graham Papers (FSU), Box 573, 6, Graham to Hay 5 April 1945.
70 Ibid, Graham to Hay, 5 April 1945.
71 For a brief account see Richard West, *Tito and the Rise and Fall of Yugoslavia* (New York: Carol and Graf, 1994), pp. 201-16; see, too, Marcus Tanner, *Croatia: A Nation Forged in War* (New Haven: Yale University Press, 2001), pp. 168-83. For a personal recollection of this time see Ljubo Sirc, *Between Hitler and Tito* (London: Deutsch, 1989), pp. 74-94.

ideological and geopolitical tensions between East and West threatened to explode into a Third World War. The household at Frith Street was forced once again to draw on the stores of resilience that had served its residents so well over the previous few years.

One immediate problem faced by Stephen and Vera was a result of their unorthodox domestic situation. Since Vera did not have a British passport – she was not of course married to Graham – she was regarded as a stateless person in the eyes of the British authorities. There was even a risk that she might be regarded as a Yugoslav subject (raising the horrifying prospect of repatriation). Vera herself was deeply anxious, particularly after she lost her job at the BBC, not least because she was well aware that many Britons wanted foreigners to be deported back to their own countries. She spent the final months of 1945 redecorating Frith Street, half-dreading a call from the Ministry of Labour assigning her to the construction of "prefabricated houses or something of the kind". She also carried out the household chores, shopping in the streets around Soho, where the rapid withdrawal of American forces had left "our platinum blondes" short of cash.[72]

Graham kept his job at the BBC, for which he was thankful, since "the prospects of picking up money by writing remain precarious". He was particularly appalled by the price of alcohol, a lament that ran through many of his letters, in which he half-jestingly blamed enforced abstinence for "a shockingly adverse effect on the character of a lot of people who have gone sour since victory".[73] Although Stephen and Vera did not go without food in the years following the War – not even in the harsh winter of 1946-47 – the daily shortages continued to irk them. Friends regularly sent parcels from America containing luxury foods and items of clothing that could not be obtained in London. Such largesse could not make up altogether for the day-to-day problems facing residents of an increasingly cheerless post-war Britain. Graham was frustrated by the impossibility of buying a new typewriter (he had not been able to replace the one damaged in the bombing of 1940). Nor, given the financial obstacles, were he and Vera able to escape from the frustrations of daily life by resuming their pre-war travels across Europe. The only significant breaks from London life took the form of short holidays to the Isle of Wight or the Hebrides, and a rather longer trip to Ireland, where Graham was delighted to see a number of his books on sale in Dublin.

---

72 Graham Papers (FSU), Box 573, 6, Vera Mitrinović to Hay, 3 November 1945
73 Ibid, Graham to Hay, 3 November 1945.

Graham's work at the BBC now took place against the backdrop of worsening East-West relations. By the spring of 1946 politicians on both sides of the Atlantic were becoming convinced of the need to prepare for a long-drawn out struggle to contain the threat posed by Soviet communism. Both the Marshall Plan of 1947 and the Brussels Treaty of 1948 were products of this new Cold War mindset. A good deal of attention was also placed on the need to fight a propaganda war, leading the BBC to establish a new Russian Service in the summer of 1946, designed to give listeners in the Soviet Union "a comprehensive picture of life in Britain today".[74] The broadcasts quickly acquired a large following and, amazingly, many letters were sent to Bush House from across the USSR.[75] At some point in 1946, Graham was transferred to the new Russian Service, working once again as a language supervisor, which meant that his role was still largely technical rather than editorial. He wrote little about his duties, not least because of the demands for secrecy, but occasional fragments in his letters suggest that he was sceptical about the value of his work. After three years of working for the new Russian Service, he told a friend that he had become weary of getting up at 2.30 in the morning to go to Bush House "to help tell the Russians their number is up".[76]

Graham's attitude towards international and domestic politics during the second half of the 1940s was marked by a degree of cynicism that had been absent earlier in his life. He complained bitterly about the "terrible ignorance" of the British Foreign Secretary Ernest Bevin and the US Secretary of State James Byrnes, dismissing them as incapable of mending "the broken eggshells" of a world that had come to resemble "a hundred humpty-dumpties". He was particularly negative about the Labour government, describing its leader Clement Atlee as "a prune",[77] who lacked the qualities to lead his country through such difficult times. He was also surprisingly concerned about the growth of a Cold War culture in the West, particularly given his recent war-time criticism of attempts by the British government to develop closer relations with the USSR and

---

74 *BBC Yearbook 1947*, p. 117.
75 For the establishment of the Russian Service, along with further discussion of the BBC in the early Cold War, see Alban Webb, 'Auntie Goes to War Again: The BBC External Services, the Foreign Office and the Early Cold War', Media History, 12, 2 (2006), pp. 117-32.
76 Graham Papers (FSU), Box 573, 6, Graham to Hay, 10 March 1949.
77 Ibid, Graham to Hay, 3 November 1945.

Tito's partisans. In April 1946, he wrote to his friend Marion Hay in Florida telling her that the British government lacked any sense of direction since it slavishly followed the anti-Soviet policies of the US administration.[78] By August he was railing against the "smiling hypocrisy" of British politicians who sought to present themselves to the world as the saviour of liberty and freedom.[79] He added rather elliptically that there were some "fine people in the background" but they were unable to influence politics for the good.

Graham's letters during this period were full of scepticism about the efficacy of capitalism, despite its pivotal place in the ideological struggle between East and West, suggesting that there could not be lasting peace until a new economic order was established both at home and abroad: "I have nothing against capitalism except that I do not think it can function much longer".[80] Eighteen months later, in 1948, he noted that the appeal of communism was rooted in the poverty and deprivation created by the failures of capitalism. Although such sentiments at first seem odd coming from a man who had always been a bitter critic of the Soviet regime, throughout his life Graham had expressed doubts about "capitalism", condemning it as a destructive force that undermined traditional societies, and created financial and spiritual poverty for many in more advanced countries like Britain and the United States. He was by instinct reluctant to accept a Manichean dualism that counter-posed the evil of communism with the unalloyed superiority of western liberalism and market economics. Graham was as a result for a time curiously muted in his criticism of the USSR.

During the second half of the 1940s, Graham spent a good deal of time collecting material for a book on Russia that was designed to counter "the stupid anti-Soviet talk" of "those who just as stupidly put over Soviet propaganda a little while back",[81] noting that he planned to show life in the USSR "in positive terms […] I think it might come as a surprise to some that there is no adverse criticism of the regime".[82] He was unable to interest a publisher in his project, although a version did eventually appear in 1951 under the title *Summing-up on Russia*, in which he was indeed

---

78 Ibid, Graham to Hay, 28 April 1946.
79 Ibid, Graham to Hay, 25 August 1946.
80 Ibid, Graham to Hay, 14 January 1946.
81 Ibid, Graham to Hay, 14 January 1946.
82 Ibid, Graham to Hay, 3 November 1945.

surprisingly restrained in discussing such questions as Stalin's treatment of the Orthodox Church.[83] Whilst he duly condemned the "slave-labour" nature of the Soviet regime, which he accused of betraying the Russian nation, he was ready to acknowledge certain "admirable features" of Soviet life, including the emphasis on education and the attempt to liberate art and literature from the taint of "commercialism". It would be wrong to see Graham's words as a complete reassessment of the evils of Soviet Russia. In 1949, he himself noted that whilst he was not "very keen" on the prospect of another war, it might be worthwhile if it liberated the satellite states from Soviet control, words that would not have sounded out of place on the lips of the most zealous proponent of the need to "roll back" communism.[84] The softening of Graham's views towards the USSR during the early Cold War reflected, above all, his sense that neither side could claim a complete monopoly of virtue. It was a position consistent with all he had ever written. He had for decades been convinced that capitalism and communism were *both* grounded in a materialistic view of life that could never meet the deepest needs of human beings.

The burgeoning Cold War had immediate resonance at Frith Street given the parlous situation of Vera's family. In the months that followed Tito's rise to power, the new government in Yugoslavia dismembered any potential source of opposition with great ruthlessness, killing many of its opponents, including the execution by firing squad of Mihailović in July 1946. Vera tried desperately to keep in contact with her family, sending them parcels of clothes and food through an intermediary, at least until the communist authorities took objection to the visitor and barred them from entry to the country. Although she continued to send parcels through the regular post, many were returned, whilst others failed to reach their destination. Nor was the plight of the Yugoslav *diaspora* in London much better. At the end of 1947, when it had become clear that those who opposed Tito could never return home, Graham told Marion Hay in Florida that the émigrés from the Balkans had become "a melancholy lot". The women worked in shops whilst their husbands "walk about with empty brief cases pretending to be on important state business". The only thing that kept them hopeful was a pathetic belief that the United States would soon declare war on Russia and

---

83 Stephen Graham, *Summing-up on Russia* (London: Ernest Benn, 1951).
84 Graham Papers (FSU), Box 573, 6, Hay to Graham, 10 March 1949.

promote a "counter-revolution in the Balkan countries [that would] put a series of Slav De Gaulles in power".[85]

The "melancholy" of the situation facing Yugoslav émigrés in Britain was not as desperate as the plight of Yugoslavs who remained on the continent. The British government was surprisingly slow to grasp the nature of the regime that Tito began to establish soon after his rise to power. Many officials in London continued to fret more about the possible escape of Nazi sympathisers from Yugoslavia than about the victims of the new communist government. The decisions that flowed from this suspicion were sometimes tragic in their consequences. When British soldiers handed over a large number of Yugoslav soldiers and civilians to the partisans in May 1945, they effectively, if unintentionally, sent thousands of innocent people to their deaths. In the months and years that followed, countless Yugoslavs who escaped their country ended up in displaced persons' camps in Italy and Germany, where allied forces worked hard to identify anyone who might previously have played a role in assisting the axis powers. The rights and wrongs of this tangled story still defy easy analysis decades later, and it is perhaps too easy to forget how sheer confusion and weariness warped the judgement of politicians and soldiers during the chaotic years after 1945. Stephen and Vera did not themselves have any detailed knowledge of the intricacies of British policy towards Tito's government. They were, however, only too well-aware of the plight of those luckless enough to end up in the camps set up to house displaced persons.

Many of the Yugoslav displaced persons were still languishing in camps in Germany and Italy more than two years after the War had ended. At the end of 1947, Vera continued to receive countless "pitiful letters" pleading for help to ameliorate the plight of "those with wrecked bodies [...] the old and infirm, unemployable women and children". Graham was appalled at the problems faced by "these frozen and starved people", and was scathing in his attacks on the allied powers responsible for supervising them, believing that the British authorities were waiting for them to "die off" so that "the problem [can] be said to have been solved".[86] By the start of 1948, the displaced persons in German camps had become the "chief interest" for Stephen and Vera, and they routinely dispatched sacks of clothes to those who were virtually destitute. Graham was incensed by the British authorities' treatment of Yugoslav refugees. One of his old friends,

---

85 Ibid, Graham to Hay, 9 December 1947.
86 Ibid, Graham to Hay, 9 December 1947.

a former editor of a leading pre-war paper, was detained in conditions of "semi-starvation", even though he had always been "very anti-Hitler" and behaved "almost as if he were a British agent [...] I suppose he has been denounced as a German agent".[87] Graham wrote to the Foreign Office complaining about the case but received only the blandest of responses. The British authorities were in 1948 still determined to identify and punish those who might have played some part in helping the occupying forces in Yugoslavia during the War, even if the country was now on the other side of the Iron Curtain, leading Graham to rail impotently against "cold-blooded" British officials who refused to be moved by the refugees' plight. He was reluctant to acknowledge, even in his own mind, that some who had fled the Tito regime were responsible for what today would be called war crimes. Not all the victims of communism had themselves led blameless lives. The tragic complexities of the Balkans created new ironies and contradictions, as the hatred and enmities of the Second World War gave place to a fresh set of ideological and political conflicts.

By the start of the 1950s, Graham was resigned to the existence of what he scathingly called "Titoland". When Vera's young niece Gordana travelled from Yugoslavia to stay with her aunt at Frith Street, he was appalled by the extent to which she had already become fluent in the Marxist-Leninist verbiage served up in the country's schoolrooms. Graham was also perturbed by her antipathy towards the vigorously anti-communist Serbian émigré population in London. He nevertheless remained sceptical of the Cold War rhetoric that dominated discussion of international politics on both sides of the Atlantic. He told Marion Hay in Florida that there was something futile about broadcasting to eastern Europe – "telling the Russians what scoundrels they are" – and he fretted at the prospect of a McCarthy style witch hunt being imported into Britain.[88] He also questioned the wisdom of the huge military build-up that began in 1949 with the creation of NATO. When *Summing-up on Russia* was finally published in 1951, it was judged insufficiently anti-Soviet to find a US publisher, at a time when the 'Red Scare' was dominating the news, although the British Foreign Office ordered 250 copies for distribution at home and abroad.[89] Graham's jaundiced view of British and American politicians – even Churchill was judged to be "a moral coward" by the early 1950s – meant that he still

---

87 Ibid, Graham to Hay, 28 January 1948.
88 Graham Papers (FSU), Box 573, 7, Graham to Hay, 15 May 1950.
89 Ibid, Graham to Hay, 6 December 1951.

refused to become a cold warrior committed to the view that the West was in every respect superior to its adversary behind the iron curtain.[90]

Graham never lost his interest in politics, whether domestic or international, but he was by the early 1950s more interested in other topics. He had from his youth been a voracious reader of poetry, writing his fair share of doggerel before he first went to live in Russia, although he was honest enough to acknowledge that he had few talents as a writer of verse. In the early 1950s he became actively involved in the Poetry Society, which at this stage still had its headquarters at Portman Square in London, and in 1952 he gave a lecture there on the topic of Modern Poetry. Graham's talk was not a panegyric to recent literary developments. He attacked the tendency of "modern" poets "to change gold into rags and tatters", and condemned those who claimed that "there is more poetry in honest dirt than the collected works of Tennyson", before going on to criticise all those who "reject the beautiful of a past age". He concluded with a rousing declaration that "The tradition of poetry is with sounds and rhythms rather than with a process of images. If our English poetry is to be one with Keats and Shelley, Milton and Shakespeare, the continuity has to be preserved".[91]

Graham did not content himself with rousing perorations against anything that smacked of the modern. In the same year, 1952, he published an anthology, *100 Best Poems in the English Language,* which consisted in large part of the pieces that he liked to recite aloud whilst walking the roads of Essex when still a teenager. His choices were both traditional and predictable. Shakespeare and Donne were well-represented. So too were Wordsworth and Coleridge. Shelley's *To Night* and Browning's *Rabbi Ben Ezra* were also included. The most modern poem amongst Graham's selection was Yeats's *The Lake Isle of Innisfree*. 'Moderns' such as T.S. Eliot and W.H. Auden were conspicuous by their absence.[92] Nor does contemporary poetry seem to have featured much in the poetry-reading evenings that still took place from time-to-time at Frith Street. There had always been something accidental about Graham's engagement with the characteristic motifs of modernism in the 1910s and 1920s. His concern with the themes of anomie and dislocation had been rooted above all in a nostalgic sense that they were products of the modern era that could best be countered by

---

90 Ibid, Graham to Hay, 18 March 1952.
91 Graham Papers (FSU), Box 574, 16a (Jottings for a speech to Poetry Society).
92 Stephen Graham (ed.), *100 Best Poems in the English Language* (London: Ernest Benn, 1952).

a re-emphasis on spirituality and tradition. Although a close reading of Eliot might have shown Graham that many of his concerns were actually shared by the author of *The Wasteland* and the *Four Quartets*, he was by the 1950s convinced that the importance of real poetry rested on the beauty of its language rather than the depth of its thematic concerns.

Graham was by the early 1950s increasingly conscious of the passing years, and he peppered his correspondence with complaints about illness. Nor was the change limited to his physical health. Although he remained quite vigorous until the late 1960s, by the time Queen Elizabeth came to the throne in 1952 Graham was increasingly retreating to a private world of family and friends. He frequently visited the flat of Maysie and Max Murray when they were in London – the couple were inveterate globe-trotters – and played host to Delano and Kit Ames on their visits to Britain from their home in Spain. Frith Street also played host for a time to the "crazy poet" John Gawsworth, who had spent much of the War in Africa and India,[93] and repaid Graham's hospitality by appointing his host to a dukedom in the fantasy world of Redonda. The Indian publisher Susil Gupta – who had met Gawsworth in Calcutta – also spent some months at 60 Frith Street (the address was at one point listed as the home of Gupta's London office). A longer-term tenant was the actor and writer Maurice Braddell, who understudied Noel Coward in the original production of *Private Lives*, and later wrote the children's book *Little Gorky of the Black Swans*. Among other frequent visitors to Frith Street was the writer Hugh Cleveley who was, like Ames, the author of numerous works of detective fiction, including some of the Sexton Blake series of novels. Graham's old friend Bernard Newman was also a regular guest. Less welcome was Vera's brother Dimitrije ("a powerful personality used to bending everyone to his will"). Graham was by the start of the 1950s convinced that members of the New Europe group headed by Dimitrije were all "mad as hatters", sending delegates around the globe to canvass for a new world order, but without any clear sense of how to achieve their leader's passion for "the union of humanity".[94] Such acerbic comments said more about the strained personal relationship between the two men than it did about the activities of the New Europe group itself.

---

93 For an insight into Gawsworth's time on active service see G.S. Fraser, *A Stranger and Afraid* (Manchester: Carcanet New Press, 1983), p. 163 ff.
94 Graham Papers (FSU), Box 573, 7, Graham to Hay, 2 October 1950.

The rigours of exchange control meant that Graham's penchant for globetrotting remained doomed to frustration during the early 1950s, although he was frequently overcome by the desire to escape from the confines of London, torn as ever between his love for urban street-scenes and the call of the wild (or at least the gently pastoral). He and Vera tried to spend several days each month on the south coast, walking the cliffs of Sussex, and often headed off to stay on the Isle of Wight. A summer holiday in the Hebrides in 1949 was not a success – the rain and the mosquitoes dampened the mood – with the result that the Grahams subsequently preferred the more welcoming climate of the Channel Islands and the Isles of Scilly. Graham found the Scilly Isles idyllic, enthusing about the traditional rhythms of life in a place where "the post box has a public telephone so that the postman can watch for the coming of the mail launch and put his old horse to the shafts to bring up the food packets and letters from the landing stage".[95] He also retained his enthusiasm for fishing, developed so many years before in Yugoslavia, and spent days on the rocks casting out his line to catch plaice and mackerel. The annual trip to the Scillies became one of the highpoints of Graham's year, and descriptions of his time on the island of St Martin's filled his correspondence. The vast spaces of Russia that dominated his youthful imagination had now given way to a hankering for the more confined life of a small island situated just thirty miles off Land's End.

The narrowing of Graham's geographical horizons was not only a matter of financial necessity. When Stalin died in 1953, Graham was already sixty nine years old. His work for the Russian Section of the BBC continued for many years, although his hours (and income) were cut sharply in 1954, as his seventieth birthday approached. He continued to write at an almost frenetic pace, but publishers were less and less inclined to value the work of a man whose interests seemed remote from the demands of a modern readership. His comments on the films and plays he saw in the West End also became increasingly caustic as he struggled to come to terms with contemporary tastes. Graham had in the 1930s been young in mind and body. By the early 1950s he was becoming old both in years and outlook. The echoes of his former self nevertheless still continued to flicker from time-to-time. Although his unappealingly trite 1949 book *Thinking of Living* consisted mostly of a series of platitudes about the need to "make of your

---

95 Ibid, Graham to Hay, 2 September 1951.

life what you will", he still took care to insist that "the miraculous force is at the inmost centre of being and drives outwards from there".[96] Even as he approached old age, Graham remained convinced that the world could not be reduced to the sum of its visible parts. Whilst the last twenty years of his life were dominated by financial concerns and worries about his health, he continued to search for the "miraculous force" that had inspired his early trips to Russia so many years before.

---

96 Stephen Graham, *Thinking of Living* (London: Ernest Benn, 1949), pp. 23, 77.

9. The Pilgrim Reborn?

The last twenty years of Graham's life were dogged by ill-health and, perhaps even more, by concerns about ill-health, for it is hard to avoid the impression that both he and Vera became border-line hypochondriacs in their advancing years. Long descriptions of their aches and pains filled Graham's voluminous correspondence with his old friend Marion Hay, a Professor of Education at Florida State University, who in her spare time ran a travel agency that specialised in providing guided tours of Europe for wealthy Floridians. Graham and Hay first became acquainted in the 1930s, when Hay spent time organising courses for the *Centro de Estudios Históricos* in Madrid, before later making a dramatic flight from Spain following the outbreak of the civil war. During the difficult days of rationing in the 1940s, it was Hay who sent parcels of food and other essential supplies to her old friend, generosity which Graham later repaid by organising hotel accommodation and theatre tickets for her tour groups when they visited London. Hay herself stayed at Frith Street at least once a year during the 1950s and 1960s, and, when back in the USA, she helped to manage Graham's financial affairs, liaising with his American publishers to ensure that his royalty cheques were forwarded to Soho.

Graham was enthralled by the accounts that Hay regularly sent of her long trips through remote areas of the globe, ranging from Latin America to Russia, but the constraints of health and money meant that his own life was increasingly confined to the streets and buildings of central London. His notebooks show that in the silence of his study his mind often turned back to his sojourns in Russia and America so many years before. He also continued to ruminate on the meaning of the world around him, privately musing over the ideas that had intrigued him when he was still a young man, once again becoming enthralled by an "idealism" that retained a luminosity even as it seemed increasingly elusive in the face of advancing years and uncertain

http://dx.doi.org/10.11647/OBP.0040.09

finances. Graham's situation was not easy in the twenty years before his death. He had always worked hard to exploit the commercial potential of his work, but his lifestyle had never been particularly frugal, and his finances were in a parlous state by the time he entered his eighth decade. After Graham's hours at the BBC were reduced in 1954, he devoted more time to his writing, in the hope of earning extra money, but the work he produced was too old-fashioned for a modern audience. His letters throughout the final two decades of his life were filled with mournful reflections about the cost of living, descending on occasion to gloomy descriptions of how he and Vera were forced to sit in the cold at Frith Street, surviving on a diet of cold macaroni cheese and tea. The picture was exaggerated. Although money was tight, Stephen and Vera continued to go on regular holidays, whilst Graham himself remained a fixture at many of the more convivial London literary meetings.

Graham's novels of the 1930s had not made him wealthy, but they did produce a solid income in advances and royalties, and he only abandoned fiction after the legal furore that followed the publication of *African Tragedy* in 1938. It was seventeen more years before his next (and final) novel appeared in 1955. *Pay as You Run* was a sequel to his earlier *Everybody Pays*, perhaps his most inoffensively tedious book, which had charted the unlikely romance between the tax inspector Henry Pillguard and the nightclub dancer Clara Lehman. In *Pay as you Run*, Pillguard is charged by his office with investigating the financial affairs of one Monty Sandburn, a raffish con-man, who made his money through the twin activities of selling dubious antiques and befriending lonely widows (Graham was, it seems, still fascinated by the way in which individuals could succeed in presenting a false *persona* to the world). The book is most politely described as forgettable – it attracted few reviews – but its obsession with taxes and taxmen echoed its creator's perennial resentment at having to hand over a large part of his earnings to the government. Graham started the novel whilst on a holiday in Guernsey, and continued work on it throughout the winter of 1954-55, a time when he was consuming twelve oranges and several pints of milk every day (a diet which, for some unknown reason, he hoped would ease his chronic digestive problems).[1] When the book finally appeared in the autumn of 1955, he held a cocktail party at Frith Street for more than fifty guests, ranging from publishers and booksellers to a restorer of old paintings. A number of tax inspectors were also present (Graham had met them when carrying out research for the book). One of the inspectors enjoyed the hospitality rather

---

1   Graham Papers (FSU), Box 573, 7, Graham to Marion Hay, 14 May 1954.

too eagerly, and had to be walked swaying to the local bus stop, but other guests remained into the small hours, consuming the left-over food in the kitchen.² The eclectic crowd was very different from the one that would have assembled at a launch-party for a book by one of Graham's more celebrated contemporaries. He was, however, always something of an outsider in the London literary world, and had no hesitation in pronouncing the Frith Street party a great success, even though it did little to push sales of the book.

Although 1954 and 1955 were dominated by Graham's work on *Pay as you Run* and his duties at the BBC, he and Vera still found time for holidays in Cornwall and the Channel Islands. They also made numerous trips to Epping Forest, where they relished the peace of the woodland that Graham had known when he was a boy living in nearby Chigwell. They planned a trip to Italy to visit one of Vera's sisters, but were forced to cancel because of poor health, although various members of the Mitrinović clan descended on London from time to time to see them (Vera and Stephen eventually managed their first trip together to Yugoslavia in 1960, but few records of their impressions remain). Graham continued to view the British political scene with a morose eye, writing to Marion Hay in 1955 that he and Vera expected the Tories to win the forthcoming election, "but we are not in love with them. But don't think much of Atlee and Company either".³ Nor was life easy on the domestic front. Although Graham and Vera were fiercely committed to staying at Frith Street, repainting the walls and moving around furniture to keep the house aired and fresh, the winters were often grim. The temperature in the living room was on occasion just above freezing, and the lavatory was only kept working by the use of an oil heater. The two of them nevertheless continued to accept such hardship as the price of living in one of London's most distinctive enclaves. Soho in the 1950s was still a cosmopolitan quarter, a fitting home for an aging writer living with a foreigner to whom he was not married. Graham continued to find Soho a place where he could relish life as "one of London's living bricks".⁴

The death of Rose Graham early in 1956, in Somerset, made it possible for Stephen and Vera to marry. It is not clear why Stephen and Rose never divorced, despite their long separation, but the bitterness of Graham's occasional comments suggests that his wife refused to bring their marriage to a formal close. Within a few months of his wife's death, Graham wrote to Marion Hay in Florida, telling her that "Vera and I are now married in the

---
2   Ibid, Graham to Hay, 18 September 1955.
3   Ibid, Graham to Hay, 25 May 1955.
4   The phrase is taken from Graham's earlier book, *Twice Round the London* (London: Ernest Benn, 1933), p. 224.

letter as well as the spirit. Decided to get married as quietly as possible and have a celebration much later when I am completely restored to health. Still cannot face a round of any big excitement".[5] There were only two guests at the wedding, which took place at Caxton Hall registry office in Westminster. Although Graham blamed his health for the quiet ceremony, he was, like his father so many years before, conventional enough to have been embarrassed about his irregular marital status, and was both gratified and perturbed when "some of the newspapers got hold of the event and gave us a write-up". Graham was happy to meet a reporter from the *Daily Mail*, telling him that he and Vera planned to have a short honeymoon at Hove, but the story he told the journalist about how and when they had met was decidedly at odds with the truth.[6] He was even more disingenuous in speaking to the *Evening News*, although he warmly praised Vera as "a wonderful companion", and told how she had helped him to learn Serbo-Croat many years earlier.[7] Graham was torn between a desire to celebrate his wedding and unease at drawing attention to the unorthodox nature of his living arrangements over the previous twenty five years.

Figure 9: Photograph of Stephen and Vera Graham on the 13 August 1957 (photographer unknown). Courtesy Private Collection.

---

5 Graham Papers (FSU), Box 573, 7, Graham to Hay, 27 October 1956.
6 *Daily Mail*, 20 October 1956.
7 *Evening News*, 20 October 1956.

Within a few months of his marriage, Graham was suddenly faced with the alarming prospect of losing his lease on Frith Street, a result of the controversial 1957 Rent Act, introduced to help increase the supply of rented property by removing restrictions on the amount landlords could charge their tenants. He had to spend a good deal of effort during the following years bargaining with the freeholder, and it looked for a time as though he and Vera might have to move out, although they eventually agreed a new lease in 1961. A good deal of restoration and repair was carried out to the building in the late 1950s, creating extensive disruption for its residents, but Graham nevertheless continued to write. He found it increasingly difficult to find a publisher for his work, though, an ironic state of affairs given that he continued to lecture on the theme of 'How to Get a Book Published'. Graham produced at least four long manuscripts in the ten years after 1958 which never appeared in print. The first of these was a biography of the humourist and poet Thomas Hood (1799-1845), a rather curious project, given Hood's comparative obscurity and the existence of a competent biography published many years earlier.[8] Graham nevertheless spent many hours in the British Library working on the manuscript (which was completed at the end of 1958). The book was written in Graham's usual style, and contained scenes that must have been speculative in character, including a detailed account of how visitors to the bookshop run by Hood's father "came in from the busy street, took their time, not rushing in to buy a book, but staying often half an hour or more browsing about".[9] The manuscript failed to catch the complex shades of light and dark in Hood's personality, which allowed him to be both a comic writer and a serious poet. Graham's biography ended with the kind of archaic flourish that was unlikely to appeal to a contemporary audience: "He quit the world with everlasting farewells and with oft-repeated hopes of reunion in heaven. Then he faded away. Late on the night of May Day 1845 he entered a coma. He died at noon on the 3rd of May". Graham was proud of the manuscript of *The Life and Times of Tom Hood*, so much so that he mentioned it in the will he made in 1957, but publishers were unwilling to accept a manuscript on a topic that was "not on a sufficiently large scale to attract a wide reading audience".[10]

Although there was no interest in Graham's biography of Hood, some of his earlier work continued to attract attention. In 1959 Ernest Benn reissued the collection of *Great Russian Short Stories* that Graham had edited

---

8   Walter Jerrold, *Thomas Hood: his Life and Times* (London: Alston Rivers, 1907).
9   Graham Papers (FSU), Box 583 (Typed manuscript of *The Life and Times of Tom Hood*).
10 Ibid, S. Lawrence (Atlantic Monthly Press) to Graham, 30 November 1961.

thirty years before, complete with a new Preface and an additional piece by the Soviet satirist Mikhail Zoschenko. Of greater excitement was the decision by the BBC to produce a radio drama based on Graham's book about the murder of King Alexander of Yugoslavia at Marseilles. The BBC was running a series on 'The Assassins', and in July 1960 Graham was approached by the Corporation seeking permission "for a dramatized version of your book".[11] A few days later, though, the BBC got back in touch saying they had found another source, an unpublished thesis by one George Csrenyi, with the result that the programme would "not really [be] a dramatisation of your book, but will be based on both sources". Graham was not pleased by the revelation – pointing out that he had himself given help and advice to Cserenyi – adding for good measure that "one has to bear in mind that the Hungarians were involved in the terrorist activities of the *Ustasha*" (Cserenyi is a Hungarian name and Graham seems to have been hinting that its author was not unbiased in his account). He nevertheless gave his permission on the condition that his own book was cited as "the chief source". The dramatisation was subsequently broadcast on the Home Service and the World Service in the final months of 1960. 'Murder at Marseilles' lasted for thirty minutes, and was narrated by a storyteller who introduced the various characters as they recounted their lives in the days leading up to the assassination of Alexander. Ante Pavelić was portrayed in the drama – as Graham had described him in his book – as a fanatical terrorist determined to hunt down the King and destroy the state of Yugoslavia ("only by the destruction of Yugoslavia can a free Croatia be born"). The actors' voices combined to capture the drama of the assassination itself, describing the scenes of chaos following the murder of Alexander in his open-topped car, as the police and soldiers responsible for guarding them rushed to capture their killer. Graham was not involved in the production, even though he was still doing some work for the BBC at the age of seventy six, but he was delighted to receive two cheques for twenty guineas at a time when his finances were at a low ebb.

Graham was less successful at finding a publisher for a collection of the short stories he had written over the previous forty years (many of which had already appeared in various magazines and anthologies). Some, like '5,000 Enemy Planes over London' and 'Kitchener at Archangel', reflected

---

11 BBC Archives (Caversham), Correspondence related to, and transcript of, *Murder at Marseilles* (transmitted 17 August 1960).

Graham's life-long interest in the macabre and ghostly.[12] Others, including 'Ilya Vilka' and 'Aha', were based on his experiences long before in Russia. Graham also continued to write new works of fiction, including an unlikely fantasy called 'Bakunin at the Dresden Zoo', a rather shapeless piece of work loosely based on the celebrated Russian anarchist's time in Germany. He even seems to have made a fitful effort to publish some of the poems he had written throughout his life. Graham did however develop his career as a literary critic in the late 1950s and early 1960s, mainly in *Poetry Review*, where his pieces revealed a sensitivity that had sometimes been missing in his earlier writing. Some of his reviews examined the works of poets like Edith Sitwell, whose *Collected Poems* he warmly praised, although he criticised Sitwell's preface for spending too long talking about technique in a way that was "professorial rather than practical [...] The lover of poetry can enjoy effects without grasping how they are achieved, just as beautiful sculpture can hush the soul without a knowledge of anatomy". Graham also lauded Arthur Waley's translations of Chinese poems for helping readers to understand that China had its own rich cultural history, and was not simply the menacing Yellow Peril of western imagination. Most of Graham's reviews were of biographies and critical works, including Renato Poggioli's *The Poets of Russia*, which he praised for its sensitive understanding of the way in which Russia's national identity had shaped the development of a unique poetic tradition. In other pieces he mounted an enthusiastic defence of poets as varied as Rudyard Kipling and Edward Thomas (a poet he admired unreservedly for his sensitivity to nature and landscape). Most of Graham's pieces in *Poetry Review* were no longer than five hundred words or so, forcing him to abandon his usual prolix style, and they revealed his acute understanding of both English and world literature.[13]

By the early 1960s, as he approached his eightieth birthday, Graham was in an increasingly reflective mood as he looked back over his long life and realised how few of the people he knew in his younger years were still alive. It was partly for this reason that he sought out the company of Vernon Hill, the illustrator who had provided the drawings for *Tramping with a Poet in the Rockies* many years before, staying with him on a number

---

12 For some correspondence on possible publication, see Gawsworth Papers (University of Reading Library), Box 9, Graham to Gawsworth, 26 May 1961. For copies of these stories see Graham Papers (FSU), Box 580.
13 For copies of these reviews see Graham Papers (FSU), Box 574, 16a.

of occasions at Hill's cottage in Sussex.[14] Graham's mind also turned to writing his autobiography, a decision prompted in part by the hope that it might prove a commercial success, but still more by the need to make sense of his life on the threshold of his ninth decade. When *Part of the Wonderful Scene* finally appeared, in 1964, he pondered on the way in which his life, like all lives, displayed "no obvious pattern", but was instead a jumble of "experiences and activities".[15] Graham worked with great diligence on the text of *Wonderful Scene* throughout 1962-63, producing a number of drafts, as he struggled to shape the telling of his "experiences and activities" in a way that made sense both to himself and his readers. In doing so he told a story that highlighted particular aspects of his life and left others shrouded in a cloud of obscurity. The contents of Graham's autobiography were determined in part by the dictates of the publishers – Collins – who believed that readers would be most interested in Graham's time in Russia before the First World War. More than half the book therefore deals with his life between 1907 and 1917. Graham resented his publisher's request, believing that his readers would be equally interested in his travels in America, and in the years after *Wonderful Scene* appeared he worked fitfully on a second edition designed to give more details about his travels in the 1920s. The text of the book was not, however, only determined by commercial requirements. It was also moulded by the mature Graham's desire to portray his life in a way that reflected his contemporary sensitivities as much as the attitudes and adventures of his younger self.

It was noted in an earlier chapter that *Part of the Wonderful Scene* carefully concealed as much as it revealed. Graham tellingly started work on the book less as a formal autobiography, and more as a description of the people he had met throughout his long life, which he initially planned to call *Pictures of My Friends*. He told one of his correspondents, the biographer Margaret Carpenter, that he loathed "debunking" and preferred to adopt a creed "that the best in a person is that person".[16] A few years later, after *Part of the Wonderful Scene* appeared in print, he wrote in another letter to Carpenter

---

14 Graham Papers (FSU), Box 578, 40 (Journal for 1959, entry dated 17 May 1959). Graham's Journals in his later years in fact really take the form of notes scribbled in diaries. The actual dates of entries are themselves unreliable, since Graham recorded his thoughts in a chaotic and unsystematic manner, and are included here simply to identify the source of quotations.
15 Stephen Graham, *Part of the Wonderful Scene* (London: Collins, 1964), p. 307.
16 Margaret Haley Carpenter Papers (University of Virginia), Accession No. 10656, Box 10, 18, Graham to Carpenter, 29 June 1962.

that "a man's books have to stand for him, not the silly things he may have said 'off the record' or physical facts known only to his doctor". He went on to note that "I am more vain of my books than I am of my actual adventures in life, because writing is art & I would rather have written Gray's elegy than taken Quebec".[17] It was a philosophy that shaped the account he told of his own life.

Graham said nothing in *Part of the Wonderful Scene* about the unorthodox nature of his early family life, only discussing his father perfunctorily, and was silent about the way in which Anderson Graham abandoned his family when the children were still young. Nor did Graham say anything about his emotional crisis of the mid-1920s, which was closely linked to the break-down of his relationship with Rose, whilst his cursory discussion of his time in Yugoslavia in the 1930s avoided discussing the nature of his relationship with Vera. Nor was it only the personal details of his life that Graham sought to refashion or obscure. Whilst he wrote a good deal in *Wonderful Scene* about his life-long "idealism" and suspicion of materialism, he was much less forthcoming about his early interest in Theosophy. He made no mention of the youthful metaphysical vision he had outlined in Ygdrasil (his youthful unpublished meditation on Nordic myth which had reflected his essentially dualistic vision of the world). The most obvious explanation for Graham's desire to distance himself from the esoteric interests of his earlier years was simply that he had long abandoned them. It is certainly true, as the previous chapters have shown, that the middle aged Graham developed a more prosaic set of intellectual and literary interests than the ones that had preoccupied his youthful self. In his old age, though, Graham's notebooks and diaries show that he was, once again, turning his mind to the questions that had so preoccupied him when he was a young man. He was simply reluctant to make too much in public of his esoteric view of life which he feared could earn him a reputation as a "crank".[18]

Graham was sharply critical in *Wonderful Scene* of gurus like P.D. Uspensky and G.I. Gurdjieff, who had been so popular in Britain in the 1920s, but during the years following the book's publication his mind often returned to that period. He seemed tantalised by the memory of an age

---

17 Ibid, Graham to Carpenter, 1 May 1966.
18 For Graham's awareness of this danger, told through the prism of his reflections on the life of his friend Vachel Lindsay, see Margaret Haley Carpenter Papers (University of Virginia), Box 10, 18, Graham to Carpenter, 1 February 1962.

when there was still a widespread hunger to reject a "materialism that rots the soul".[19] Despite Graham's professed dislike of anything that smacked of black magic, he met the writer John Symmonds, who had written a book about the controversial occultist Aleister Crowley. He also read numerous works on Christian theology and history, ranging from the books of Maude Royden through to David Strauss's nineteenth-century classic *Life of Jesus*, which had caused a huge storm when it was published in Germany by denying the divinity of Christ. Schopenhauer and Schweitzer also figured in his reading. Graham remained convinced that "The world is not what it seems [...] it is full of magic and the most extraordinary things", and recalled how he had once asked in one of his books "What is our life if it is not miraculous?", a sentiment that he continued to espouse deep into old age.[20] Graham remained sceptical of the main churches, although he still pondered from time to time the possibility of going over to Rome. He was particularly critical of the modern Anglican obsession with social problems. Graham was also still instinctively wary of formal theology, since "it works no miracles and it cannot inspire", instead praising "holy men" such as St Francis of Assisi, who had devoted his life to preaching the gospel of love to the ordinary peasants of northern Italy.[21]

Some of the other maxims that filled Graham's notebooks point still more strongly towards his reinvigorated sense that Christianity was simply one of "many mansions" in the spiritual domain, of value above all for capturing certain truths about the nature of the universe, rather than for articulating particular dogmas and principles. Sometimes these speculations bordered on an esoteric obscurantism that makes them hard to unravel, including such claims as "God is not a name of the Deity: it is a word not a name, but it becomes the equivalent of a name",[22] a phrase that seems to hint at its author's sense that certain phenomena could not easily be captured in words. Vera also seemed to share such views – despite being a regular worshipper at the Serbian Orthodox Church in London – speculating that "Man arrived on the planet from God knows where. Hence the myth of Lucifer and his rebel angels. Man is descended from these rebel angels".[23] Graham's notebooks contained speculations about

---

19 Graham Papers (FSU), Box 578, 21 (Journal for 1967, entry dated 4 January).
20 Graham Papers (FSU), Box 577, 10 (Journal for 1963, entry dated 24 May).
21 Ibid (Journal for 1963, entry dated 4 September). See, too, Graham Papers (FSU), Box 577, 13E (Journal for 1964, entry dated 20 June).
22 Graham Papers (FSU), Box 577, 13A (Journal for 1965, entry dated 13 January).
23 Ibid (Journal for 1965, entry dated 15 January).

the nature of a world in which "Times goes on forever because you cannot imagine a day which has no tomorrow. The whole universe may dissolve but there must be a day after [...] What we call the universe is something complete in itself [...] outside the universe – what?"[24] Such speculations were peppered with the kind of reflections about self-improvement that Graham had jotted down for more than sixty years, although these were by now tinged with a realism that had once eluded him: "In a day a man does many wrong things. It is utopian to try to give up all wrong things, but a man could very well reduce the number of wrong things he does in a day".[25] Although there were times when Graham seemed to slip into a kind of depression in the period following publication of *Wonderful Scene*, he was aware of the dangers of living in the past, writing that "I must push on to the next turning in the road. It is as if it was long ago when I first tramped into the Caucasus, from the sunbathed [...] foothills towards the heights in the snow".[26] The wistful remembrance of the strength and emotional exuberance of his youth was matched by a melancholy realism that he was facing a time of inevitable decline and death.

When not working in his wood-panelled study on the first floor of 60 Frith Street, Graham spent a good deal of time fretting about money. Whilst he was always delighted to hear from readers who had come across his books for the first time, he never lost his resentment at how little he had earned from his writing. He nevertheless found the money for a trip to Yugoslavia with Vera in 1966, when the two of them visited Belgrade, before heading on to the town of Vela Luka, on the Dalmatian island of Korcula, where Vera's niece and her husband owned a summer house.[27] Graham's financial situation became a little easier following his return from Vela Luka, when he received some extra money from the BBC, and he returned to the Adriatic for each of the following two summers. Graham always found the journey to Yugoslavia tiring, especially given the bureaucratic headaches involved in buying plane and train tickets. He only survived the heat of Vela Luka by buying dark sunglasses and sitting in the shade throughout the heat of the day. One visitor to the house recalled that Graham struck the assembled company of artists and scholars as "quite old and sombre", seldom joining in the lively conversations about art and politics, although

---

24 Ibid (Journal for 1965, entries dated 14 April, 14 June).
25 Graham Papers (FSU), Box 578, 21 (Journal for 1966, entry dated 4 January).
26 Graham Papers (FSU), Box 577, 13A (Journal for 1965, entry dated 17 March).
27 Graham Papers (FSU), Box 573, 8, Graham to Hay, 20 June 1966.

Graham's own notes show that he was impressed by the growing freedom with which members of the country's intelligentsia were able to discuss controversial topics. Whilst he never reconciled himself to the reality of communist Yugoslavia, Graham was convinced that life in the country had improved since he and Vera first went there in 1960, at least as measured by the growing number of cars and the large projects to build new houses for the population. He was also struck by the extent to which "friendly equality and good manners permeate social behaviour".[28] Graham loathed Belgrade – a city he had never liked since first going there in 1920 – but he was still captivated by the beauty of the Dalmatian coast which he so lovingly described forty years earlier in his novel *Midsummer Music*.

Within a few weeks of returning from his visit to Dalmatia in the summer of 1967, Graham began preparing for his first trip outside Europe since he and Vera had gone to South Africa some thirty years before. For many years he had wanted to return to the United States – his last visit had been in 1930 – but the difficult financial circumstances of the post-war years meant that such a trip had always been out of the question. The receipt of his severance payment from the BBC finally gave Graham the means to return to the country he had not seen for thirty seven years. The detailed preparations he made for the trip could hardly have compared more starkly with his insouciant approach to travel in his younger years, when he crossed oceans with nothing more than a rucksack, and the eighty-three year old Graham was as apprehensive as he was excited about the prospect of another long journey. His correspondence with Marion Hay was full of the practical details involved in applying for a visa and getting permission to take sterling out of the country (the normal allowance of fifty pounds permitted by the British governments to its citizens travelling abroad was quite inadequate for a three-month trip). Graham and Vera even fretted about the practical business of closing up Frith Street, taking meter readings and making arrangements for their upstairs tenant to keep an eye on the flat, which had been burgled during one of their earlier trips to Yugoslavia. Both of them also predictably worried about how their health would stand up to the rigours of the journey. At the start of November 1967, the two of them finally left Heathrow on a BOAC flight to New York, where they had booked a double room on the seventeenth floor of the art deco Hotel Edison, located in midtown Manhattan near Times Square.

---

28 Graham Papers (FSU), Box 580, 37A ('Yugoslavia is Getting Happier').

Graham planned to write a book about his return to America after almost four decades, and was determined to use his trip to revisit the places he had known long before, although most of the friends and acquaintances he had once known were long since dead.[29] He realised as soon as he arrived in New York how much the city had changed. The cheap lodgings he had taken during his first visit in 1913 had long been swept away, replaced by a red-brick skyscraper with swing doors policed by "a man in buttons". The formerly run-down area around Third Avenue near Gramercy Park had become clean and respectable. The only person in the city who remembered Graham from the 1920s was Helen Worden, now a twice-widowed stately matron, but then one of the bright young things who had introduced him to the social life of New York. The two of them met in her apartment to chat about the changes that had taken place in the city, by now a more dangerous place than in the 1920s, as many of its prosperous white residents had fled to the suburbs.

Graham and Vera only stayed in New York for a few days, before taking a plane southwards to stay with Marion Hay in Tallahassee, a city Graham had visited almost half a century before when collecting material for *Children of the Slaves*. He was stunned by the changes that had taken place. Although he found that the South was still "a different country" from the North, maintaining its culture of "early Victorian morals and piety", Tallahassee itself was no longer "a collection of small shops and genteel residences" clustered round the domed Capitol. It had instead become a city of "lurid billboards and advertising sticks". He was however enchanted by Marion Hay's home, which was located in woodland on the fringes of the city, where he and Vera sat in the garden watching the local wildlife. Graham declared Florida "heavenly".

Graham stayed in Tallahassee for about six weeks, meeting many of Hay's friends and fellow professors at Florida State University, as well as attending various concerts and plays. He also visited New Orleans, some three hundred and fifty miles along the Gulf coast, and was once again stunned to find how the rotting wooden city he had known half a century earlier had become a place of packed streets and convention hotels. Graham also had the opportunity to visit Houston, where he went to the Harry Ransom Center at the University of Texas, in order to see a collection of his

---

29 All quotations in the following paragraphs unless otherwise stated from Graham Papers (FSU), Box 580, 2 ('America after Fifty Years') or Graham Papers (FSU), Box 582, 39 (Various notes on United States).

papers that had been deposited there. He was awed by the size of Texas – "a state at which the traveller can only nibble" – and the wealth of Houston (a city he believed had more millionaires than New York City). In the early 1920s Graham had hoped to find in the south and west of the United States a place uncontaminated by the materialism and industrialisation of the north. In the late 1960s he seemed almost happy to leave the New South, heading northwards for Chicago, a city he found enveloped "half in factory smoke [and] half in lake mist". The soaring architecture had once again destroyed most of the landmarks Graham had known, for when he first visited Chicago, in 1913, it had been a place of grim tenements and poverty, whilst on his last visit there in 1929 he had gone to hidden nightclubs guarded by gangsters with machine guns. Graham had not come to Illinois simply to see Chicago. He also wanted to visit the places connected with two of the men who had played a major role earlier in his life: the poet Vachel Lindsay and the Serbian priest Nikolai Velimirović.

Graham left Vera in Chicago for a few days and took the train to Lindsay's hometown of Springfield, trudging from the station through the rain to Vachel's old house, which had by now become a museum. The house was locked and bolted, but the local newspaper office got in touch with the curator, who came over to open up the building for him. Graham was uneasy about the change that had taken place inside: "I saw not indeed the house where the poet lived but a transfigured place where all that had looked shabby had been removed". After being guided round the house, which he populated in his mind's eye with images of his old friend, he was then taken across to the local museum where he was asked to make a recording of some of Lindsay's verse. Graham was intensely aware that Lindsay was no longer a living presence in Springfield, but had instead become transmogrified into a kind of literary ghost, and his search for the spirit of the man who had once played such a large role in his life proved to be forlorn. Although memories of his time with Vachel in the 1920s came flooding back, he could find no echo of his friend in a town that had been transformed into a modern urban conglomeration, far from the place Lindsay had envisioned in his *Golden Book of Springfield* as a city destined to transform the American psyche by rejecting the materialist civilisation of the East Coast.

On returning to Chicago, Graham rejoined Vera, and the two of them made their way out to the monastery of St Sava at Libertyville, in the northwestern suburbs of the city, to visit the grave of Fr Nikolai Velimirović. It was bitterly cold and snowing when they got there, and they had some difficulty in finding the grave, "a rectangle of sacred earth, some withered flowers, a broken holder for candles and a low Orthodox wooden cross with his name on the crossbeam". The two of them stood by the grave in the drifting snow, and Graham watched as "tears came from Vera's eyes and crept down her cheeks", a rare event for a woman who "never cries". Graham's visits to Springfield and Libertyville represented a kind of pilgrimage designed to reconnect him with two of the people who had shaped his past. The unpublished notes of his visit have an elegiac quality, evidence perhaps that he was trying to make sense of a life increasingly permeated by a sense of loss and intimations of mortality.[30]

After leaving Chicago, the Grahams returned to New York, briefly visiting Washington in order to see Stephen's niece who taught at Howard University. They flew back to London at the start of February 1968, from where Graham wrote to Marion Hay, thanking her for her help in making their trip "so memorable".[31] He was not particularly happy to be home. The tenant in the upstairs flat at Frith Street had become a drug addict, with the result that questionable characters were coming and going at all hours of the day and night. A few days later he heard that yet another old friend, Bernard Newman, had died. Graham was appalled by the pall of "social depression" that hung over British life,[32] whilst his mood was made worse by the need to confront, once again, his money worries, now made worse by the cost of the American trip. He had written to a number of prominent writers the previous year, asking them to support his application for a pension from the civil list, but apparently without any positive results, and he was forced once again to try to earn some money from writing. It was no easy task for a man entering his mid-eighties.

Graham had for a number of years been working fitfully on a history of Russia, provisionally entitled *From Barbarism to Tsarism*, and the manuscript suggests that he had carried out a good deal of research for the project. It nevertheless lacked both the historical and literary merit needed to attract a publisher. The book sought to defend the idea of Holy Russia, arguing that the Russian peasantry had by temperament been inclined to adopt the Russian Orthodox faith after the conversion of the Grand Prince Vladimir

---

30 For details of Velimirović's later life see Graham Papers (FSU), Box 581, 23a ('Nikolai Velimirović').
31 Graham Papers (FSU), Box 573, 8. Graham to Hay, 11 February 1968.
32 Ibid, Graham to Hay, 1 March 1968.

in 988 A.D., but its author did not have the depth of knowledge needed to make his thesis convincing. Graham was on firmer ground in trying to write a book on the theme of *America after Fifty Years*, describing his recent trip, but he never turned his copious notes into anything approaching a polished manuscript. Although some of those who knew Graham in the late 1960s recall that he was still remarkably vigorous, despite constantly fretting about his health, his reserves of mental and physical energy were fading fast. The literary projects he continued to devise in his head were too demanding for his increasingly limited powers.

Graham became more and more reclusive during the last years of his life, a consequence both of indifferent health and the loss of so many old friends. He and Vera continued to see a good deal of the publisher and bookseller Susil Gupta, who lived with his family in south London. They also saw a fair amount of Maysie Grieg, who moved permanently to London in 1966, following the death of her second husband Max Murray. Graham's correspondence during the last ten years of his life reflects his unhappiness about the changes taking place both in Britain and across the world. He was appalled by the development of the sex industry in Soho – one strip club was opened just a few doors from his home – and dismayed by the growth of street prostitution in the area. He was also angered by the number of strikes in the second half of the 1960s, and his letters were full of denunciations of the industrial unrest that grew remorselessly during the time of Harold Wilson's first Labour government.

Graham was equally perturbed by the changes taking place beyond Britain's shores. He was bitterly critical of the British government's treatment of the white Rhodesian government, following its Unilateral Declaration of Independence in 1965, and complained angrily that Wilson and his ministers had no sympathy for the white minority there ("if these people were Jews you would never hear the end of it"). He also predictably condemned the decision to impose sanctions. Graham's language was equally virulent when he wrote to Hay about the race riots that erupted in the United States in 1968. He criticised Martin Luther King for his "whining Christianity", which he thought promoted "envy", by encouraging "the individual coloured man [to] believe he was a wronged man".[33] Graham also condemned the demonstrations that followed King's murder, anxiously writing to Hay to check that she had not been caught

---

33 Ibid, Graham to Hay, 24 April 1968.

up in the race riots that swept Tallahassee, adding that his own niece had been forced to leave her teaching post at Howard University because of the anti-white feeling on campus (Howard was historically a black institution). 1968 was indeed an *annus horribilis* for Graham. He anxiously followed the events in Paris in May – his sympathies were entirely with De Gaulle rather than the demonstrators – and was by August "all in a frenzy" about the Soviet invasion of Czechoslovakia.[34] As he sat in his study in Frith Street, increasingly remote from the world around him, Graham felt more and more disoriented by the tide of modernity sweeping away the landmarks of his life.

Graham's worries about his health were sometimes exaggerated, but by the end of the 1960s his medical problems were becoming more serious, although he proudly noted a few days after his eighty-sixth birthday in March 1970 that he was still "going strong" despite a problem with his leg. He also felt well enough to appear in a BBC television documentary on John Gawsworth, and in the summer he travelled with Vera to Spain, staying in the town of San Juan in Alicante, close to his old friend Susil Gupta. By the autumn Graham was feeling less well again, though, and he started to fret about what would happen if Vera should ever become incapacitated.[35] His last published article appeared in 1970, a piece on Rasputin, which was printed in a magazine *Men, Myth and Magic* that was devoted to the supernatural.[36] Graham was almost childishly happy to see his name in print once more, but by Christmas his mood was still glum, as he reflected on the state of "beleaguered Britain" with its power shortages and endless strikes.[37] By the following spring he was complaining to Marion Hay in Tallahassee that strikes by postal workers and newspaper printers meant that he and Vera felt increasingly cut off from the world. Graham had in fact collapsed early in 1971 when he was found unconscious in his bedroom by Vera – probably a minor heart attack – and by the end of the year he could only walk with the benefit of two sticks. His poor sight also made it hard for him to read and write. Beset by gloom about his failing powers, Graham was depressed throughout 1972 by the "imbroglio of bad news" that filled the papers every day, and anxious about the growing inflation that was wiping out the value of his few savings. Things were not made any easier

---

34 Ibid, Graham to Hay, 23 August 1968.
35 Graham Papers (FSU), Box 573, 9, Graham to Hay, 8 December 1970.
36 A copy of the article can be found in Graham Papers (FSU), Box 581, 29a.
37 Graham Papers (FSU), Box 573, 9, Graham to Hay, 8 December 1970.

320 Beyond Holy Russia

by a fire that broke out at Frith Street at the end of the year, which was caused by an oil stove Vera had left burning in an attempt to keep the old house heated. Her husband was at least able to find comfort in the fact that the damage was limited to the bedroom.

Graham continued to read as much as he could, despite his poor eyesight, and during the course of 1973 he consumed many of the books and stories by the Soviet dissident writer and Nobel Prize winner Alexander Solzhenitsyn (Graham rather ambitiously thought he could have written *August 1914* "better" than the author).[38] He now spent most of his time living on the ground floor in order to avoid the stairs, although the arrival of a wheelchair in the spring of 1973 allowed him to leave the "very stuffy" house for outings into the Soho streets. An invitation to a Royal Garden Party at Buckingham Palace caused a flourish of excitement in July, but Graham was realistic enough to know that he was too frail to attend, although the invitation was kept in pride of place on the mantelpiece. A few weeks earlier he had another excitement when the *Evening News* sent a journalist to interview him about recent developments in the USSR, following Leonid Brezhnev's dramatic trip to America as part of the detente process. The subsequent half-page article described Graham's early trips to Russia before 1917, when his writings made him "a world authority on Russia", and quoted his views that the Soviet regime was only now seeking better relations with the West because it needed foreign investment. The article concluded with a description of "the wonderful elderly gentleman who now leans comfortably back in his armchair and says: "Life is too short – now I'm washed on the shores of time. But I am quite happy just sitting around the house, musing [...] and remembering".[39] Graham was putting on a brave face for the readers of the *Evening News*. At least some who knew him at this time recall a hidden sadness in his mood – a recognition not only that his life was drawing to a close – but also a pervasive sense that there had to use Wordsworth's words "passed away a beauty from the earth". The material cares of daily life – health and money – now seemed far more real than the elusive ideals lurking behind the mundane façade of the world. The visionary in Graham struggled in his final years to preserve the sense of the miraculous that had once been so powerful a feature of his life.

The last full year of Graham's life, 1974, began with illness and continued with more expressions of concern about the state of Britain. The miners'

---

38 Ibid, Graham to Hay, 25 January 1973.
39 *Evening News*, 30 June 1973.

strike and the return of a Labour government in February did nothing to improve his mood, and he was convinced that the country could only survive if "it ceases to be an industrial one and becomes an agricultural one".[40] A brief holiday at Littlehampton lightened his mood, and he enjoyed his time in "the lovely place", relishing the sea air as Vera pushed him up and down the esplanade in his wheel chair. Their return to Frith Street was once again accompanied by concerns about rising prices and shortages of such basic goods as lavatory paper. The year ended on a high note with a "blizzard" of Christmas cards and a "glorious" Christmas dinner, complete with a four-pound duck with all the trimmings, but Graham's health was by now fading fast. A few weeks later, on 21 February 1975, he told Marion Hay in America that he and Vera were "not in the best of health. Vera gets so easily tired and suffers from aches and pains. I get weaker daily".[41] It was the last letter he sent his old friend.

Stephen Graham died on 16 March 1975, just four days short of his ninety-first birthday. For reasons that remain obscure, Vera insisted that his funeral should be a private affair. She had become increasingly protective of her husband during his final years, discouraging visitors who might tire him out, and did not seem to realise that there were still people who held him in high regard and were upset at being excluded. They were, however, consoled by the memorial service held at All Saints Church in Margaret Street, a few hundred yards from Frith Street, a month after Graham's death. There were about thirty people in attendance to celebrate the life of a man who had, for more than six decades, been a permanent if sometimes neglected member of the British literary establishment.

---

40 Graham Papers (FSU), Box 573, 9, Graham to Hay, 3 June 1974
41 Ibid, Graham to Hay, 21 February 1975.

Final Thoughts

No record exists of what was said at Graham's Memorial Service. Anyone who has ever given an address at such an occasion will know how hard it is to compress the details of even the most ordinary life into a ten-minute eulogy. The challenge must have been particularly difficult for whoever was charged with selecting a few details to capture the spirit of a man as complex as Graham. Graham himself noted in his memoirs that "how much takes place in a lifetime you will hardly know until you attempt to write it down". He added that as he looked back he realised how he had often led "a double or even a triple life" – divided between "idealism, travel and intense literary work" – which meant that he tended to live in separate compartments, each with their own set of friends and acquaintances.[1] It was a shrewd observation. Graham's life was not defined by a neat narrative arc (to use that most tiresome of literary phrases). It was instead like all lives messy and uncertain, shaped by circumstances and chance meetings, yet still displaying certain enduring motifs and attitudes. The time has long gone when it is possible to believe that even the most formidable person, not even one of Carlyle's "greats", can develop an unproblematic sense of self founded on an acute awareness of inner motivation and drive. And yet most of us believe, to a greater or lesser extent, that a ghost does still live in the machine. Whatever the religious or metaphysical foundation for such a belief, and whatever the ruminations of the neuroscientists, all of us behave as though we possess coherent identities and live amongst others who have an equally strong sense of self. And the prevalence of this belief in a very real sense makes it so.

Some useful clues to Graham's awareness of his own *persona* can be found in his most popular book, *The Gentle Art of Tramping* (1926), written

---

1 Stephen Graham, *Part of the Wonderful Scene* (London: Collins, 1964), p. 307.

roughly half-way through his life at a time when he was going through a deep personal crisis. The book was like so much of his work a curious mixture of the reflective and the mundane. Advice about how to brew coffee or find shelter from a storm was interspersed with philosophical reflections on landscape and destiny. The wistful tone of the book was rooted in its author's sense that the young carefree vagabond, who had walked through alien landscapes, and peered beneath their surface to see deep meanings and profound truths, was somehow losing his vision as the cares of middle age began to intrude. Graham was still happy to quote Novalis to the effect that nature was "an encylopaedical index of our own souls", with the result that the tramp could by looking outwards obtain a deeper insight into their own psyche, but the tone of *Gentle Art* leaves no doubt that the effortless sense of meaning was fast fading away. Its author noted sadly that it was often only ten years after a particular moment in time that one looked back and realised "How wonderful it was [...] I was happy then". Graham urged his readers to keep some kind of diary that would allow them to capture not just the events of the day, but also its more elusive meanings, warning that "the details of your spiritual adventures fade out unless you have a good memory or an aide-memoire". And yet he was under no illusion that "poetic rhapsodies" or "intellectual notes" could fully capture particular experiences or insights. It was therefore important for each individual to appropriate for themselves the rare moments of illumination that they experienced whether on the road or in other settings of their daily lives. Every person, Graham wrote in *Gentle Art*, was an artist. All men and women were involved in a constant attempt to make sense of their lives as something more than a simple journey through the prosaic realities of day-to-day living.[2]

Graham used *Gentle Art of Tramping* to reflect on the similarity between tramping and pilgrimage as forms of "spiritual adventure", insisting that both the tramp and the pilgrim should focus on the experience of the journey rather than the final destination. It was advice rooted in his sense that "the world is not a straight line [...] it is an area, a broad surface [...] Life is not length of time but breadth of human experience. Life is not a chain of events, but an area – something spreading out from a hidden centre

---

2 Stephen Graham, *The Gentle Art of Tramping* (New York: Appleton, 1926), pp. 209, 215, 216.

and welling at once towards all points of the compass".[3] The final chapter of *Gentle Art* was headed 'A Zigzag Walk'. Graham described how he had in the past when visiting big cities like Paris or New York cultivated the habit of exploring them by pursuing a diagonal path, turning first left and then right, repeating the sequence at each junction, in a way that led him away from the major thoroughfares and into back streets and courtyards he would otherwise have missed. The metaphor did not escape him. He noted on the final page of *Gentle Art* that "I am still on the zigzag way, pursuing the diagonal between the reason and the heart".[4] The references to reason and heart are not accidental. The previous chapters have shown that Graham was throughout the first half of his life torn between a love of the "Little World" of everyday experiences and a longing for the "Somewhere-Out-Beyond". His love of travel was the product *both* of his desire to see new things *and* his hope of discovering places that could speak to his need to find a deeper meaning in the world. He was, to use the language of theology, searching for a sense of transcendence in the immanent, hoping that art or religion or nature could offer him an insight into the numinous, a hint of something eternal that was rooted in realities that lay beyond the material world.

The process of maturity is sometimes said to be rooted in giving up illusions and accepting the realities of life. That at least was Freud's view. But it can perhaps be argued that real maturity consists of accepting the world as a disenchanted place where personal epiphanies and echoes of the transcendent are at best fleeting and partial. The fundamental things are not necessarily absent; they simply cannot be known in their entirety. It was this realisation that gradually dawned on Graham during the 1920s. Although he wrote little on the subject, Graham was throughout his life intrigued by the philosophy of Plato, and above all by the notion of Platonic 'forms' that represented the real essences of the things in the world. The celebrated allegory of the cave – which describes how men sitting in the dark, with their backs to the fire, would mistake the shadows on the wall for the things that cast the shadows – serves as a useful image for Graham's own youthful view of the world. He may or may not have had this metaphor in mind when he later wrote how he had as a young man abandoned the

---

3   Ibid, p. 193.
4   Ibid, p. 271.

"shadow" of secure employment in search of the "substance" he hoped to find in Russia.

The youthful Graham's decision to tone down some of the more abstruse speculations that appeared in early books like *A Tramp's Sketches* and *Undiscovered Russia* was governed in part by his recognition that it would broaden the market for his work. As time went by, he began to use his travel books to provide descriptions of the places he visited and the things he saw, a move that became more pronounced once the 1917 Revolution destroyed the country that had dominated his imagination for so many years. Graham was never really able to find a substitute for Holy Russia, nor the ideals it inspired in him, although his private diaries show that he remained true to many of his earlier ideas even as he wrote such seemingly prosaic works as *Children of the Slaves* and *Europe Quo Vadis*. The journalist in Graham could write fluently about people and places. The artist-thinker continued to seek (in the words of one critic of his work) "the deeper meaning of it all". The crisis that followed in the mid 1920s was not simply a personal crisis resulting from the death of his parents and the disintegration of his marriage. It was also rooted in a dawning realisation that any sense of transcendence or epiphany could only be temporary and partial, something to be stored away and remembered, but doomed to be swept away in time by the prosaic cares and problems of the world.

Graham's later work continued to be intimately shaped by his experiences but in a new way from before. Some novels such as *Lost Battle*, *Balkan Monastery* and *African Tragedy* drew extensively on his own life or the lives of those he knew. Others like *The Padre of St Jacobs* and *One of the Ten Thousand* displayed a fascination with the presentation of self in everyday life that was rooted in their author's personal interest in the porous and shifting nature of identity. None of Graham's later work really sought, though, to convey its author's life-philosophy. This was in large part because his earlier sense that religion and nature could provide insights into profound truths about the world had largely evaporated. Or, more accurately, he now recognised that it was difficult if not impossible to talk unproblematically about such things. The shift was not of course a precise one. The younger Graham had written numerous books and articles that focused on the surface of the world, providing deft pen portraits of people and places whose liveliness and significance did not rest simply on their ability to articulate some deeper truth. The radical change in the nature of his work after the mid 1920s was nevertheless unmistakeable. The character of Graham's books was increasingly determined by the question of market.

The change meant that his later work was seldom marred by the obscurantism and verbosity that sometimes marred his more youthful writings. But nor did it have the fire. It was not so much that the older Graham was content to paint the shadows, rather than peer towards the flames to see the forms that were casting them. It was that he no longer believed whole-heartedly in the poetics of Plato's cave. It was only in the final ten or fifteen years of his life that he seemed to become enthralled once again by the insights and inspirations that had dominated his youth. Perhaps Graham's awareness that his life was slowly drawing to a close led him to a philosophy of consolation that sought to transcend the material fact of extinction. Or perhaps – and *contra* Freud – he realised once more that life in its fullest sense consists of more than the here and now.

When Graham was still a young man he wrote a piece for the *English Review* on 'The Death of Yesterday's Books',[5] describing how some books died at birth, strangled by reviewers, whilst other flared up for a short time, only gradually to fade and die, passing from bookshelf to second-hand bookseller to jumble sale. He went on to note how "benevolent readers stare at rows of dead books and wonder if there may not be one of them that belies its title and its appearance. Many a man or woman has raised dead books to life as a result of searching the dusty stacks". Most of Graham's fifty plus books today firmly belong to the category of dead books, something that would doubtless mortify their author, who told a correspondent a few years before his death that he was prouder of his literary work than his status as a world traveller. It seems unlikely that any of his books are about to enjoy a spectacular rebirth, even if some of them continue to sell in dribs and drabs, beneficiaries of the print-on-demand phenomenon that has helped to raise "dead books to life". Graham wrote too fast and too frequently, a result both of the need to earn money, and of what at times seemed a particularly obsessive form of graphomania. He was always a writer of insight and flair rather than sustained thought. And, as he himself acknowledged, he was at his best when writing directly from his own experience rather than through the second-hand medium of novels and biographies. And yet, for all their weaknesses, there is hidden away in the best of Graham's books an intensity of vision that endures despite their archaic language and prolix style.

---

5   Stephen Graham, 'The Death of Yesterday's Books', *English Review*, November 1923.

Graham lived a fascinating life that was fuelled not only by the desire to travel, but also by a desire to use his travel as a quest for something more important than the mere accumulation of experiences. Many of Graham's youthful journeys became pilgrimages, prompted by a yearning for something that was half-sensed but little known, and by a determination to treat the journey itself as part of the search for meaning. His later life was shaped by a desire to come to terms with the loss of his earlier vision – or at least with the loss of his sense that the vision could be made actual in the world – a kind of 'reconciliation with reality' to use a phrase associated with the nineteenth-century Russian writer Vissarion Belinsky. To live is in a way to become disillusioned. Or, to quote the French writer Marcel Pagnol, it is to accept that life is "a few joys, quickly obliterated by unforgettable sorrows". And yet any life worth the name is also about venturing out to search for what is important and true, even if what is important and true can never be fully known. Graham in old age occasionally jotted down notes about St Paul, and it is perhaps worth ending with a quote from the apostle's first epistle to the Corinthians: "For now we see through a glass, darkly, but then face to face: now I know in part; but then shall I know even as also I am known".

Bibliography

Archival Sources

The biggest collections of Stephen Graham's manuscripts and letters can be found in the Harry Ransom Center (University of Texas) and the Strozier Library (Florida State University). Graham was not systematic in the way he wrote or recorded his thoughts. I have therefore in the text, when using material from the Harry Ransom Center and Strozier Library, given definite titles (eg 'Journal for 1921') to works that often took the form of rough notes and sketches. The problem is compounded by Graham's penchant for using engagement diaries to record his thoughts and activities, ignoring the actual dates of the pages on which he wrote. I have noted where this is a particular issue in the footnotes.

Abraham Lincoln Presidential Library (Springfield, IL)
Catherine Blair Papers
Vachel Lindsay Papers

British Broadcasting Corporation Archives (Caversham)
Various records relating to Graham's career at the BBC and on policy relating to broadcasts to the USSR.

Bradford University Library (Special Collections)
New Atlantis Archive

British Library (India Office Library and Records)
Evelyn Wrench Papers
Viscount Reading Papers

Cambridge University Library (Special Collections)
Papers of the Royal Society of Literature

University of Chicago Library (Special Collections)
Harriet Monroe Papers
Harriet Moody Papers

Columbia University Library (Rare Books and Manuscripts)
Charles Crane Papers

Florida State University (Strozier Library, Special Collections)
Stephen Graham Papers
Marion Hay Papers

Garrick Club Library Collections
Dorothy Allhusen Papers

Harry Ransom Center (University of Texas)
Stephen Graham Papers
Vachel Lindsay Papers
Wilfrid Ewart Papers
T.I.F. Armstrong (John Gawsworth) Papers
Christopher Morley Papers
P.E.N. Papers
Alice Henderson Papers

Haverford College Library (Special Collections)
Christopher Morley Papers

Indiana University at Bloomington (Lilly Library)
Lewis Browne Papers

Lambeth Palace Library
Papers of the Anglican and Eastern Churches Association
W.J. Birkbeck Papers
Randall Davidson Papers
William Temple Papers

The National Archives (Kew)
FO 371 (General Correspondence of the Foreign Office)
WO 95 (First World War and Army of Occupation War Diaries)

National Library of Scotland
Letter from Stephen Graham to Malcolm Bulloch

University of Nottingham Library (Special Collections)

Letters from Stephen Graham to Janko Lavrin

University of Pennsylvania (Rare Book and Manuscript Library)

Van Wyck Brooks Papers

University of Reading

T.I.F. Armstrong (John Gawsworth) Papers

University of Virginia (Albert and Shirley Small Special Collections Library)

Margaret Hayley Carpenter Papers
Vachel Lindsay Papers

Material in Private Hands

Letters between Stephen Graham and Lulu Smith
Sundry photographs and letters relating to Graham's later years

Journals and Newspapers

Athenaeum
Atlantic Monthly
Current History
Country Life
Daily Express
Daily Mail
Daily Mirror
Daily Telegraph
The Eastern Churches Broadsheet
English Review
Evening News
Evening Standard
Evening Times
Fortnightly Review
Harper's Magazine
Jewish Chronicle
Jewish World
John O'London's Weekly
Letopis'
Manchester Guardian
Montreal Gazette
National Observer

New Britain
New York Evening Post
New Yorker
New York Times
Observer
Orthodox Church Bulletin
Poetry Review
Proceedings of the Anglo-Russian Literary Society
Quest
Radio Times
Rech'
Russkaia Mysl'
Saturday Review of Literature
Scribner's Magazine
Speculum
Spiritual Issues of the War
Stephen Graham's Newsletter about the Orthodox Churches in War-Time
Sunday Pictorial
The Academy
The Beacon
The Bookman
The Century Magazine
The Crisis
The Globe
The Living Age
The New Age
The Sunday Times
The Times
The Times Literary Supplement
The Tramp
The Weekly Westminster
Western Morning News

Books written by Stephen Graham

Many of Graham's works were published in the USA as well as Britain, sometimes under other titles. The list below only gives details of the first British publication or the American version when the book was initially published in the United States. The electronic version identified in the text is not necessarily the version used in the research for the book. When a version other than the first British publication has been used in this book details are given in the footnotes. For fuller details see the valuable list in Marguerite Helmers, 'Stephen Graham', *Dictionary of Literary Biography*, vol. 195, pp. 137–54.

A Vagabond in the Caucasus with Some Notes on His Experiences among the Russians (London: John Lane, 1911).
Undiscovered Russia (London: John Lane, 1912).
A Tramp's Sketches (London: Macmillan, 1912).
Changing Russia (London: Macmillan, 1913).
With the Russian Pilgrims to Jerusalem (London: Macmillan, 1913).
With Poor Immigrants to America (London: Macmillan, 1914).
Russia and the World: A Study of the War and a Statement of the World-Problems that Now Confront Russia and Great Britain (London: Cassel, 1915).
The Way of Martha and the Way of Mary (London: Macmillan, 1915).
Christmas in the Heart (London: A.T. Stevens, 1916).
Through Russian Central Asia (London: Cassell, 1916).
Priest of the Ideal (London: Macmillan, 1917).
Russia in 1916 (London: Cassell, 1917).
The Quest of the Face (London: Macmillan, 1918).
A Private in the Guards (London: Macmillan, 1919).
Children of the Slaves (London: Macmillan, 1920).
The Challenge of the Dead: A Vision of the War and the Life of a Common Soldier in France, Seen Two Years Afterwards between August and November, 1920 (London: Cassell, 1921).
Europe Whither-Bound? (Quo Vadis Europa?): Being Letters of Travel from the Capitals of Europe (London: Butterworth, 1921).
Tramping with a Poet in the Rockies (London: Macmillan, 1922).
Under-London (London: Macmillan, 1923).
In Quest of El Dorado (London: Macmillan, 1924).
Life and Last Words of Wilfrid Ewart (London: Putnam, 1924).
London Nights (London: Hurst and Blackwood, 1925).
Russia in Division (London: Macmillan, 1925).
The Gentle Art of Tramping (New York: Appleton, 1926).
Midsummer Music (London: Hurst and Blackett, 1926).
New York Nights (New York: George H. Doran, 1927).
The Lay Confessor (London: Ernest Benn, 1928).
Peter the Great: A Life of Peter I of Russia (London: Ernest Benn, 1929).
The Death of Yesterday (London: Ernest Benn, 1930).
St Vitus Day (London: Ernest Benn, 1930).
A Modern Vanity Fair (London: Ernest Benn, 1931).

Stalin: An Impartial Study of the Life and Work of Joseph Stalin (London: Ernest Benn, 1931).
Everybody Pays (London: Ernest Benn, 1932).
Ivan the Terrible: The Life of Ivan IV of Russia (London: Ernest Benn, 1932).
Twice Round the London Clock and More London Nights (London: Ernest Benn, 1933).
Boris Godunof (London: Ernest Benn, 1933).
One of the Ten Thousand (London: Ernest Benn, 1933).
Lost Battle (London: Ivor Nicholson and Watson, 1934).
The Padre of St Jacobs (London: Ivor Nicholson and Watson, 1934).
Balkan Monastery (London: Ivor Nicholson and Watson, 1935).
A Life of Alexander II: Tsar of Russia (London: Ivor Nicholson and Watson, 1935).
Characteristics (London: Rich and Cowan, 1936).
African Tragedy (London: Rich and Cowan, 1937).
Alexander of Jugoslavia: Strong Man of the Balkans (London: Cassell, 1938).
The Moving Tent: Adventures with a Tent and Fishing Rod in Southern Jugoslavia (London: Cassell, 1939).
From War to War: A Date-Book of the Years Between 1917 and 1939 (London: Hutchinson, 1940).
Liquid Victory (London: Hutchinson, 1940).
Thinking of Living (London: Ernest Benn, 1949).
Summing-Up on Russia (London: Ernest Benn, 1951).
Pay as you Run (London: Ernest Benn, 1955).
Part of the Wonderful Scene (London: Collins, 1964).

Books Edited / Introduced / Translated by Stephen Graham

Bogoras, Vladimir, *Sons of the Mammoth* (New York: Cosmopolitan Books, 1929).
Briusov, Valery, *The Republic of the Southern Cross and Other Stories* (London: Constable, 1918).
Chirikov, E., *Marka of the Pits* (London: Alston Rivers, 1930).
Doroshevich, Vlas, *The Way of the Cross* (London: Constable, 1916).
Dostoievskaia, L.F., *The Emigrant* (London: Constable, 1916).
Frolov, Yury, *Fish Who Answer the Telephone and Other Studies in Experimental Biography* (London: Kegan Paul, 1937).
Gogol, Nikolai, *Dead Souls* (London: Unwin, 1915).
Gul', Roman, *General B.O.* (London: Ernest Benn, 1930).
Great American Short Stories (London: Ernest Benn, 1931).
Great Russian Short Stories (London: Ernest Benn, 1929).
Kuprin, Alexander, *A Slav Soul and Other Stories* (London: Constable, 1916).
Novikov, Olga, *Russian Memories* (London: Herbert Jenkins, 1917).

One Hundred Best Poems in the English Language (London: Ernest Benn, 1952).

Romanov, Panteleimon, *Without Cherry Blossom* (London: Ernest Benn, 1930).

— *Three Pairs of Silk Stockings* (London: Ernest Benn, 1931).

Sologub, Fedor, *The Sweet-Scented Name and other Fairy-Tales* (London: Constable, 1915).

Solovyof, Vladimir, *The Justification of the Good* (London: Constable, 1916).

— *War and Christianity from the Russian Point of View* (London: Constable, 1915).

The Tramp's Anthology (London: Peter Davies, 1928).

Other Contemporary Writings and Memoirs Referred to in the Notes

Allies in Art: A Collection of works in Modern Art by the Artists of the Allied Nations (London: Colour, 1917).

Baedeker, Karl, *Russia: A Handbook for Travellers* (London, 1914).

Baring, Maurice, *The Mainsprings of Russia* (London: Nelson, 1914).

— *The Puppet Show of Memory* (London: Cassell, 1987).

Bell, G.K.A., *Randall Davidson: Archbishop of Canterbury* (London: Oxford University Press, 1939).

Blackwood, Algernon, *The Centaur* (London: Macmillan, 1911).

— *The Listener* (London: Eveleigh, Nash and Grayson, 1907).

— *Pan's Garden: A Volume of Nature Stories* (London: Macmillan, 1912).

Blavatsky, Helen, *The Key to Theosophy* (London: Theosophical Publishing Society, 1891).

Bury, Right Reverend Herbert, *Russian Life Today* (London: Mowbray, 1915).

Bynner, Witter, *A Canticle of Pan* (New York: Alfred Knopf, 1920).

Camp, Denis, ed., *The Prose of Vachel Lindsay* (Peoria, IL: Spoon River Press, 1988).

Campbell, R.J. *The New Theology* (London: Mills and Boon, 1907).

Chenétier, Marc, ed., *Letters of Vachel Lindsay* (New York: Burt Franklin, 1979).

Dunbar, Oliva Hoard, *A House in Chicago* (Chicago: University of Chicago Press, 1947).

Ellis, Havelock, 'The Genius of Russia', *Contemporary Review*, 80 (1901), pp. 419-33.

Ewart, Wilfrid, *Scots Guard* (London: Rich and Cowan, 1934).

— *Scots Guard on the Western Front, 1915-1918* (Stevenage: Strong and Oak Press, 2001).

— *Way of Revelation* (London: G.P. Putnam, 1921).

— *When Armageddon Came* (London: Rich and Cowan, 1933).

— et al., *The Scots Guard in the Great War, 1914-18* (London: John Murray, 1925).

Falk, Bernard, *He Laughed in Fleet Street* (London: Hutchinson, 1937).

Farson, Daniel, *Never A Normal Man* (London: Harper Collins, 1997).

Farson, Negley, *Going Fishing* (London: Country Life, 1942).

— *A Mirror for Narcissus* (London: Victor Gollanz, 1956).
— *Way of a Trangressor* (London: Victor Gollanz, 1935).
Fraser, G.S., *A Stranger and Afraid* (Manchester: Carcanet New Press, 1983).
Gardiner, Alfred George, *The Warlords* (London: J.M. Dent, 1915).
Garston, Denis, *Friendly Russia* (London: Fisher Unwin, 1915).
Gawsworth, John, *Above the River* (London: Ulysses, 1931).
— ed., *Strange Assembly* (London: Unicorn Press, 1932).
— ed., *Thrills Crimes and Mysteries* (London: Associated Press, 1936).
Graham, P. Anderson, *All the Year with Nature* (London: Smith and Elder, 1893).
— *Country Pastimes for Boys* (London: Longmans, 1897).
— *Highways and Byways in Northumbria* (London: Macmillan, 1920).
— *Lindisfarne* (London: Knight, Frank and Rutley, 1920).
— *Nature in Books* (London: Methuen, 1891).
— 'The Abuse of Kindness', *National Observer*, 30 March 1895.
— *The Collapse of Homo Sapiens* (London: G.P. Putnam, 1923).
— *The Rural Exodus* (London: Methuen, 1892).
Harman, Neal, *Crown Colony* (London: Arthur Barker, 1939).
— *Death and the Archdeacon* (London: Arthur Barker, 1949).
Henderson, A.C., ed., *The Turquoise Trail: An Anthology of New Mexico Poetry* (Boston: Houghton Mifflin, 1928).
Henley, W.E., *Views and Reviews* (London: David Nutt, 1890).
Heyking, Baron A., *The Main Issues Confronting the Minorities of Lativa and Esti* (London: King, 1922).
Hicks, Stephen and Ewart, Wilfrid H.G., *Practical Poultry Keeping for Smallholders* (London: Feathered World, 1912).
Jerrold, Walter, *Thomas Hood: his Life and Times* (London: Alston Rivers, 1907).
Kipling, Rudyard, *The Irish Guards in the Great War: the First Battalion* (Staplehurst: Spellmount, 1997).
Kirkpatrick, Ivonne, 'Calling Europe', *BBC Yearbook 1943*.
— *The Inner Circle* (London: Macmillan, 1959).
Lachman, Gary, *In Search of P.D. Ouspensky: The Genius in the Shadow of Gurdjieff* (Wheaton, IL: Quest, 2004).
Latimer, R.S., *Under Three Tsars* (London: Morgan and Scott, 1907).
Lindsay, Vachel, *Adventures Whilst Preaching the Gospel of Beauty* (New York: Mitchell Kennerley, 1914).
— *A Handy Guide for Beggars* (New York: Macmillan, 1916).
— *Going-to-the-Stars* (New York: Appleton, 1926).
— *Going-to-the-Sun* (New York: Appleton, 1923).
— *The Art of the Moving Picture* (New York: Macmillan, 1922).
— 'The New Localism', *Vision: A Quarterly Journal of Aesthetic Appreciation of Life*, 4

(1912).

Lodge, Oliver, *Raymond, or Life and Death: With Examples of the Survival of Memory and Affection after Death* (London: Methuen, 1916).

Maclean, Fitzroy, *Eastern Approaches* (London: Cape, 1949).

Mairet, Philip, *Autobiographical and Other Papers* (Manchester: Carcanet, 1981).

Maugham, W. Somerset, *Collected Short Stories*, vol. 3 (London: Pan, 1976).

Merkurieva, Vera, *Tshcheta: sobranie stikhotvorenii* (Moscow: Vodolei Publishers, 2007).

Miliukov, Paul, *Russia Today and Tomorrow* (New York: Macmillan, 1922).

Nesterov, M.V., *Pis'ma izbrannye* (Leningrad: Iskusstvo, 1988).

Newman, Bernard, *Albanian Back Door* (London: Herbert Jenkins, 1936).

Olmsted, Frederick Law, *A Journey in the Seaboard Slave States with Remarks on their Economy* 2 vols. (New York: Dix and Edwards, 1856).

Pares, Bernard, *Russia and Reform* (London: Constable, 1907).

Pisarava, E.S., *The Light of the Russian Soul: A Personal Memoir of Early Russian Theosophy* (Wheaton, IL: Quest, 2008).

Ralston, W.R.S., *Krilof and his Fables* (London: Strahan, 1869).

Ransome, Arthur, *Bohemia in London* (London: Chapman and Hall, 1907).

Rowlands, John, ed., *Path and Pavement: Twenty New Tales of Britain* (London: Eric Grant, 1937).

Sirc, Ljubo, *Between Hitler and Tito: Nazi Occupation and Communist Oppression* (London: Deutsch, 1989).

Spender, Stephen, *World Within a World: The Autobiography of Stephen Spender* (London: Hamish Hamilton, 1951).

Stead, W.T., *The M.P. for Russia*, 2 vols. (London: Andrew Melrose, 1909).

Stoddart, T. Lothrop, *Present-Day Europe: Its National States of Mind* (New York: Century, 1917).

Synnott, Edward Fitzgerald, *Five Years' Hell in a Country Parish* (London: Stanley, Paul and Co, 1920).

Tietjens, Eunice, *The World at My Shoulder* (New York: Macmillan, 1938).

Turner, Samuel, *Siberia: A Record of Travel, Climbing and Exploration* (London: Unwin, 1905).

Untermeyer, Louis, *From Another World: the Autobiography of Louis Untermeyer* (New York: Harcourt Brace and Co, 1939).

Velimirović, Nikolai, *Christianity and War* (London: Faith Press, 1918).

— *Serbia in Light and Darkness* (London: Longmans, 1916)

— *The Agony of the Church* (London: Student Christian Movement, 1917).

West, Rebecca, *Black Lamb and Grey Falcon* (Edinburgh: Canongate Books, 1993).

— ed., *Selected Poems of Carl Sandburg* (New York: Harcourt Brace and Co, 1926).

Williamson, Kennedy, *W.E. Henley: A Memoir* (London: Harold Shaylor, 1930).

Zangwill, Israel, *Works of Israel Zangwill: the War for the World* (New York: American Jewish Book Company, 1921).

Secondary Sources

A full list of the secondary sources used in writing this book would be enormous. The books and articles listed below are those cited in the footnotes along with a small number of others that have been of particular use.

Alston, Charlotte, *Russia's Greatest Enemy: Harold Williams and the Russian Revolutions* (London: I.B. Tauris, 2007).

Ashley, Mike, *Starlight Man* (London: Constable, 2000).

Atkinson, Damien, ed., *The Selected Letters of W.E. Henley* (Aldershot: Ashgate, 2000).

Bell, Helen, *London was Ours: Diaries and Memoirs of the London Blitz* (London: I.B. Tauris, 2008).

Bell, Philip, *John Bull and the Bear: British Public Opinion, Foreign Policy and the Soviet Union, 1941-1945* (London: Edward Arnold, 1990).

Benjamin, Walter, *The Arcades Project* (Cambridge, MA: Harvard University Press, 1999).

Bird, Robert, *The Russian Prospero: The Creative Universe of Viacheslav Ivanov* (Madison, WI: University of Wisconsin Press, 2006).

Blakesley, Rosalind P., *The Arts and Crafts Movement* (London: Phaidon, 2006).

Bourke, Joanna, *An Intimate History of Killing in Twentieth Century Warfare* (London: Granta, 1999).

Briggs, Asa, *The War of Words* (London: Oxford University Press, 1970).

Brooker, Peter, *Bohemia in London* (Basingstoke: Palgrave, 2007).

Bullock, Philip Ross, *Rosa Newmarch and Russian Music in Late Nineteenth and Early Twentieth-Century England* (Aldershot: Ashgate, 2009).

Burchardi, Kristiane, *Die Moskauer Religios-Philsophische Vladimir Solov'ev Gesellschaft, 1905-1918* (Wiesbaden: Harrassowitz, 1998).

Carlton, David, *Churchill and the Soviet Union* (Manchester: Manchester University Press, 1999).

Cecil, Hugh, *The Flower of Battle: British Fiction Writers of the First World War* (London: Secker and Warburg, 1995).

Cline, Lynn, *Literary Pilgrims: The Santa Fe and Taos Writers' Colonies, 1917-1950* (Alberquerque, NM: University of New Mexico Press, 2007).

Collins, David, 'Anglophone Travellers in the Russian Altai, 1848-1904', *Sibirica* 2, 1 (2002), pp. 43-68 (http://dx.doi.org/10.1080/1361736022000007390)

Cook, Andrew, *To Kill Rasputin: The Life and Death of Grigori Rasputin* (London: The History Press, 2006).

Cross, Anthony, ed., *A People Passing Rude: British Responses to Russian Culture* (Cambridge: Open Book Publishers, 2012). (http://dx.doi.org/10.11647/obp.0022)

David, Hugh, *The Fitzrovians: A Portrait of a Bohemian Society, 1900-1950* (London: Michael Joseph, 1988).

Davidson, A.P., *Rossiia i Britaniia: Sviazi i vzaimnye predstavleniia XIX–XX veka* (Moscow: Nauka, 2006).

Davies, Horton, *Worship and Theology in England: the Ecumenical Century* (Cambridge: Erdmans, 1996).

Dedijer, Vladimir, *The Road to Sarajevo* (London: Macgibbon and Kee, 1967).

De Fortis, Paul, ed., *The Kingdom of Redonda, 1865-1990: A Celebration* (Wirral: Aylesford Press, 1991).

Erickson, John, *The Road to Stalingrad* (London: Weidenfeld and Nicholson, 1975).

Faivre, Antoine, *Accès de l'ésotérisme occidental* (Paris: Gallimard, 1986).

Feldman, Eliyahu, 'British Diplomats and British Diplomacy and the 1905 Pogroms in Russia', *Slavonic and East European Review*, 65, 4 (1987), pp. 579-608.

Frisby, David, *Cityscapes of Modernity* (Cambridge: Polity, 2001).

Fussell, Paul, *The Great War and Modern Memory* (New York: Oxford University Press, 1975).

Gardiner, Juliet, *The Blitz: The British Under Attack* (London: Harper Press, 2011).

Garafola, Lynn and Van Norman Baer, Nancy, eds., *The Ballets Russes and its World* (New Haven, CT: Yale University Press, 1999).

Garnett, David, *The Secret History of PWE: The Political Warfare Executive, 1939-1945* (London: St Ermin's Press, 2002).

Garnett, Richard, *Constance Garnett: An Heroic Life* (London: Faber, 2009).

Gatrell, Peter, *Russia's First World War: A Social and Economic History* (Harlow: Pearson Longman, 2005).

Gitelman, Zvi Y., *A Century of Ambivalence: The Jews of Russia and the Soviet Union, 1881 to the Present* (Bloomington, IN: Indiana University Press, 2001).

Gleason, Abbott, 'Russkii inok: The Spiritual Landscape of Mikhail Nesterov', *Cultural Geographies*, 7, 3 (2000), pp. 299-312 (http://dx.doi.org/10.1177/096746 080000700304).

— et al, eds., *Bolshevik Culture: Experiment and Order in the Russian Revolution* (Bloomington, IN: Indiana University Press, 1985).

Gleason, John Howes, *The Genesis of Russophobia in Great Britain* (Cambridge, MA: Harvard University Press, 1950).

Glover, Jonathan, *Humanity: A Moral History of the Twentieth Century* (London: Jonathan Cape, 1999).

Graham, Margaret, *Edgar Wallace: Biography of a Phenomenon* (London: Book Club, 1938).

Gray, Paul H., 'Performance and Bardic Ambition of Vachel Lindsay', *Text and Performance Quarterly*. 9, 3 (1989), pp. 216-23.

Harris, Mark, *City of Discontent* (New York: Boobs Merrill, 1952).

Hewison, Robert, *Under Siege: Literary Life in London, 1939-45* (London: Weidenfeld and Nicolson, 1977).

Hollingsworth, Barry, 'The Society of Friends of Russian Freedom: English Liberals and Russian Socialists, 1890-1917', *Oxford Slavonic Papers*, 3 (1970), pp. 45-64.

Holmes, Richard, *Footsteps: Adventures of a Romantic Biographer* (London: Harper Perennial, 2005).

Holt, Tonie and Valmai, *My Boy Jack* (Barnsley: Pen and Sword, 2008).

Hopkirk, Stephen, *The Great Game: The Struggle for Empire in Central Asia* (London: John Murray, 2006).

Hughes, Michael, *Conscience and Conflict: Methodism, Peace and War in the Twentieth Century* (Peterborough: Epworth, 2008).

— *Diplomacy before the Russian Revolution: Britain, Russia and the Old Diplomacy, 1894-1917* (Basingstoke: Macmillan, 2000).

— 'Diplomacy or Drudgery? British Consuls in Russia during the Early Twentieth Century', *Diplomacy and Statecraft*, 6, 1 (1995), pp. 76-95 (http://dx.doi.org/10.1080/09592299508405958).

— *Inside the Enigma: British Officials in Russia, 1900-1939* (London: Hambledon Press, 1997).

— 'Picturesque Visions and Hopeful Dreams: W.J. Birkbeck, Stephen Graham and British Responses to Russian Orthodoxy on the Eve of Revolution', *Sobornost*, 33, 2 (2011), pp. 6-27.

— 'Searching for the Soul of Russia: British Perceptions of Russia during the First World War', *Twentieth-Century British History*, 20, 2 (2009), pp. 198-226 (http://dx.doi.org/10.1093/tcbh/hwp017).

— 'The Traveller's Search for Home: Stephen Graham and the Quest for London', *The London Journal*, 36, 3 (2011), pp. 211-24 (http://dx.doi.org/10.1179/174963211X13127325480271).

— 'The Visionary Goes West: Stephen Graham's American Odyssey', *Studies in Travel Literature*, 14, 2 (2010), pp. 179-96 (http://dx.doi.org/10.1080/13645141003747264).

Hutchings, Stephen C., *Russian Modernism: The Transfiguration of the Everyday* (Cambridge: Cambridge University Press, 1997).

Johnson, Sam, 'Making or Breaking the Silence: British Jews and East European Relief, 1914-1917', *Modern Judaism*, 30, 1 (2010), pp. 95-119.

Kay, M.A., 'The Yugoslav Government-in-Exile and the Problems of Restoration', *East European Quarterly*, 25, 1 (1991), pp. 1-19.

Kaznina, Olga, *Russkie v Anglii: Russkaia emigratsiia v kontekste russko-angliskikh sviazei v pervoi polovine XX veka* (Moscow: Nasledie, 1997).

Kirby, Dianne, *Church, State and Propaganda: The Archbishop of York and International Relations. A Study of Cyril Foster Garbett, 1942-55* (Hull: Hull University Press, 1999).

— 'The Church of England and "Religions Division" during the Second World War: Church-State Relations and the Anglo-Russian Alliance', *Electronic Journal of International History*, 4.

Klier, John and Lambrozo, Shlomo, eds., *Pogroms: Anti-Jewish Violence in Modern Russian History* (Cambridge: Cambridge University Press, 2004).

Koss, Stephen, *The Rise and Fall of the Political Press in Britain* (London: Hamilton, 1981).

Kramer, Dale, *Chicago Renaissance: The Literary Life of the Midwest, 1900-1930* (New York: Appleton-Century, 1966).

Kurapovna, Marcia Christoff, *Shadows on the Mountain: the Allies, the Resistance and the Rivalries that Doomed WWII* (Hoboken, NJ: Wiley, 2011).

Lane, Anne, 'Perfidious Albion? Britain and the Struggle for Mastery of Yugoslavia, 1941-44: A Reexamination in the Light of "New" Evidence', *Diplomacy and Statecraft*, 7, 2 (1996), pp. 345-77 (http://dx.doi.org/10.1080/09592299608406007).

Leatherbarrow, William, ed., *Dostoevsky and Britain* (Oxford: Berg, 1995).

Lees, Michael, *The Rape of Serbia: The British Role in Tito's Grab for Power* (San Diego, CA: Harcourt, Brace, Jovanovich, 1990).

Letley, Emma, *Maurice Baring: A Citizen of Europe* (London: Faber and Faber, 1991).

Lopate, Philip, ed., *Writing New York* (New York: Library of America, 1998).

Mackay, Robert, *Half the Battle: Civilian Morale in Britain during the Second World War* (Manchester: Manchester University Press, 2002).

Mairet, Philip, *A.R. Orage: A Memoir* (London: J.M. Dent, 1936).

Makarova, N.V. and Morgunova, O.A., eds., *Russkoe prisutstvie v Britanii* (Moscow: Sovremennaia ekonomika i pravo, 2009).

Malcolm, Noel, *Bosnia: A Short History* (London: Papermac, 1996).

Marias, Javier, *Dark Back of Time* (London: Vintage, 2004).

Martin, Wallace, *The New Age under Orage* (Manchester: Manchester University Press, 1967).

Masters, Edgar Lee, *Vachel Lindsay: A Poet in America* (New York: Scribners, 1935).

Miner, Steven Merritt, *Stalin's Holy War: Religion, Nationalism and Alliance Politics, 1941-45* (Chapel Hill, NC: University of North Carolina Press, 2003).

Montefiore, Simon Sebag, *Jerusalem: The Biography* (London: Phoenix, 2011).

Morrison, Alexander, *Russian Rule in Samarkand, 1868-1910: A Comparison with British India* (Oxford: Oxford University Press, 2008).

Muchnic, Helen, *Dostoevsky's English Reputation, 1881-1936* (New York: Octagon Books, 1969).

Neilson, Keith, *Britain and the Last Tsar: British Policy and Russia, 1894-1917* (Cambridge: Cambridge University Press, 1995).

— 'Joyrides? British Intelligence and Propaganda in Russia, 1914-1917', *Historical Journal*, 24, 4 (1981), pp. 885-906 (http://dx.doi.org/10.1017/S0018246X00008256).

Nicholas, Sian, 'Partners Now: Problems in the Portrayal of the Soviet Union and the United States of America, 1939-1945', *Diplomacy and Statecraft*, 3, 2 (1992), pp. 243-71.

Oppenheim, Janet, *The Other World: Spiritualism and Psychic Research in England, 1850-1914* (Cambridge: Cambridge University Press, 1985).

Overy, Richard, *Russia's War: A History of the Soviet Effort, 1941-1945* (Harmondsworth: Penguin, 1998).

Palavestra, Predrag, *Dogma i utopija Dimitrija Mitrinovića* (Belgrade: Slovo ljubve, 1977).

Pavlowitch, Steven K., 'Out of Context: The Yugoslav Government in London, 1941-45', *Journal of Contemporary History*, 16, 1 (1981), pp. 89-118.

Polonsky, Rachel, *Molotov's Magic Lantern: a Journey in Russian History* (London: Faber and Faber, 2010).

Pyman, Avril, *A History of Russian Symbolism* (Cambridge: Cambridge University Press, 1994).

Ramet, Sabrina and Listhaug, Ola, eds., *Serbia and the Serbs in World War Two* (Basingstoke: Palgrave, 2011).

Ritchie, Sebastian, *Our Man in Yugoslavia: the Story of a Secret Service Operative* (London: Frank Cass, 2004).

Rigby, Andrew, *Dimitrije Mitrinović: A Biography* (York: William Sessions, 2006).

Robbins, Keith, *England, Ireland, Scotland, Wales: The Christian Church, 1900-2000* (Oxford: Oxford University Press, 2008).

Roberts, Andrew, *The Holy Fox: A Life of Lord Halifax* (London: Weidenfeld, 1991).

Roberts, Walter R., *Tito, Mihailović and the Allies* (Durham, NC: Duke University Press, 1973).

Robson, Roy R., *Solovki: The Story of Russia Told Through its Most Remarkable Islands* (New Haven, CT: Yale University Press, 2004).

Rosenthal, Bernice Glatzer, ed., *The Occult in Russian and Soviet Culture* (Ithaca: Cornell University Press, 1997).

Ruggles, Eleanor, *The West-Going Heart: A Life of Vachel Lindsay* (New York: Norton, 1959).

Rutherford, H.C., *The Religion of Logos and Sophia: From the Writings of Dimitrije Mitrinović on Christianity* (London: New Atlantis Foundation, 1966).

— ed., *Certainly, Future: Selected Writings by Dimitrije Mitrinović* (New York: Columbia University Press, 1987).

Ruud, Charles, *Russian Entrepreneur: Publisher Ivan Sytin of Moscow* (Montreal: McGill University Press, 1990).

Sahedo, Jeff, *Russian Colonial Society in Tashkent, 1865-1923* (Bloomington, IN: Indiana University Press, 2007).

Sansom, William, *The Blitz: Westminster at War* (Oxford: Oxford University Press, 1990).

Scheijen, Sjeng, *Diaghilev: A Life* (London: Profile, 2009).

Siegel, Jennifer, *Endgame: Britain, Russia and the Final Struggle for Central Asia* (London: I.B. Tauris, 2002).

Stanley, David and Fletcher, Elaine, eds., *Cowboy Poets and Cowboy Poetry* (Urbana, IL: University of Illinois Press, 2000).

Steinberg, Marc and Coleman, Heather, *Sacred Stories: Religion and Spirituality in Modern Russia* (Bloomington, IN: Indiana University Press, 2007).

Stevens, Winifred, *The Soul of Russia* (London: Macmillan, 1916).

Stites, Richard, *Revolutionary Dreams: Utopian Visions and Experimental Life in the Russian Revolution* (New York: Oxford University Press, 1989).

Stone, Norman, *The Eastern Front, 1914-1917* (London: Hodder and Stoughton, 1975).

Strong, Sir Roy, *Country Life, 1897-1997: An English Arcadia* (London: Country Life Books, 1997).

Sutton, Jonathan, *The Religious Philosophy of Vladimir Solovyov: Towards a Reassessment* (Basingstoke: Macmillan, 1988).

Sweet, Matthew, *The West End Front: The Wartime Secrets of London's Great Hotels* (London: Faber and Faber, 2011).

Tanner, Marcus, *Croatia: A Nation Forged in War* (New Haven: Yale University Press, 1994).

Tret'iakova, S. Nikolaevna, 'Angliskii pisatel'-puteshestvennik Stefan Grekhem o Rossii nachala XX veka', *Voprosy istorii*, 11 (2002), pp. 156–60.

Trew, Simon C., *Britain, Mihailović and the Chetniks, 1941-42* (Basingstoke: Macmillan, 1998).

Tryphonopolous, Demetres P. and Surette, Leon, eds., *Literary Modernism and the Occult Tradition* (Orono, ME: National Poetry Foundation,1996).

Waddington, Patrick, ed., *Ivan Turgenev and Britain* (Oxford: Berg, 1995).

Ware, Carolyn F., *Greenwich Village: 1920-1930* (New York: Houghton Mifflin, 1935).

Webb, Aldan, 'Auntie Goes to War Again: the BBC External Services, the Foreign Office and the Early Cold War', *Media History*, 12, 2 (2006), pp. 117-32 (http://dx.doi.org/10.1080/13688800600807965).

West, Richard, *Tito and the Rise and Fall of Yugoslavia* (New York: Carroll and Graf, 1994).

Wheeler, Mark, *Britain and the War for Yugoslavia, 1941-1945* (New York: Columbia University Press, 1980).

Whittel, *Extreme Continental* (London: Indigo, 1995).

Wilkinson, Alan, *The Church of England and the First World War* (London: SPCK, 1978).

Winter, Jay, *Sites of Memory, Sites of Mourning: the Great War in European Cultural History* (Cambridge: Cambridge University Press, 1998).

Worrall, Nick, *The Moscow Art Theatre* (London: Routledge, 1996).

Wylie, Neville, ed., *The Politics of Strategy and Clandestine War: Special Operations Executive, 1940-1946* (London: Routledge, 2007).

Index

Above the River, by Terrence Armstrong 239
Academy, The 54
Adler, Alfred 228
Adventures Whilst Preaching The Gospel of Beauty, by Vachel Lindsay 178
Agate, James 250
Alexandrettia (now Iskenderun) 70
Alexandria 102
All the Year with Nature, by Peter Anderson Graham 19
American Legion Weekly 193
Ames, Delano 278, 300
Ames, Kit 300
Anderson, Sherwood 196
Anglican and Eastern Churches Association (AECA) 278–282
Anglo-Russian agreement (1907) 42, 54, 68
Anglo-Russian alliance 126, 281
Anglo-Russian Literary Society 106
Anglo-Russian Propaganda Bureau 98, 153
Anna Karenina, by Leo Tolstoy 28
Armstrong, Terrence. *See* Gawsworth, John
Arras 140, 144
Ashkhabad 90
Ataturk, Mustafa Kemal 159
Athenaeum 75, 122, 174
Athens 104, 158
Atlanta 171
Atlantic Monthly 176
Auden, W.H. 299

August 1914, by Alexander Solzhenitsyn 320
Autobiography of a Supertramp, by William Henry Davies 38

Babel, Isaac 237
Baku 41, 90
Balboa, Vasco Nunez de 189, 191, 194, 195
Baldwin, Stanley 212
Baltimore 172
Baring, Maurice 54, 81, 98
Barrie, J.M. 15
Batumi 70
BBC 6, 271, 276, 277, 278, 280, 286–291, 293–294, 304, 305, 308–309, 313, 314, 319
  European Service 287–288
  Russian Service 287–288, 294, 301
  Serbo-Croat Section 288–289, 290
Beacon, The 164–166, 188, 245
Beardsley, Aubrey 15
Beaverbook, Lord Max Aitken 260
Belgrade 158–160, 240–242, 243, 244, 245, 254, 255, 264, 269, 290, 292, 313, 314
Belinsky, Vissarion 328
Belloc, Joseph Hilaire 23, 38
Beloved Vagabond, by William Locke 38, 53
Bely, Andrei 45
Beneš, Eduard 160–161
Benn, Ernest 237, 307
Benningsen, Countess Olga 121

Berdiaev, Nikolai 60
Berlin 11, 161–162, 282, 292
Bevin, Ernest 294
Black and White 27
Black Lamb and Grey Falcon, by Rebecca West 255
Blackwood, Algernon 53, 81–82, 115, 136, 153, 231
Blok, Alexander 45, 51
Bokhara 90–91
Bolshevism 4, 127, 133, 139, 153, 157, 160, 211, 213, 231
Bonar Law, Andrew 123–124
Bookman, The 130, 205, 207, 217, 231
Borrow, George 228
Boston 176
Bowen, York 135
Braddell, Maurice 300
Bratislava 221
Brezhnev, Leonid 320
British Weekly, The 106
Brittain, Vera 278
Brooker, Paul 173
Buchanan, Sir George 105, 123–125
Buchan, John 106, 123
Bucharest 104
Budapest 160, 266
Bunin, Ivan 213
Burlingham, Charles 177
Burne-Jones, Edward 58
Burns, Robert 233
Bury, Bishop Herbert 98
Bynner, Witter 192
Byrnes, James 294

Cadet party 104–105, 118, 125
Cadiz 188
Caine, William 80
Cairo 102–103, 284
Campbell, Reginald John 139
Canticle of Pan, A, by Bynner Witter 192
Cape Town 260
Carlyle, Thomas 23, 25, 29, 34, 259, 323
Carmel, California 191
Carpenter, Margaret 310
Cassidy, Gerald 197

Caterham Depot. *See* Little Sparta (Guards's Training Camp)
Centaur, The, by Algernon Blackwood 54
Century Magazine, The 131
Chamberlain, Neville 269
Chaucer, Geoffery 117
Chekhov, Anton 32, 238, 291
Chernozemski, Vlado 264
Chesham, Lady Margot Hilda Layton 262–263
Chetniks 8, 284–286, 289
Chicago 11, 79, 169, 175, 177, 179, 187–188, 192, 196, 255, 316–318
Chihuahua 198
Children who Lived in a Barn, The, by Eleanor Graham 18
Churchill, Winston 5, 152, 280, 284, 291–292, 298
Church of England 4, 35, 73, 102, 281
Cleveley, Hugh 300
Cohen, Percy 100
Cold War 287, 294, 296–298
Coleridge, Samuel Taylor 299
Coleridge, Stephen 80
Collapse of Homo Sapiens, The, by Peter Anderson Graham 18
Collected Poems, by Edith Sitwell 309
Cologne 149–150
Colon 194, 195
communism 160, 229, 264, 270–271, 279, 284–285, 290, 292, 294–298, 314
Congo, The, by Vachel Lindsay 177
Constantinople 11, 62, 69, 70, 104, 158, 159–160, 251
Constantin, Stanislavsky 32
Copenhagen 154
Coptic Church 103
Cordoba 188
Cornhill Magazine 143
Coronado, Francesco Vásquez de 189
Cortes, Herman 189
Country Life 4, 14, 17, 18, 21–22, 29, 44, 45, 82, 157, 250
Country Pastimes for Boys, by Graham Peter Anderson 20

Coventry 274
Coward, Noel 300
Cram, Ralph 176
Crane, Charles 176
Crime and Punishment, by Fyodor Dostoevsky 23–25, 28
Crippen, Hawley Harvey 55
Crisis, The 175
Crowley, Aleister 312
Crown Colony, by Neal Harman 260
Csrenyi, George 308
Current History 224

Dagobert Brown, by Delano Ames 278
Daily Express 152, 240, 259, 263, 277
Daily Mail 4, 83, 98, 124, 126, 212, 231, 257, 258, 264, 306
Daily Mirror 231
Daily Telegraph 3
Dark Forest, The, by Hugh Walpole 153
Dawson, Geoffrey 83, 210
Dead Souls, by Nikolai Gogol 127
Death and the Archdeacon, by Neal Harman 260
De Gaulle, Charles 319
Denmark 170
Diaghilev, Sergei 54
Diary of a Nobody, by George and Weedon Grossmith 16
Dillard, Annie 9
Donne, John 299
Dostoevsky, Fyodor 4, 23–26, 28, 31, 32–33, 60, 65, 76, 94, 101
Doyle, Sir Arthur Conan 152
Dublin 293
Dubois, William 174
Duddington, Natasha (née Ertel) 119, 128
Dukhobors 185
Dunkirk 271
Durrell, Lawrence 238

Eastern Churches Broadsheet, The 283. See also *Stephen Graham's Newsletter about the Orthodox Churches in War Time*
Edinburgh 13–16, 20, 133

Edinburgh Courant 15
Elegy Written in an English Country Church-Yard, by Thomas Gray 113
Eliot, Thomas 299
Elmes, Rick 251
El Paso 191, 198
Ely 227
Embezzlers, The, by Valentin Kataev 237–238
Emblems, by Francis Quarles 115
English Review 58, 69, 99, 143, 327
Ertel, Aleksander 237
Ertel, Lola 120
Ertel, Natasha. *See* Duddington, Natasha (née Ertel)
Essex 12, 17, 18, 21, 26, 59, 188, 249, 273, 299
Evening News 205, 207, 306, 320
Evening Standard 18, 31, 66
Evening Times 55–57, 59, 81, 84
Evgeny, Father 72, 73
Ewart, Wilfrid 6, 8, 142–144, 146–147, 151, 153, 155, 180, 195–202, 205, 238
Excelsior 201
Extreme Continental, by Giles Whittell 9, 90

Falk, Bernard 55
Farson, Eve 36
Farson, Negley 36, 254–255
Ferdinand, Archduke Franz 94, 95, 112, 242–243
Fish Who Answer the Telephone and Other Studies in Experimental Biology, by Professor Y.P. Frovlov 259
Ford, Ford Maddox 209
Four Quartets, by Thomas Eliot 300
Freud, Sigmund 325, 327
Frith Street, 60 11, 57–59, 81–82, 137, 150, 151, 153, 170, 188, 205, 206, 212, 218, 220, 224, 232, 239, 245, 269–270, 273, 275–278, 289, 292–293, 296, 298, 299–300, 303, 304, 305, 307, 313, 314, 317–321
Fytton, Mary 238

Garbett, Cyril, Archbishop of York 281

Gawsworth, John 8, 238–240, 272, 300, 319
General B.O., by Roman Gul 237
General William Booth Enters the Kingdom of Heaven, by Vachel Lindsay 177
Gentleman from San Francisco, The, by Ivan Bunin 213
Glacier National Park 181–182
Gladstone, William 10, 80
Gloucestershire Echo 15
Godunov, Boris 252
Gogol, Nikolai 127
Going Fishing, by Negley Farson 254
Going-to-the-Sun, by Vachel Lindsay 181, 185–186
Golden Book of Springfield, by Vachel Lindsay 179–180, 316
Gorky, Maxim 32, 87, 125, 211
Gorlice 104
Grahame, Kenneth 15, 53
Graham, Eleanor 18, 232, 278
Graham, Jane Anderson 16, 214
Graham, Peter Anderson 13–22, 29, 31, 82, 213, 228, 249–250, 263–264, 311
Graham, Rosa / Rose (née Savory) 35–37, 41, 45, 57–59, 82, 113, 115, 127, 136, 154–161, 170–171, 188–189, 191, 193, 194, 198–201, 213, 214–215, 218–222, 224, 225, 228–229, 232, 234–235, 244, 258, 305, 311
Graham, Stephen, Works
  Articles
    City of Romance, A 91
    Credo, The 6, 165–167, 188, 245
    Hope for Russia, The 153
    Marriage Ruined his Life 258
    Russian Pilgrim, The 87
    Second Coming, The 56
    Soul of the British Empire, The 260
    Universal Panorama 87
    Way of the Young Man, The 245
  Published works
    5,000 Enemy Planes over London 272, 308
    100 Best Poems in the English Language 299
    African Tragedy 261–263, 304, 326

Alexander II Tsar of Russia 253
Alexander of Yugoslavia, Strong Man of the Balkans 263–266, 285, 308
America after Fifty Years 318
Balkan Monastery 257–258, 263, 326
Boris Godunov 252
Challenge of the Dead, The 154, 157
Changing Russia 62–63, 66–68, 76
Characteristics 259
Children of the Slaves 171–175, 315, 326
Death of Yesterday, The 232–233, 327
Europe Whither-Bound? (Quo Vadis Europa?) 157–158, 161, 164, 326
Everybody Pays 246–247, 250, 263, 304
From War to War 270
Gentle Art of Tramping, The 215–216, 228, 323–324
Great Russian Short Stories 237, 307
In Quest of El Dorado 190, 192–195, 202, 205
Ivan the Terrible of Russia 252
Kitchener at Archangel 239–240, 308
Last Battle 263
Lay Confessor, The 229–231, 237
Liquid Victory 270
London Nights 207, 209, 224
Lost Battle 16–18, 213–214, 249, 326
Midsummer Music 216–217, 314
Modern Vanity Fair, A 247, 250
Moving Tent, The 255–257, 267, 269
New York Nights 224–227
One of the Ten Thousand 247, 263, 326
Padre of St Jacobs, The 249, 326
Part of the Wonderful Scene 6, 8, 14, 34, 37, 310–312, 313
Pay as You Run 304–305
Peter the Great, A Life of Peter I of Russia Called the Great 231–233
Priest of the Ideal 114–118, 121, 139, 144, 151, 166, 167, 219, 250
Private in the Guards, A 134, 135, 138, 142, 146–148, 150–152, 164
Quest of the Face, The 111, 128–131, 151, 166
Russia in 1916 121–122

Russia in Division 211, 212
Stalin, An Impartial Study of the Life and Work of Joseph Stalin 252
Stephen Graham's Newsletter about the Orthodox Churches in War Time 279, 281–283, 285
Struggle Against Drunkenness, The 86
St Vitus Day 242–244, 264
Summing-up on Russia 295, 298
Thinking of Living 301
Through Russian Central Asia 93
Tramping with a Poet in the Rockies 181–184, 190, 309
Tramp's Anthology, The 228
Tramp's Philosophy, The 59
Tramp's Sketches, A 43, 62–66, 68, 75, 164, 326
Twice Round the London Clock 251–252
Under-London 22, 188, 193, 208–209, 263
Undiscovered Russia 45–46, 48–52, 53–56, 62, 120, 326
Vagabond in the Caucasus, A 38, 40, 42–44, 46, 53–56, 81, 134, 164, 167, 256
Way of Martha and the Way of Mary, The 103, 107–110, 120, 122
With Poor Immigrants to America 79–80, 83, 120
With the Russian Pilgrims to Jerusalem 69–76, 83, 120–121
  Unpublished works
  Aha 309
  Air Raid Diary 273, 276
  Bakunin at the Dresden Zoo 309
  From Barbarism to Tsarism 317
  Ilya Vilka 309
  Life and Times of Tom Hood, The 307
  Litany for a Discharged Solider, A 150
  Ygdrasil 34–36, 44, 51, 64, 166, 311
Graham, Vera (née Mitrinović) 113, 241–242, 244, 254–258, 260, 262, 263, 266, 269, 271, 273, 274–277, 286, 288–290, 292–293, 296–298, 300–301, 303–307, 311–316, 318–321
Gray, Thomas 113, 117
Green, Roger Lancelyn 18

Grey, Sir Edward 68
Grieg, Maysie 278, 318
Grossmith, George 16
Grossmith, Walter Weedon 16
Gul, Roman 237
Gupta, Susil 300, 318, 319
Gurdjieff, George 164, 167, 311

Haldane, John Burdon Sanderson 166, 188
Halifax, Lord Edward 271
Handful of Dust, A, by Evelyn Waugh 261
Handy Guide for Beggars, A, by Vachel Lindsay 177
Hardy, Thomas 102
Harman, Neal 260, 262–263
Harmsworth, Alfred, First Viscount Northcliffe. *See* Northcliffe, Lord
Harper's Magazine 69, 76, 174–175, 222
Hayes, Roland 175
Hay, Marion 295–296, 298, 303, 305–306, 314–315, 317–319, 321
Heart of Darkness, by Joseph Conrad 261
Heliopolis 103
Hemingway, Ernest 229
Henderson, Alice Corbin 185, 189, 192
Henley, William Earnest 15, 19
Henry V (film) 290
Hibbert Journal 111
hieroglyphics 115, 178, 185
Hill, Vernon 35, 181, 309
Hindenburg, Paul Von 95
Hitler, Adolf 270, 271, 279, 280, 298
Hocking, Silas 99
Hoffmann, Colonel Max 95
Holmes, Richard 10
Horizon 278
Houston 191, 315, 316
Hull 210

Ibsen, Henrik 25
idealism / idealist philosophy 111, 128, 139, 164, 166, 167
  Graham's idealism 9, 12, 34, 76, 109, 118, 130, 167–168, 176, 220, 250, 303, 311, 323

Ilinitchina, Vavara 86
Irwin, Margaret (Peggy) 218, 220–224, 229
Isaacs, Rufus, First Marquess of Reading 102
Ivanov, Viacheslav 51, 60, 88
Ivan the Terrible's Murder of his Son, by Ilya Repin 210

Jacks, Professor Lawrence Pearsall 111
Jaffa 70, 77
Jalap 202
James, William 88
Jane Hamish, by Delano Ames 278
Jealousy, by Mikhail Artsybashev 85
Jefferies, Richard 19
Jerusalem 5, 62, 69–75, 80, 85, 91
Jevtić, Bogoljub 265
Jewish Chronicle 100
Jewish World 100
Journey in the Seaboard Slave States, A, by Frederick Law Olmsted 170
Joy, Thomas Musgrove 57
Jungle, The, by Upton Sinclair 79
Justification of the Good, by Vladimir Solovev 119, 128

Kandinsky, Vasily 112
Kataev, Valentin 237–238
Keats, John 299
Kennard, Howard 31
Kharkov 26, 29
Khvostov, Alexi Nikolayevich 105
Kiev 85, 86
King Alexander I of Yugoslavia 8, 240–241, 264–266, 308–309
King Arthur and his Knights of the Round Table, by Roger Lancelyn Green 18
King, Martin Luther 318
King Peter II of Yugoslavia 283
Kipling, John 141
Kipling, Rudyard 140, 141, 232, 309
Kirkpatrick, Ivonne 287–288
Kislovodsk 121
Krasnovodsk 90
Kropotkin, Peter 213
Kuprin, Alexander 35, 127, 213

La Ciudad de Juarez 198
Lake Bohinje 246, 247, 251, 254
Lake Isle of Innisfree, The, by W.B. Yeats 299
Lake Ochrid 255–257
Lake Peipsi 12
Lake Prespa 256
Lane, John 38, 42, 51, 59, 80
Las Vegas 193
Lawrence, D.H. 192
Lawrence, Frieda (née Von Richthofen) 192
Lebedev, Nikolai 26, 29–32, 38
Le Havre 140
Lenin, Vladimir 28, 127
lepidoptery 14, 21, 208
Letopis 125
Lewis, Sinclair 196
libel case against Graham 262–263
Life of Jesus, by David Strauss 312
Life of Man, by Leonid Andreev 30
Lindsay, Elizabeth (née Connor) 233–234
Lindsay, Vachel 6, 177–187, 189–193, 195–196, 217, 225, 228, 232–234, 241, 316
Lisitchansk 29–30
Lisri, North Ossetia 42
Listener, The, by Algernon Blackwood 81, 238
Lister, Joseph 15
Little Gorky of the Black Swans, by Maurice Braddell 300
Little Joe the Wrangler, by Jack Thorpe 192
Little Sparta (Guards's Training Camp) 133–137, 139, 152
Liverpool 77
Ljubljana 245
Lloyd George, David 82, 102, 106, 122–124, 126
Locke, William 38
Lockhart, Sir Robert Bruce 122
London Blitz 10, 272–278
Longman's Magazine 18
Lower Depths, by Maxim Gorky 211
Ludendorff, Erich 95

Lutyens, Sir Edwin 154
lynching 173, 261

MacDonald, Ramsey 212
Macfarlane, Robert 9
Madrid 188, 303
Mainsprings of Russia, The, by Maurice Baring 55
Mairet, Philip 113, 229
Makarios 103
Malo-Krasnoiarsk 94
Manchester 50, 99
Manchester Courier, The 54
Manchester Guardian, The 230, 238, 240, 243, 245, 246, 255
Marias, Javier 8, 37, 200, 202
Marseilles 102, 263, 265, 308
Masaryk, Jan 176, 220
Masaryk, Tomaš 220
Masterman, Charles 82
Masters, Edgar Lee 177
materialism 68, 102, 108, 110, 112, 113, 164, 166–168, 176, 179, 181, 184, 188, 190, 191, 215, 311, 312, 316
Maugham, Somerset 125
McCarthy, Joseph 298
Mckenna, Reginald 102
Mead, George Robert Stowe 111
Men, Myth and Magic 319
Merezhkovsky, Dmitri 60, 125
Merkurieva, Vera 45, 47, 88
Mexico City 142, 198–202
Miami Herald 180
Midsummer Night's Dream, A, by William Shakespeare 217
Mihailović, Draža 8, 284–286, 289, 290, 296
Miliukov, Paul 105, 118, 125
Milton, John 299
Mir iskusstva 61
Mitrinović, Chedomir 244, 292
Mitrinović, Dimitrije 110–113, 118, 128–130, 136, 159, 163–165, 167, 228–229, 239–241, 244–245, 300
Mitrinović, Lubo 241, 243
Mitrinović, Vera. *See* Graham, Vera (née Mitrinović)

modernism 32, 58, 299
Monroe, Harriet 192
Moody, Harriet 187
Morley, Christopher 176, 180, 183, 190, 191, 196
Morning Leader 152
Morning Post 17, 18
Moscow 11, 27–28, 30–33, 35, 37, 45–47, 50–52, 56, 59, 60, 62, 86–88, 95, 97, 104–105, 120, 122, 125, 230, 251, 281
Moscow Patriarchate 282
Moscow Religious-Philosophical Society 46, 60–61
Moscow Theosophical Society 88
Munich 112, 161
Murray, Max 278, 300, 318
Murray, Maysie 278, 300
Musaryk, Jan 220

Napoleon 105, 253
National Observer 15
Nation, The 100
Nature in Books, by Peter Anderson Graham 19
Nazareth 72
Nazaroff, Alexander 232
Negra espalda del tiempo (Dark Back of Time), by Javier Marias 8, 37, 200, 202
Nesterov, Michael 46
New Age, The 32, 56, 58, 100, 122, 163, 165
New Britain 244
Newcastle 135
Newman, Bernard 254, 255, 300, 317
Newmarch, Rosa 24
New Orleans 174, 175, 191, 194, 198–199, 315
New Review, The 18
News of the World 82, 106
New Theology, The, by John Reginald Campbell 139
New York 6, 11, 57, 77–79, 152, 169, 170, 172, 175–177, 179, 180, 187–188, 195–197, 205, 222–227, 233–234, 314–315, 317, 325
New Yorker 222

New York Evening Post 180, 183, 190
New York Times 75, 78, 175, 186, 227, 232
Nicoll, Robertson 106
Nietzsche, Friedrich 25, 61, 65, 233
Nikon, Patriarch 12
Nizhni Novgorod 27
Norfolk, Virginia 173
Northcliffe, Lord 83, 85, 86, 124, 152
Novalis 324
Novikov, Olga 80, 97

Observer, The 231, 238
Odessa 70, 104
Olivier, Laurence 290
Olmsted, Frederick Law 170
Omsk 95
Operation Barbarossa 280, 281, 286
Orage, Alfred 32, 56, 163–164
Oregonian, The 180, 187
Orthodox Church Bulletin 280
Orwell, George 278
Oslo 97
Oxford 177, 184

Pagnol, Marcel 328
Pall Mall Gazette 44
Panama City 195
pantheism 43, 62–66, 168, 175
Paris 85, 102, 144, 156, 162, 212–213, 214, 215, 216, 218, 229, 237, 325
partisans (Yugoslav) 285–286, 289, 290, 292, 297
Pasha, Ali 41
Path to Rome, by Joseph Hilaire Belloc 38, 53, 54
Pavelić, Ante 264, 283–284, 288, 308
Pavlov, Ivan 259
Peggy. *See* Irwin, Margaret (Peggy)
Pennell, Joseph 80
Pentonville Prison (London) 206–207, 248
Perepletchikov, Vasily 47, 58, 60, 87–88
Peter the Great of Russia 31, 47, 232
Petrograd. *See* St Petersburg
Philadelphia 172, 176
Phoney War 271

Pickwick Papers, The, by Charles Dickens 28
Pilgrim at Tinker's Creek, by Annie Dillard 9
Plato 325, 327
Playfair, William 13
Poetry Magazine 192
Poetry Review 309–310
Poets of Russia, The, by Renato Poggioli 309
Poggioli, Renato 309
Political Warfare Executive (PWE) 6, 287–288
Prague 11, 160, 220–221
Prince Paul of Yugoslavia 265
Princess Marie-Louise of Schleswig-Holstein 138
Princip, Gavril 242–243
Pueblo Indians 191
Punch 16
Pushkin, Alexander 237

Quarles, Francis 115
Queen Elizabeth II of England 10, 300
Queen Maria of Yugoslavia 265
Queen Victoria of England 10, 138
Quest 60, 111, 128

Rabbi Ben Ezra, by Robert Browning 299
Rabinovich, Nina 88
Ralston, William 24
Rasputin, Grigori 106, 123–124, 230, 319
Red Army 161, 290
Remizov, Aleksei 88–89, 213, 237
Repin, Ilya 58, 210
Riddell, Sir George 82, 106
Robinson, Geoffrey 124
Roman Catholic Church 285
Romanov, Panteleimon 237–238
Rome 158–159, 266, 312
Roosevelt, Franklin 289
Rostov-on-Don 66, 121
Royal Central Asian Society 92–93
Royden, Maude 312
Rural Exodus, The, by Peter Anderson Graham 19, 20

Rus 27
Ruskin, John 16, 21, 23, 252
Russell, Adeline, Duchess of Bedford 102, 133
Russia, by Donald Mackenzie Wallace 24
Russian and Western Churches compared 101, 103, 107–111, 120, 122
Russian bourgeoisie 67–68
Russian émigrés 6, 77, 79, 131, 153, 160, 212–213, 237, 241
Russian Orthodox Church 4, 26, 33, 40–41, 49, 62, 86, 98, 101, 110, 119, 230, 253, 279–280, 282, 296, 317
Russian peasantry 3, 5, 49, 62, 175, 317
Russian Peasant, The, by Howard Kennard 31
Russian Revolution 9, 12, 34, 42, 66, 71, 80, 84, 126, 152, 160, 209, 210, 253, 326
  February 1917 5, 114, 118, 122, 124, 127–128, 131, 133, 230
  October 1917 4, 127, 133, 230
Russkaia Mysl 120
Ruthven, Lord Walter Hore- 138, 150, 152

Sackville-West, Vita 238
Sala, George 251
Samarkand 91, 224
Sandburg, Carl 177, 233
San Francisco 195
Sanin, by Mikhail Artsybashev 85
San Juan 189, 319
Santa Fé 189, 191–192, 194, 197–198, 208
  literary and artistic colony 191, 197–198
Sarajevo 94, 112, 242–243, 255, 269
Saturday Review 127, 216, 227
Saturday Westminster 153
Savory, Rosa. *See* Graham, Rosa /Rose (née Savory)
Sazonov, Sergei, Russian Foreign Minister 96–97, 99–100, 125
Schopenhauer, Arthur 312
Schweitzer, Albert 312

Scots Guards 5, 131, 133–134, 137, 141–143, 145, 146, 149–154, 198
  1st Battalion 141
  2nd Battalion 141, 144, 146, 148–150
  3rd (Reserve Battalion) 133
Scotsman, The 15
Scots Observer 15
Scott, Sir Walter 16
Scranton, Pennsylvania 79
Secret City, The, by Hugh Walpole 153
Secret Society (as proposed by Dimitrie Mitrinović) 110–111, 113, 118, 129, 167, 244
Sedgwick, Ellery 176
Self, Kenny 14
Semipalatnisk 94
Seraphim, Father 108
Sergeant, Elizabeth 192
Sergiev Posad 33
Servile State, The, by Joseph Hilaire Belloc 23
Seton-Watson, Robert 242
Shakespeare, William 117, 217, 238, 299
Shamil, Imam 37
Shaw, George Bernard 23
Shelley, Percy 299
Sherman, General William 171, 174
Shiel, Matthew Phipps 238
Siege of Sidney Street 57
Silver Age (of Russian culture) 59–61, 88
Simaika, Marcus Bey 103
Simpleton, William 125
Sinclair, Upton 79, 196
Sitwell, Edith 309
Smyrna 70
Sochi 63, 66
Sofia 104, 159
Sologub, Fyodor 127
Solov'ev, Vladimir 60, 119, 128
Solzhenitsyn, Alexander 320
Soul of London, The, by Ford Maddox Ford 209
Spectator 83, 143
Spender, Stephen 277
Spiritual Issues of the War 280

Spokane 187, 225, 233
Springfield, Illinois 179, 180, 187, 233, 316, 317
St Albans 17
Stalin, Joseph 252, 270, 271, 280–283, 296, 301
Stampa 269
Stanislavsky, Constantin 30
Stasov, Vladimir 25
Stepniak, Sergei 213
Stevenson, Robert Louis 15
St Francis of Assisi 312
St Helier, Lady Susan 102, 138
Stirling, Colonel John 144, 152
St James' Gazette 18, 45
Stockholm 97
St Petersburg 25, 28, 31, 37, 47, 87, 97–99, 105, 106, 123, 124, 126, 133, 153, 230
Strachey, John St Loe 83
Strauss, David 312
Struve, Peter 120
Stuart-King, Mabel 82, 231
Sukhominov, Vladimir 104
Sunday Express 260
Sunday Pictorial 106
Sunday Times, The 96, 125
symbolism
  Graham's symbolist reading of the world 5, 51, 65, 69, 80, 86, 88, 101, 115, 178
  Russian Symbolism 45, 51, 61, 88, 112, 125
Symmonds, John 312
Sytin, Ivan 120–121

Tallahassee 315, 319
Tashkent 91–92
Temple, William, Archbishop of Canterbury 281
Tennyson, Lord Alfred 299
Theosophy 8, 51, 61, 81, 88, 111, 130, 154, 176, 311
Thomas, Edward 309
Thoreau, Henry David 19
Thorp, Jack 192, 193
Three Pairs of Silk Stockings, by Panteleimon Romanov 237

Times Literary Supplement, The 87, 122, 174, 216, 227, 231, 262
Times, The 3, 9, 83, 86–87, 89, 91, 93, 95, 96, 97, 100, 103, 105, 113, 121, 122, 124, 125, 126, 152, 210, 220, 291–292
Tito, Josef 284, 285, 286, 289, 290, 292, 295, 296–298
Todd, Barbara Euphan 18
Tolstoy, Leo 3, 26, 28, 76, 87, 119, 232, 237
To Night, by Percy Shelley 299
Toynbee Hall 206
Tramp, The 53–54, 81
Travels with a Donkey in the Cevennes, by Robert Louis Stevenson 54
Treaty of Versailles 6, 150, 161
Trotsky, Leon 188
Trubetskoi, Evgeny 60
Truth about Religion in Russia, The 281
Tsar Alexander II 253
Tsar Nicholas II 27, 67, 76, 87, 104–106, 118–119, 123–124, 126, 127
Turgenev, Ivan 24, 120
Twice Round the Clock Hours of the Day and Night in London, by George Sala 251

Uncle Vanya, by Anton Chekhov 291
Upward, Allen 167
Uspensky, Peter 167–168, 311
Ustaša 264, 284, 285
Uzhgorod 221

Velimirović, Father Nikolai 36, 110, 133, 158–159, 239, 244, 255, 316
Vera Cruz 202
Vestnik Teosofy (Herald of Theosophy) 45
Vienna 11, 82, 160
Vilka, Ilya 87
Vladikavkaz 40, 42, 45, 86, 88, 89
Volga Boatmen, by Ilya Repin 210

Waley, Arthur 309
Wallace, Donald Mackenzie 24
Wallace, Edgar 55
Walpole, Hugh 153
War and Peace, by Leo Tolstoy 232
Warsaw 5, 11, 27, 85, 96, 160–161, 211

Washington 114, 116, 172, 317
Wasteland, The, by Thomas Eliot 300
Watney, Charles 55–56, 59
Watts, George Frederic 58
Way of a Transgressor, by Negley Farson 254
Way of Revelation, The, by Wilfrid Ewart 142–144, 147, 195, 198
Way of the Cross, by Vlas Mikhailovich Doroshevich 107
Weekly Westminster, The 212
Wellington Barracks 137–140
Wells, Herbert George 24, 153
Western societies (lack of spirituality) 55, 61, 89, 101, 109–111, 113, 116, 118
Westminster Gazette 81
West, Rebecca 238, 243, 255
White, William Allen 192
Whittell, Giles 9, 90
Wickham Steed, Henry 124
Wiese, Kurt 226
Wilde, Oscar 15
Wild Places, The, by Robert Macfarlane 9
Williams, Harold 210
Wilson, Harold 10, 318
Wind in the Willows, by Kenneth Grahame 53
Woodstock, New York 191
Worden, Helen 315
Wordsworth, William 19, 299, 320
Wrangel, General Pyotr 159–160
Wrench, Evelyn 83
Wurzel Gummidge, by Barbara Euphan Todd 18

Yeats, W.B. 81, 299
Young Bess, by Margaret Irwin 218
Ypres 141, 143, 155
Yugoslav refugees 297–298

Zagreb 112, 217, 288
Zangwill, Israel 100
Zinov'ev Letter 212
Zoschenko, Mikhail 308

This book does not end here...

At Open Book Publishers, we are changing the nature of the traditional academic book. The title you have just read will not be left on a library shelf, but will be accessed online by hundreds of readers each month across the globe. We make all our books free to read online so that students, researchers and members of the public who can't afford a printed edition can still have access to the same ideas as you.

Our digital publishing model also allows us to produce online supplementary material, including extra chapters, reviews, links and other digital resources. Find *Beyond Holy Russia* on our website to access its online extras. Please check this page regularly for ongoing updates, and join the conversation by leaving your own comments:

http://www.openbookpublishers.com/isbn/9781783740123

If you enjoyed this book, and feel that research like this should be available to all readers, regardless of their income, please think about donating to us. Our company is run entirely by academics, and our publishing decisions are based on intellectual merit and public value rather than on commercial viability. We do not operate for profit and all donations, as with all other revenue we generate, will be used to finance new Open Access publications.

For further information about what we do, how to donate to OBP, additional digital material related to our titles or to order our books, please visit our website.

Knowledge is for sharing

www.ingramcontent.com/pod-product-compliance
Lightning Source LLC
Chambersburg PA
CBHW060551230426
43670CB00011B/1772